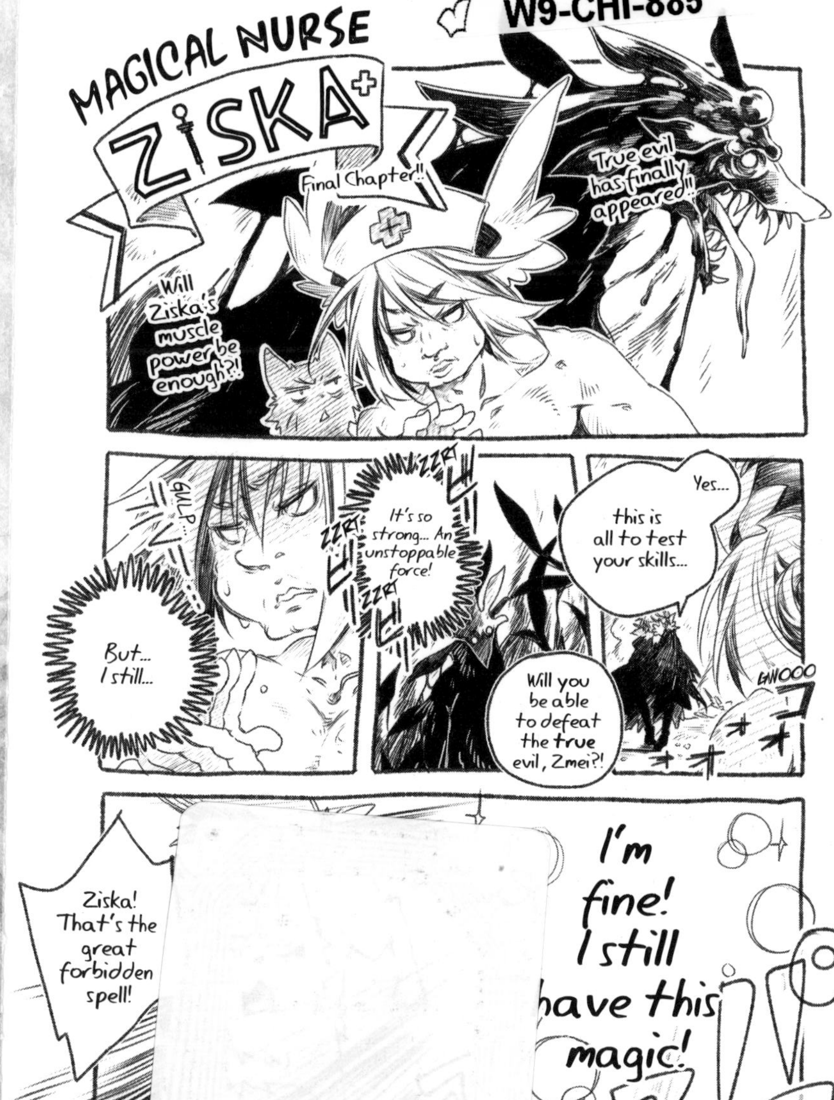
MAGICAL NURSE
ZISKA
True evil has finally appeared!!
Final Chapter!!
Will Ziska's muscle power be enough?!
Yes...
this is all to test your skills...
Will you be able to defeat the true evil, Zmei?!
GWOOO
ZZRT
It's so strong... An unstoppable force!
ZZRT
ZZRT
GULP...
But... I still...
I'm fine! I still have this magic!
PWAAAA
Ziska! That's the great forbidden spell!

How to Treat Magical Beasts

Mine and Master's Medical Journal

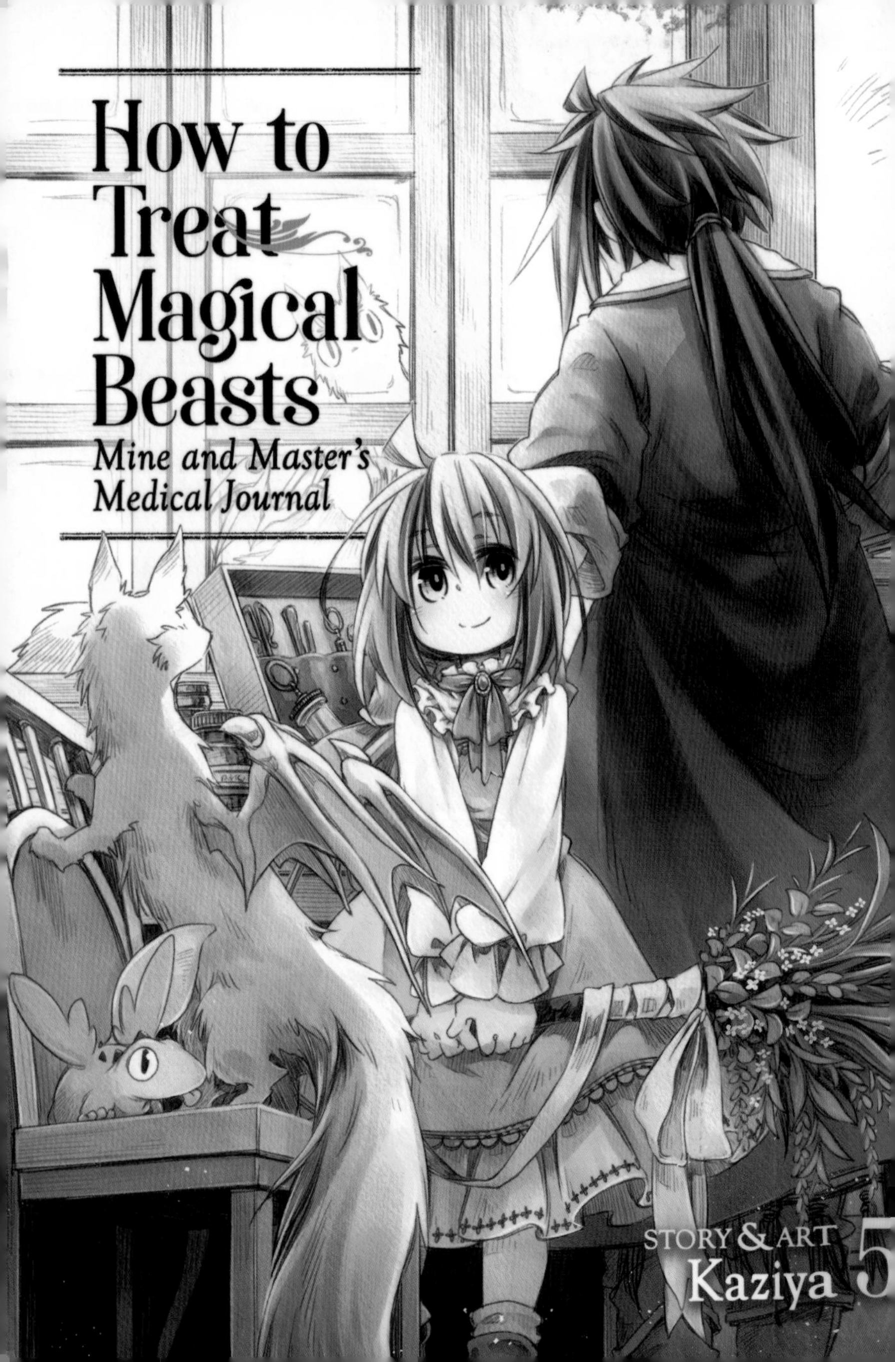

STORY & ART
Kaziya

5

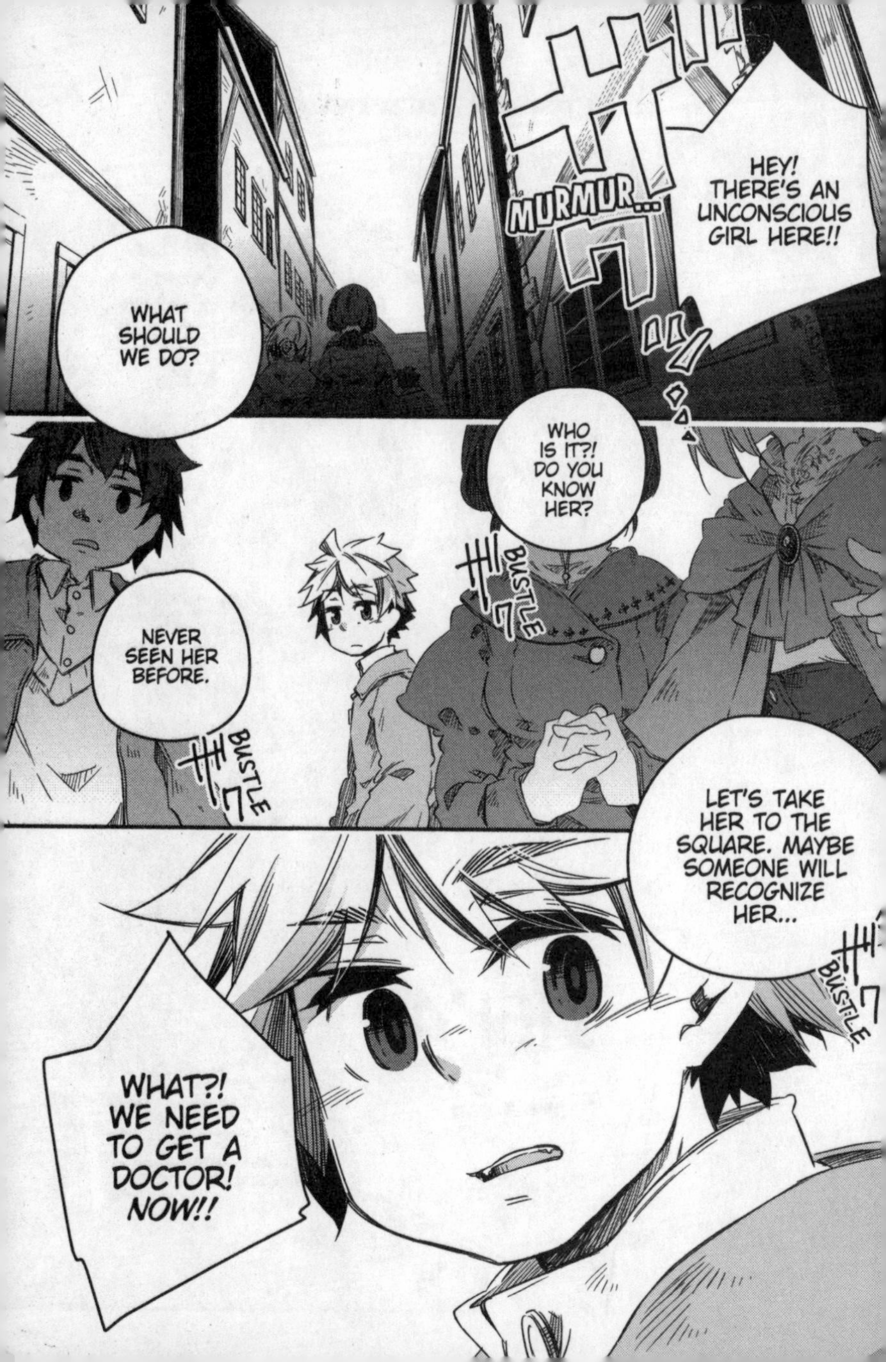
HEY! THERE'S AN UNCONSCIOUS GIRL HERE!!
MURMUR...
WHAT SHOULD WE DO?
WHO IS IT?! DO YOU KNOW HER?
BUSTLE
NEVER SEEN HER BEFORE.
BUSTLE
LET'S TAKE HER TO THE SQUARE. MAYBE SOMEONE WILL RECOGNIZE HER...
BUSTLE
WHAT?! WE NEED TO GET A DOCTOR! NOW!!

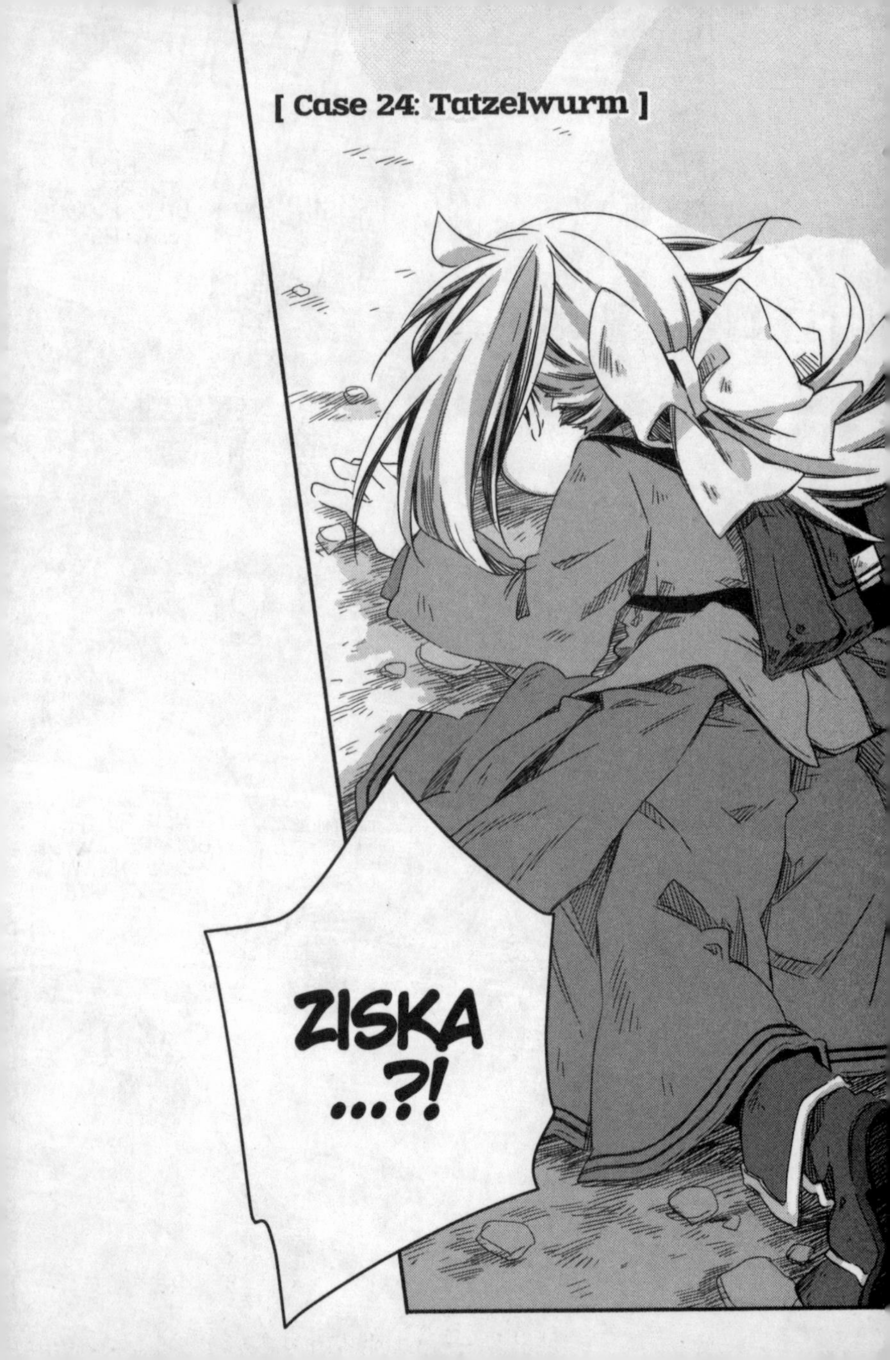
[Case 24: Tatzelwurm]
ZISKA …?!

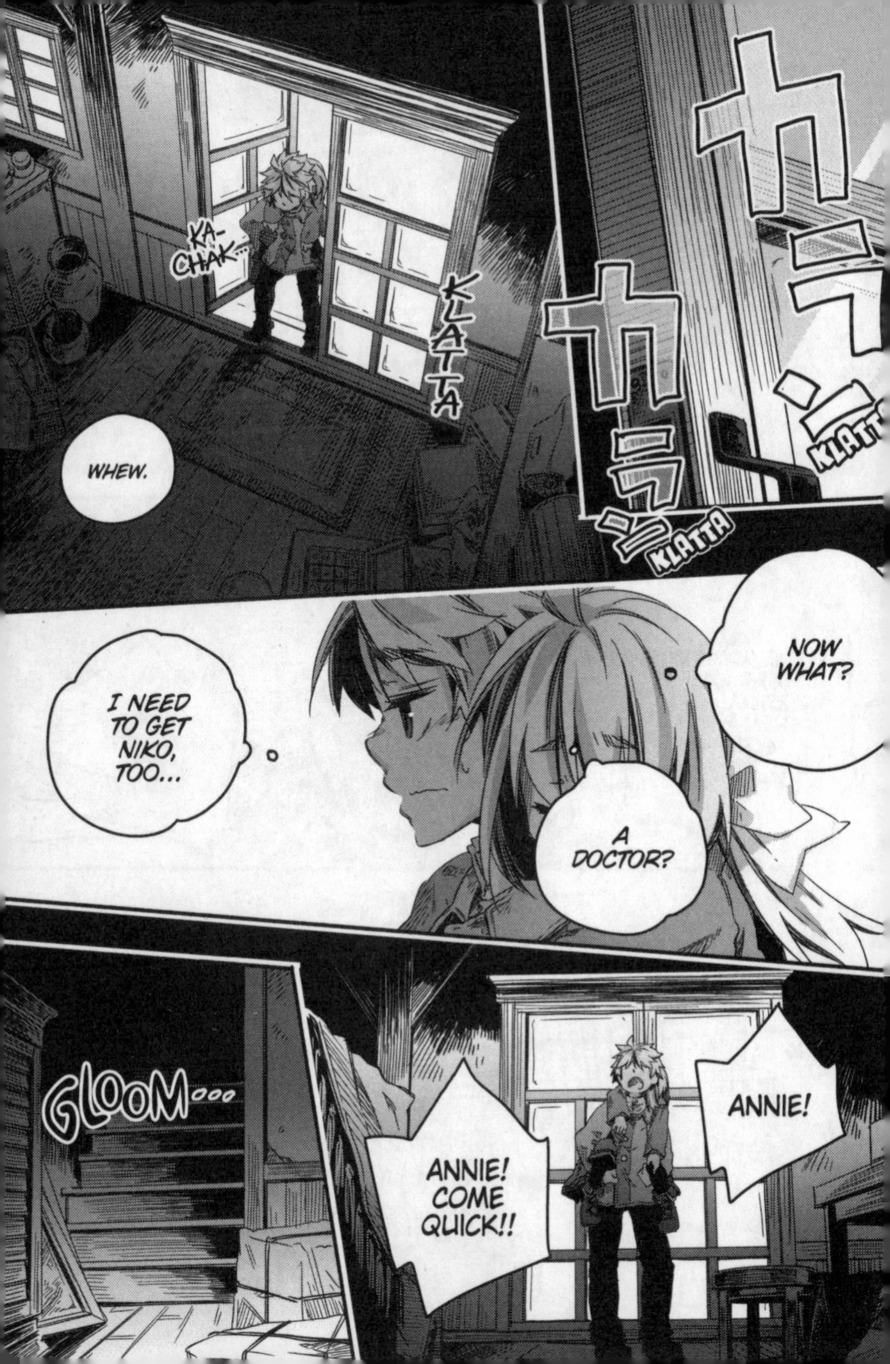

カラン
KLATTA
カラン
KLATTA
KA-CHAK...
KLATTA
WHEW.
NOW WHAT?
A DOCTOR?
I NEED TO GET NIKO, TOO...
ANNIE!
ANNIE! COME QUICK!!
GLOOM...

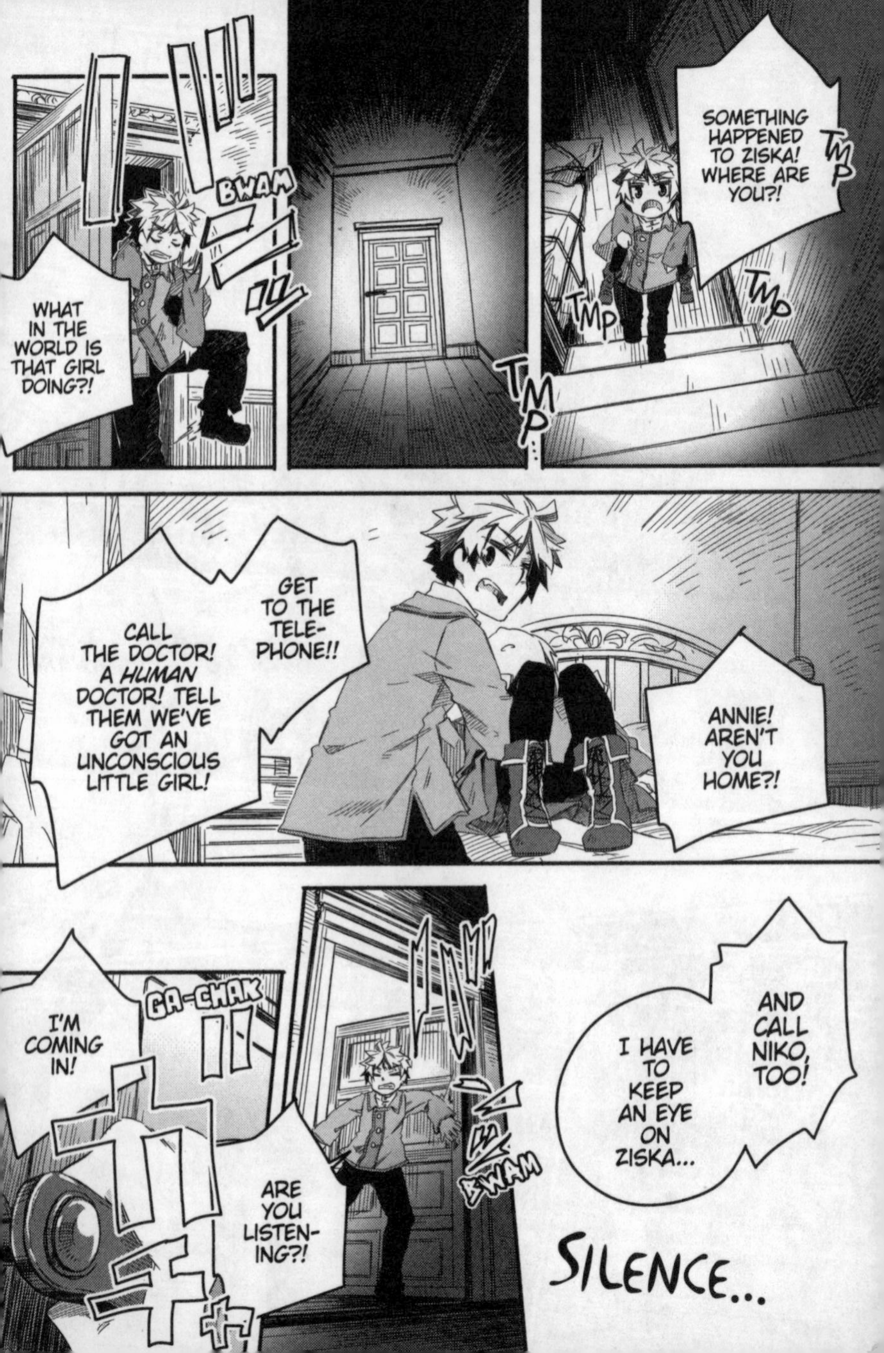
SOMETHING HAPPENED TO ZISKA! WHERE ARE YOU?!
TMP
TMP
TMP
TMP...
BWAM
WHAT IN THE WORLD IS THAT GIRL DOING?!
ANNIE! AREN'T YOU HOME?!
GET TO THE TELEPHONE!!
CALL THE DOCTOR! A *HUMAN* DOCTOR! TELL THEM WE'VE GOT AN UNCONSCIOUS LITTLE GIRL!
AND CALL NIKO, TOO!
I HAVE TO KEEP AN EYE ON ZISKA...
SILENCE...
BWAM
ARE YOU LISTENING?!
GA-CHAK
I'M COMING IN!

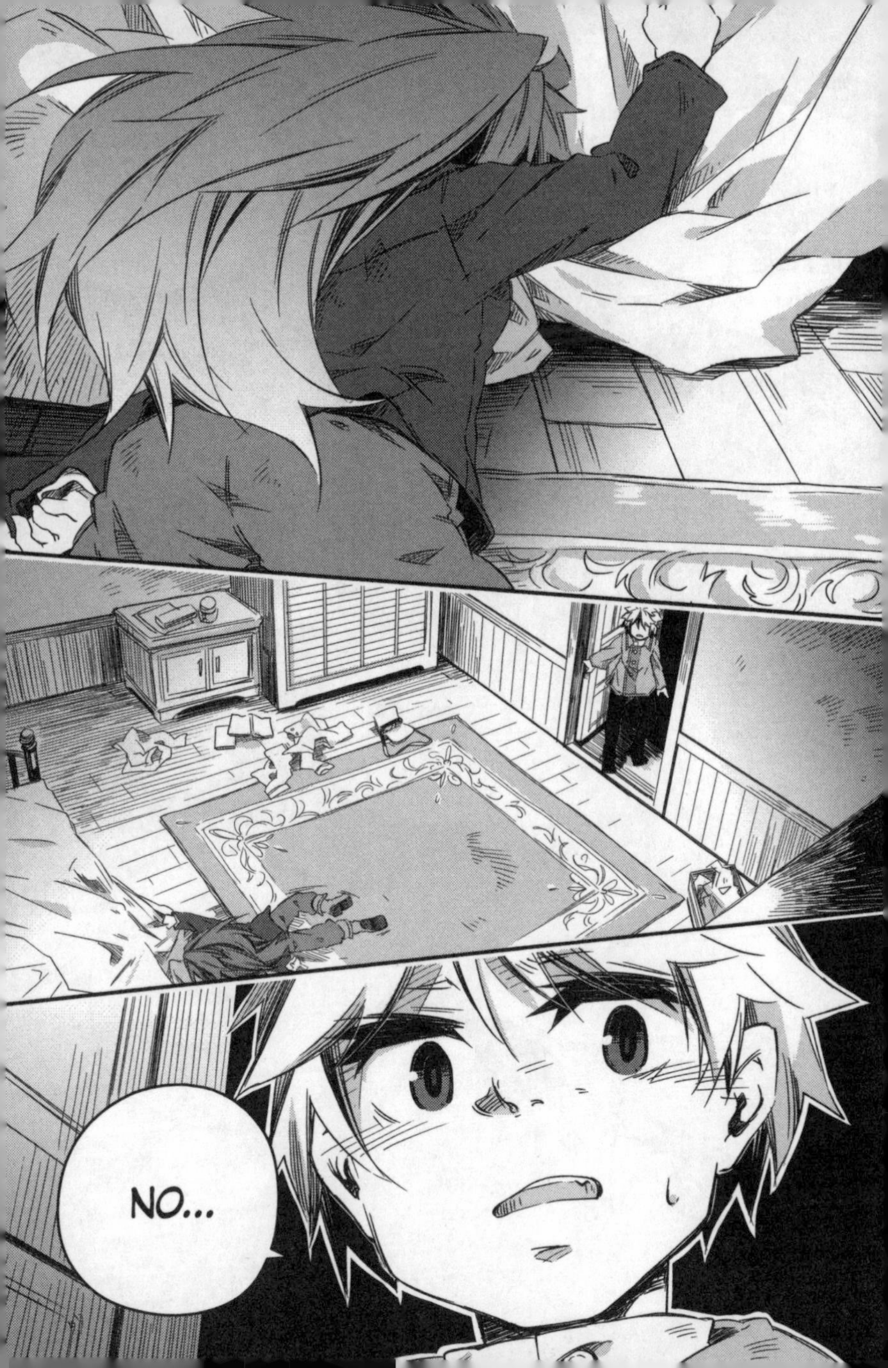
NO...

NO IDEA. THERE WAS A COMMOTION ON MY WAY BACK FROM VISITING A CUSTOMER...
WHEN I LOOKED THROUGH THE CROWD, I SAW ZISKA THERE, UNCONSCIOUS.
I HAD NO IDEA WHAT TO DO, SO I BROUGHT HER HERE.
THEN I FOUND ANNIE UNCONSCIOUS, TOO. JUST WHAT IS GOING ON?!
HAVE YOU CALLED THE DOCTOR?
I DID! THEY'RE BUSY WITH OTHER PATIENTS, SO IT MIGHT TAKE A WHILE.
I SEE... I DON'T TREAT HUMANS, SO...

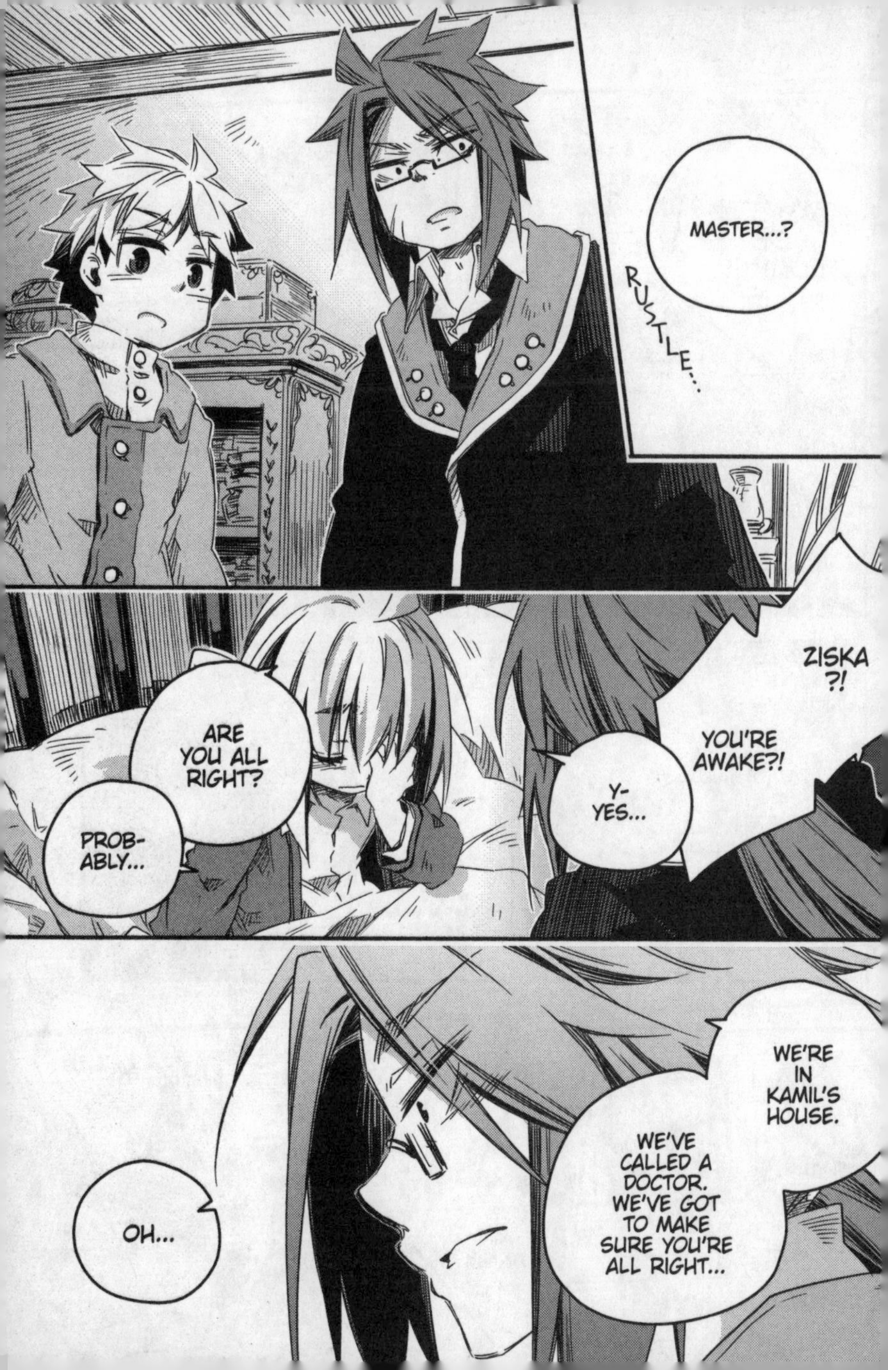
MASTER...?
RUSTLE...
ZISKA ?!
YOU'RE AWAKE?!
Y- YES...
ARE YOU ALL RIGHT?
PROB- ABLY...
WE'RE IN KAMIL'S HOUSE.
WE'VE CALLED A DOCTOR. WE'VE GOT TO MAKE SURE YOU'RE ALL RIGHT...
OH...

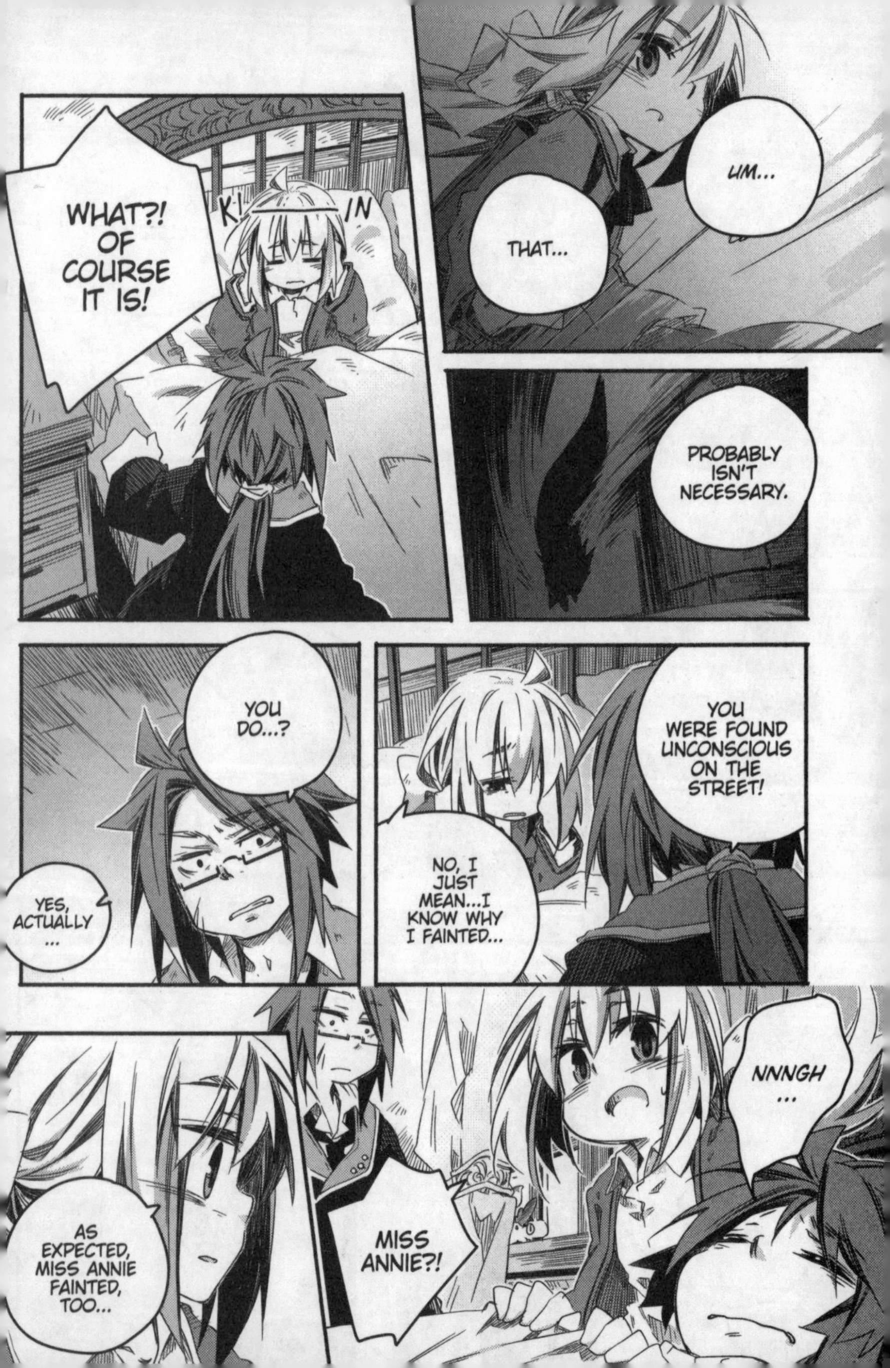

UM...
THAT...
PROBABLY ISN'T NECESSARY.
WHAT?! OF COURSE IT IS!
K! IN
YOU WERE FOUND UNCONSCIOUS ON THE STREET!
NO, I JUST MEAN...I KNOW WHY I FAINTED...
YOU DO...?
YES, ACTUALLY ...
NNNGH ...
MISS ANNIE?!
AS EXPECTED, MISS ANNIE FAINTED, TOO...

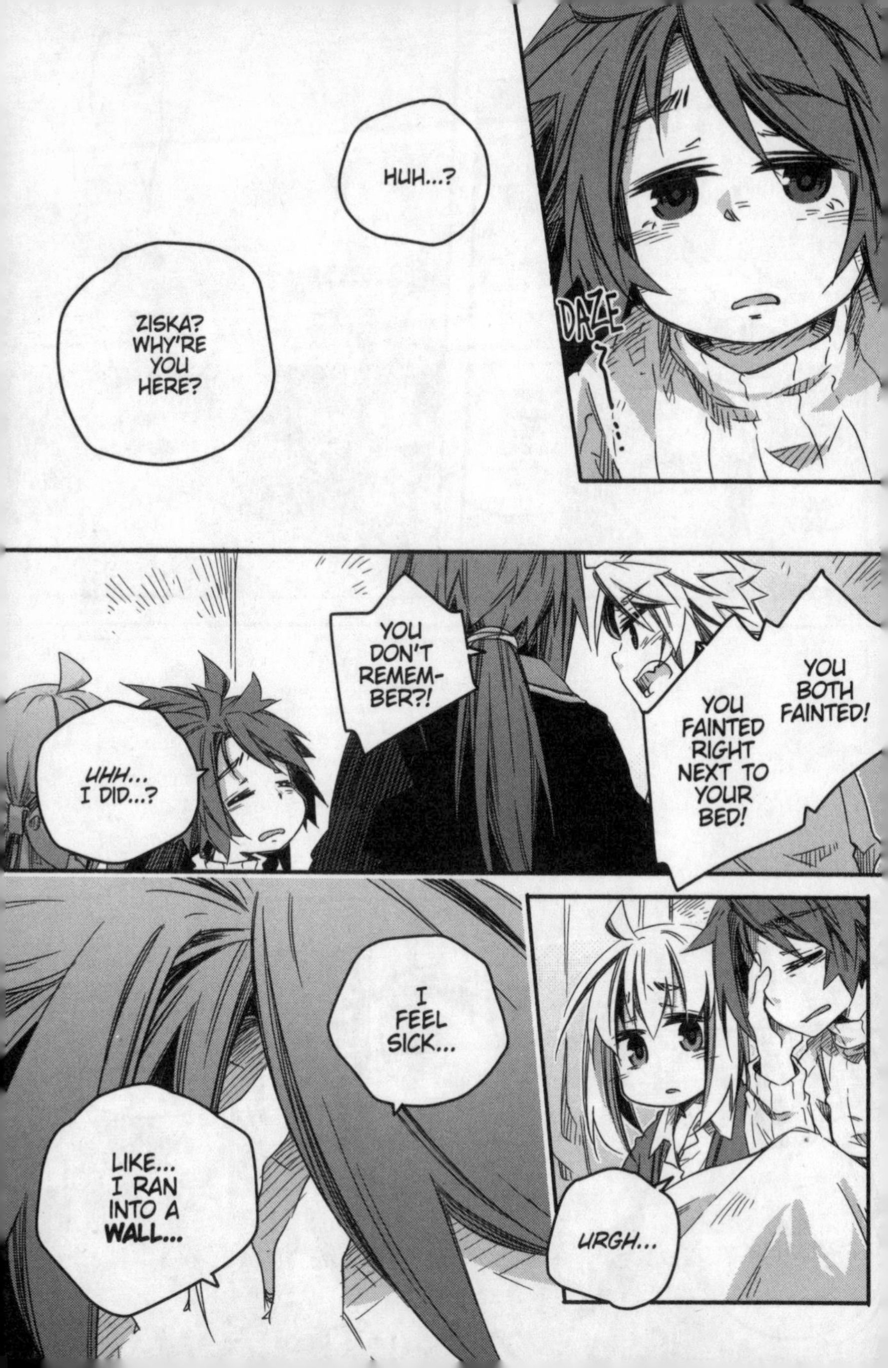
DAZE
HUH...?
ZISKA? WHY'RE YOU HERE?
YOU BOTH FAINTED!
YOU FAINTED RIGHT NEXT TO YOUR BED!
YOU DON'T REMEM-BER?!
UHH... I DID...?
URGH...
I FEEL SICK...
LIKE... I RAN INTO A WALL...

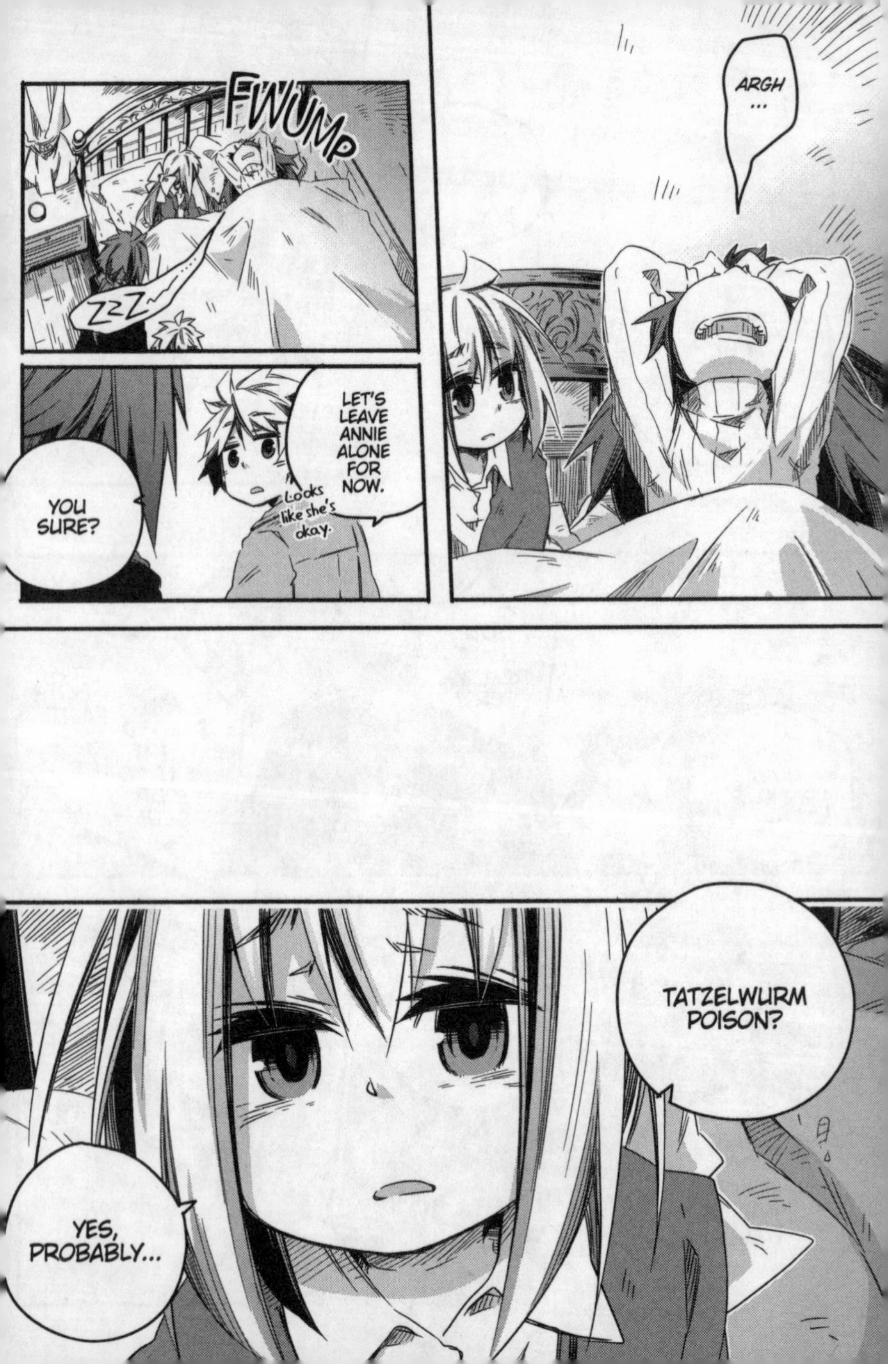
ARGH ...
FWUMP
ZzZ
LET'S LEAVE ANNIE ALONE FOR NOW.
Looks like she's okay.
YOU SURE?
TATZELWURM POISON?
YES, PROBABLY...

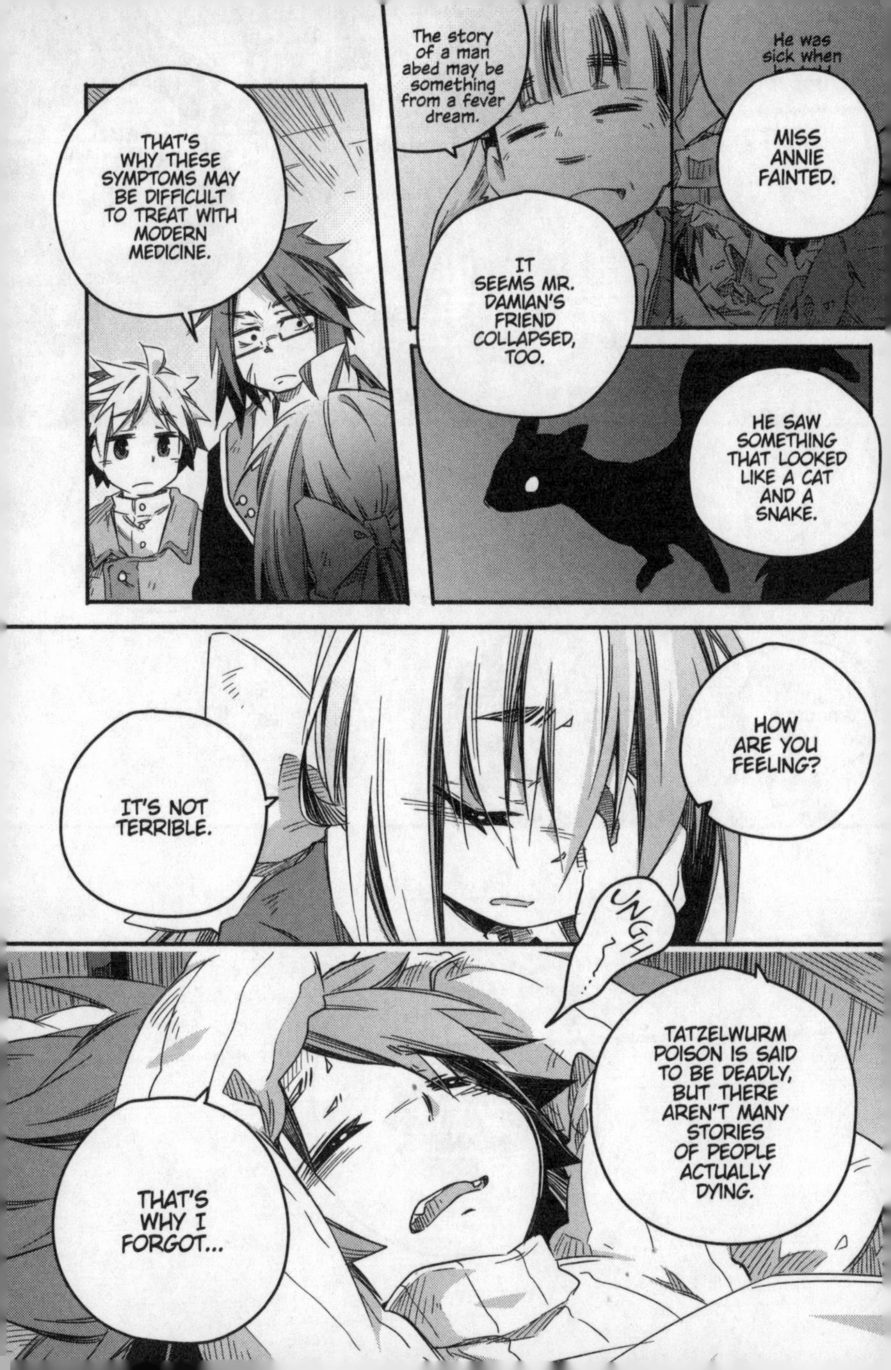
He was sick when
MISS ANNIE FAINTED.
IT SEEMS MR. DAMIAN'S FRIEND COLLAPSED, TOO.
HE SAW SOMETHING THAT LOOKED LIKE A CAT AND A SNAKE.
The story of a man abed may be something from a fever dream.
THAT'S WHY THESE SYMPTOMS MAY BE DIFFICULT TO TREAT WITH MODERN MEDICINE.
HOW ARE YOU FEELING?
IT'S NOT TERRIBLE.
UNGH...
TATZELWURM POISON IS SAID TO BE DEADLY, BUT THERE AREN'T MANY STORIES OF PEOPLE ACTUALLY DYING.
THAT'S WHY I FORGOT...

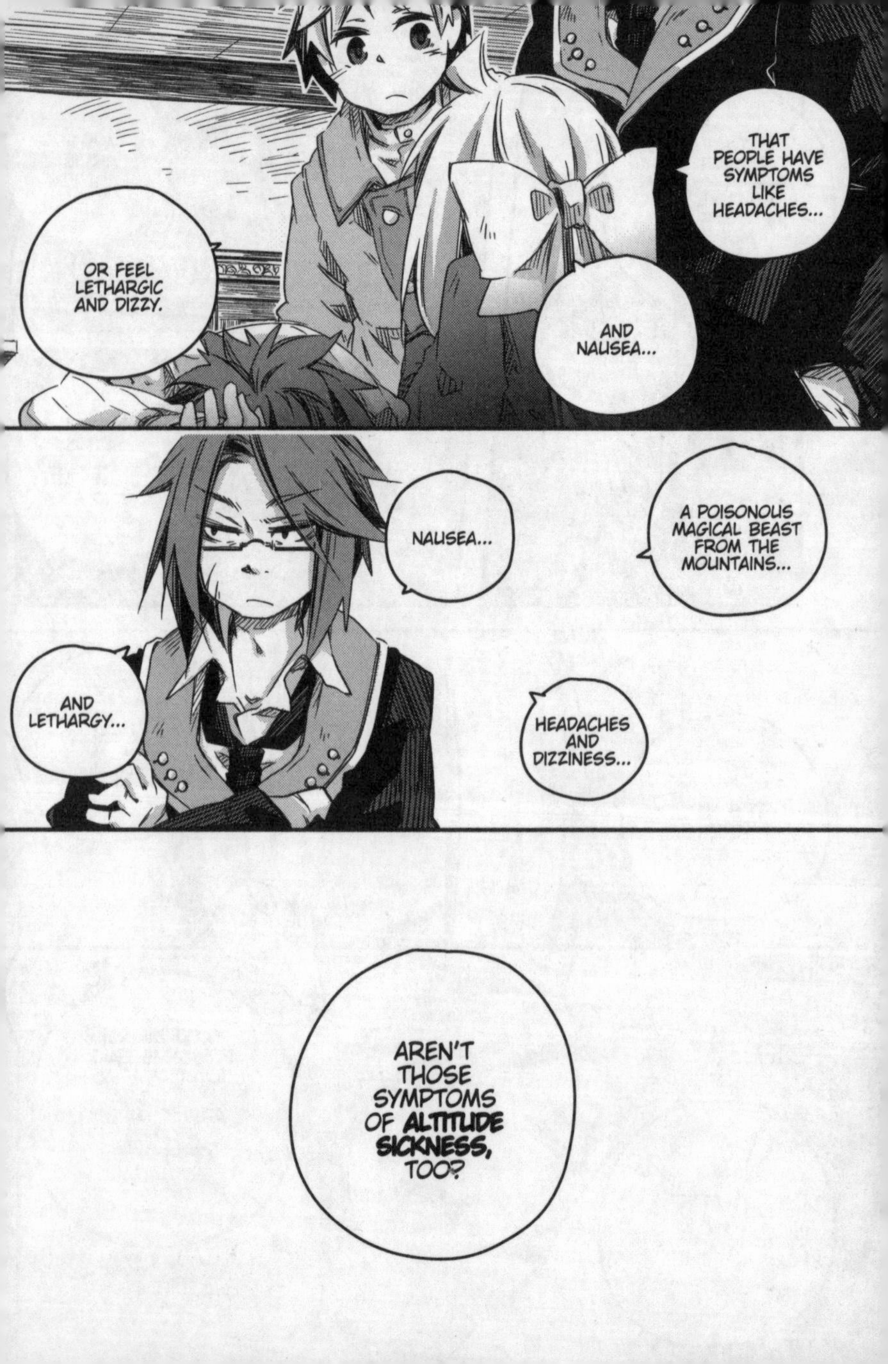
THAT PEOPLE HAVE SYMPTOMS LIKE HEADACHES...
AND NAUSEA...
OR FEEL LETHARGIC AND DIZZY.
A POISONOUS MAGICAL BEAST FROM THE MOUNTAINS...
NAUSEA...
HEADACHES AND DIZZINESS...
AND LETHARGY...
AREN'T THOSE SYMPTOMS OF **ALTITUDE SICKNESS,** TOO?

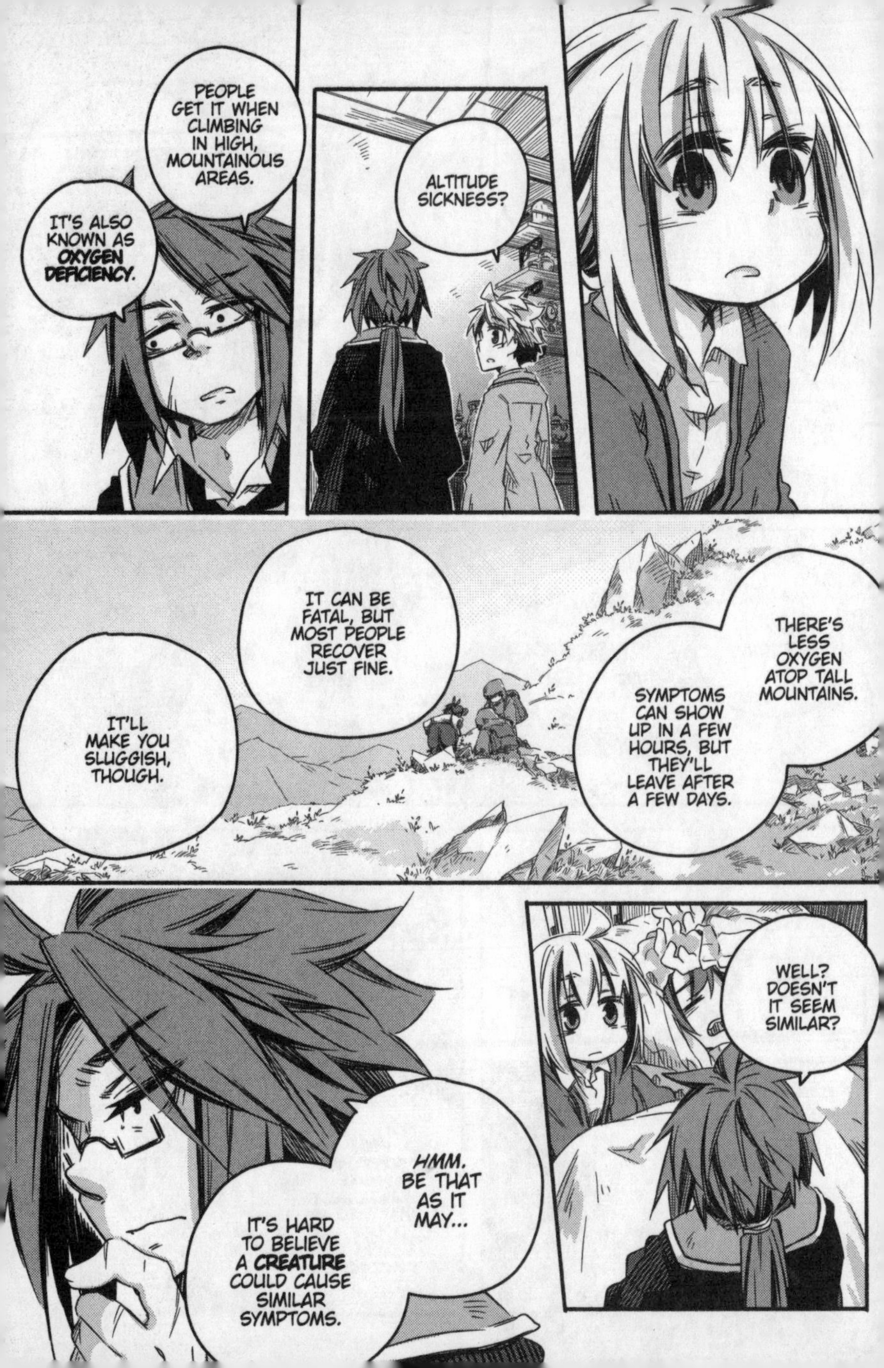
ALTITUDE SICKNESS?
PEOPLE GET IT WHEN CLIMBING IN HIGH, MOUNTAINOUS AREAS.
IT'S ALSO KNOWN AS **OXYGEN DEFICIENCY.**
THERE'S LESS OXYGEN ATOP TALL MOUNTAINS.
SYMPTOMS CAN SHOW UP IN A FEW HOURS, BUT THEY'LL LEAVE AFTER A FEW DAYS.
IT CAN BE FATAL, BUT MOST PEOPLE RECOVER JUST FINE.
IT'LL MAKE YOU SLUGGISH, THOUGH.
WELL? DOESN'T IT SEEM SIMILAR?
HMM. BE THAT AS IT MAY...
IT'S HARD TO BELIEVE A **CREATURE** COULD CAUSE SIMILAR SYMPTOMS.

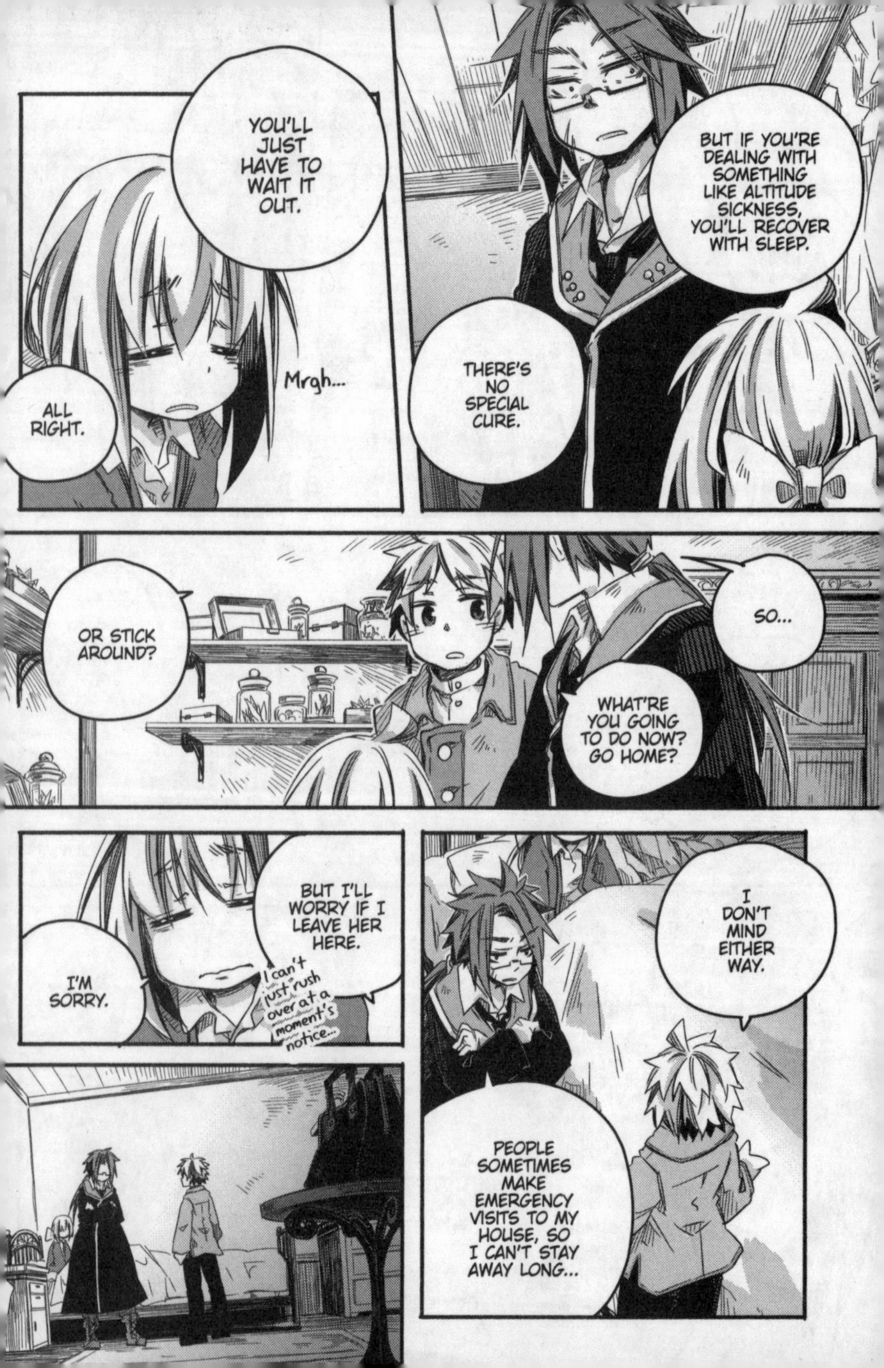
BUT IF YOU'RE DEALING WITH SOMETHING LIKE ALTITUDE SICKNESS, YOU'LL RECOVER WITH SLEEP.
THERE'S NO SPECIAL CURE.
YOU'LL JUST HAVE TO WAIT IT OUT.
Mrgh...
ALL RIGHT.
SO...
WHAT'RE YOU GOING TO DO NOW? GO HOME?
OR STICK AROUND?
I DON'T MIND EITHER WAY.
PEOPLE SOMETIMES MAKE EMERGENCY VISITS TO MY HOUSE, SO I CAN'T STAY AWAY LONG...
BUT I'LL WORRY IF I LEAVE HER HERE.
I can't just rush over at a moment's notice...
I'M SORRY.

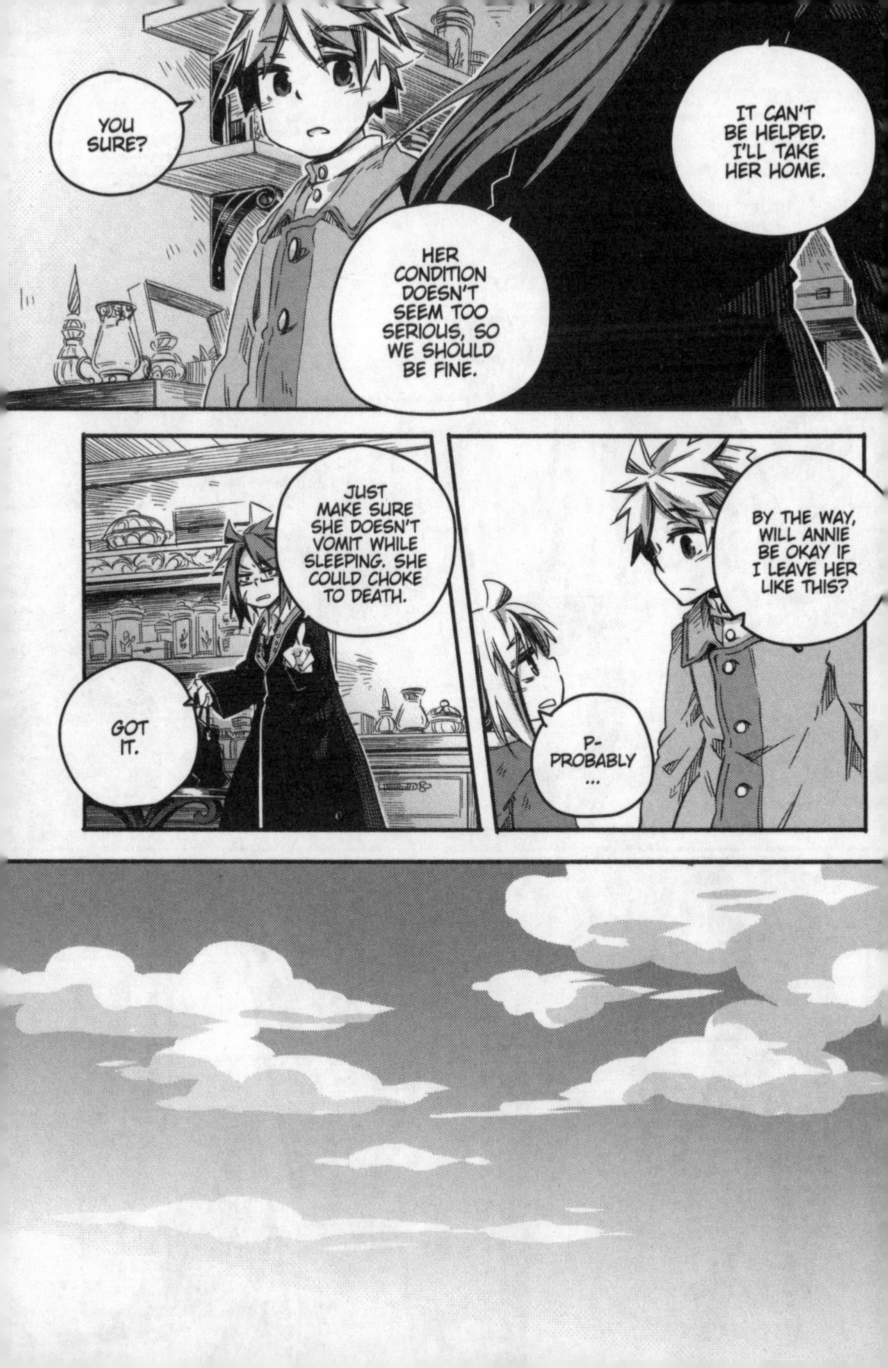
IT CAN'T BE HELPED. I'LL TAKE HER HOME.
YOU SURE?
HER CONDITION DOESN'T SEEM TOO SERIOUS, SO WE SHOULD BE FINE.
BY THE WAY, WILL ANNIE BE OKAY IF I LEAVE HER LIKE THIS?
P-PROBABLY ...
JUST MAKE SURE SHE DOESN'T VOMIT WHILE SLEEPING. SHE COULD CHOKE TO DEATH.
GOT IT.

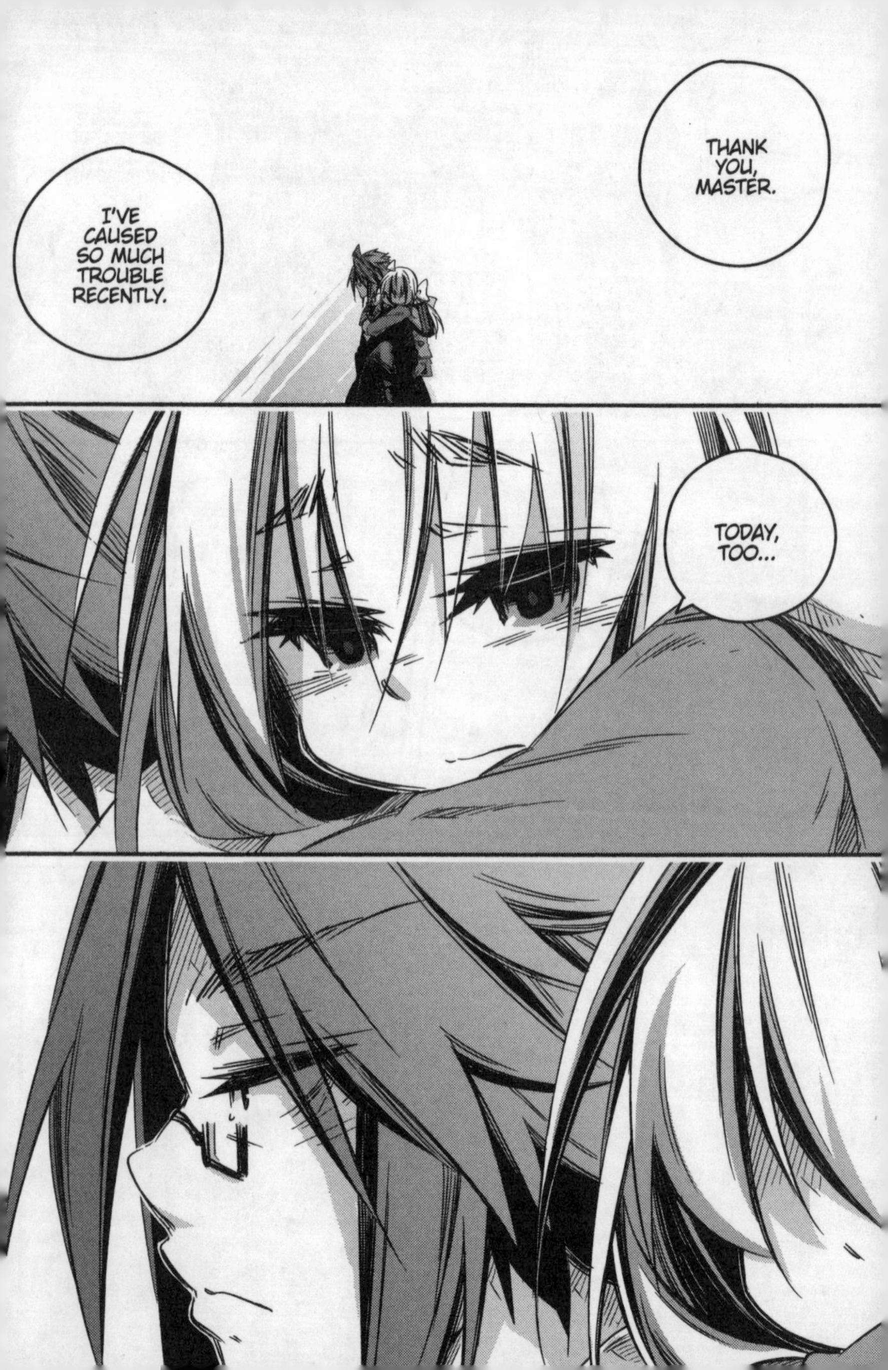
THANK YOU, MASTER.
I'VE CAUSED SO MUCH TROUBLE RECENTLY.
TODAY, TOO...

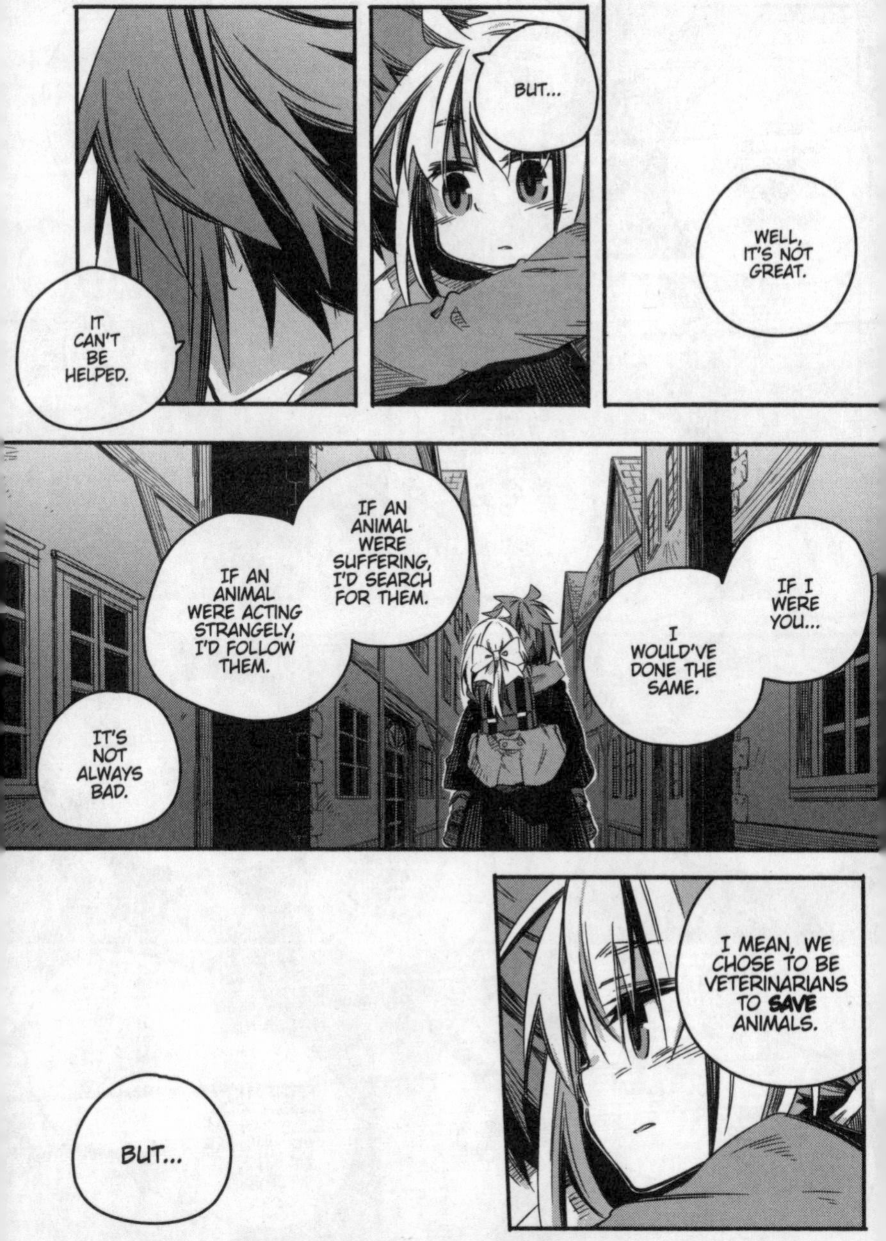
WELL, IT'S NOT GREAT.
BUT...
IT CAN'T BE HELPED.
IF I WERE YOU...
I WOULD'VE DONE THE SAME.
IF AN ANIMAL WERE SUFFERING, I'D SEARCH FOR THEM.
IF AN ANIMAL WERE ACTING STRANGELY, I'D FOLLOW THEM.
IT'S NOT ALWAYS BAD.
I MEAN, WE CHOSE TO BE VETERINARIANS TO **SAVE** ANIMALS.
BUT...

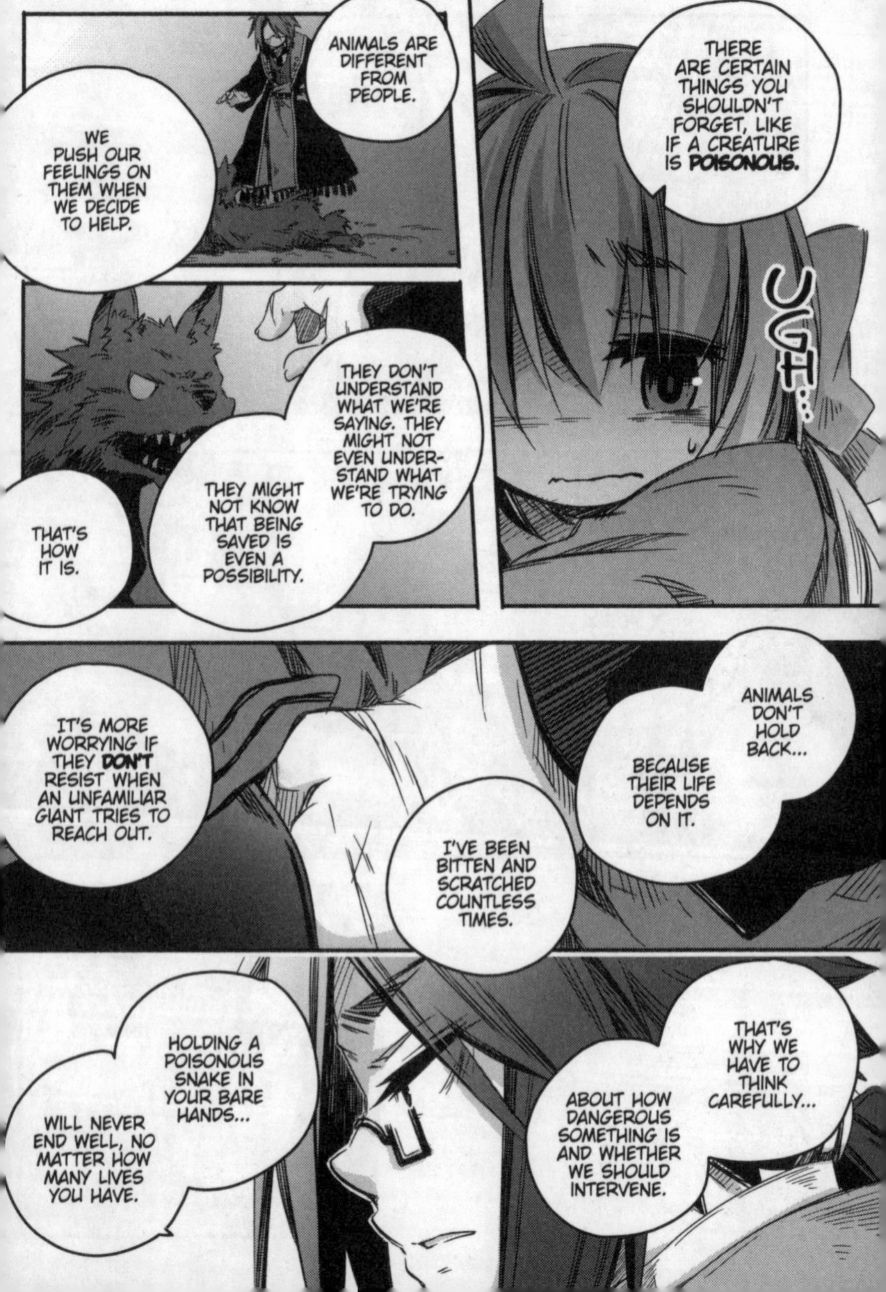
THERE ARE CERTAIN THINGS YOU SHOULDN'T FORGET, LIKE IF A CREATURE IS **POISONOUS.**
UGH...
ANIMALS ARE DIFFERENT FROM PEOPLE.
WE PUSH OUR FEELINGS ON THEM WHEN WE DECIDE TO HELP.
THEY DON'T UNDERSTAND WHAT WE'RE SAYING. THEY MIGHT NOT EVEN UNDER-STAND WHAT WE'RE TRYING TO DO.
THEY MIGHT NOT KNOW THAT BEING SAVED IS EVEN A POSSIBILITY.
THAT'S HOW IT IS.
ANIMALS DON'T HOLD BACK...
BECAUSE THEIR LIFE DEPENDS ON IT.
I'VE BEEN BITTEN AND SCRATCHED COUNTLESS TIMES.
IT'S MORE WORRYING IF THEY **DON'T** RESIST WHEN AN UNFAMILIAR GIANT TRIES TO REACH OUT.
THAT'S WHY WE HAVE TO THINK CAREFULLY...
ABOUT HOW DANGEROUS SOMETHING IS AND WHETHER WE SHOULD INTERVENE.
HOLDING A POISONOUS SNAKE IN YOUR BARE HANDS...
WILL NEVER END WELL, NO MATTER HOW MANY LIVES YOU HAVE.

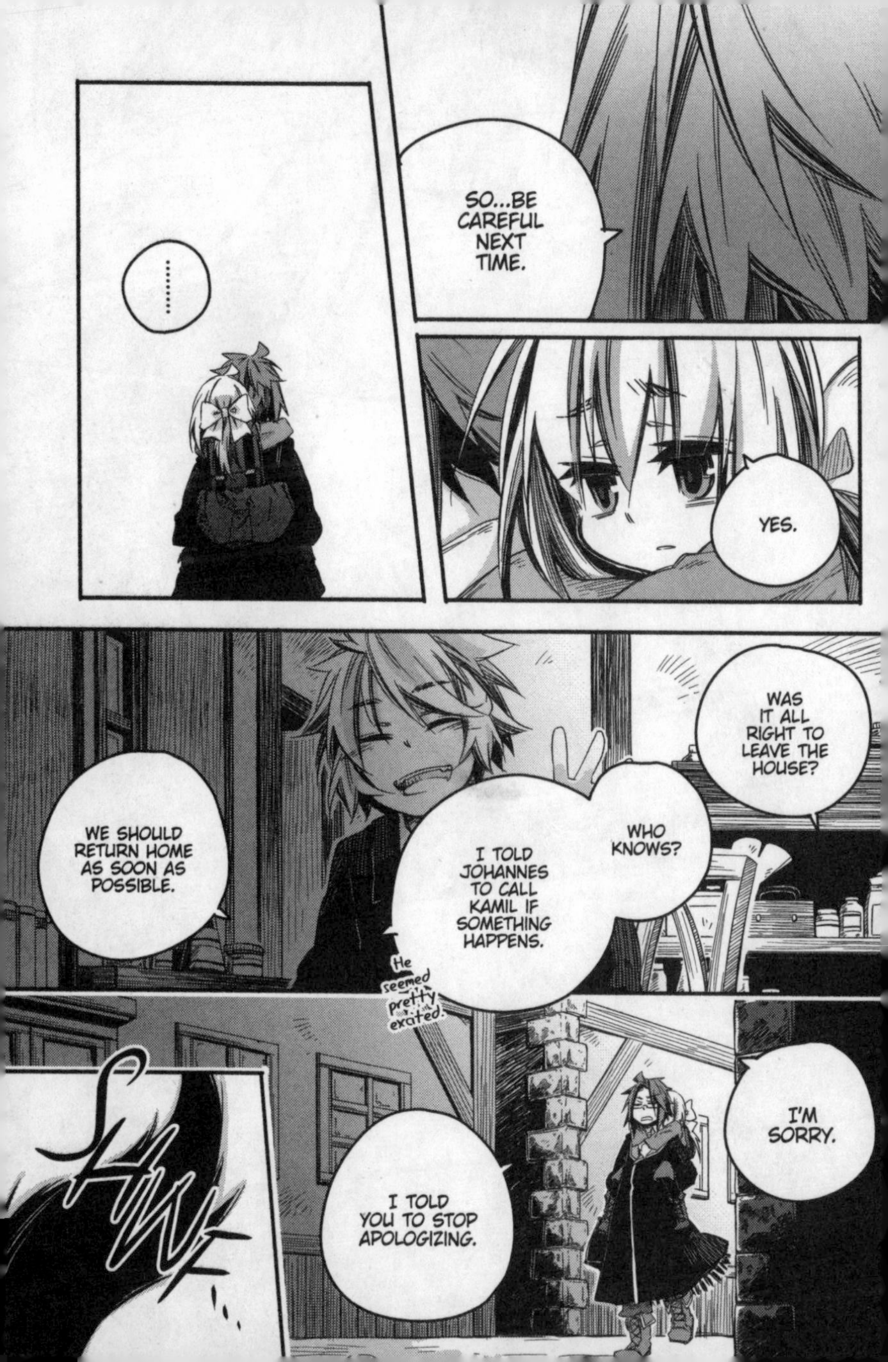
SO...BE CAREFUL NEXT TIME.
YES.
......
WAS IT ALL RIGHT TO LEAVE THE HOUSE?
WHO KNOWS?
I TOLD JOHANNES TO CALL KAMIL IF SOMETHING HAPPENS.
He seemed pretty excited.
WE SHOULD RETURN HOME AS SOON AS POSSIBLE.
I'M SORRY.
I TOLD YOU TO STOP APOLOGIZING.
SHW
!..

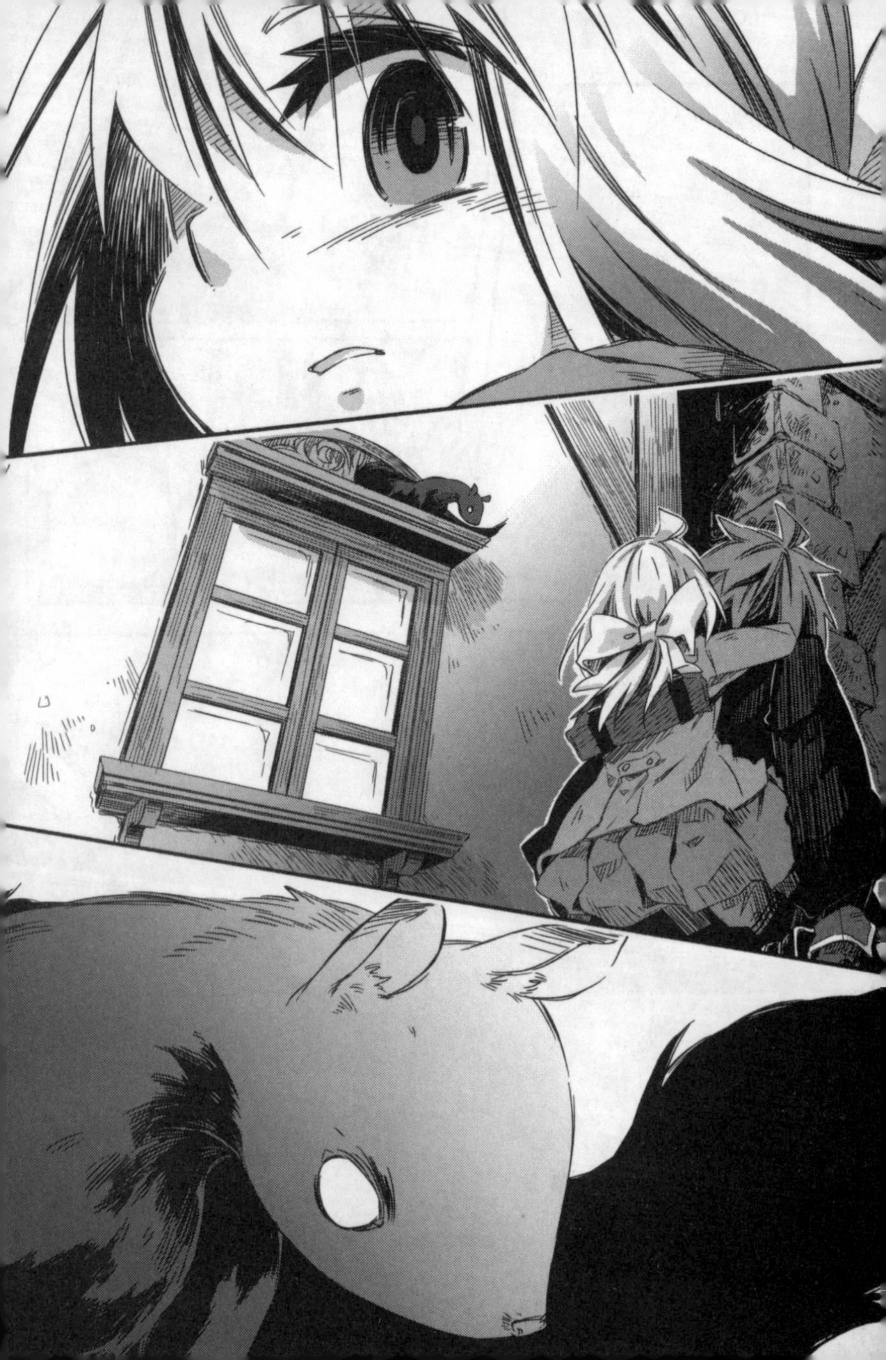

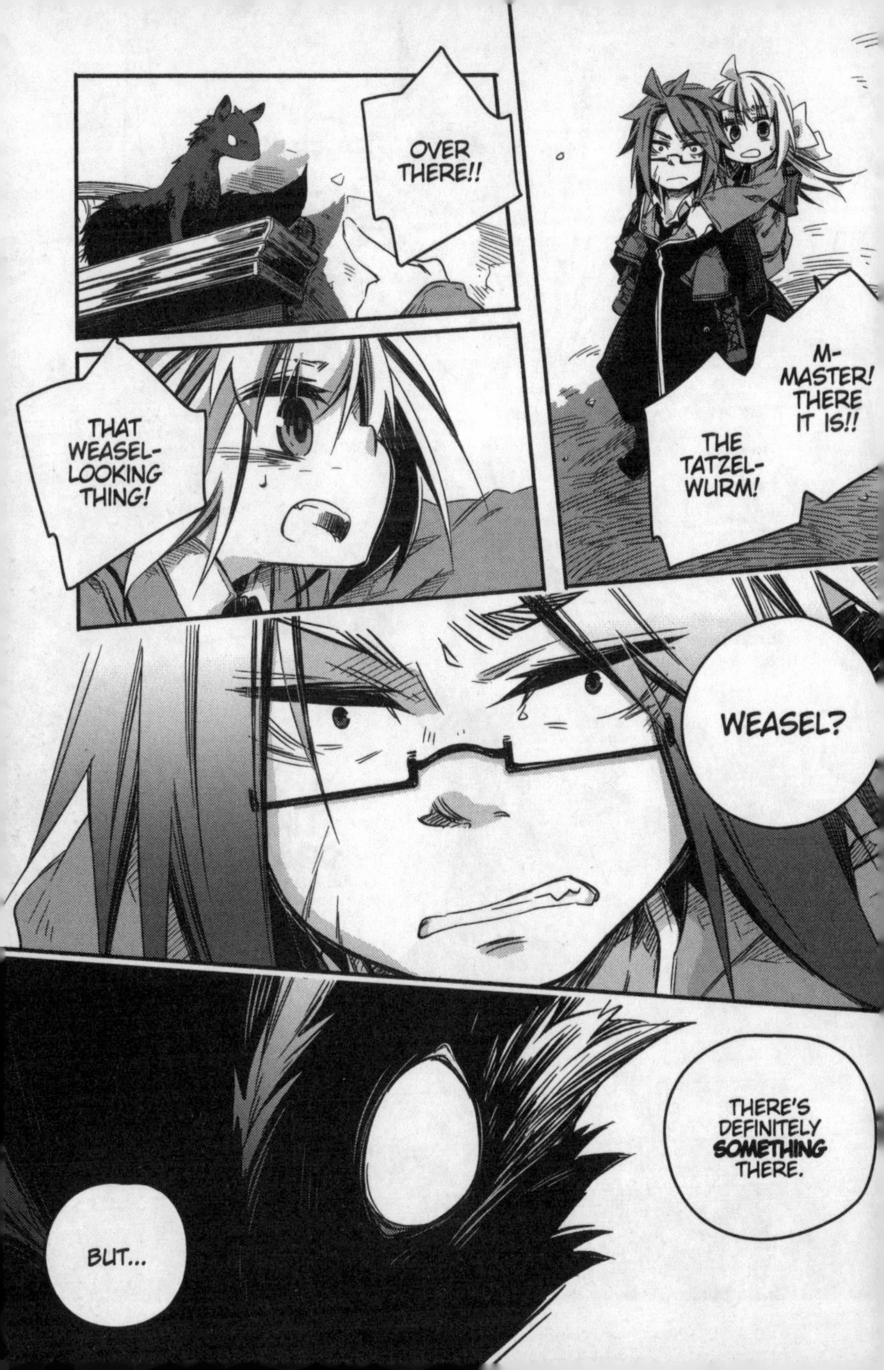
M-MASTER! THERE IT IS!!
THE TATZELWURM!
OVER THERE!!
THAT WEASEL-LOOKING THING!
WEASEL?
THERE'S DEFINITELY **SOMETHING** THERE.
BUT...

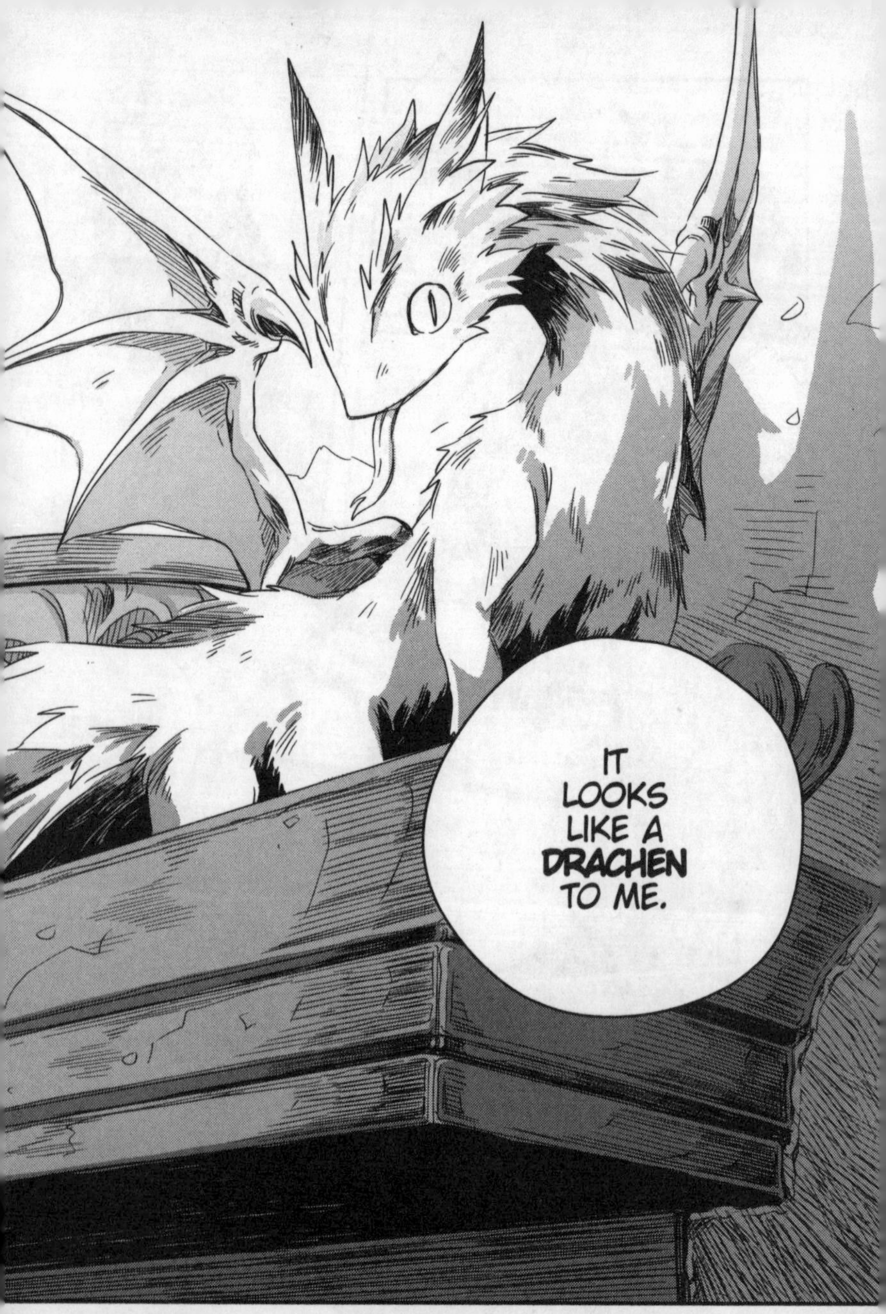
IT LOOKS LIKE A DRACHEN TO ME.

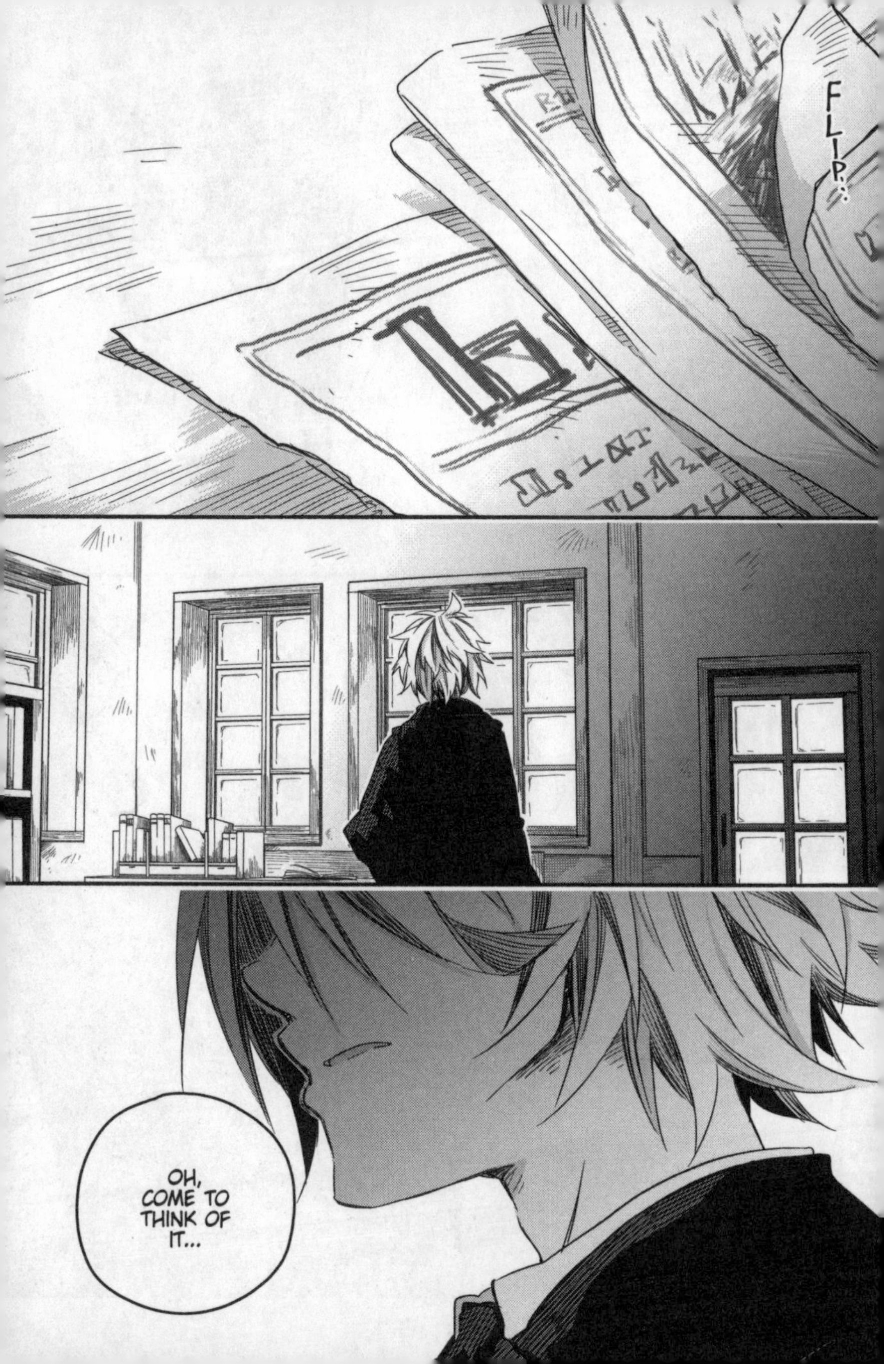
FLIP...
OH, COME TO THINK OF IT...

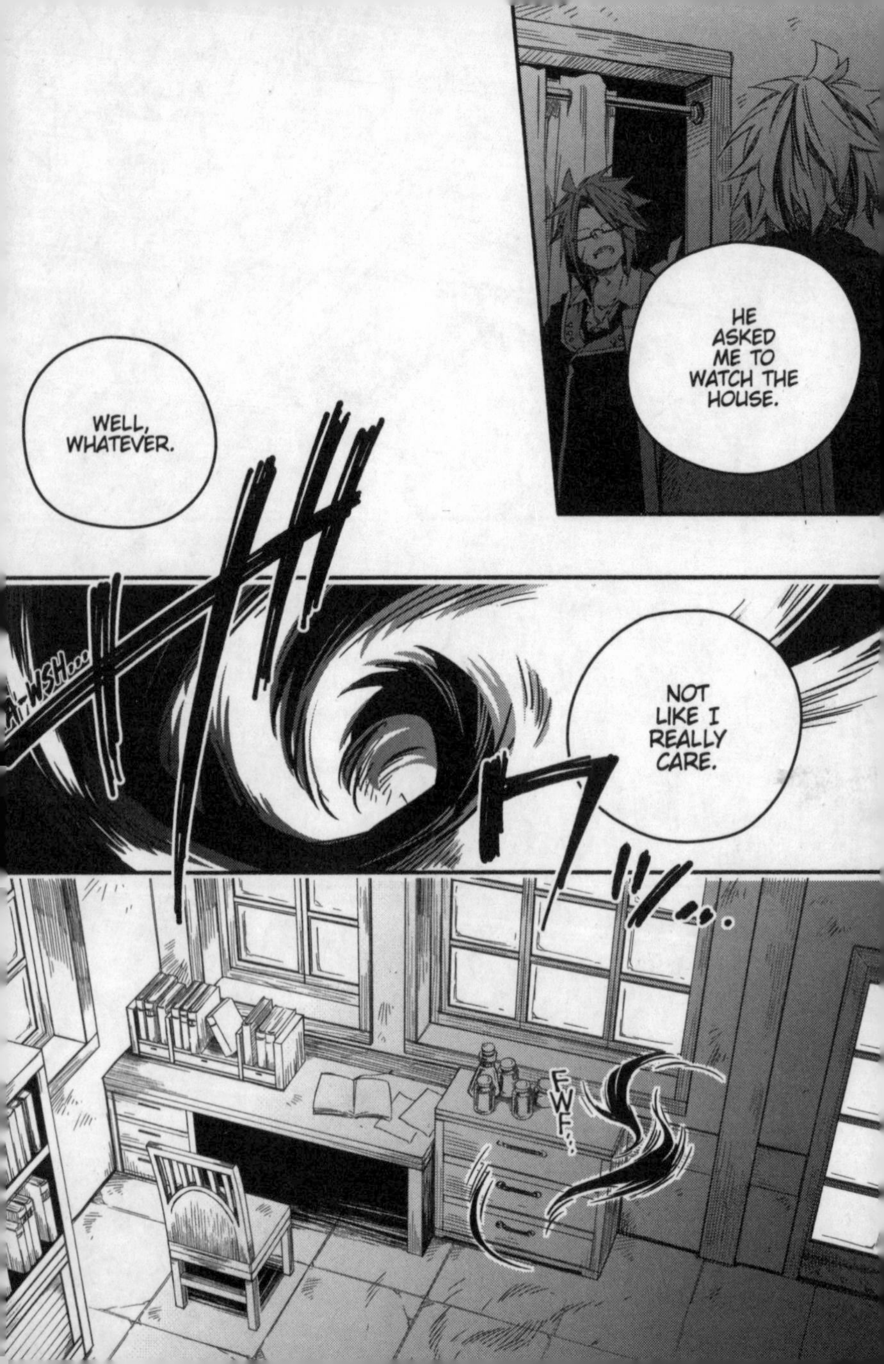
HE ASKED ME TO WATCH THE HOUSE.
WELL, WHATEVER.
NOT LIKE I REALLY CARE.
A-WSH...
FWF...

[Case 25: Truth And Imagination]

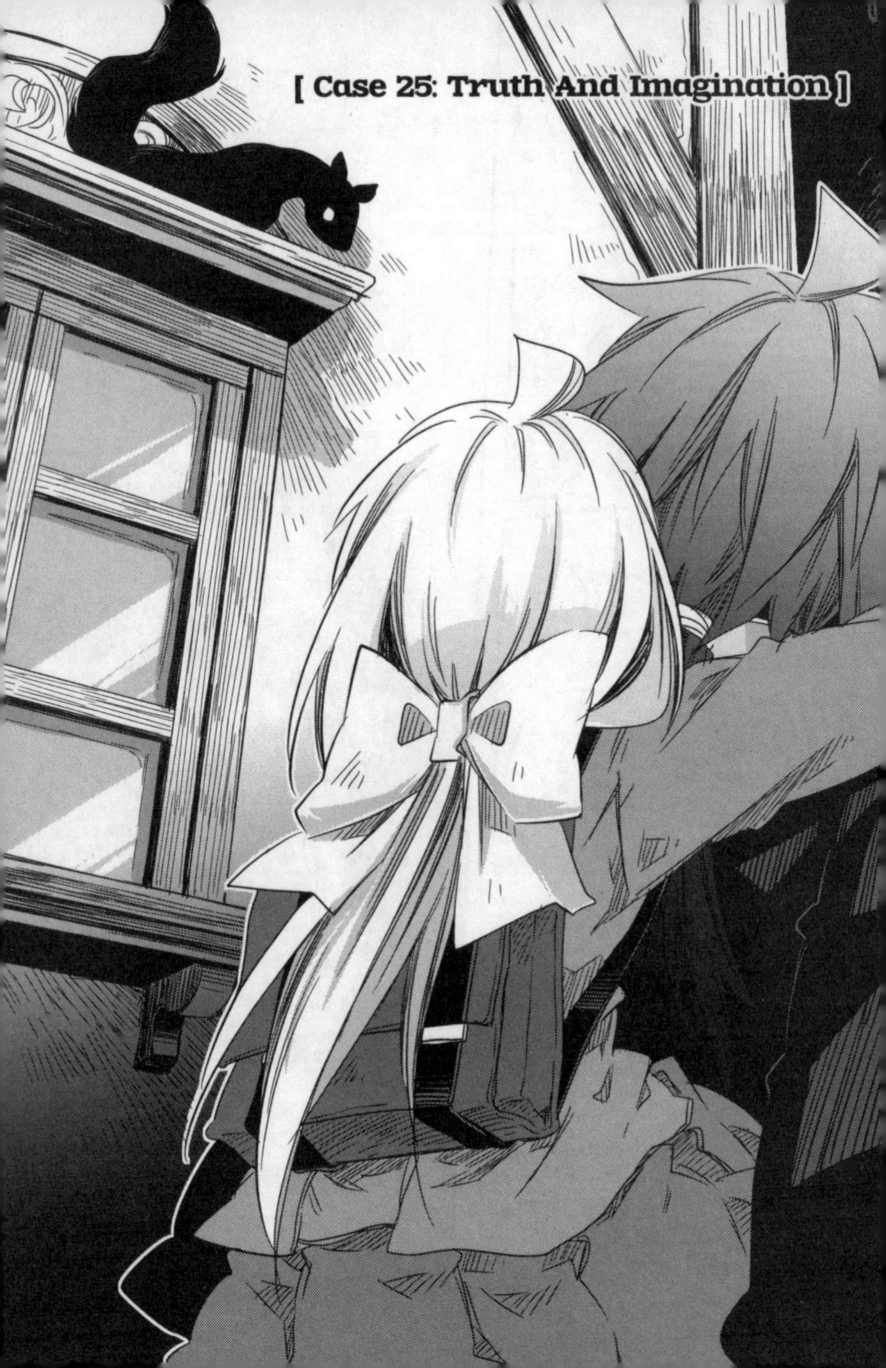

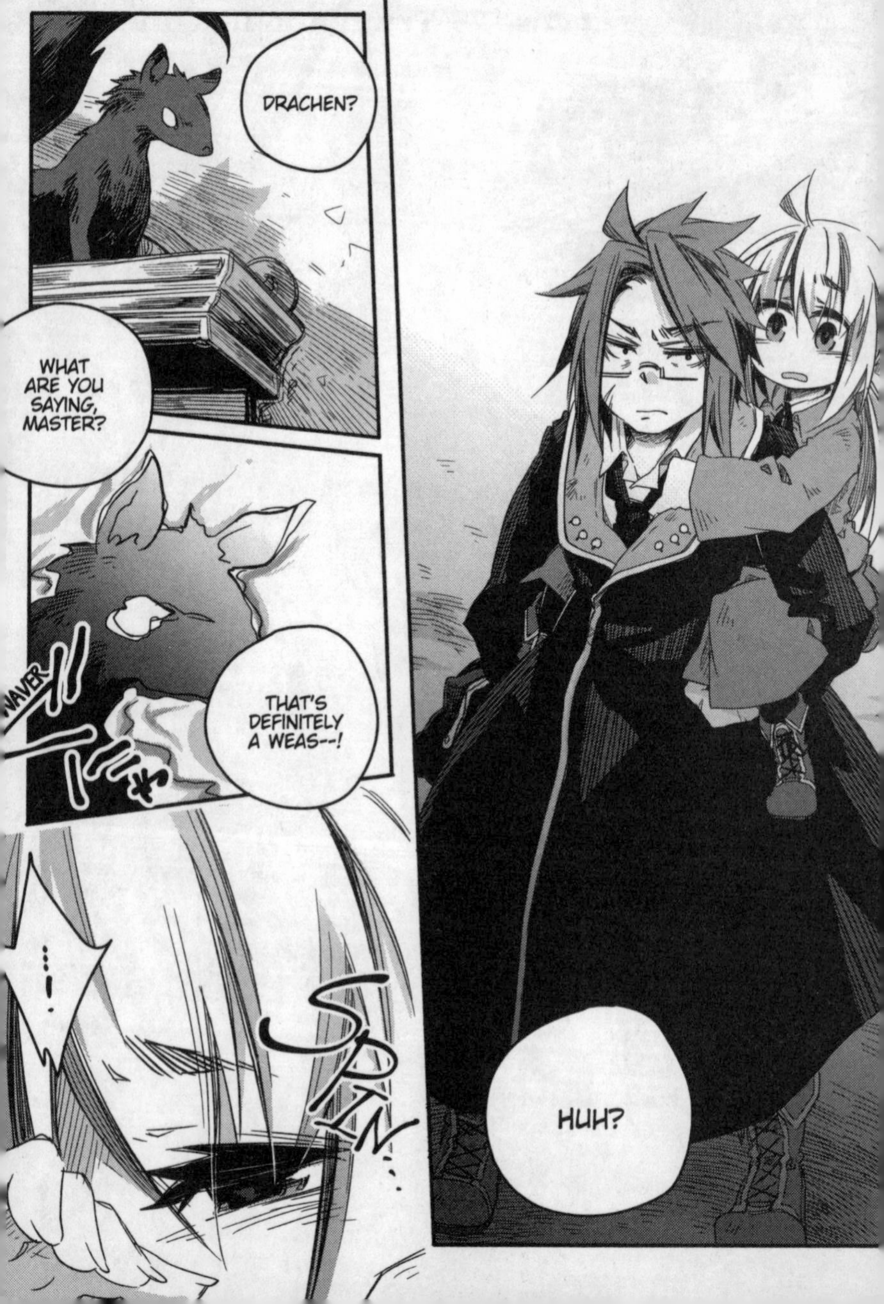
HUH?
DRACHEN?
WHAT ARE YOU SAYING, MASTER?
THAT'S DEFINITELY A WEAS--!
WAVER
...!
SPIN

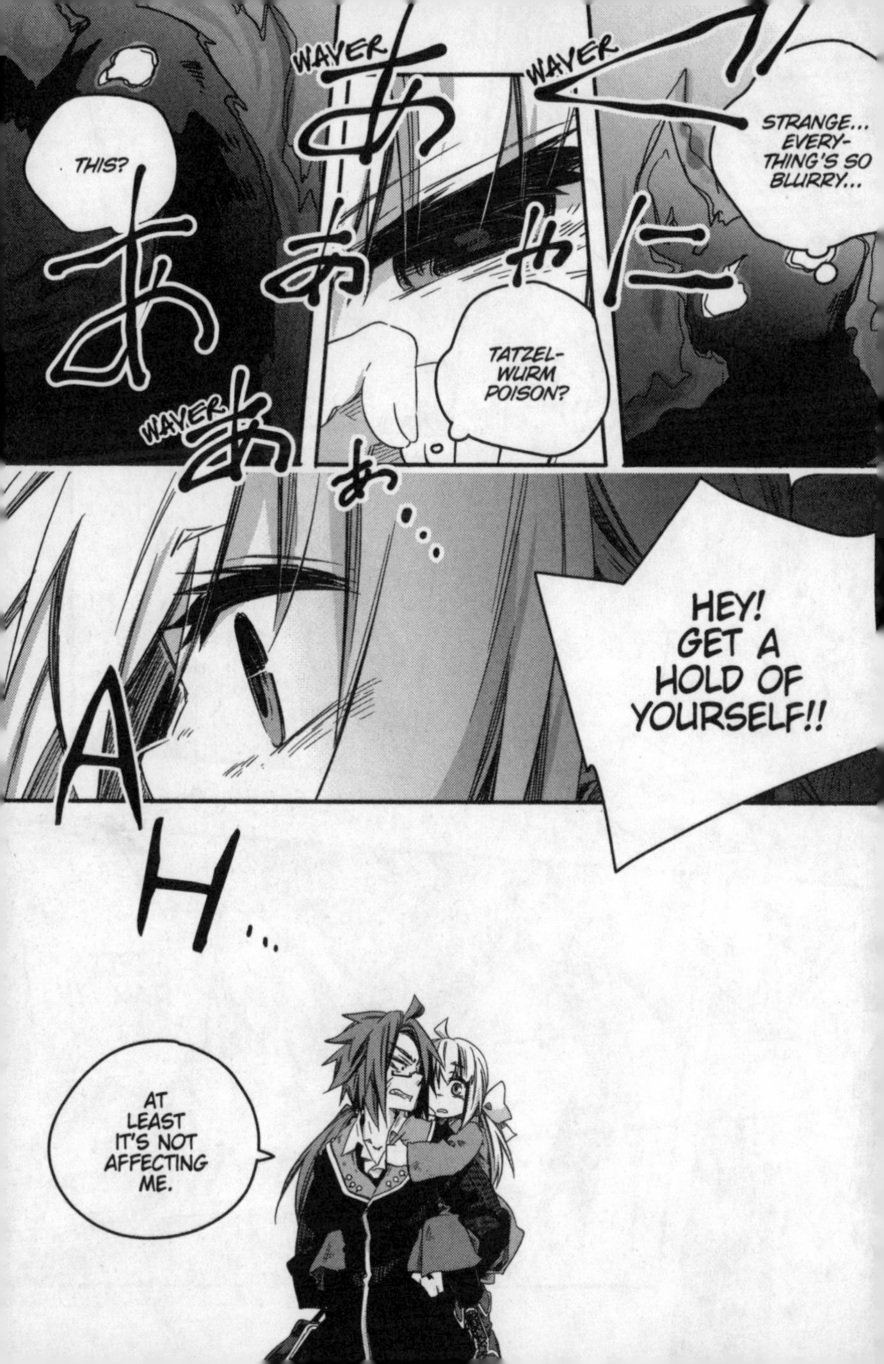

WAVER
STRANGE... EVERYTHING'S SO BLURRY...
WAVER
TATZELWURM POISON?
THIS?
WAVER
HEY! GET A HOLD OF YOURSELF!!
AH...
AT LEAST IT'S NOT AFFECTING ME.

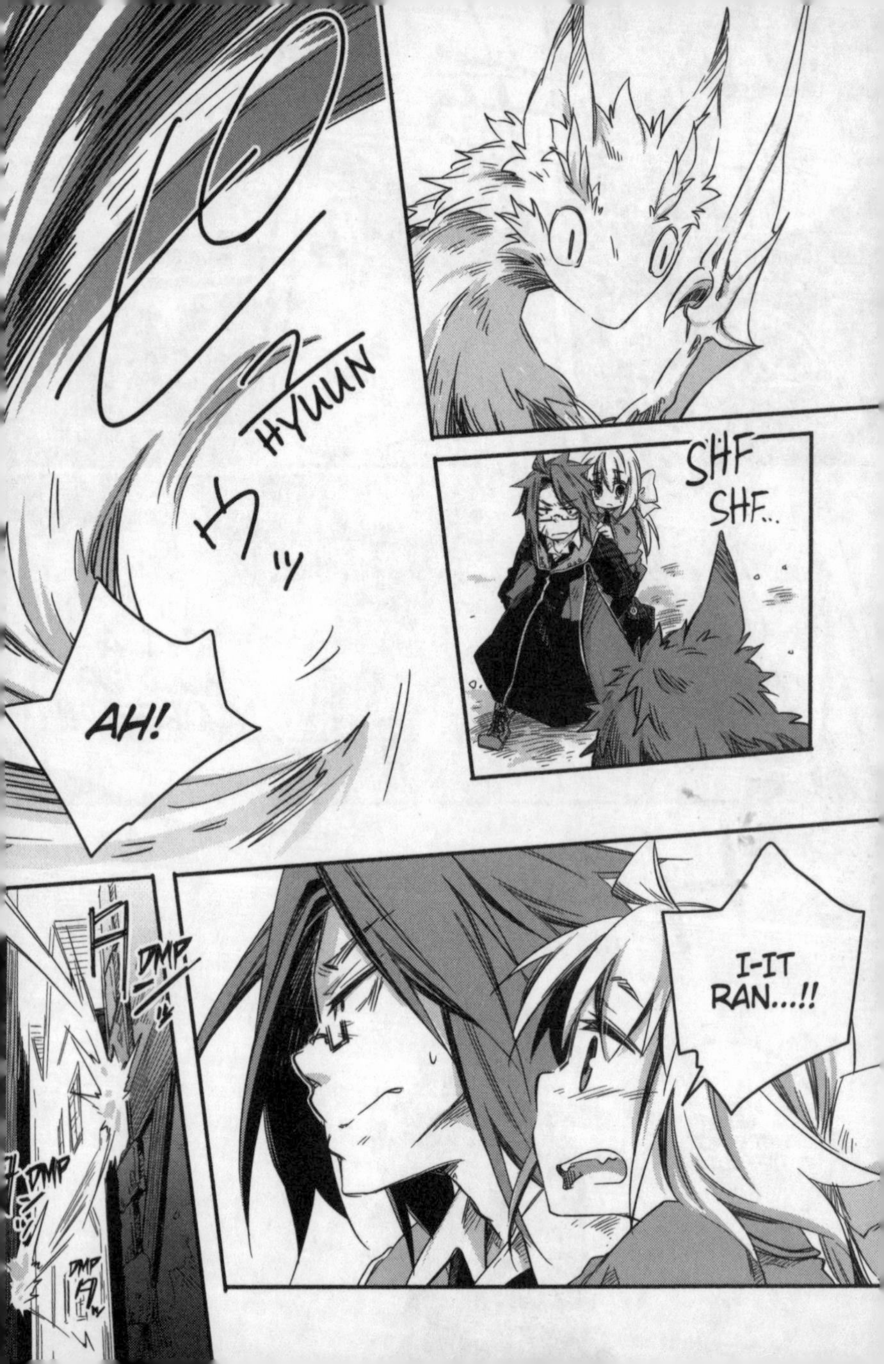
SHF
SHF...
HYUUN
AH!
I-IT RAN...!!
DMP
DMP
DMP

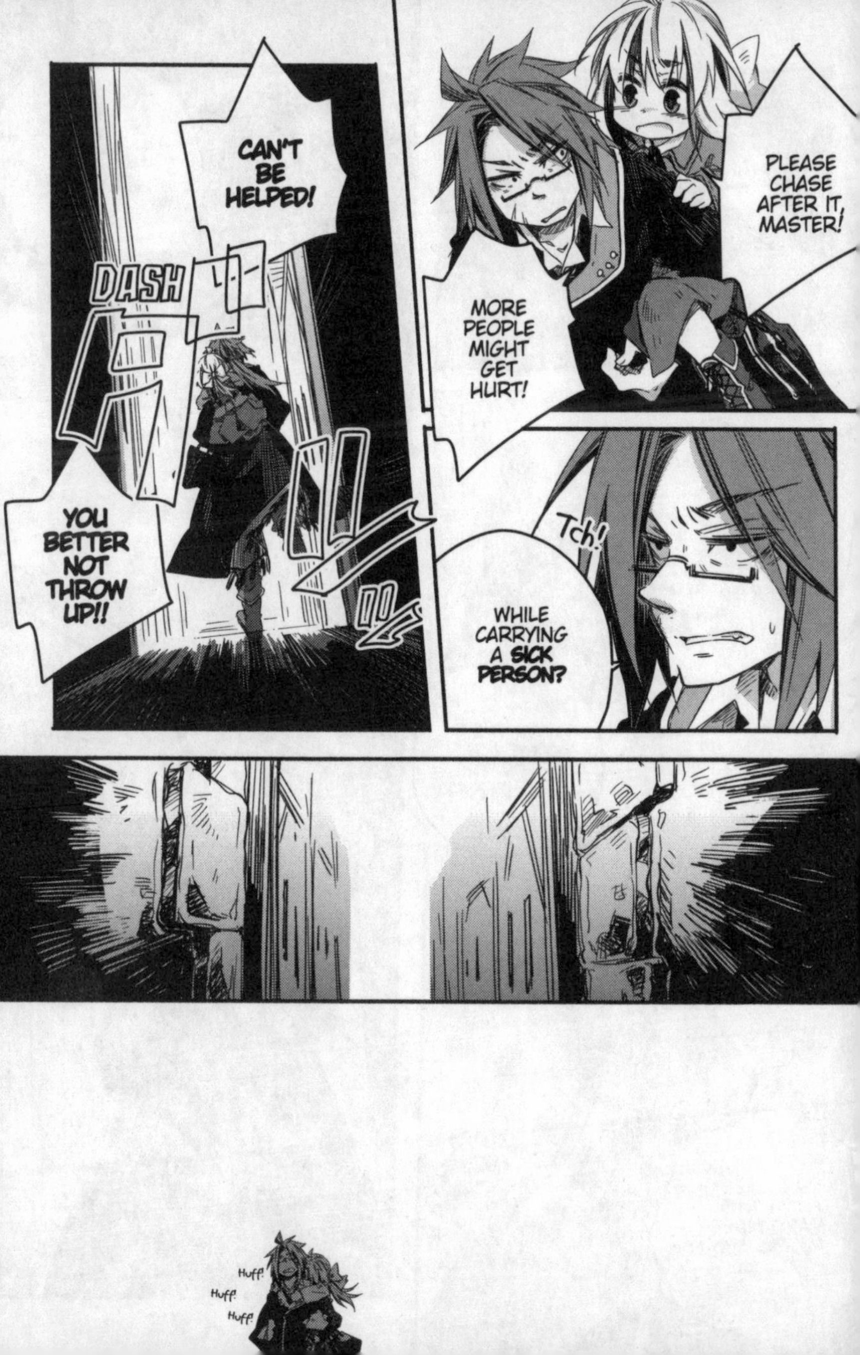
PLEASE CHASE AFTER IT, MASTER!
MORE PEOPLE MIGHT GET HURT!
Tch!
WHILE CARRYING A SICK PERSON?
CAN'T BE HELPED!
DASH
YOU BETTER NOT THROW UP!!
Huff!
Huff!
Huff!

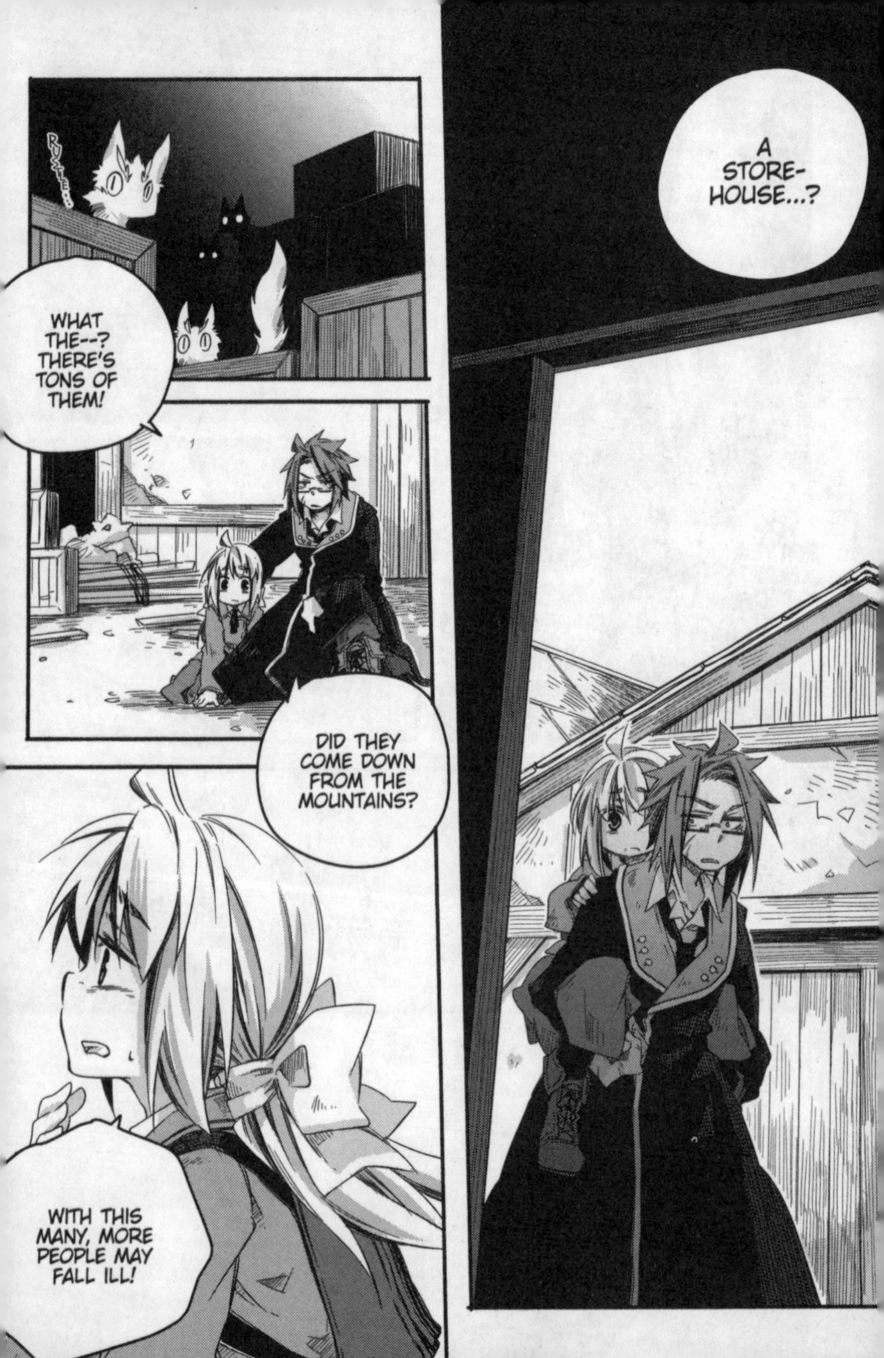
A STORE-HOUSE...?
RUSTLE...
WHAT THE--? THERE'S TONS OF THEM!
DID THEY COME DOWN FROM THE MOUNTAINS?
WITH THIS MANY, MORE PEOPLE MAY FALL ILL!

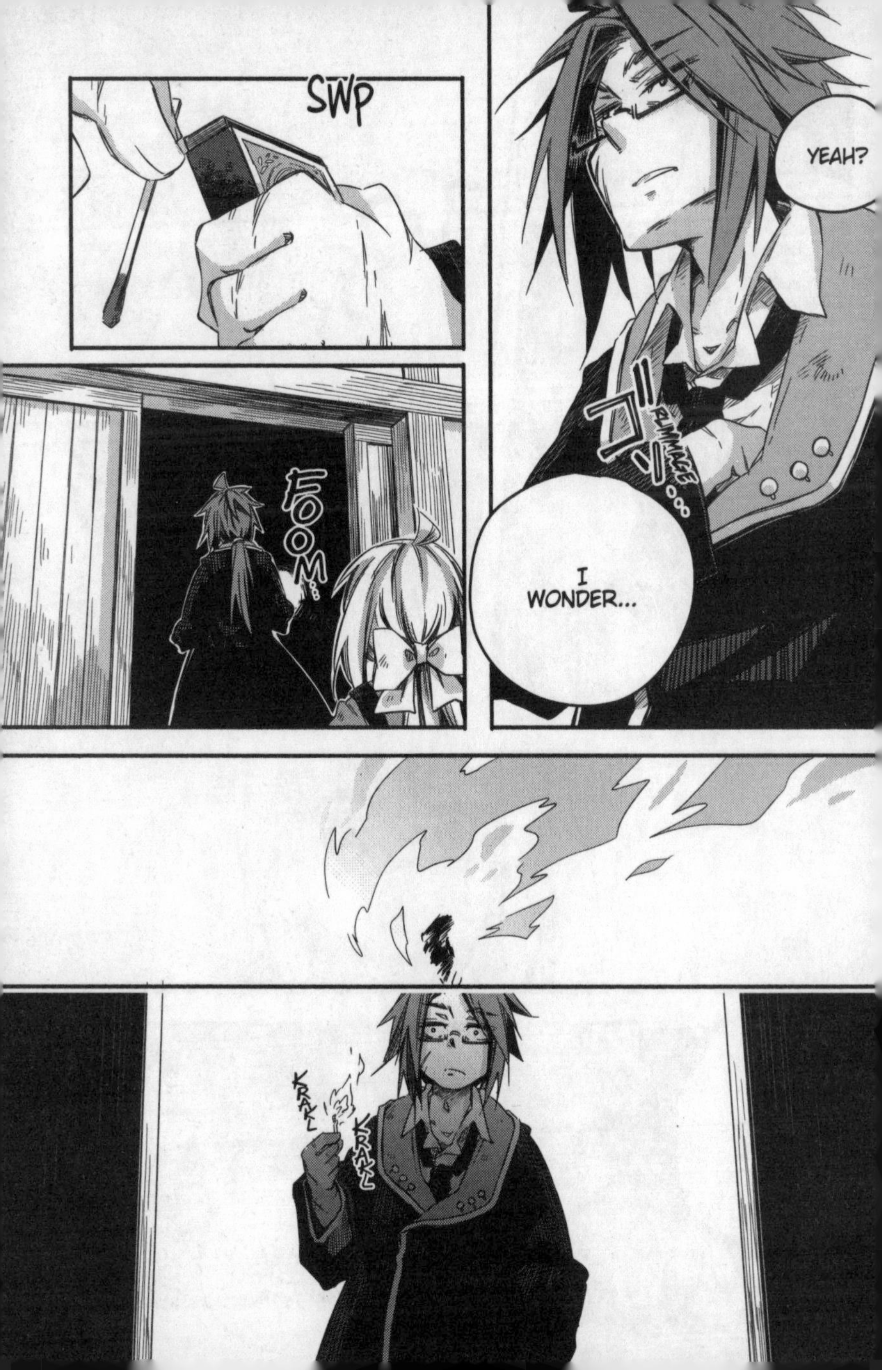
YEAH?
RUMMAGE...
I WONDER...
SWP
FOOM...
KRAKL
KRAKL

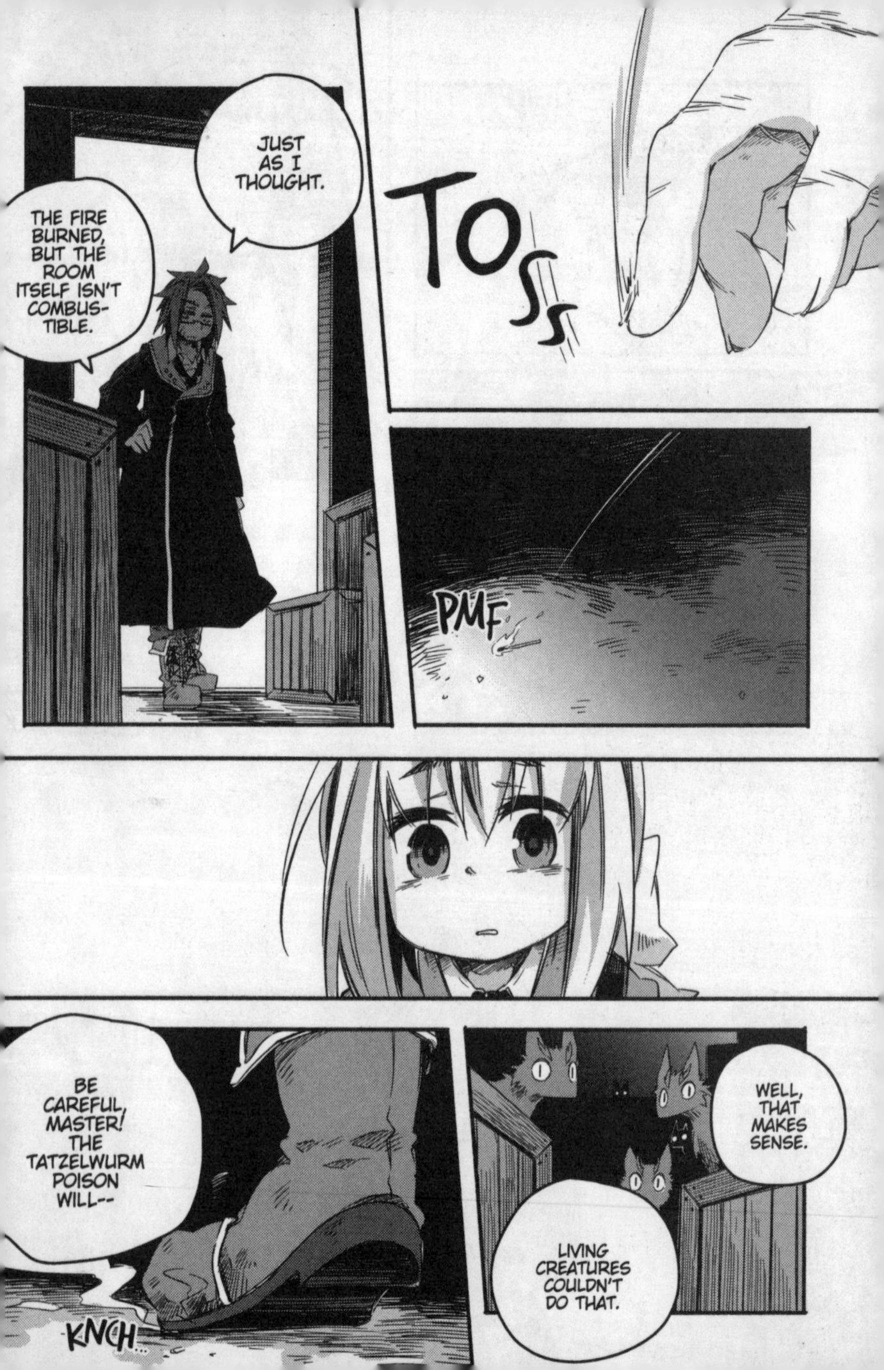
TOSS
PMF
JUST AS I THOUGHT.
THE FIRE BURNED, BUT THE ROOM ITSELF ISN'T COMBUSTIBLE.
WELL, THAT MAKES SENSE.
LIVING CREATURES COULDN'T DO THAT.
BE CAREFUL, MASTER! THE TATZELWURM POISON WILL--
KNCH...

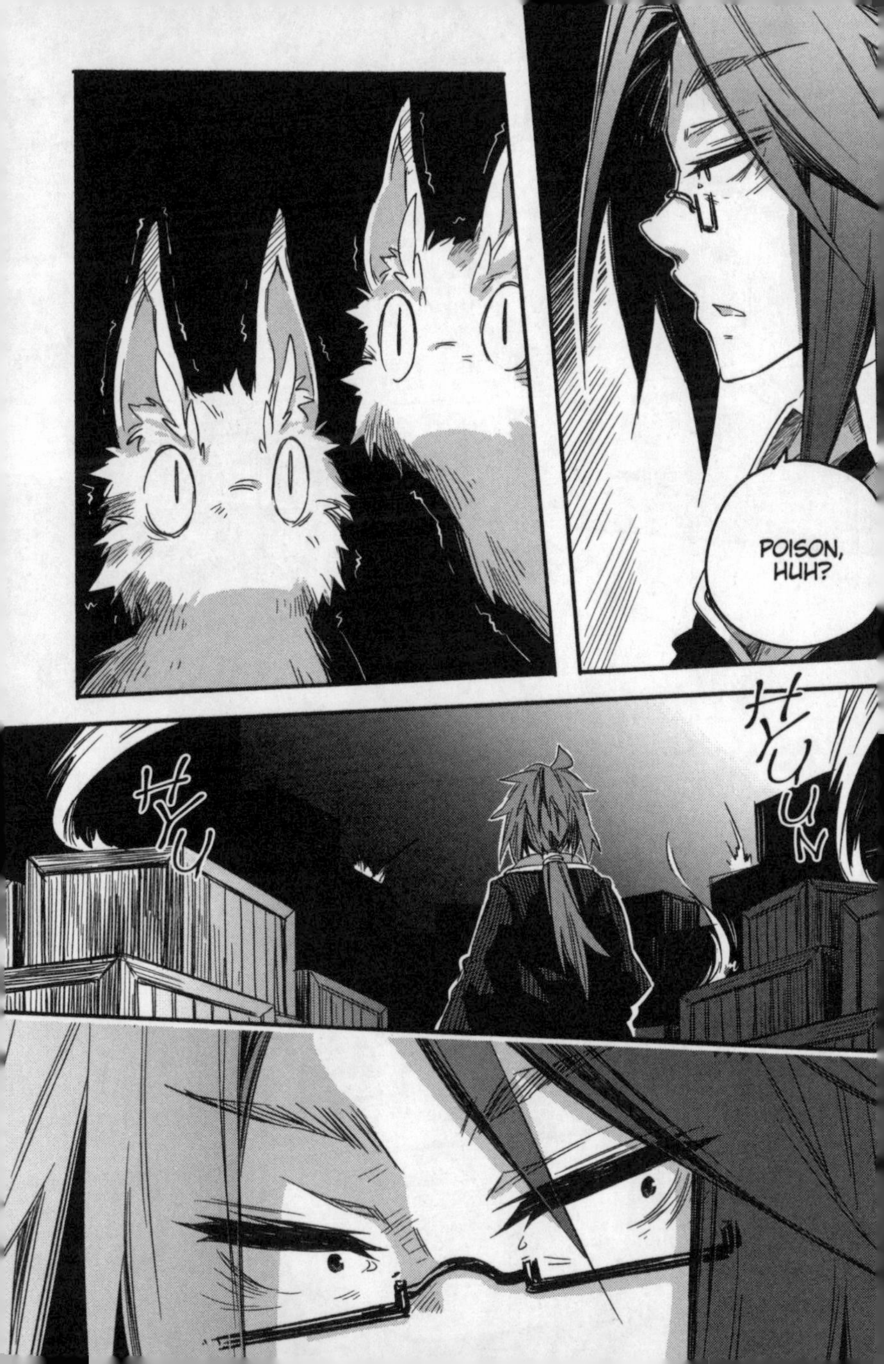
POISON, HUH?
HYUUN
HYU

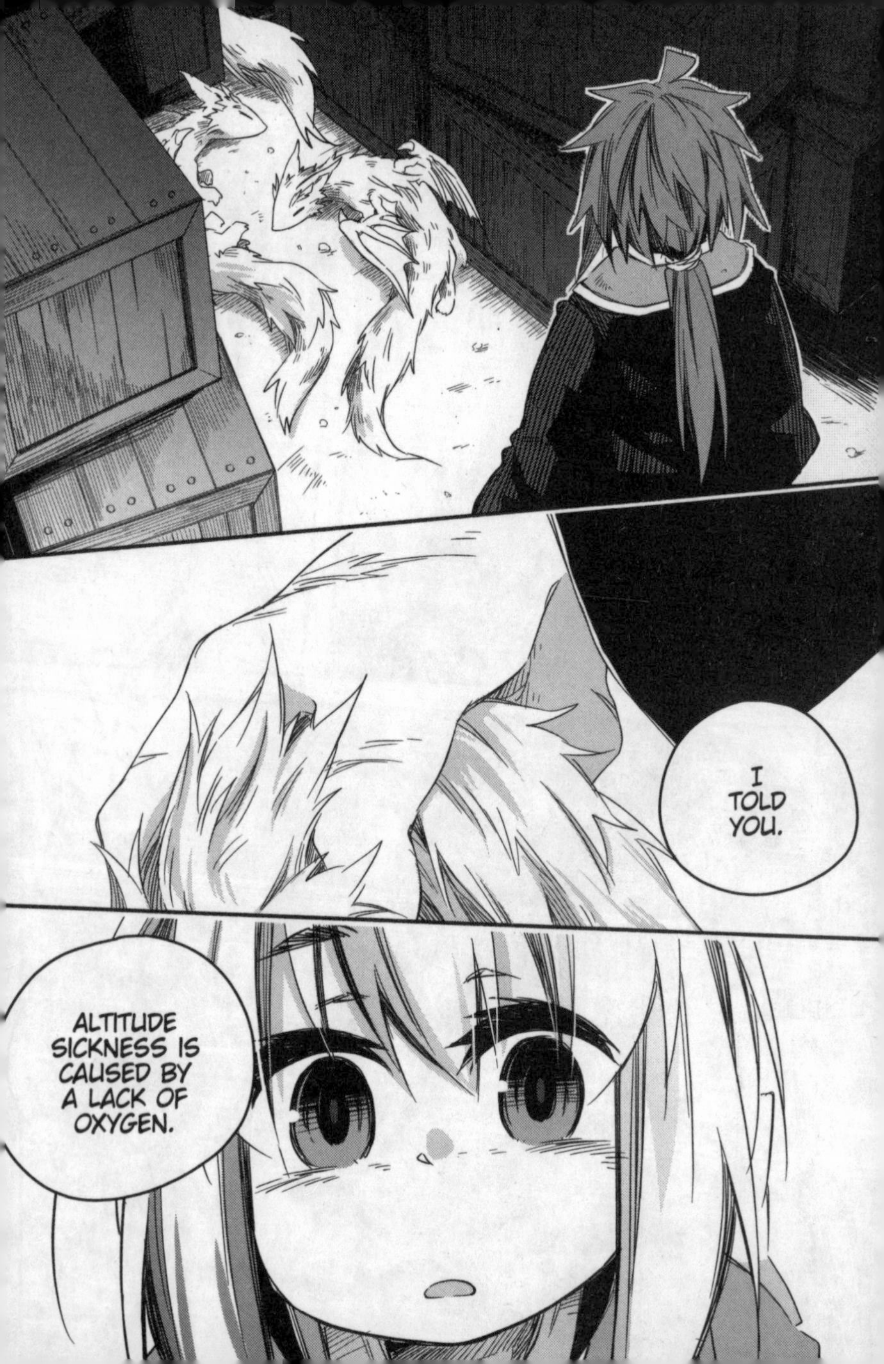
I TOLD YOU.
ALTITUDE SICKNESS IS CAUSED BY A LACK OF OXYGEN.

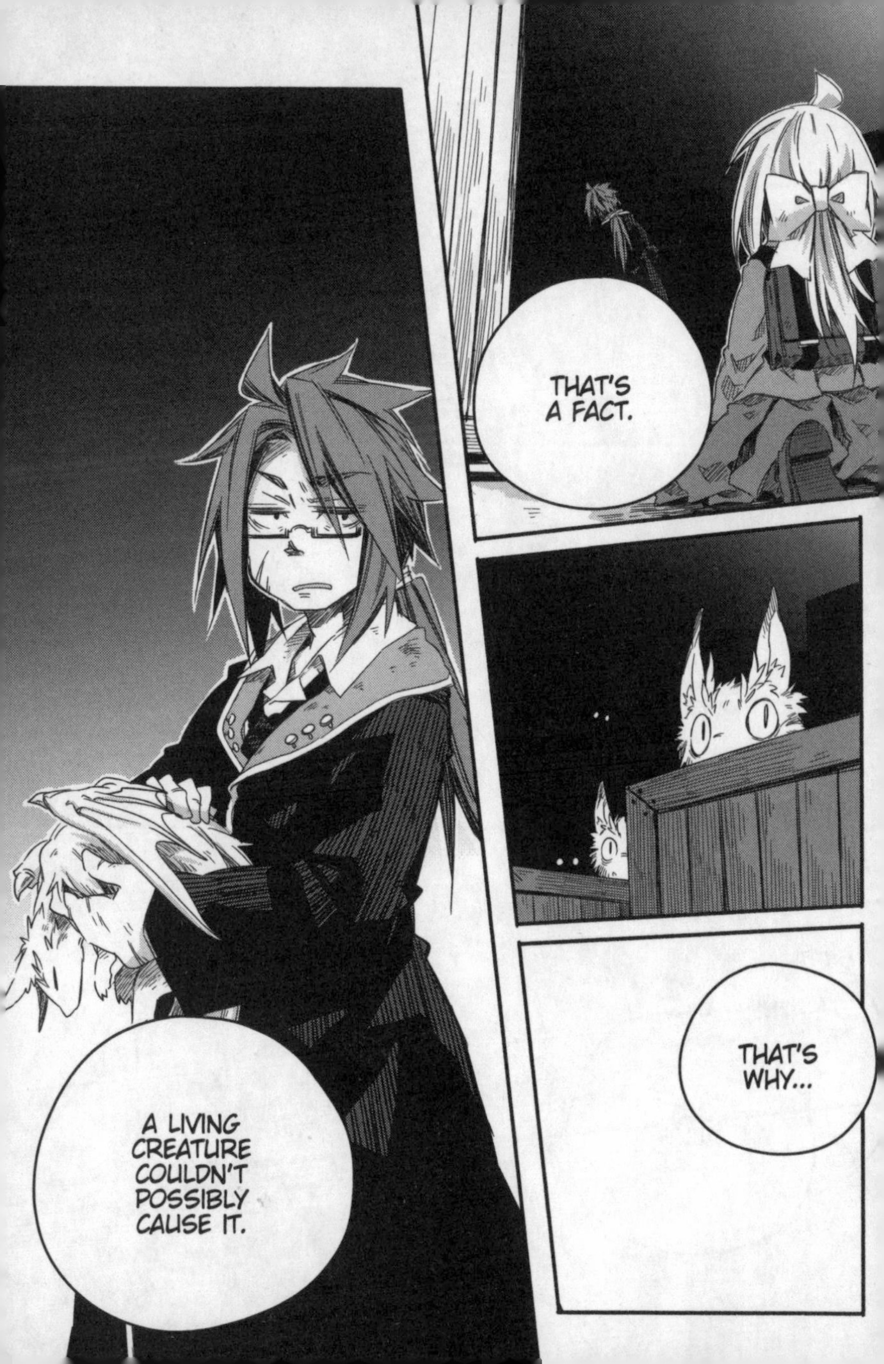
THAT'S A FACT.
THAT'S WHY...
A LIVING CREATURE COULDN'T POSSIBLY CAUSE IT.

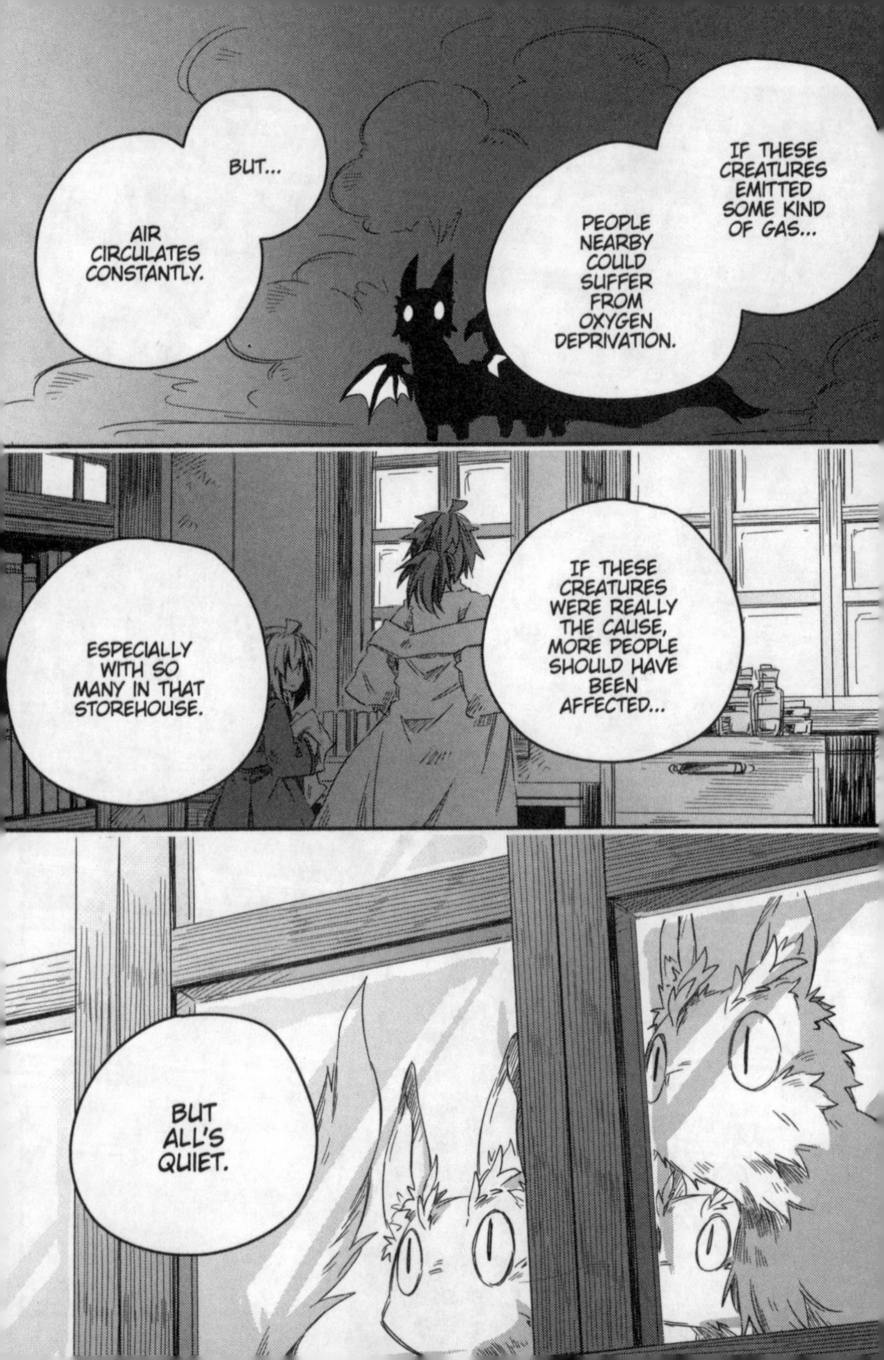
IF THESE CREATURES EMITTED SOME KIND OF GAS...
PEOPLE NEARBY COULD SUFFER FROM OXYGEN DEPRIVATION.
BUT...
AIR CIRCULATES CONSTANTLY.
IF THESE CREATURES WERE REALLY THE CAUSE, MORE PEOPLE SHOULD HAVE BEEN AFFECTED...
ESPECIALLY WITH SO MANY IN THAT STOREHOUSE.
BUT ALL'S QUIET.

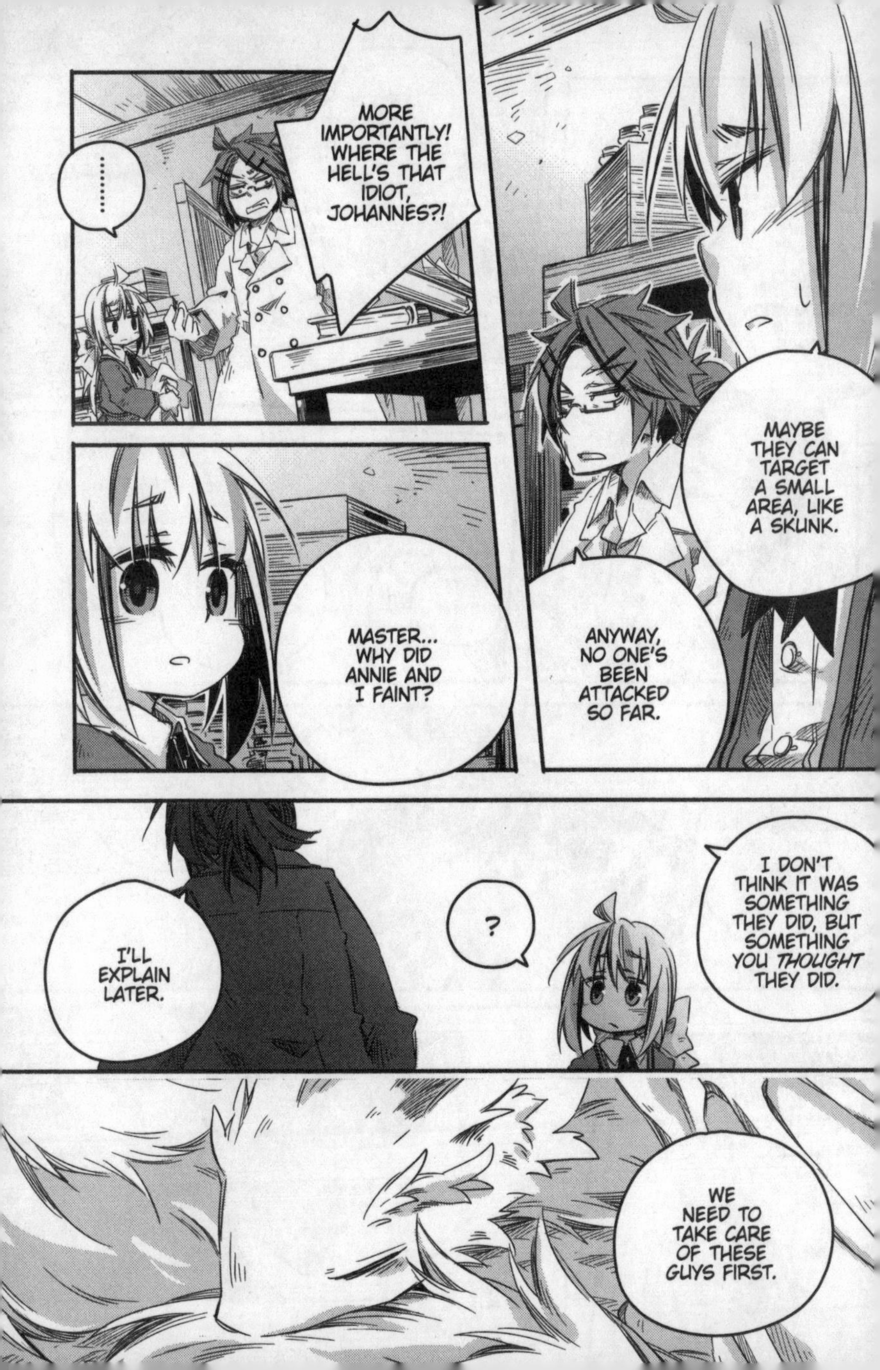
MAYBE THEY CAN TARGET A SMALL AREA, LIKE A SKUNK.
ANYWAY, NO ONE'S BEEN ATTACKED SO FAR.
MORE IMPORTANTLY! WHERE THE HELL'S THAT IDIOT, JOHANNES?!
......
MASTER... WHY DID ANNIE AND I FAINT?
I DON'T THINK IT WAS SOMETHING THEY DID, BUT SOMETHING YOU *THOUGHT* THEY DID.
?
I'LL EXPLAIN LATER.
WE NEED TO TAKE CARE OF THESE GUYS FIRST.

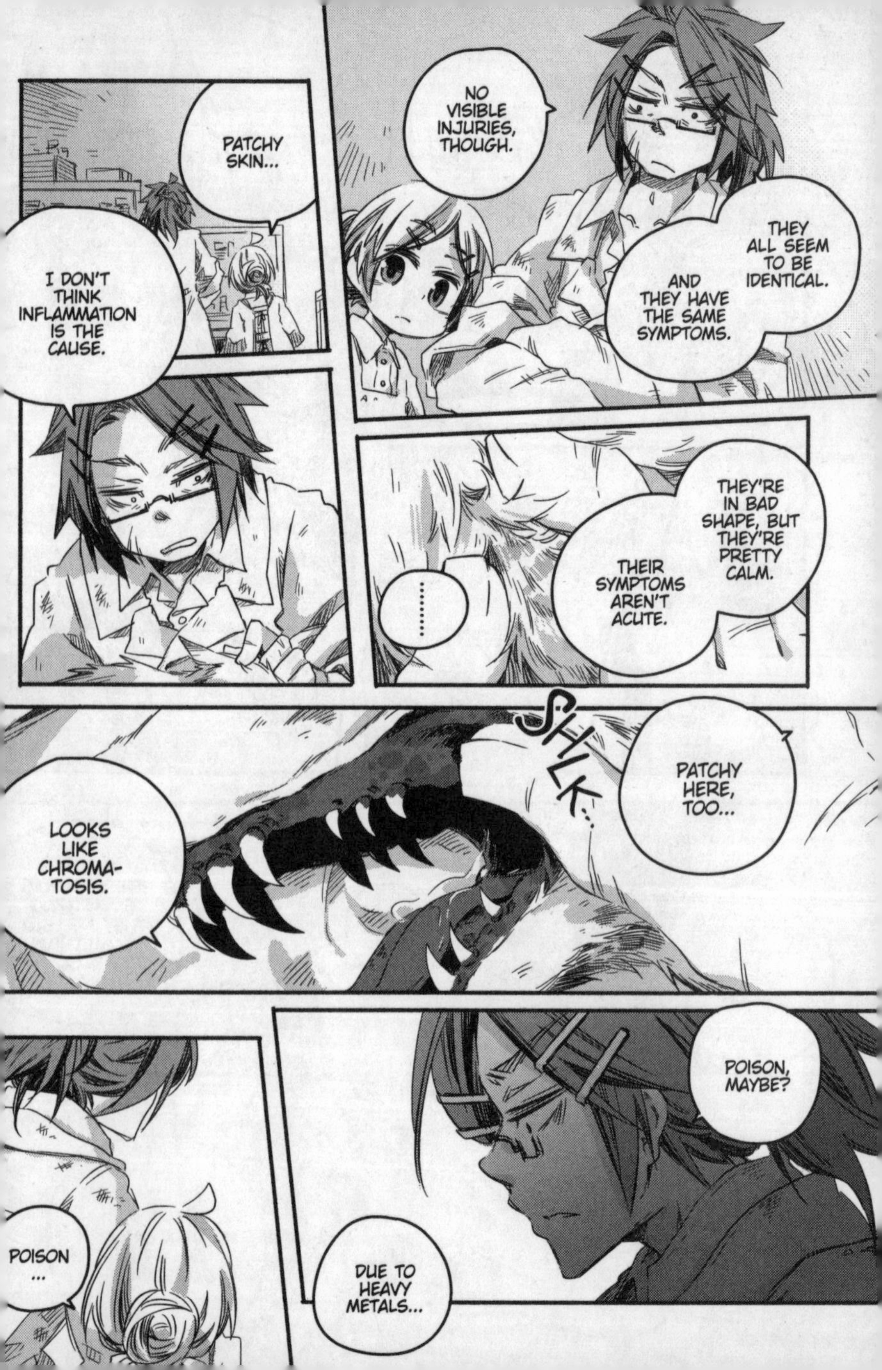
NO VISIBLE INJURIES, THOUGH.
THEY ALL SEEM TO BE IDENTICAL.
AND THEY HAVE THE SAME SYMPTOMS.
PATCHY SKIN...
I DON'T THINK INFLAMMATION IS THE CAUSE.
THEY'RE IN BAD SHAPE, BUT THEY'RE PRETTY CALM.
THEIR SYMPTOMS AREN'T ACUTE.
......
PATCHY HERE, TOO...
SHLK...
LOOKS LIKE CHROMA-TOSIS.
POISON, MAYBE?
DUE TO HEAVY METALS...
POISON ...

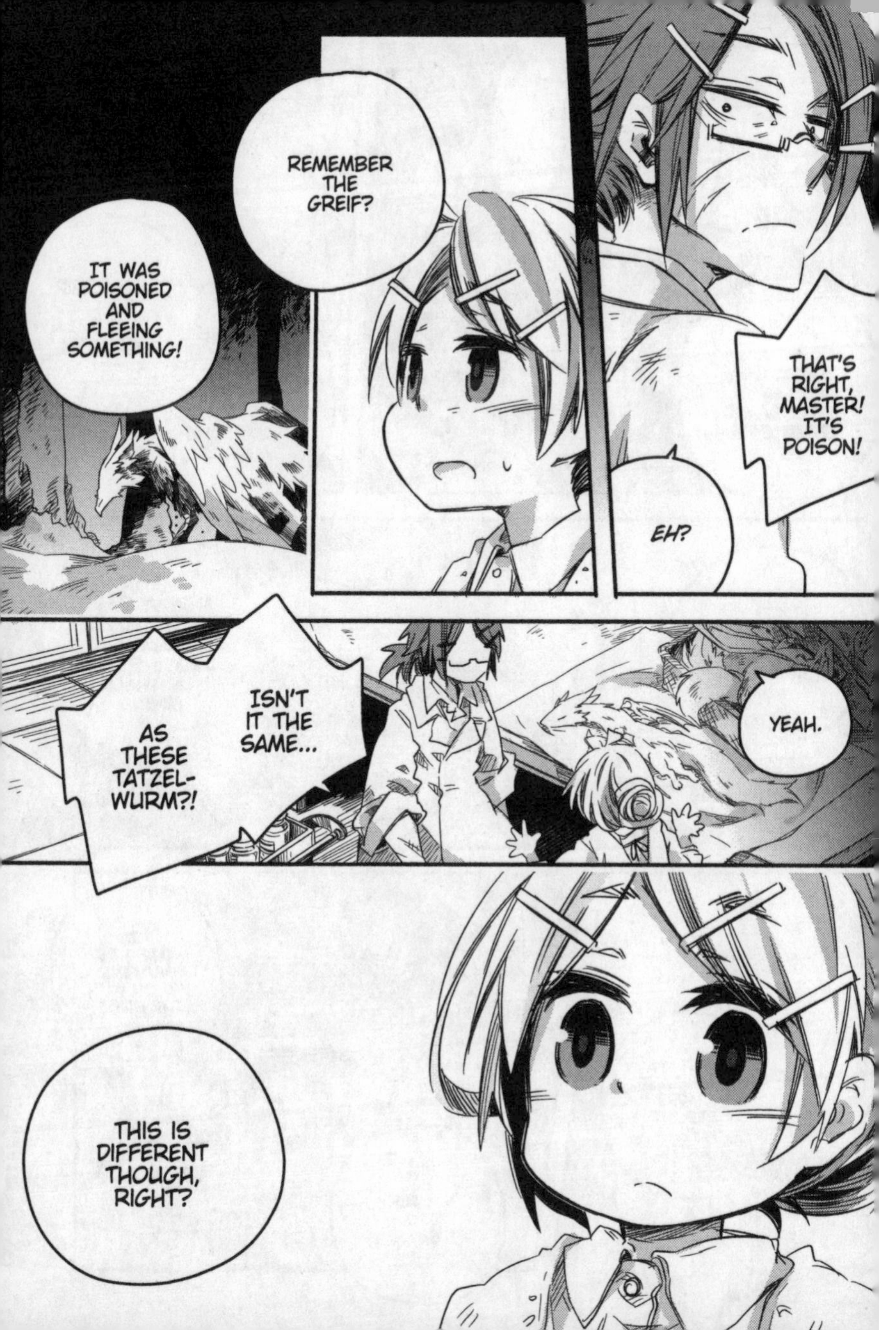
THAT'S RIGHT, MASTER! IT'S POISON!
EH?
REMEMBER THE GREIF?
IT WAS POISONED AND FLEEING SOMETHING!
YEAH.
ISN'T IT THE SAME...
AS THESE TATZEL-WURM?!
THIS IS DIFFERENT THOUGH, RIGHT?

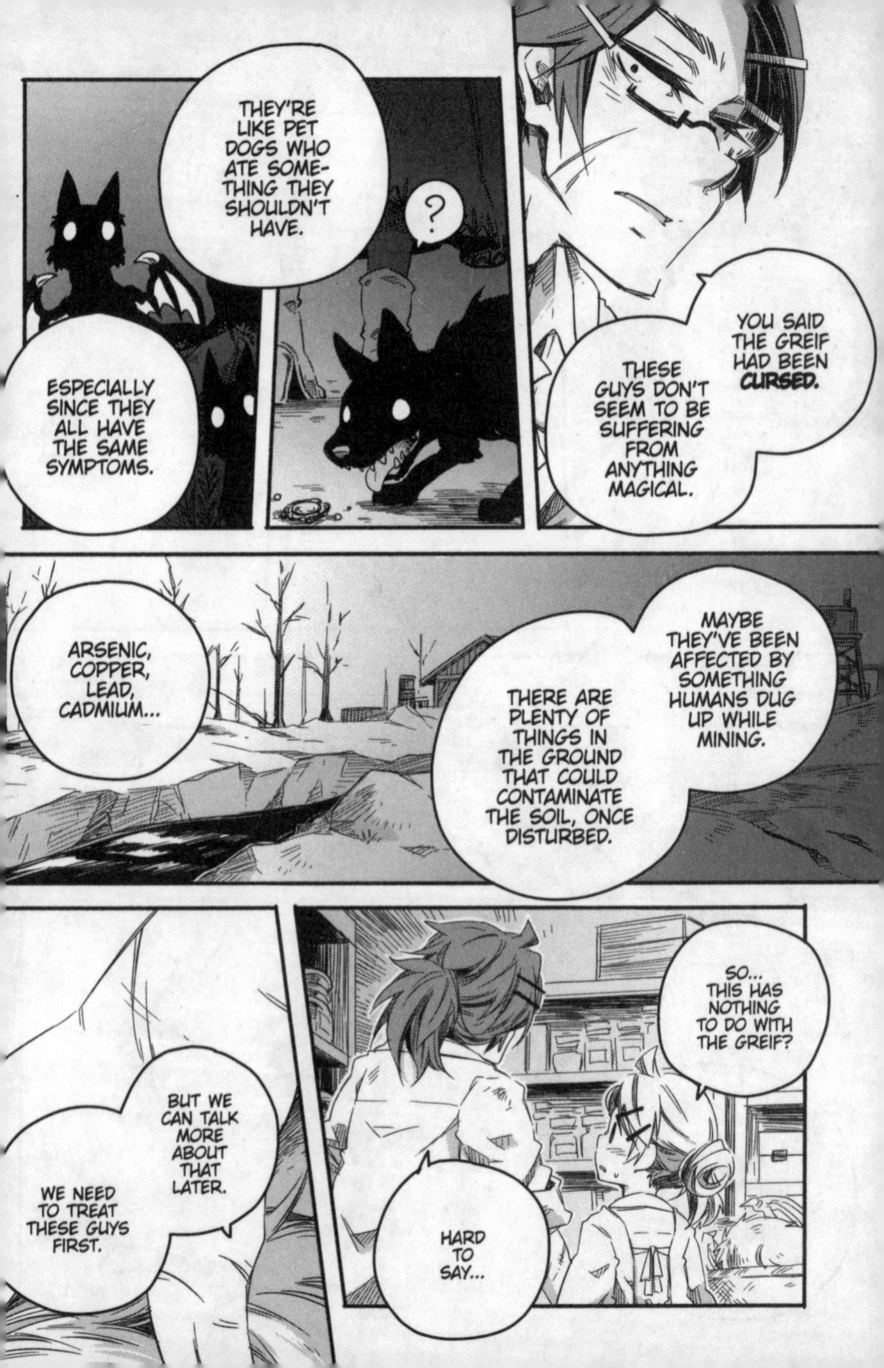
YOU SAID THE GREIF HAD BEEN **CURSED.**
THESE GUYS DON'T SEEM TO BE SUFFERING FROM ANYTHING MAGICAL.
THEY'RE LIKE PET DOGS WHO ATE SOME-THING THEY SHOULDN'T HAVE.
?
ESPECIALLY SINCE THEY ALL HAVE THE SAME SYMPTOMS.
MAYBE THEY'VE BEEN AFFECTED BY SOMETHING HUMANS DUG UP WHILE MINING.
THERE ARE PLENTY OF THINGS IN THE GROUND THAT COULD CONTAMINATE THE SOIL, ONCE DISTURBED.
ARSENIC, COPPER, LEAD, CADMIUM...
SO... THIS HAS NOTHING TO DO WITH THE GREIF?
HARD TO SAY...
BUT WE CAN TALK MORE ABOUT THAT LATER.
WE NEED TO TREAT THESE GUYS FIRST.

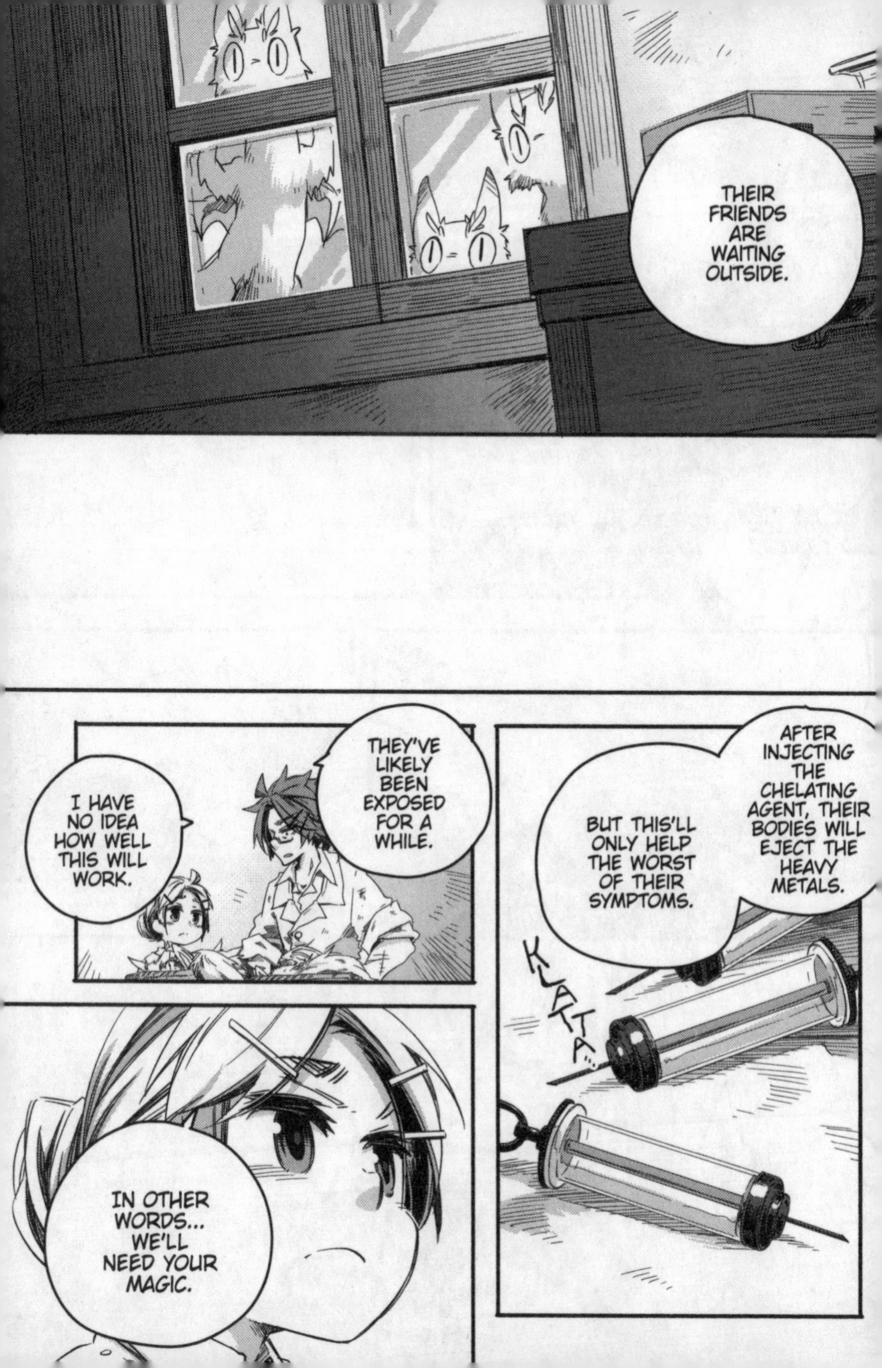
THEIR FRIENDS ARE WAITING OUTSIDE.
AFTER INJECTING THE CHELATING AGENT, THEIR BODIES WILL EJECT THE HEAVY METALS.
BUT THIS'LL ONLY HELP THE WORST OF THEIR SYMPTOMS.
KLATTA...
THEY'VE LIKELY BEEN EXPOSED FOR A WHILE.
I HAVE NO IDEA HOW WELL THIS WILL WORK.
IN OTHER WORDS... WE'LL NEED YOUR MAGIC.

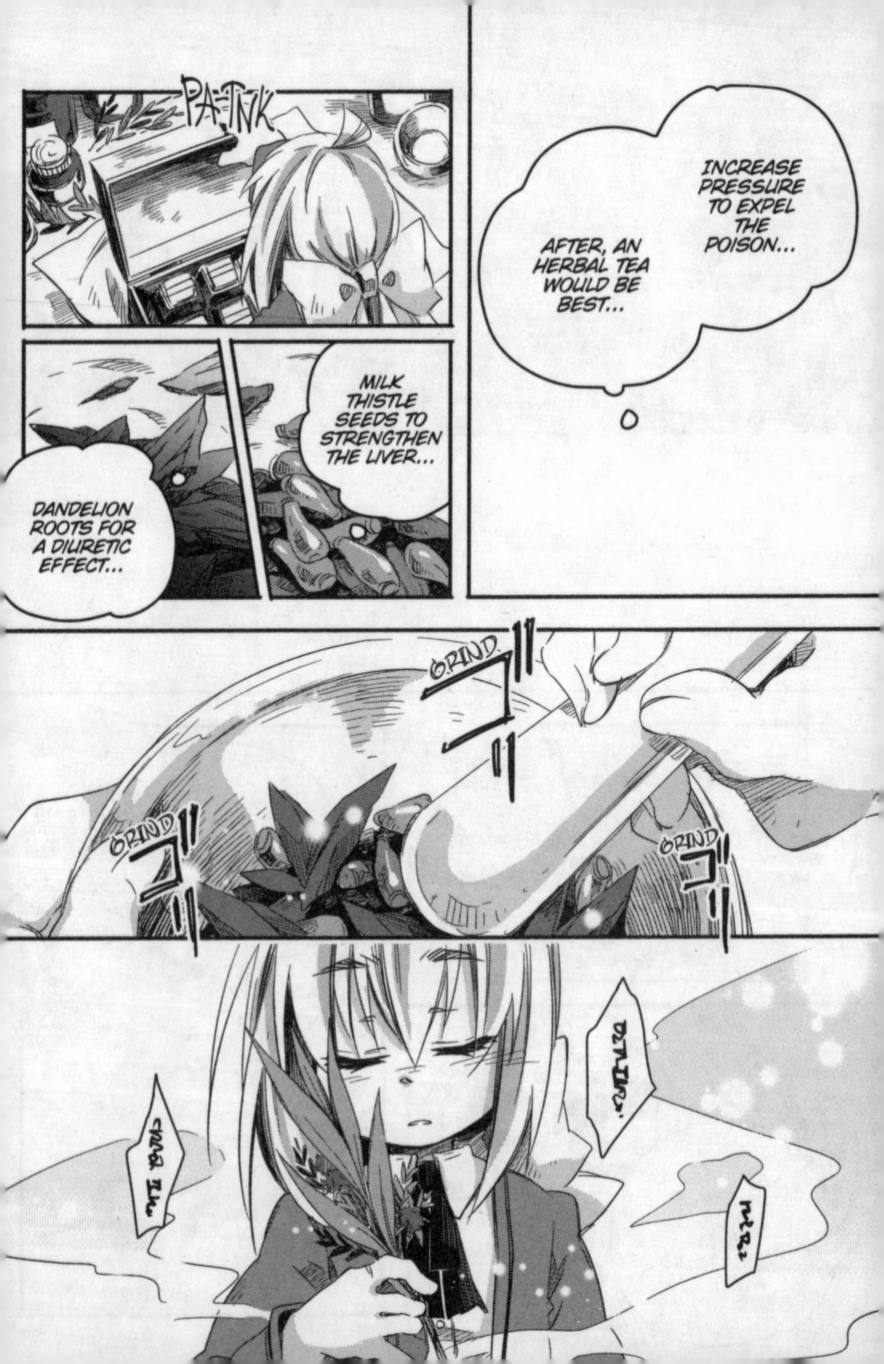
INCREASE PRESSURE TO EXPEL THE POISON...
AFTER, AN HERBAL TEA WOULD BE BEST...
PA-TINK
MILK THISTLE SEEDS TO STRENGTHEN THE LIVER...
DANDELION ROOTS FOR A DIURETIC EFFECT...
GRIND
GRIND
GRIND

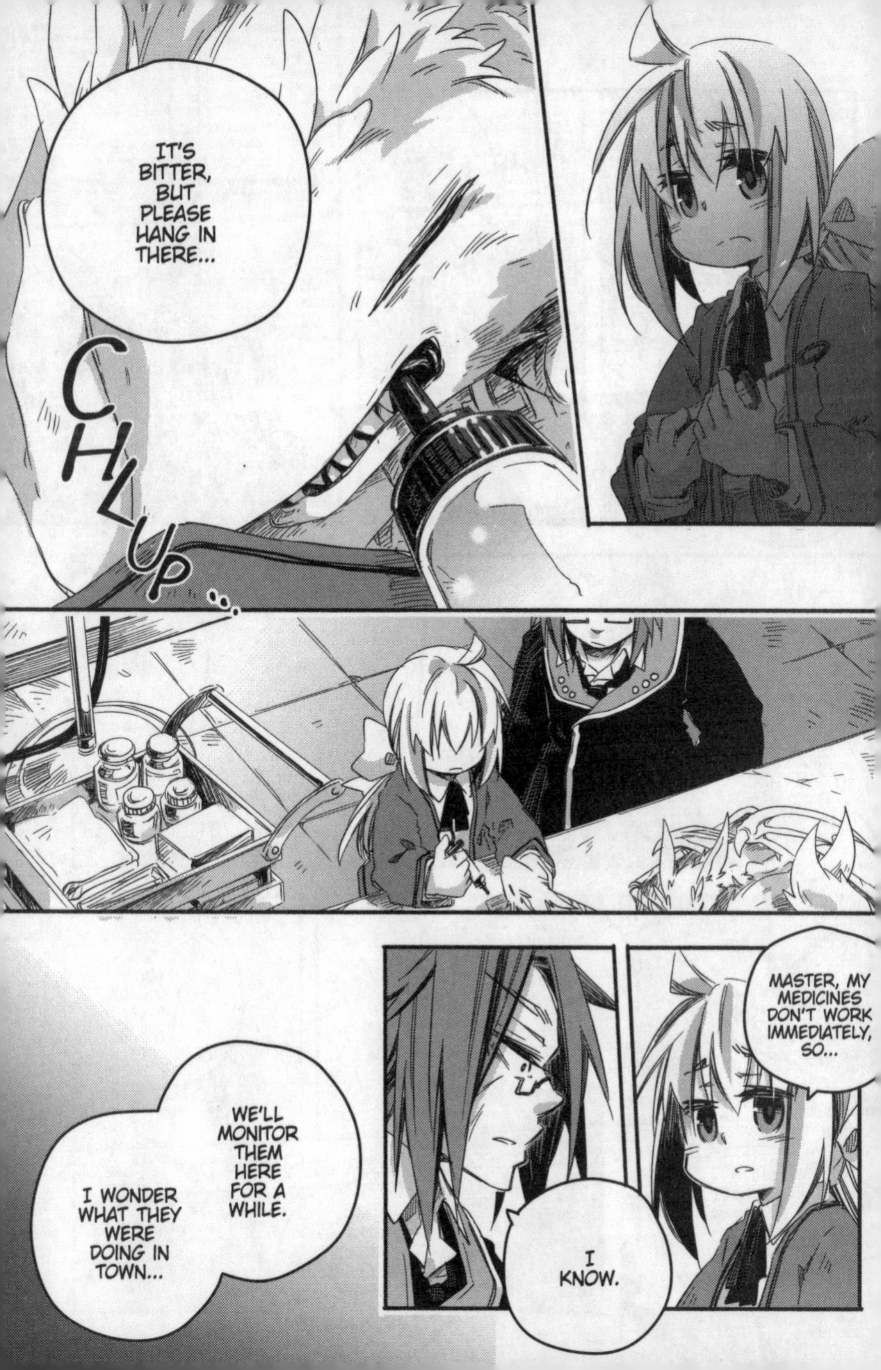
IT'S BITTER, BUT PLEASE HANG IN THERE...
CHLUP
...
MASTER, MY MEDICINES DON'T WORK IMMEDIATELY, SO...
I KNOW.
WE'LL MONITOR THEM HERE FOR A WHILE.
I WONDER WHAT THEY WERE DOING IN TOWN...

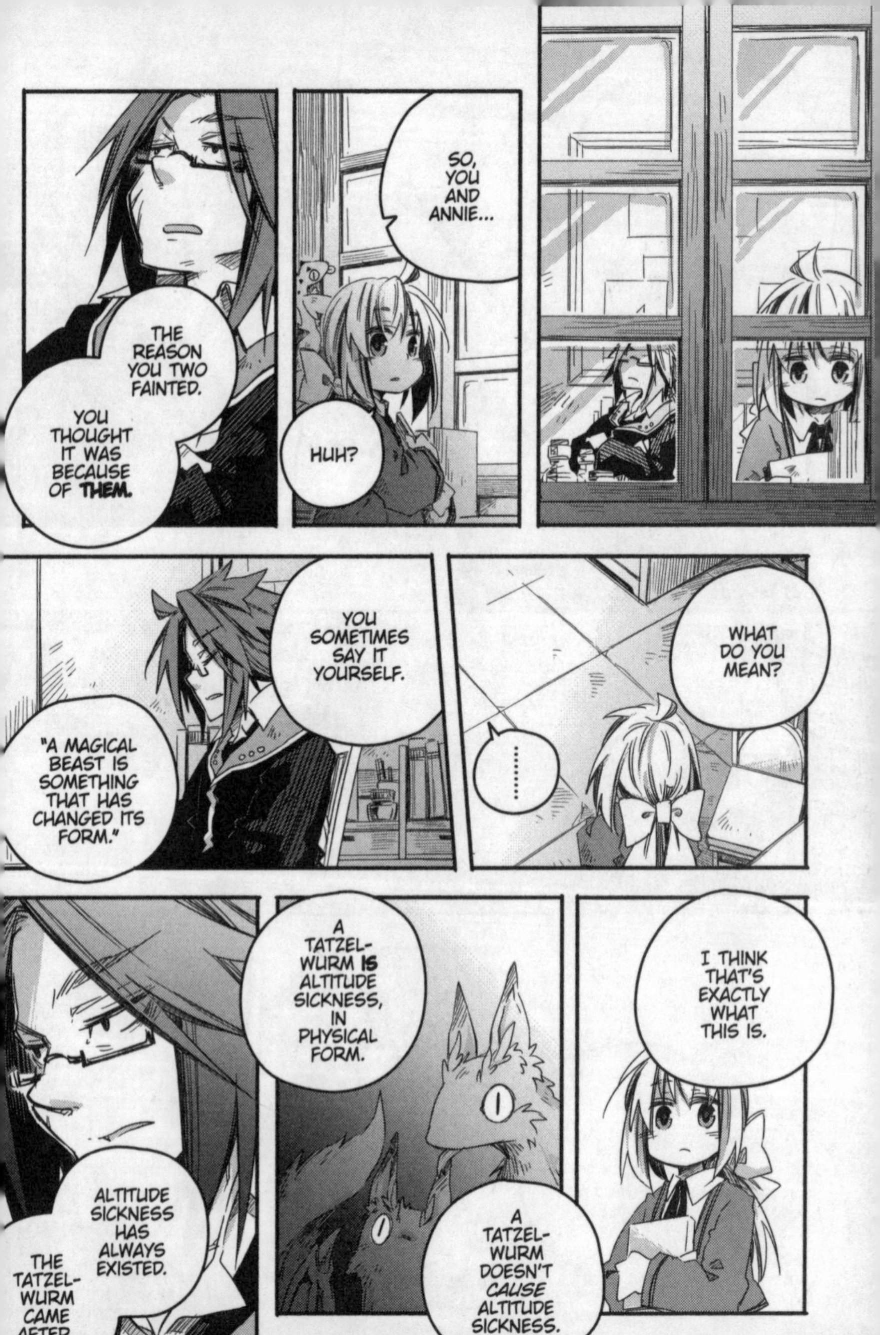
SO, YOU AND ANNIE...
HUH?
THE REASON YOU TWO FAINTED.
YOU THOUGHT IT WAS BECAUSE OF **THEM.**
WHAT DO YOU MEAN?
......
YOU SOMETIMES SAY IT YOURSELF.
"A MAGICAL BEAST IS SOMETHING THAT HAS CHANGED ITS FORM."
I THINK THAT'S EXACTLY WHAT THIS IS.
A TATZEL-WURM DOESN'T *CAUSE* ALTITUDE SICKNESS.
A TATZEL-WURM **IS** ALTITUDE SICKNESS, IN PHYSICAL FORM.
ALTITUDE SICKNESS HAS ALWAYS EXISTED.
THE TATZEL-WURM CAME AFTER.

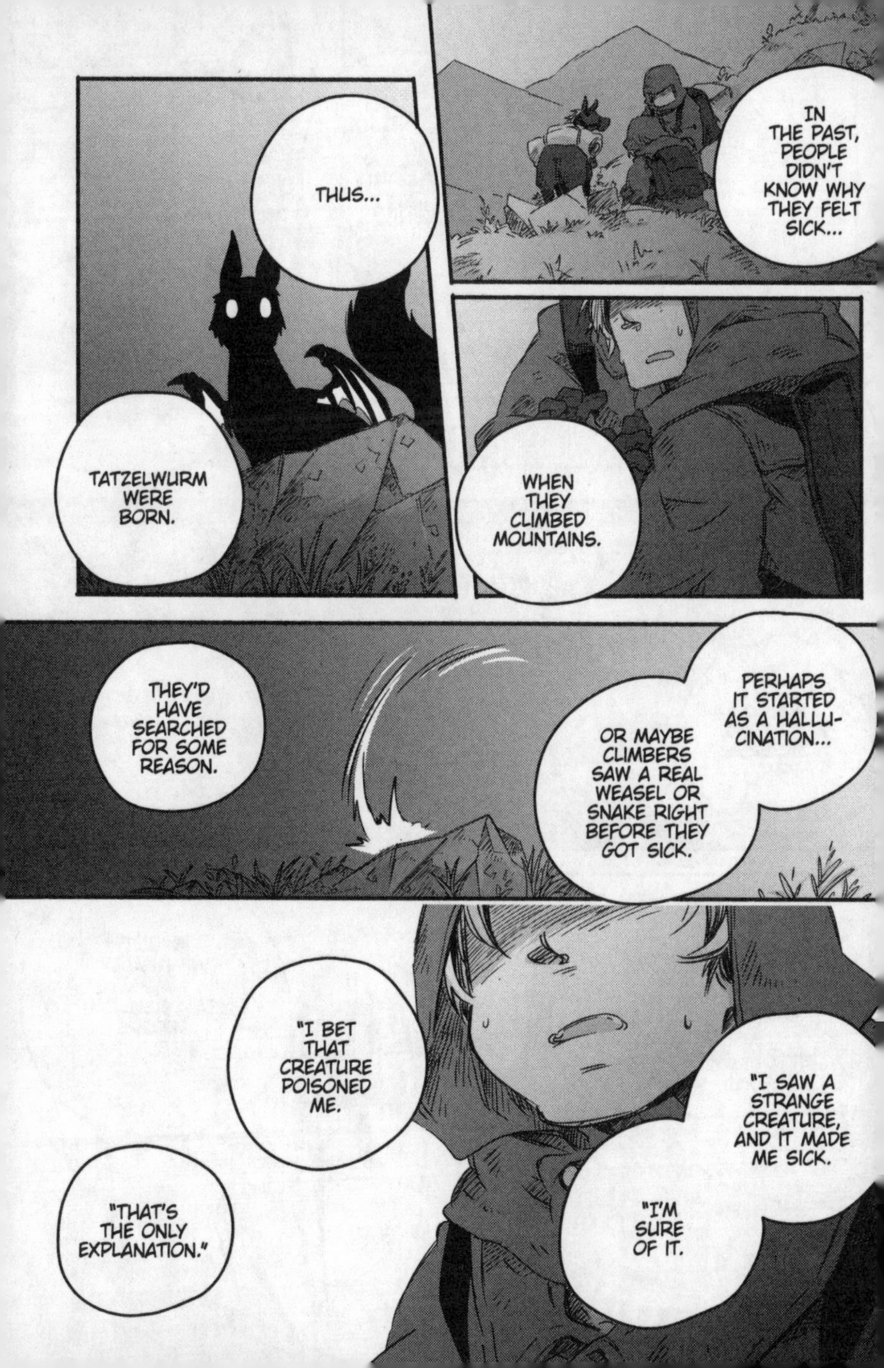
IN THE PAST, PEOPLE DIDN'T KNOW WHY THEY FELT SICK...
WHEN THEY CLIMBED MOUNTAINS.
THUS...
TATZELWURM WERE BORN.
PERHAPS IT STARTED AS A HALLUCINATION...
OR MAYBE CLIMBERS SAW A REAL WEASEL OR SNAKE RIGHT BEFORE THEY GOT SICK.
THEY'D HAVE SEARCHED FOR SOME REASON.
"I SAW A STRANGE CREATURE, AND IT MADE ME SICK.
"I'M SURE OF IT.
"I BET THAT CREATURE POISONED ME.
"THAT'S THE ONLY EXPLANATION."

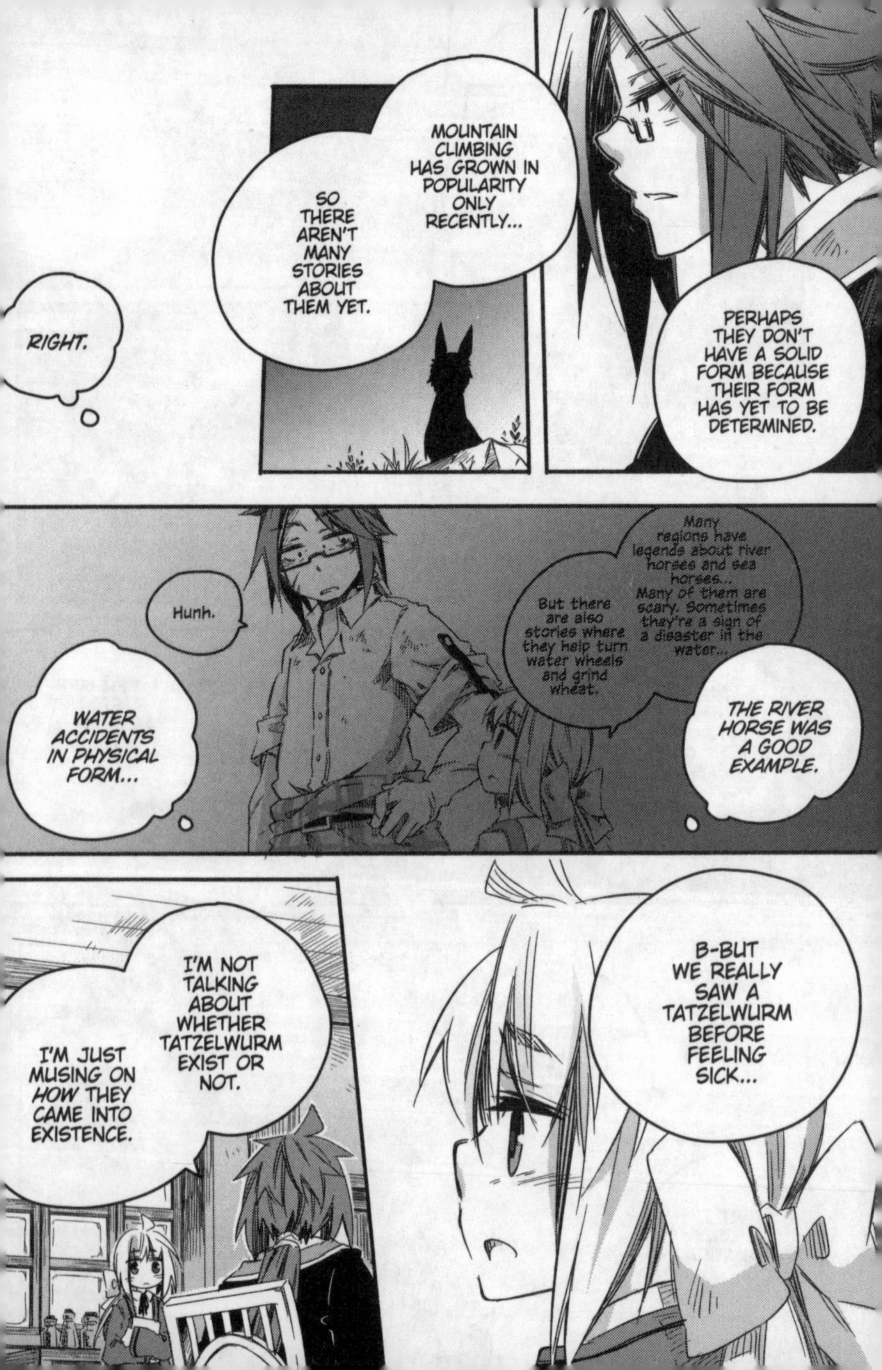
PERHAPS THEY DON'T HAVE A SOLID FORM BECAUSE THEIR FORM HAS YET TO BE DETERMINED.
MOUNTAIN CLIMBING HAS GROWN IN POPULARITY ONLY RECENTLY...
SO THERE AREN'T MANY STORIES ABOUT THEM YET.
RIGHT.
Many regions have legends about river horses and sea horses... Many of them are scary. Sometimes they're a sign of a disaster in the water...
But there are also stories where they help turn water wheels and grind wheat.
THE RIVER HORSE WAS A GOOD EXAMPLE.
Hunh.
WATER ACCIDENTS IN PHYSICAL FORM...
B-BUT WE REALLY SAW A TATZELWURM BEFORE FEELING SICK...
I'M NOT TALKING ABOUT WHETHER TATZELWURM EXIST OR NOT.
I'M JUST MUSING ON *HOW* THEY CAME INTO EXISTENCE.

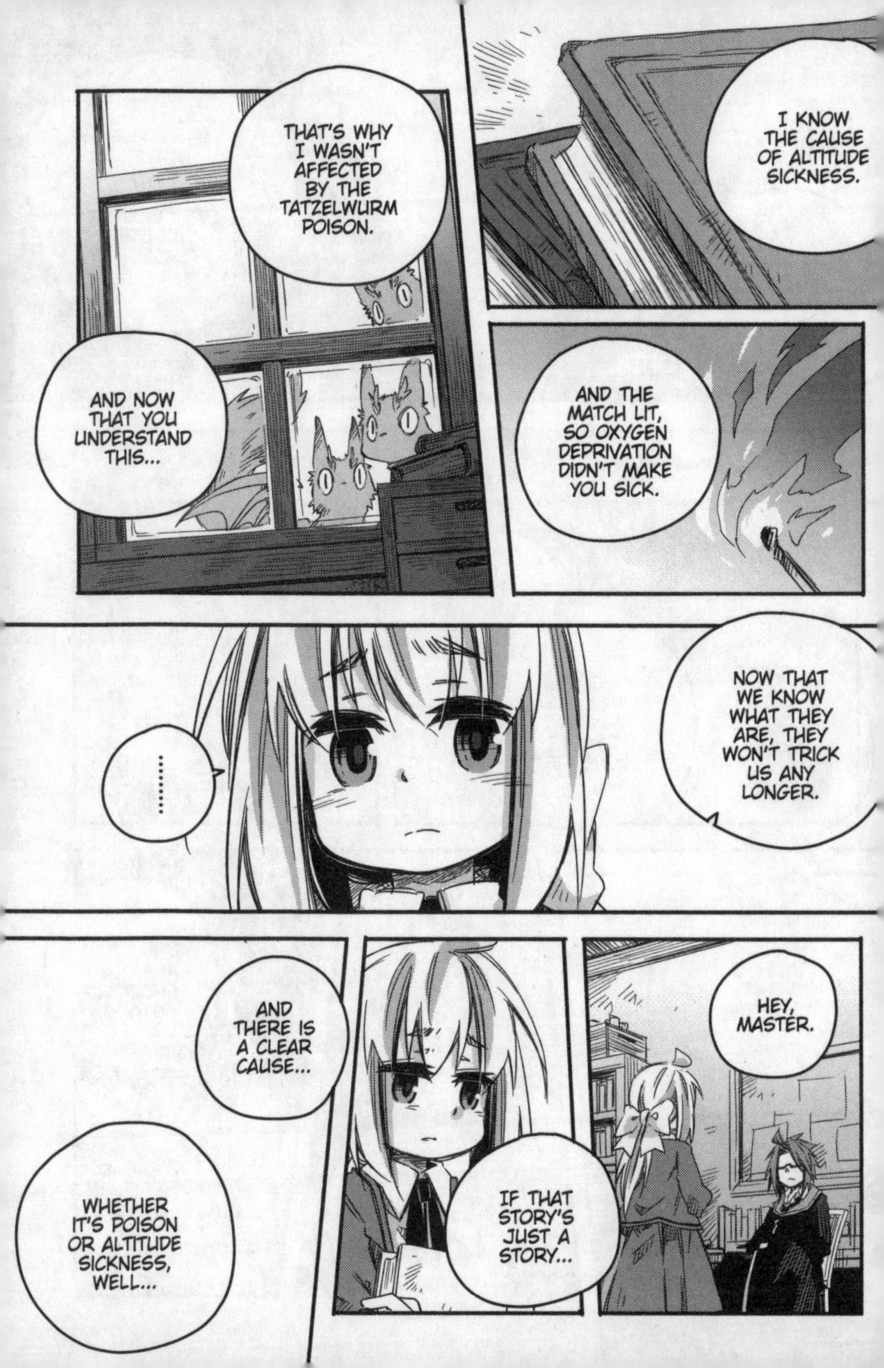
I KNOW THE CAUSE OF ALTITUDE SICKNESS.
AND THE MATCH LIT, SO OXYGEN DEPRIVATION DIDN'T MAKE YOU SICK.
THAT'S WHY I WASN'T AFFECTED BY THE TATZELWURM POISON.
AND NOW THAT YOU UNDERSTAND THIS...
NOW THAT WE KNOW WHAT THEY ARE, THEY WON'T TRICK US ANY LONGER.
....
HEY, MASTER.
IF THAT STORY'S JUST A STORY...
AND THERE IS A CLEAR CAUSE...
WHETHER IT'S POISON OR ALTITUDE SICKNESS, WELL...

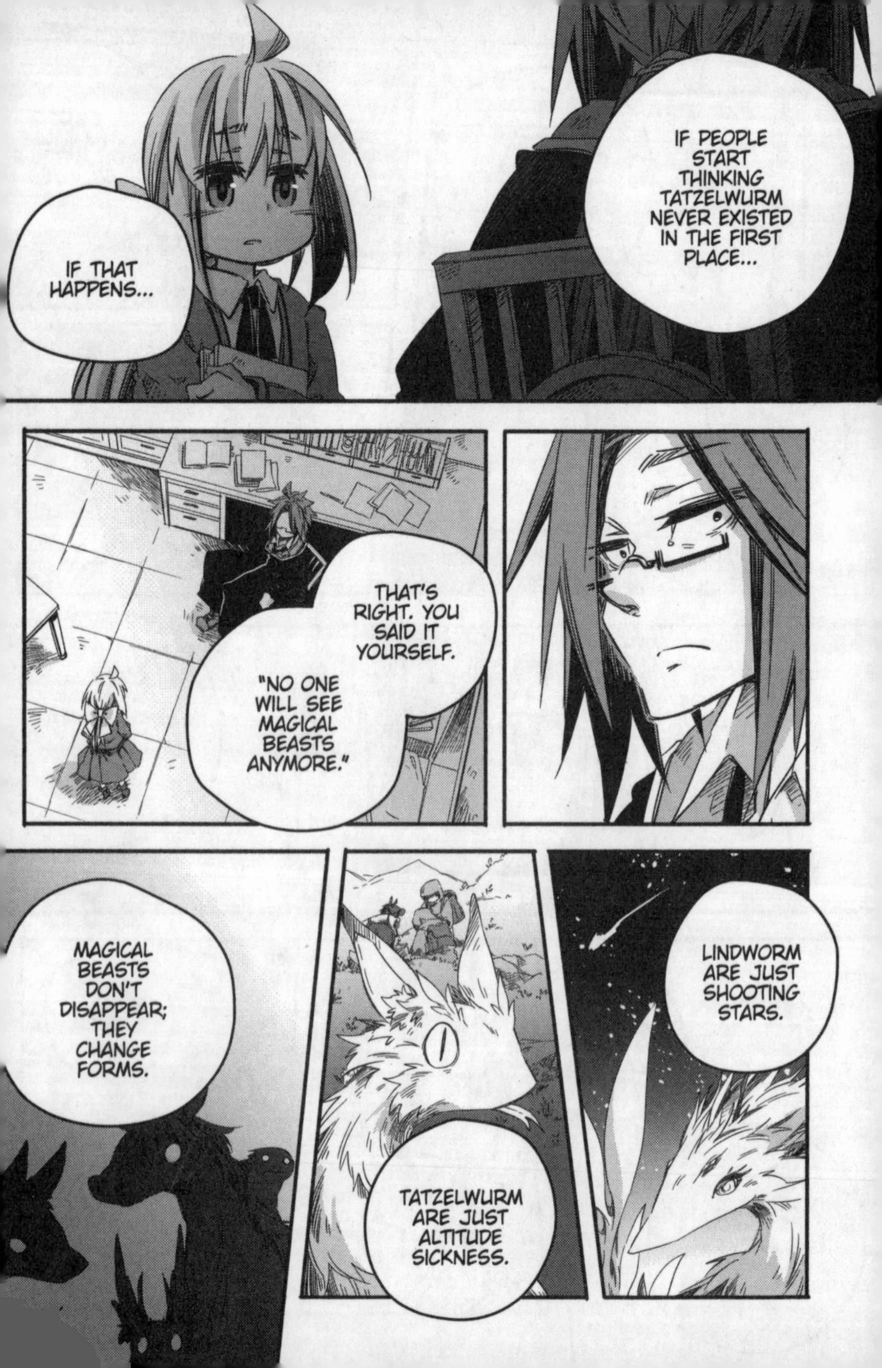
IF PEOPLE START THINKING TATZELWURM NEVER EXISTED IN THE FIRST PLACE...
IF THAT HAPPENS...
THAT'S RIGHT. YOU SAID IT YOURSELF.
"NO ONE WILL SEE MAGICAL BEASTS ANYMORE."
LINDWORM ARE JUST SHOOTING STARS.
TATZELWURM ARE JUST ALTITUDE SICKNESS.
MAGICAL BEASTS DON'T DISAPPEAR; THEY CHANGE FORMS.

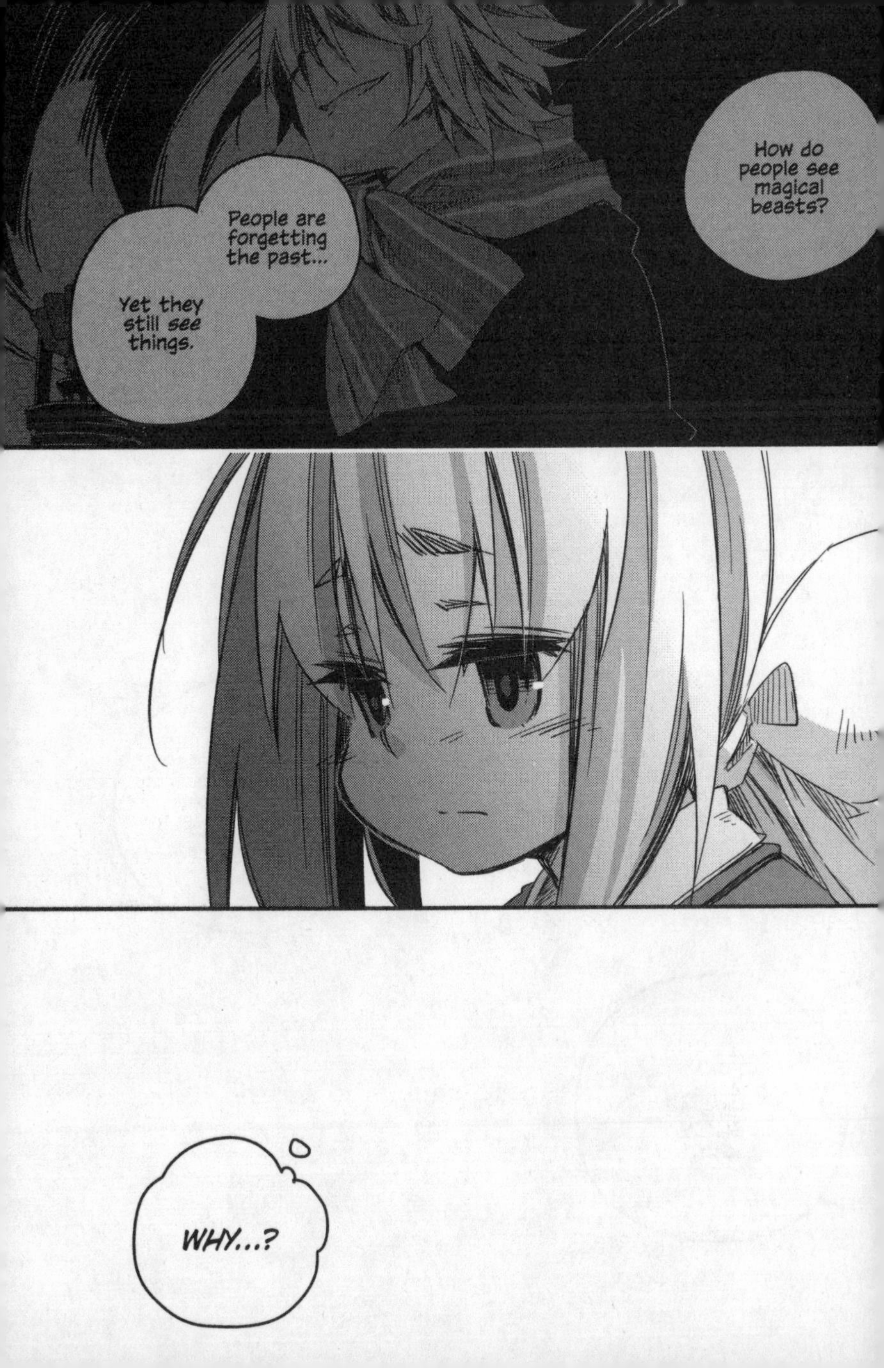
How do people see magical beasts?
People are forgetting the past...
Yet they still see things.
WHY...?

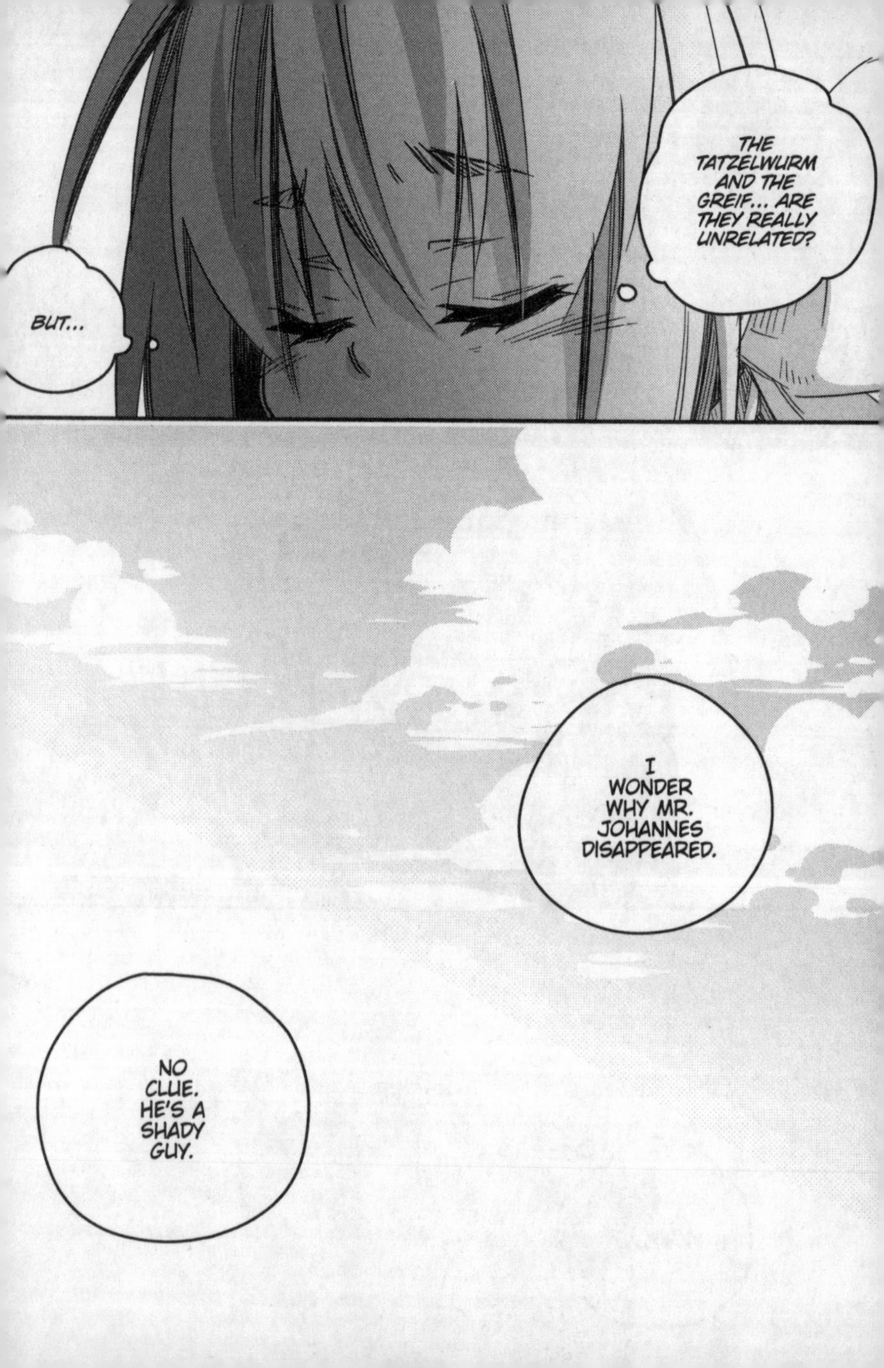
THE TATZELWURM AND THE GREIF... ARE THEY REALLY UNRELATED?
BUT...
I WONDER WHY MR. JOHANNES DISAPPEARED.
NO CLUE. HE'S A SHADY GUY.

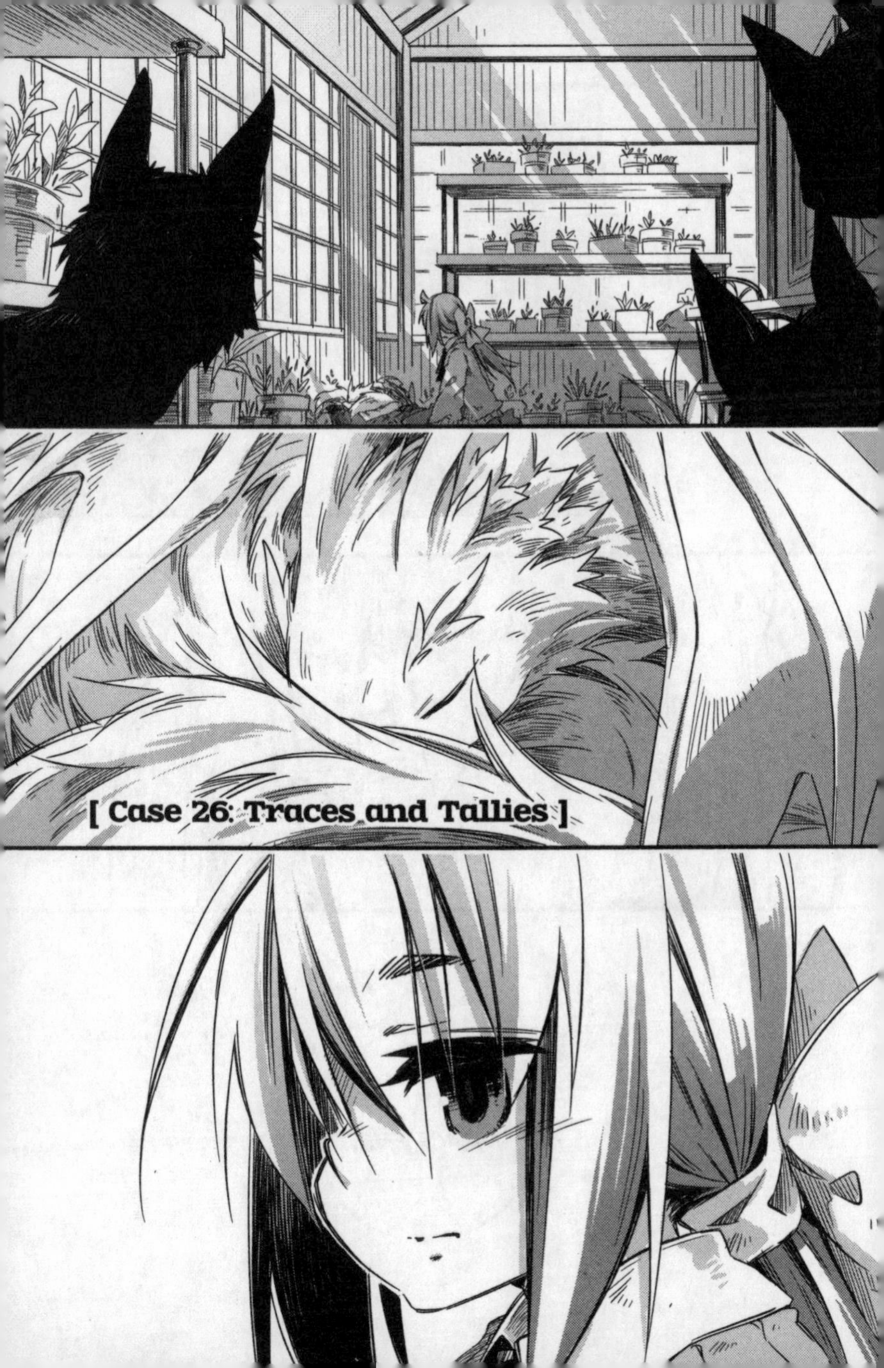
[Case 26: Traces and Tallies]

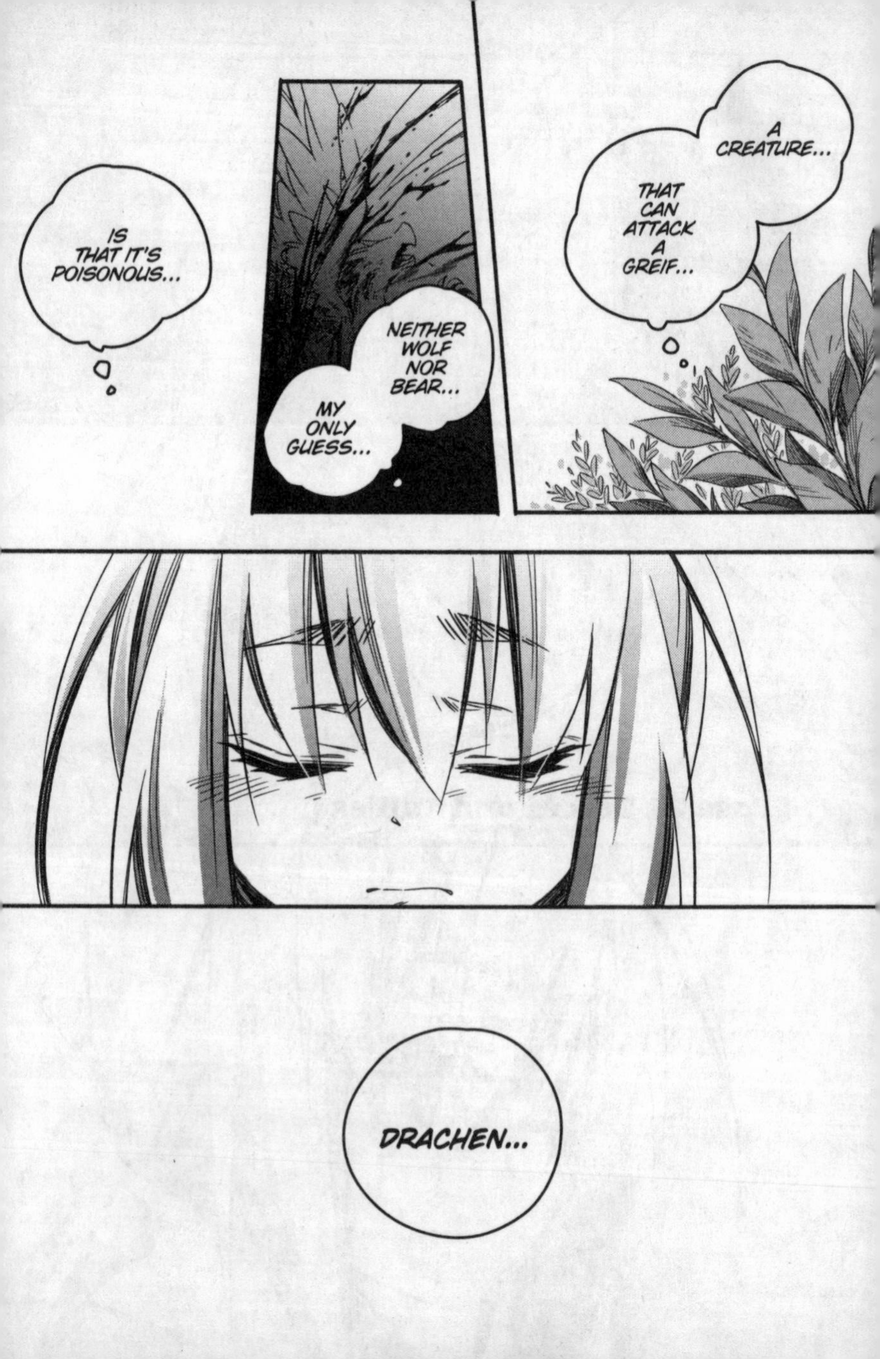
A CREATURE...
THAT CAN ATTACK A GREIF...
NEITHER WOLF NOR BEAR...
MY ONLY GUESS...
IS THAT IT'S POISONOUS...
DRACHEN...

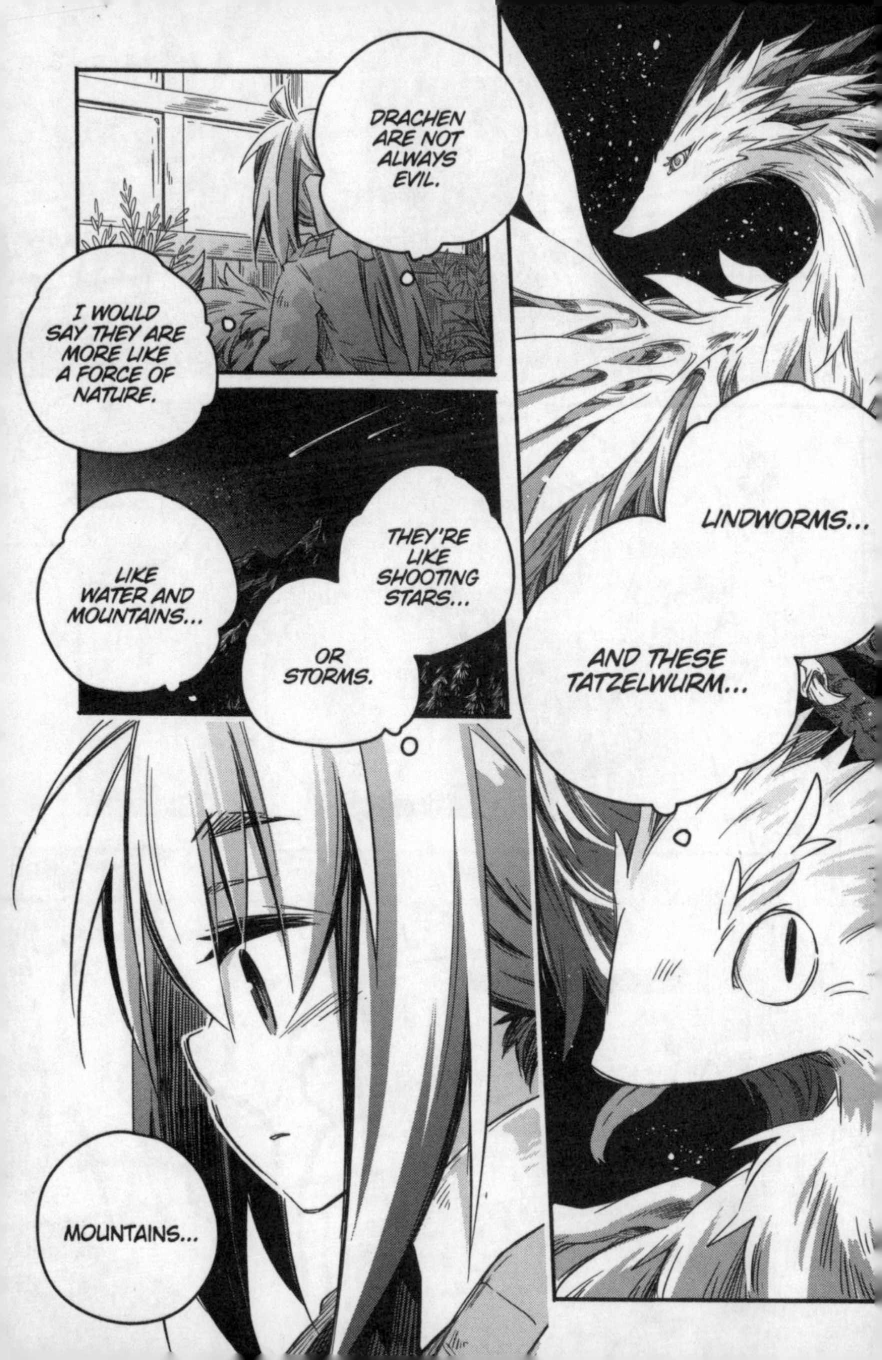
LINDWORMS...
AND THESE TATZELWURM...
DRACHEN ARE NOT ALWAYS EVIL.
I WOULD SAY THEY ARE MORE LIKE A FORCE OF NATURE.
THEY'RE LIKE SHOOTING STARS...
OR STORMS.
LIKE WATER AND MOUNTAINS...
MOUNTAINS...

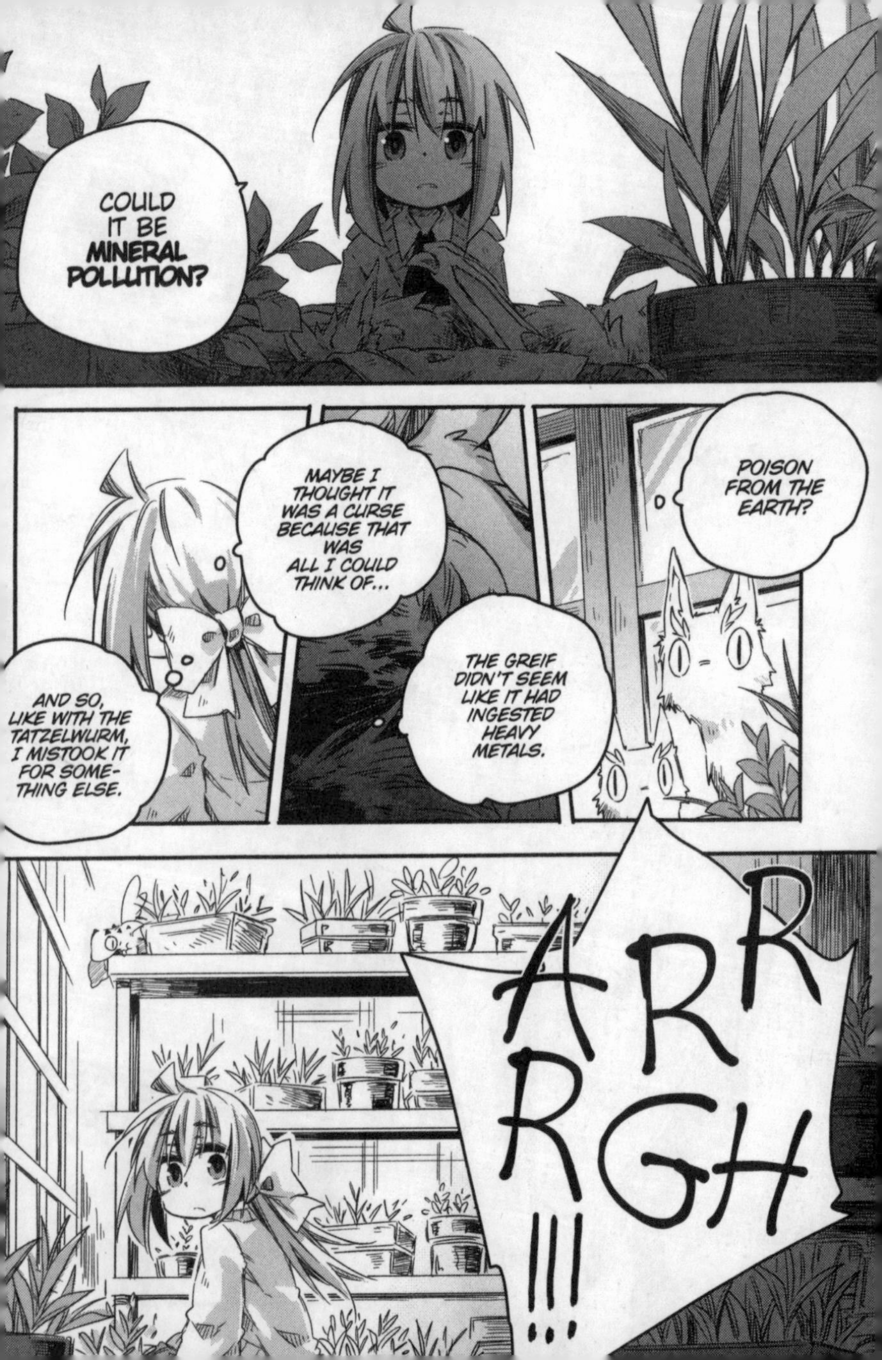
COULD IT BE **MINERAL POLLUTION?**
POISON FROM THE EARTH?
THE GREIF DIDN'T SEEM LIKE IT HAD INGESTED HEAVY METALS.
MAYBE I THOUGHT IT WAS A CURSE BECAUSE THAT WAS ALL I COULD THINK OF...
AND SO, LIKE WITH THE TATZELWURM, I MISTOOK IT FOR SOME-THING ELSE.
ARRRGH!!!

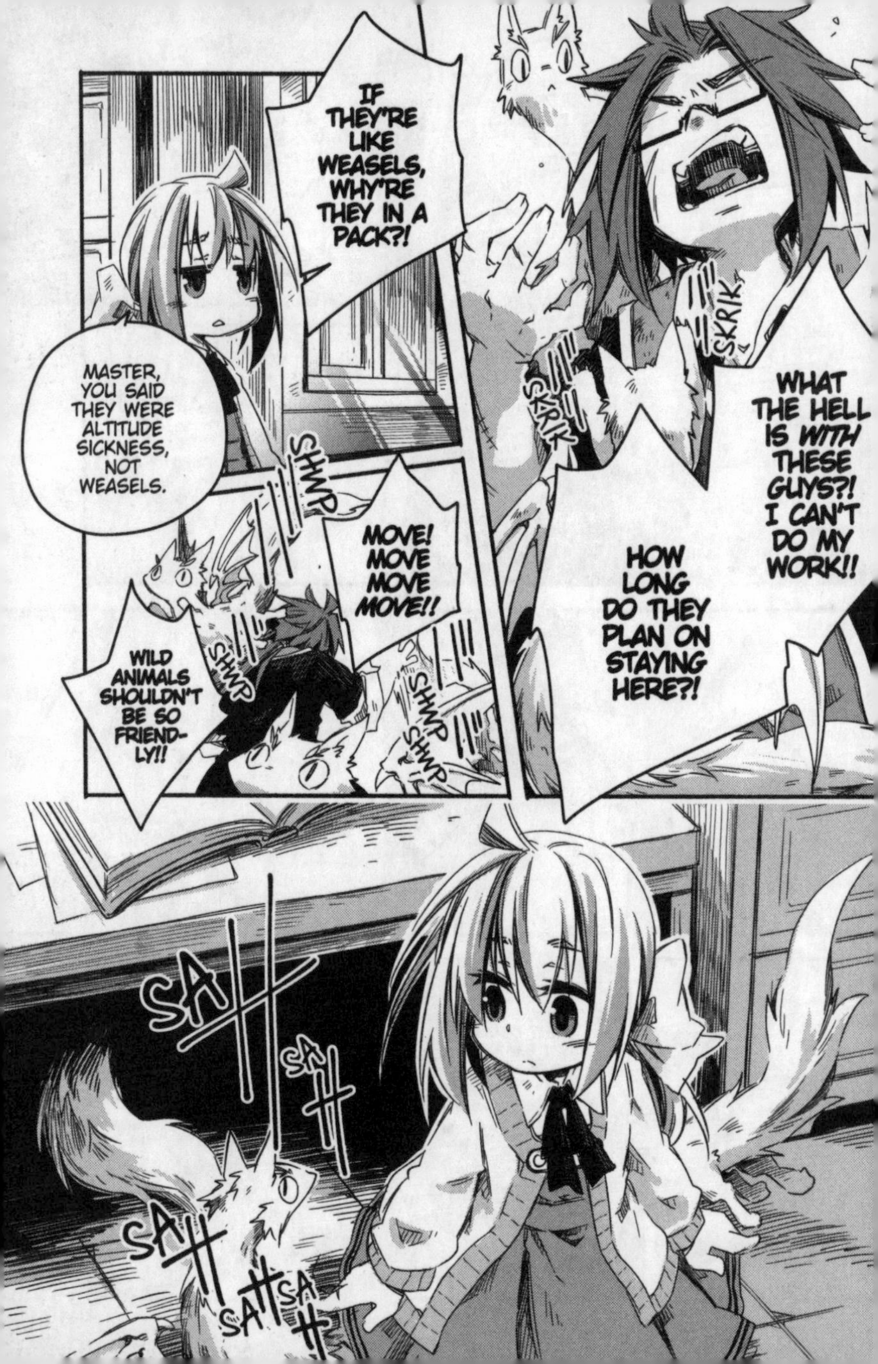

WHAT THE HELL IS *WITH* THESE GUYS?! I CAN'T DO MY WORK!!
HOW LONG DO THEY PLAN ON STAYING HERE?!
SKRIK
SKRIK
IF THEY'RE LIKE WEASELS, WHY'RE THEY IN A PACK?!
MASTER, YOU SAID THEY WERE ALTITUDE SICKNESS, NOT WEASELS.
SHMP
MOVE! MOVE MOVE *MOVE!!*
WILD ANIMALS SHOULDN'T BE SO FRIEND-LY!!
SHMP
SHMP
SHMP
SA
SA
SA
SA
SA

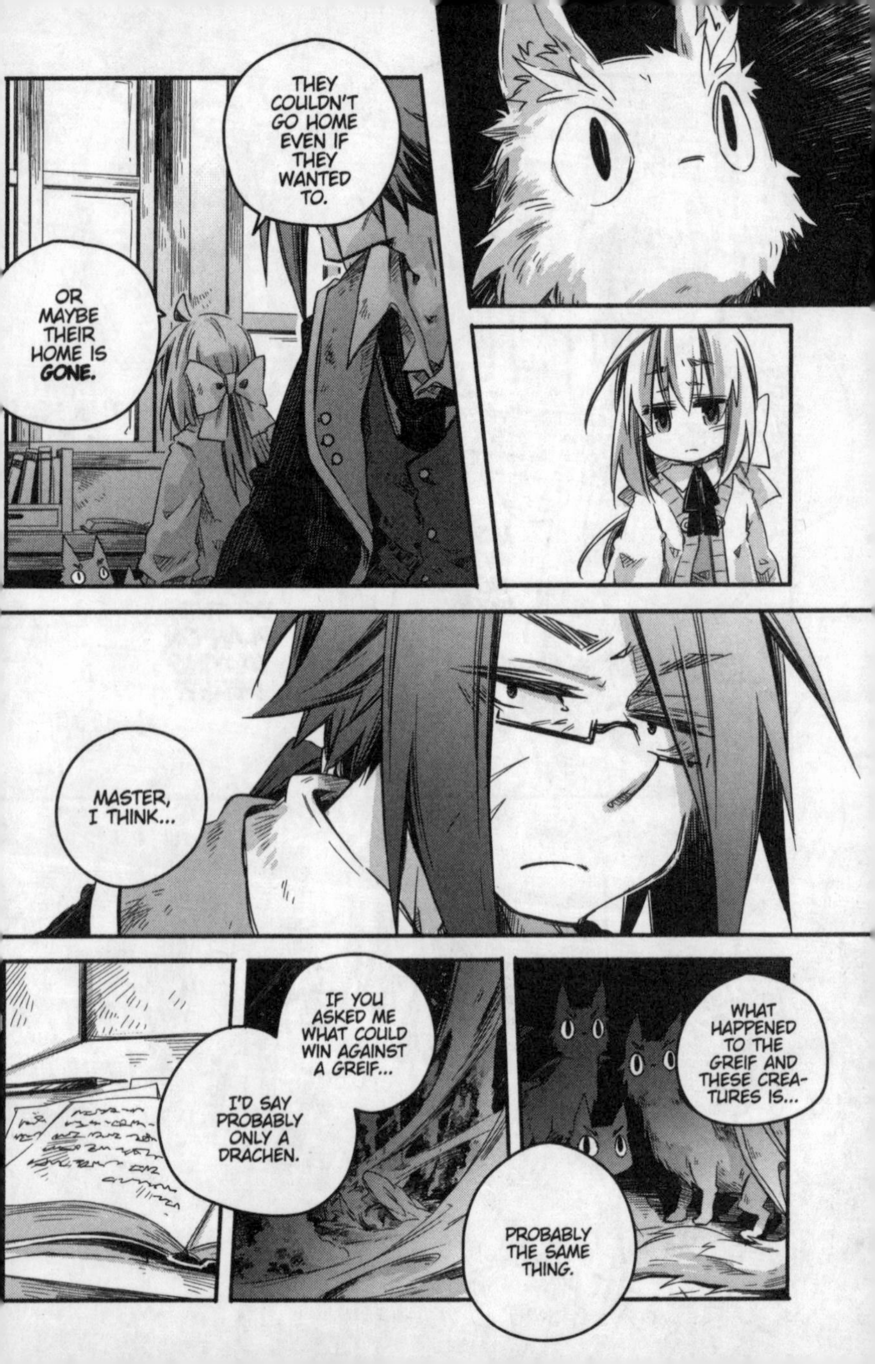
THEY COULDN'T GO HOME EVEN IF THEY WANTED TO.
OR MAYBE THEIR HOME IS **GONE.**
MASTER, I THINK...
WHAT HAPPENED TO THE GREIF AND THESE CREA-TURES IS...
PROBABLY THE SAME THING.
IF YOU ASKED ME WHAT COULD WIN AGAINST A GREIF...
I'D SAY PROBABLY ONLY A DRACHEN.

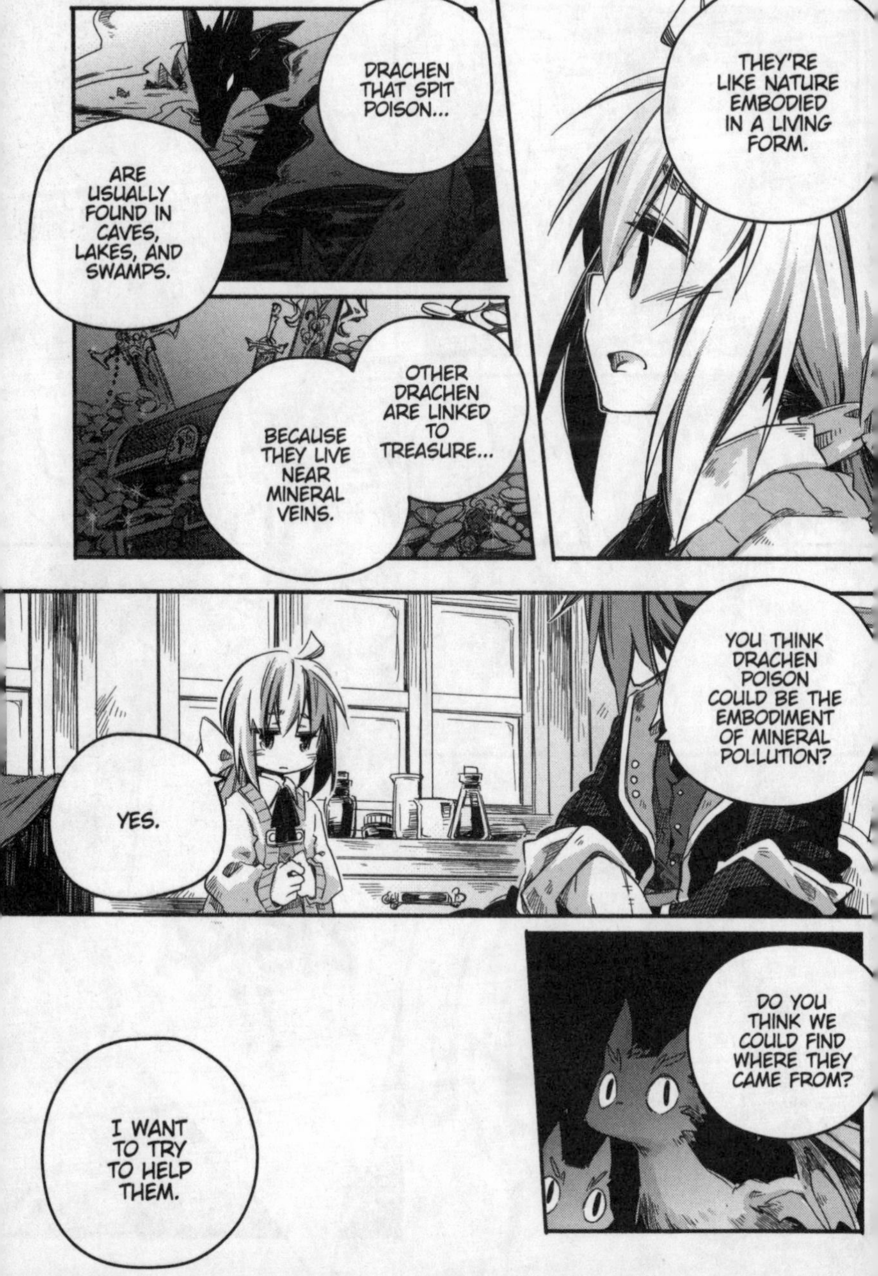
THEY'RE LIKE NATURE EMBODIED IN A LIVING FORM.
DRACHEN THAT SPIT POISON...
ARE USUALLY FOUND IN CAVES, LAKES, AND SWAMPS.
OTHER DRACHEN ARE LINKED TO TREASURE...
BECAUSE THEY LIVE NEAR MINERAL VEINS.
YOU THINK DRACHEN POISON COULD BE THE EMBODIMENT OF MINERAL POLLUTION?
YES.
DO YOU THINK WE COULD FIND WHERE THEY CAME FROM?
I WANT TO TRY TO HELP THEM.

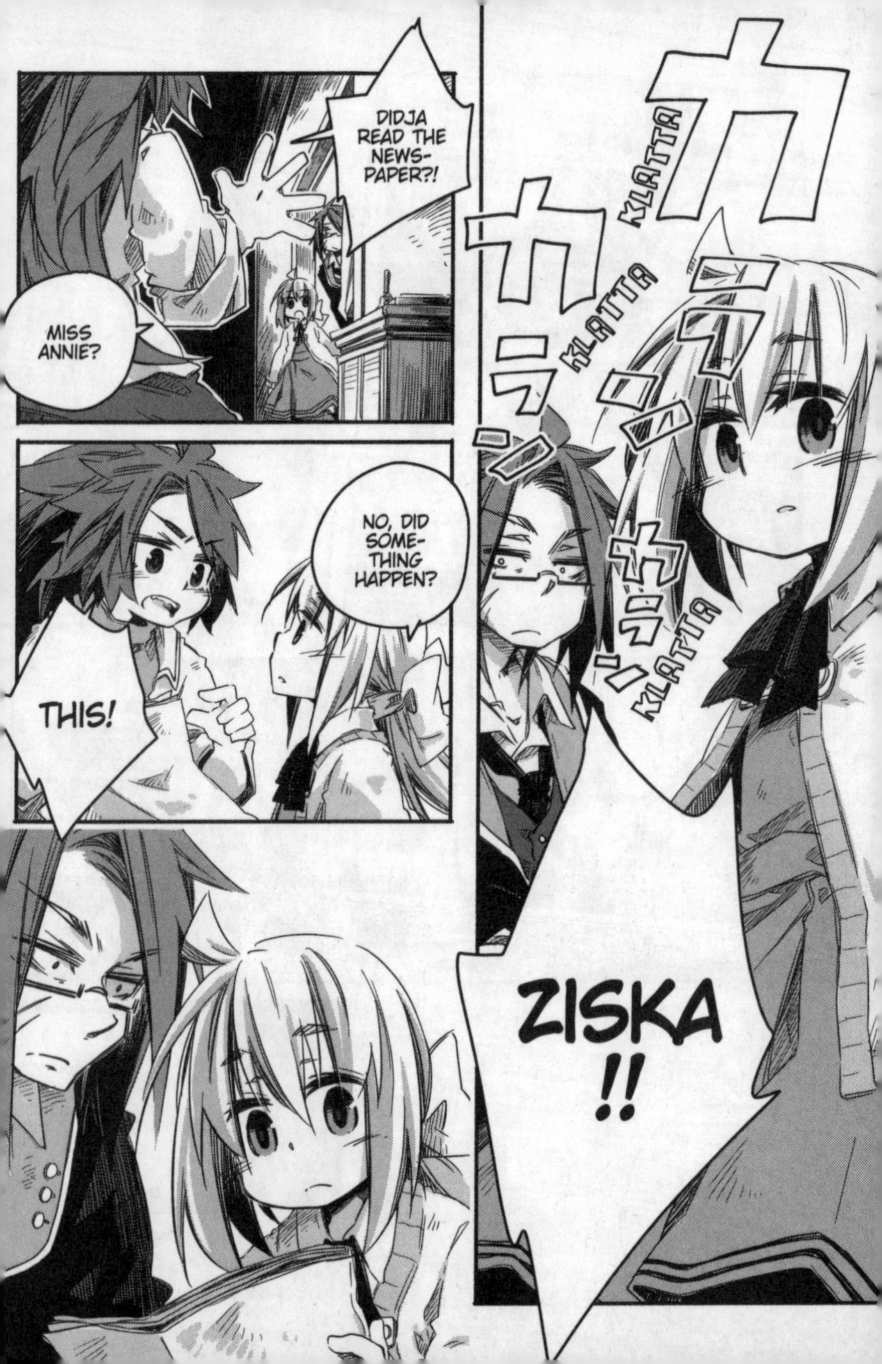
KLATTA
KLATTA
KLATTA
KLATTA
ZISKA !!
DIDJA READ THE NEWS-PAPER?!
MISS ANNIE?
NO, DID SOME-THING HAPPEN?
THIS!

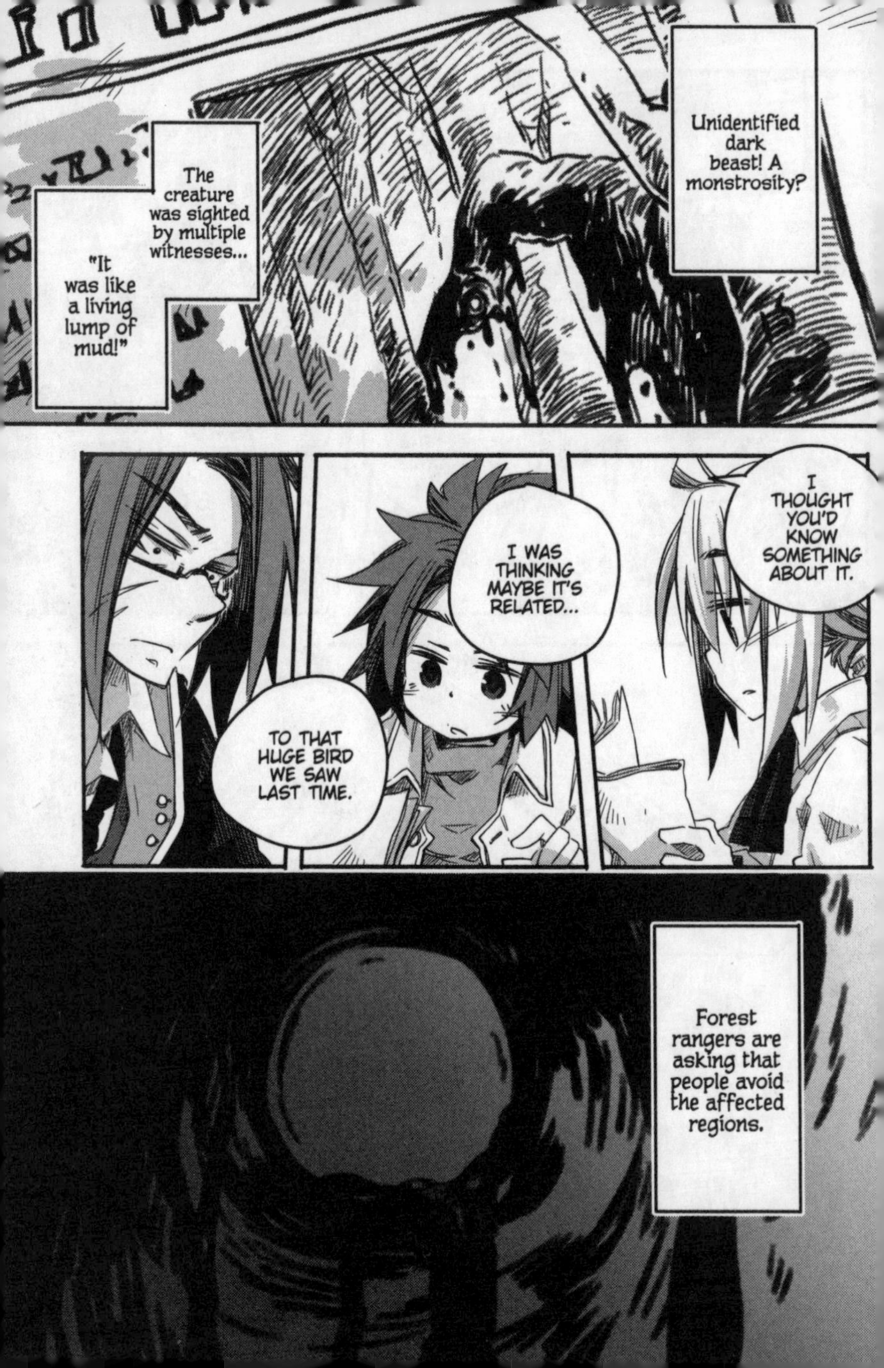
Unidentified dark beast! A monstrosity?
The creature was sighted by multiple witnesses...
"It was like a living lump of mud!"
I THOUGHT YOU'D KNOW SOMETHING ABOUT IT.
I WAS THINKING MAYBE IT'S RELATED...
TO THAT HUGE BIRD WE SAW LAST TIME.
Forest rangers are asking that people avoid the affected regions.

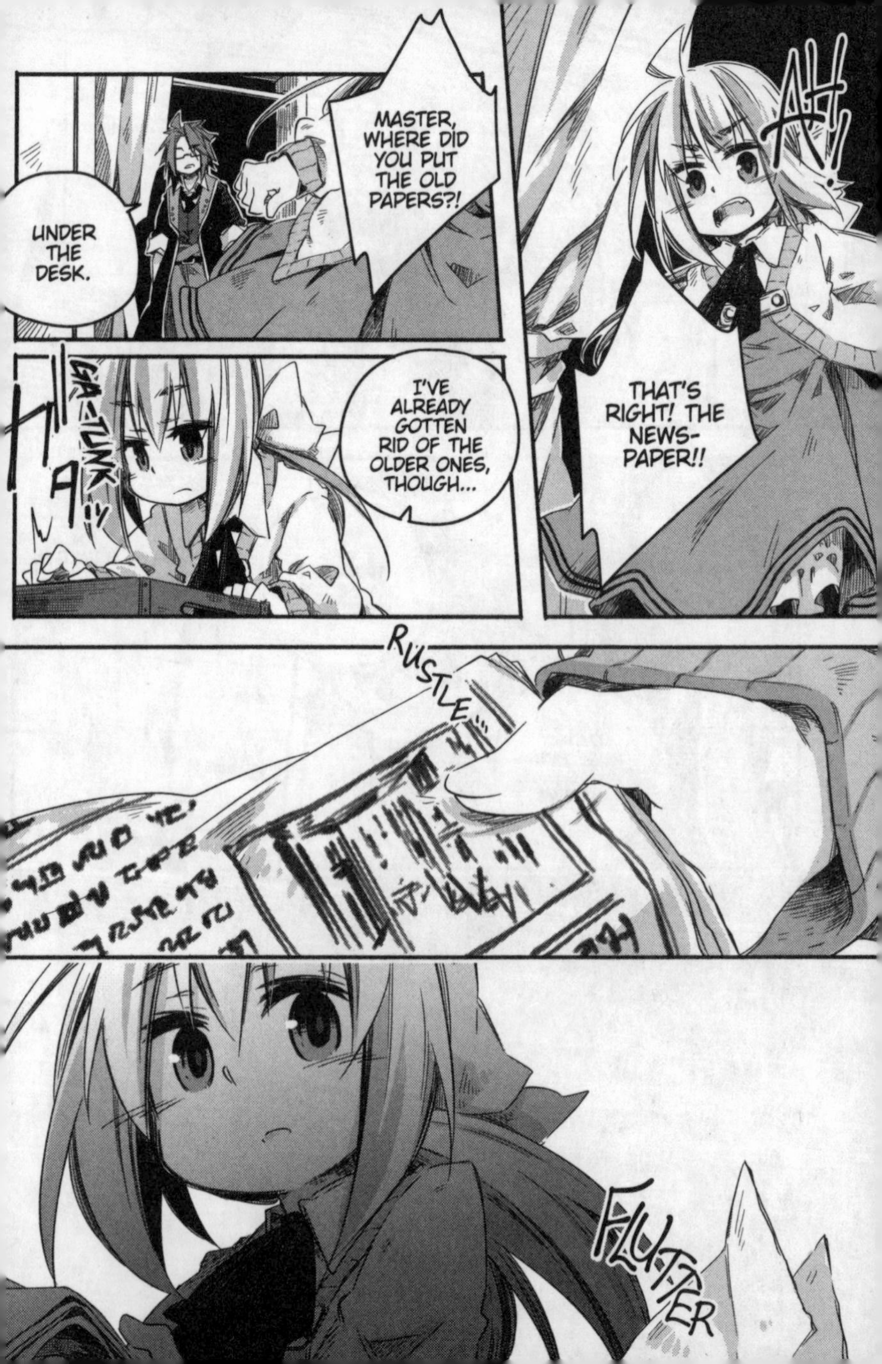
AH!
THAT'S RIGHT! THE NEWS-PAPER!!
MASTER, WHERE DID YOU PUT THE OLD PAPERS?!
UNDER THE DESK.
GA-TUNK
I'VE ALREADY GOTTEN RID OF THE OLDER ONES, THOUGH...
RUSTLE...
FLUTTER

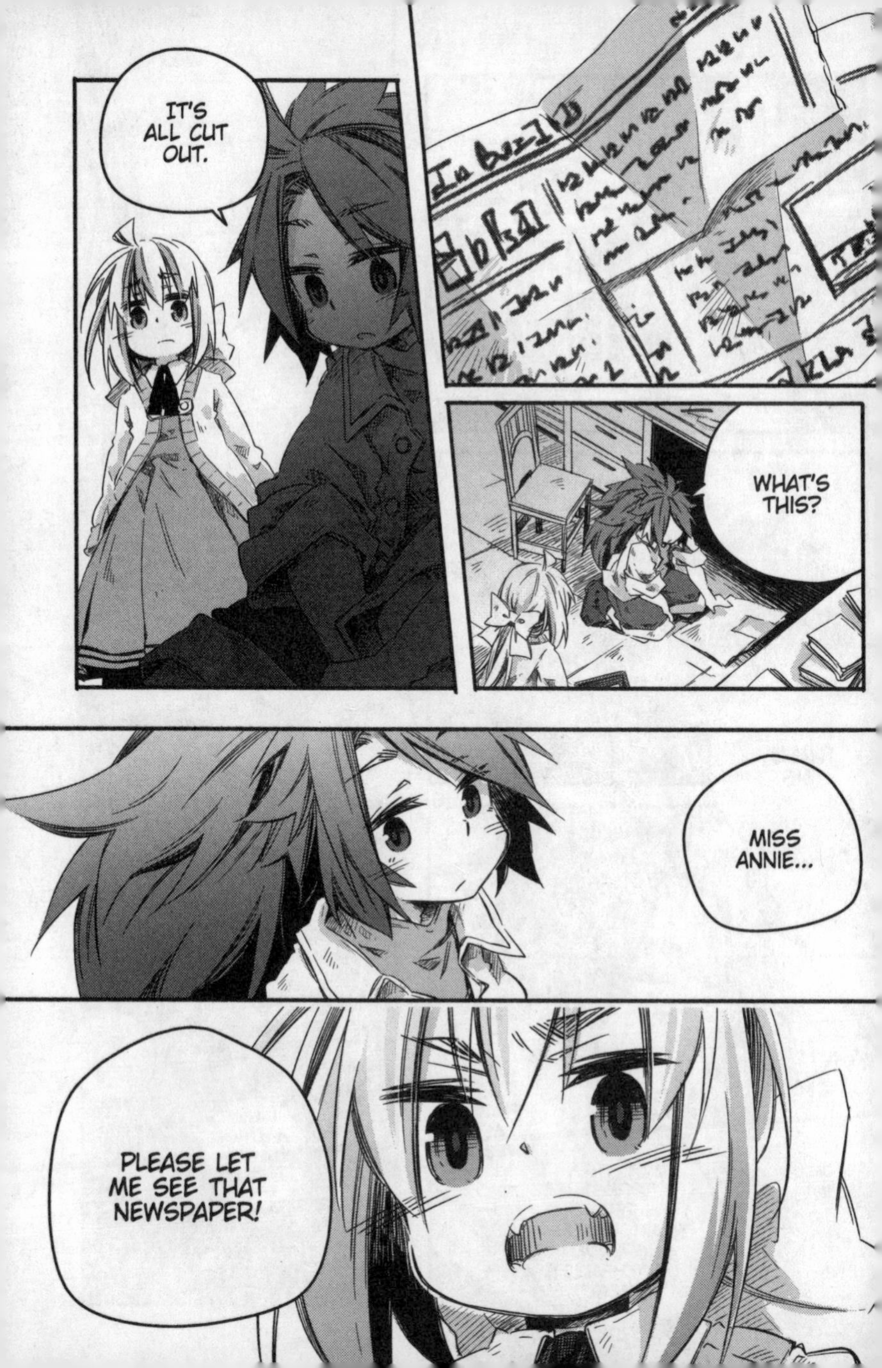
WHAT'S THIS?
IT'S ALL CUT OUT.
MISS ANNIE...
PLEASE LET ME SEE THAT NEWSPAPER!

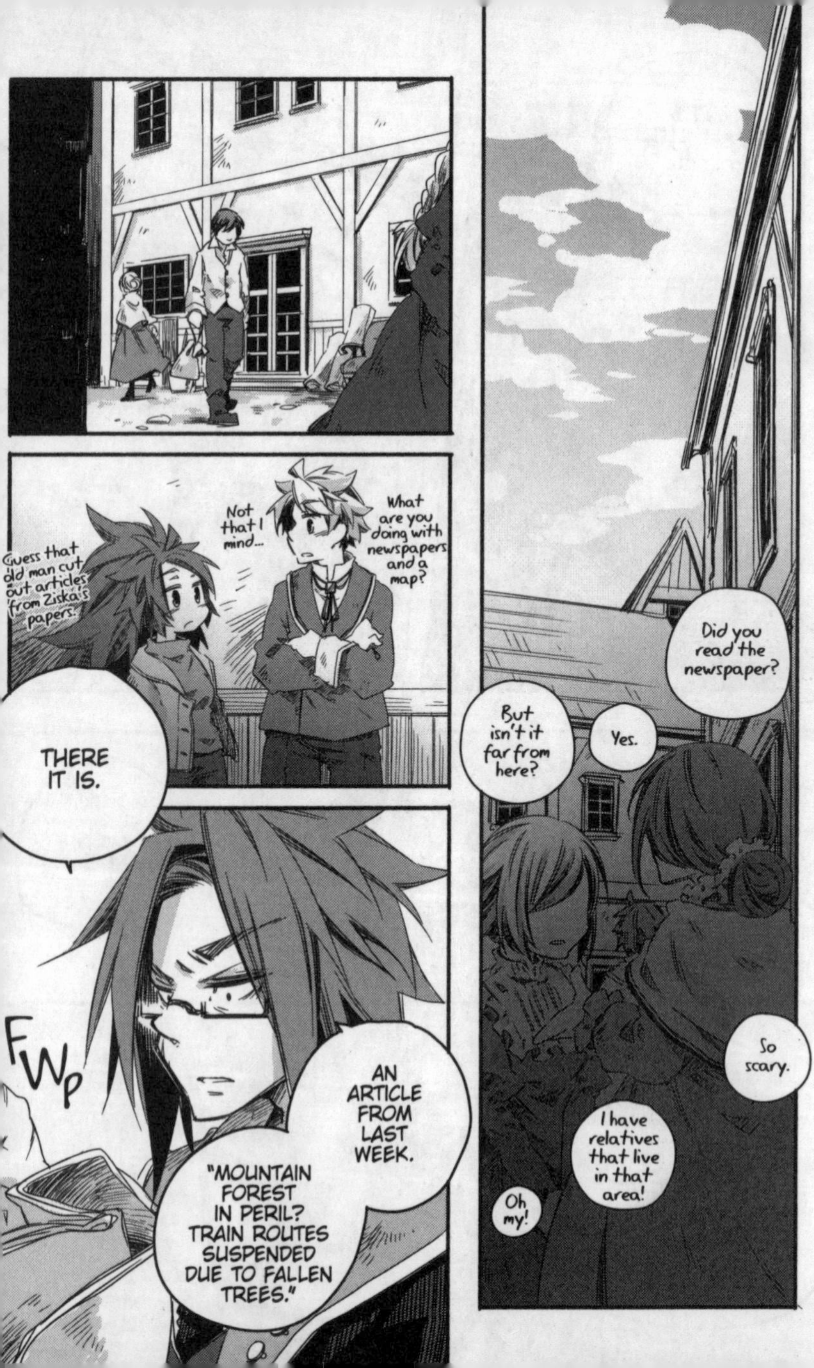
Did you read the newspaper?
Yes.
But isn't it far from here?
So scary.
I have relatives that live in that area!
Oh my!
What are you doing with newspapers and a map?
Not that I mind...
Guess that old man cut out articles from Ziska's papers.
THERE IT IS.
FWP
AN ARTICLE FROM LAST WEEK.
"MOUNTAIN FOREST IN PERIL? TRAIN ROUTES SUSPENDED DUE TO FALLEN TREES."

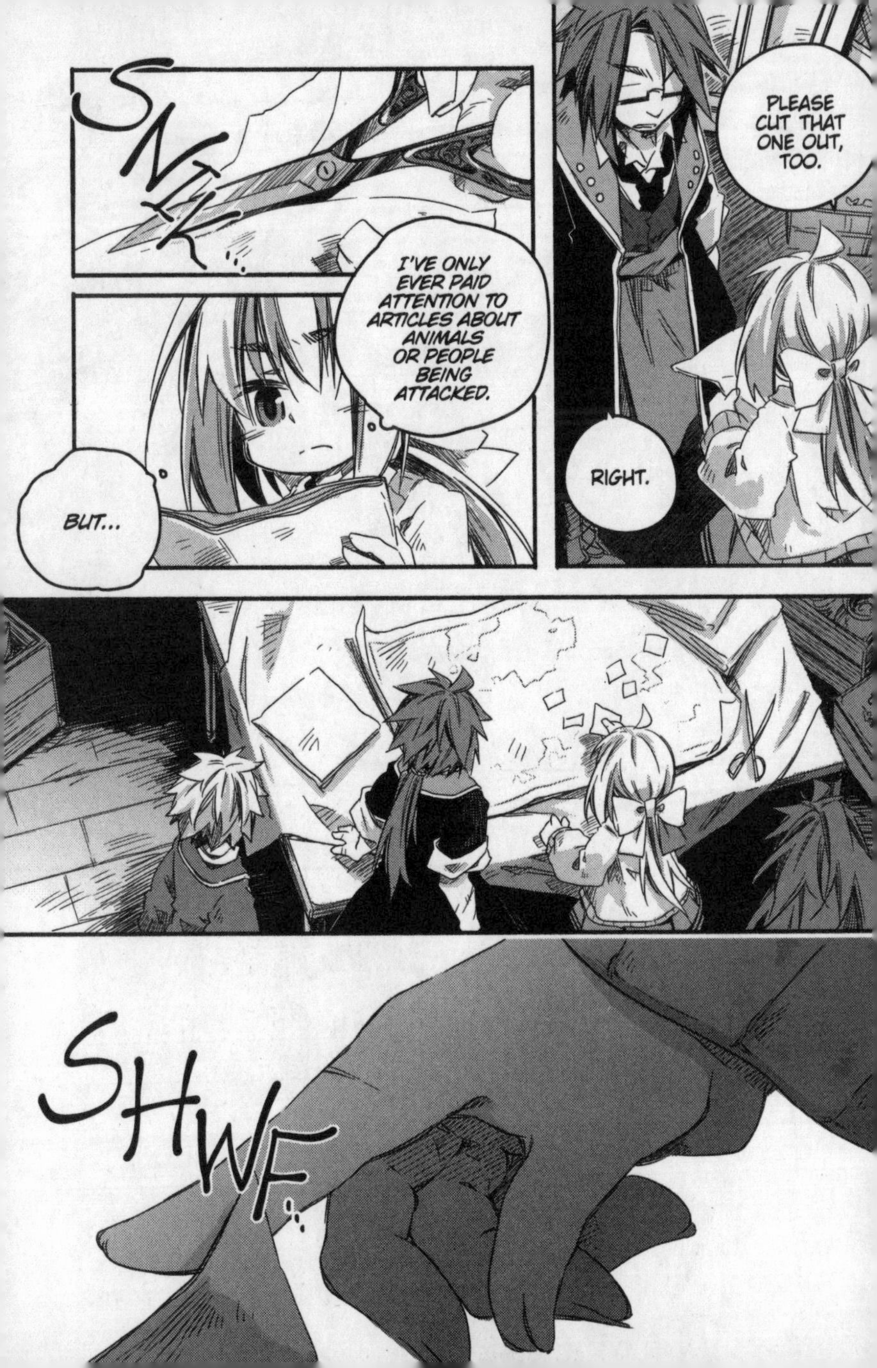
PLEASE CUT THAT ONE OUT, TOO.
RIGHT.
SNIK
I'VE ONLY EVER PAID ATTENTION TO ARTICLES ABOUT ANIMALS OR PEOPLE BEING ATTACKED.
BUT...
SHWF

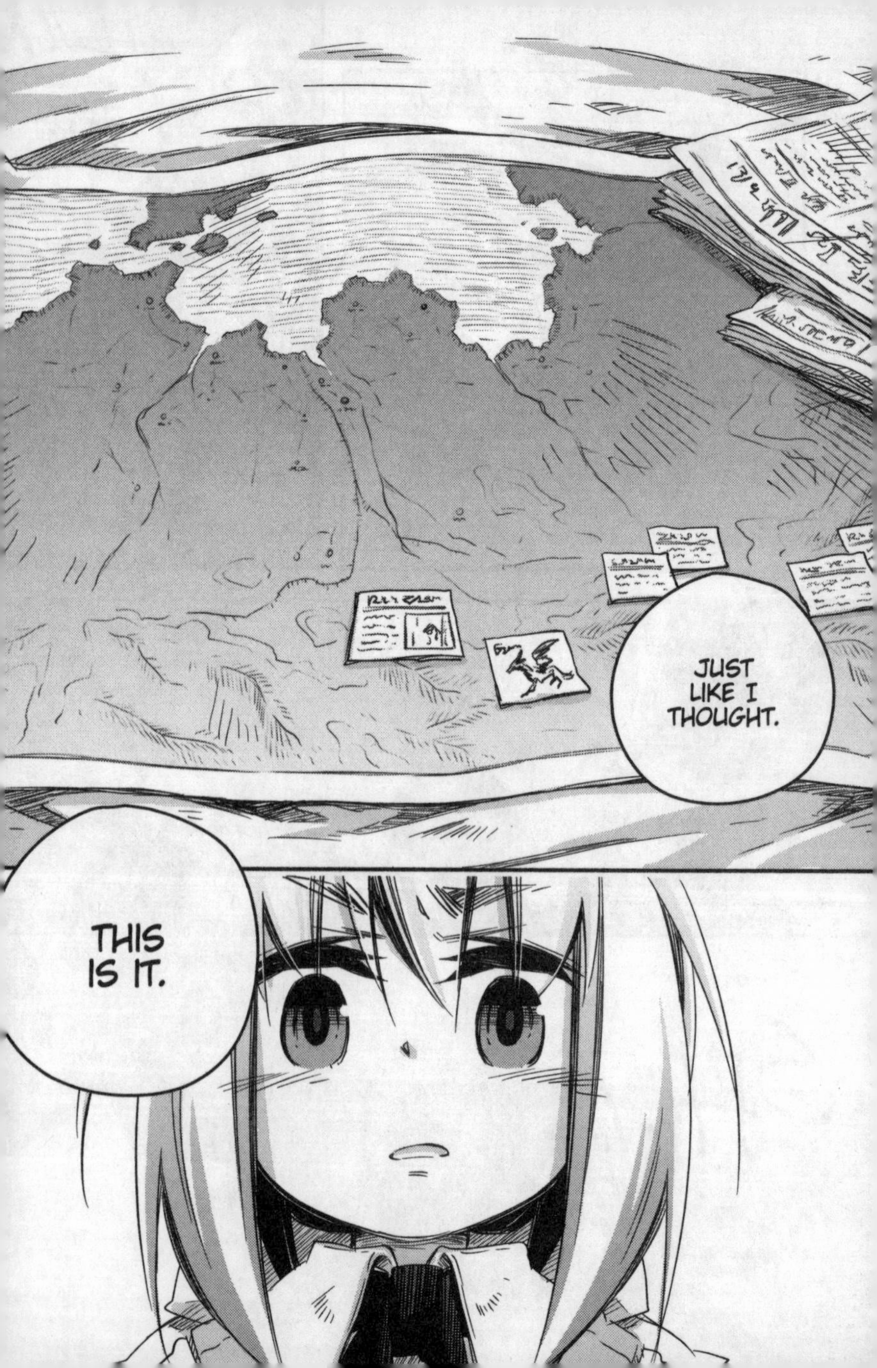
JUST LIKE I THOUGHT.
THIS IS IT.

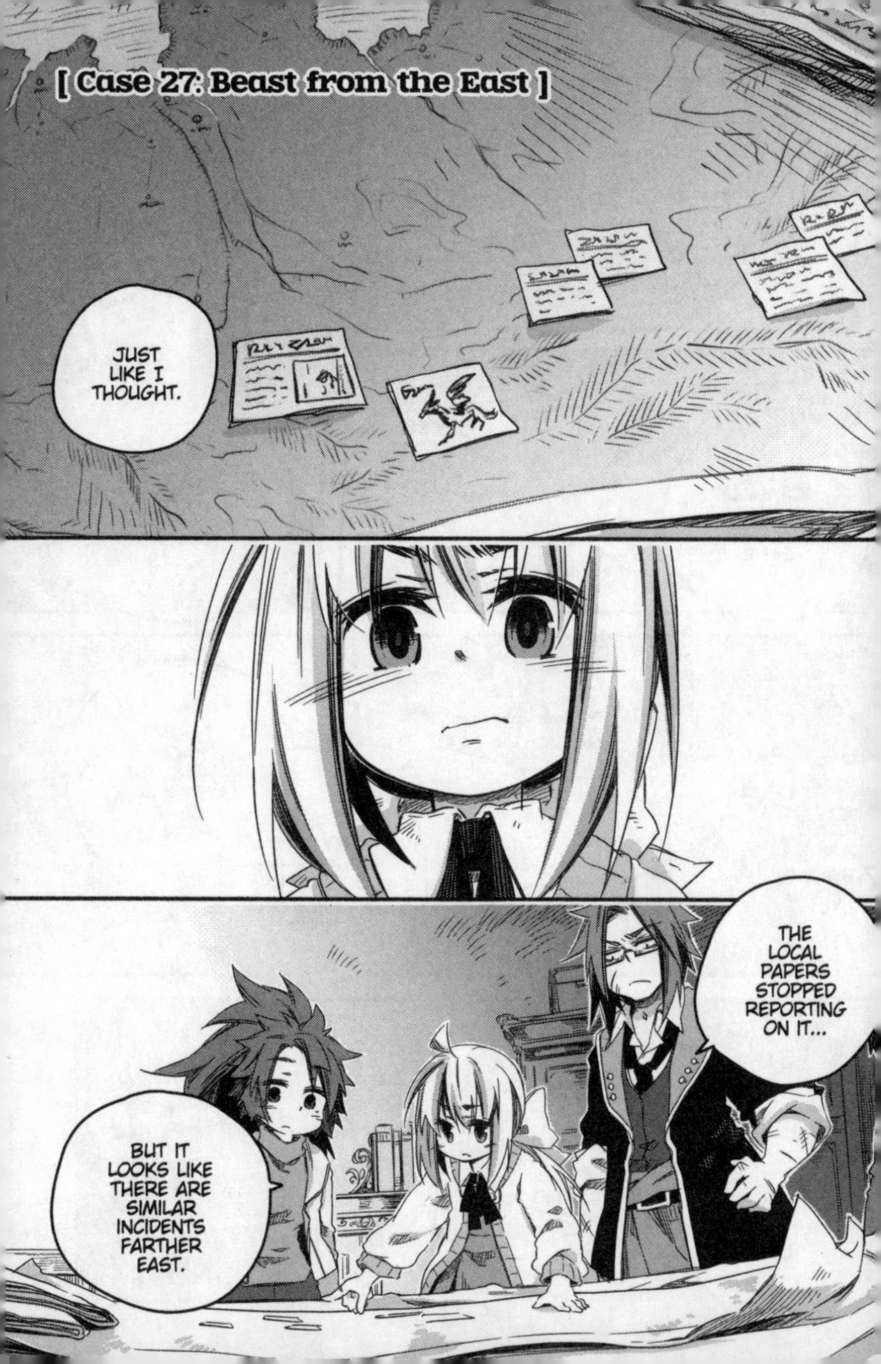
[Case 27: Beast from the East]
JUST LIKE I THOUGHT.
THE LOCAL PAPERS STOPPED REPORTING ON IT...
BUT IT LOOKS LIKE THERE ARE SIMILAR INCIDENTS FARTHER EAST.

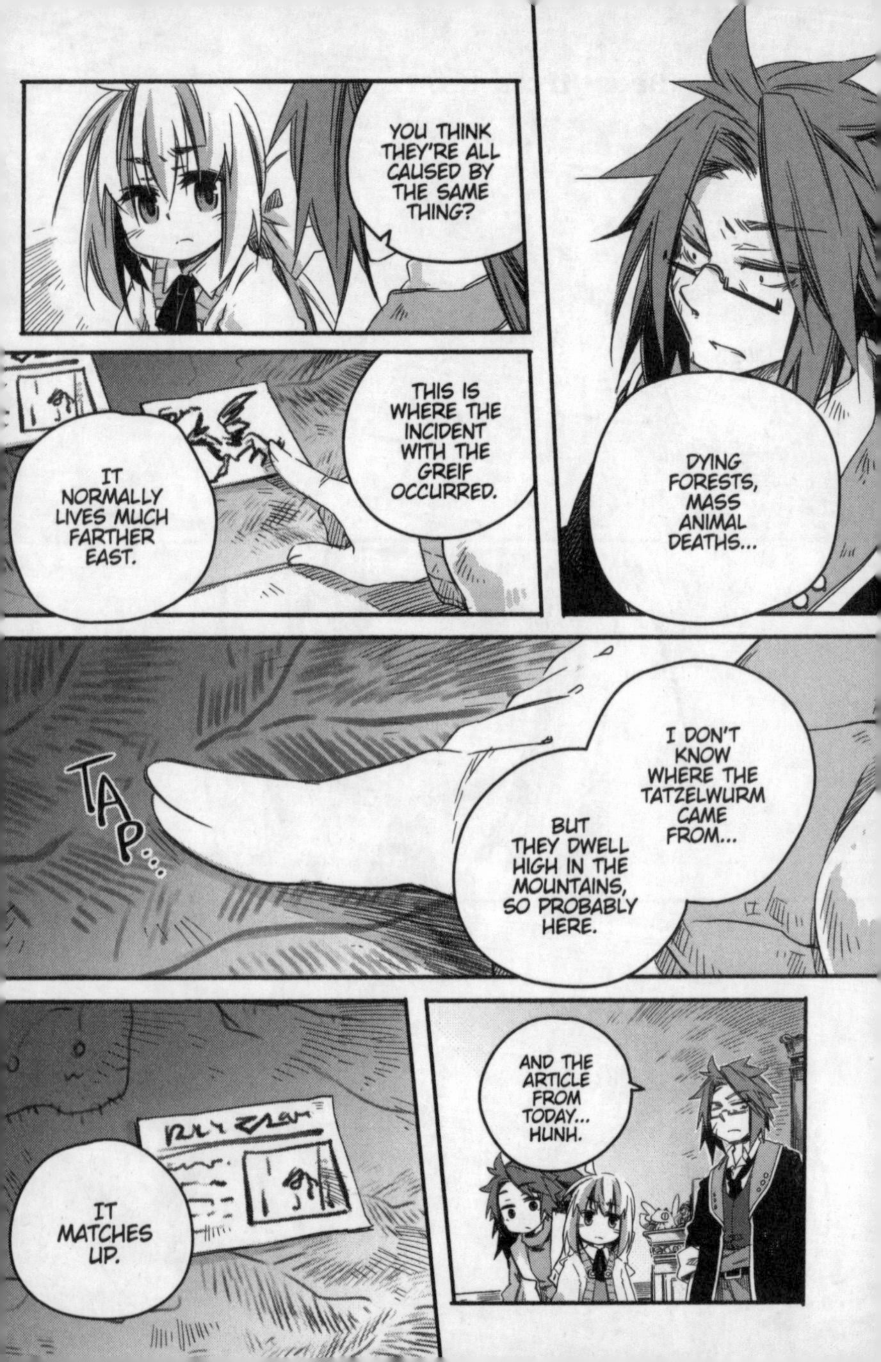
DYING FORESTS, MASS ANIMAL DEATHS...
YOU THINK THEY'RE ALL CAUSED BY THE SAME THING?
THIS IS WHERE THE INCIDENT WITH THE GREIF OCCURRED.
IT NORMALLY LIVES MUCH FARTHER EAST.
I DON'T KNOW WHERE THE TATZELWURM CAME FROM...
BUT THEY DWELL HIGH IN THE MOUNTAINS, SO PROBABLY HERE.
TAP...
AND THE ARTICLE FROM TODAY... HUNH.
IT MATCHES UP.

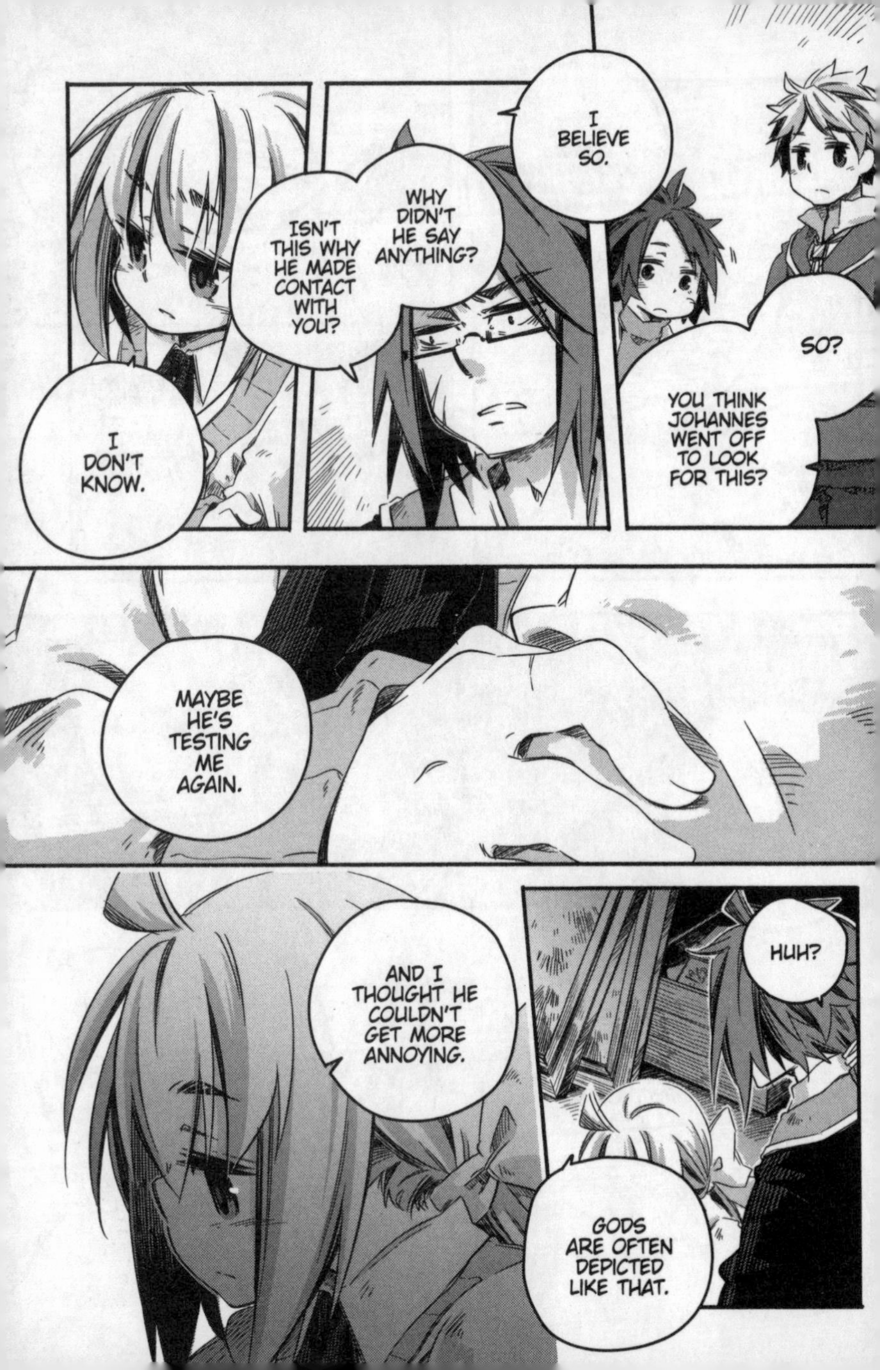
SO?
YOU THINK JOHANNES WENT OFF TO LOOK FOR THIS?
I BELIEVE SO.
WHY DIDN'T HE SAY ANYTHING?
ISN'T THIS WHY HE MADE CONTACT WITH YOU?
I DON'T KNOW.
MAYBE HE'S TESTING ME AGAIN.
HUH?
GODS ARE OFTEN DEPICTED LIKE THAT.
AND I THOUGHT HE COULDN'T GET MORE ANNOYING.

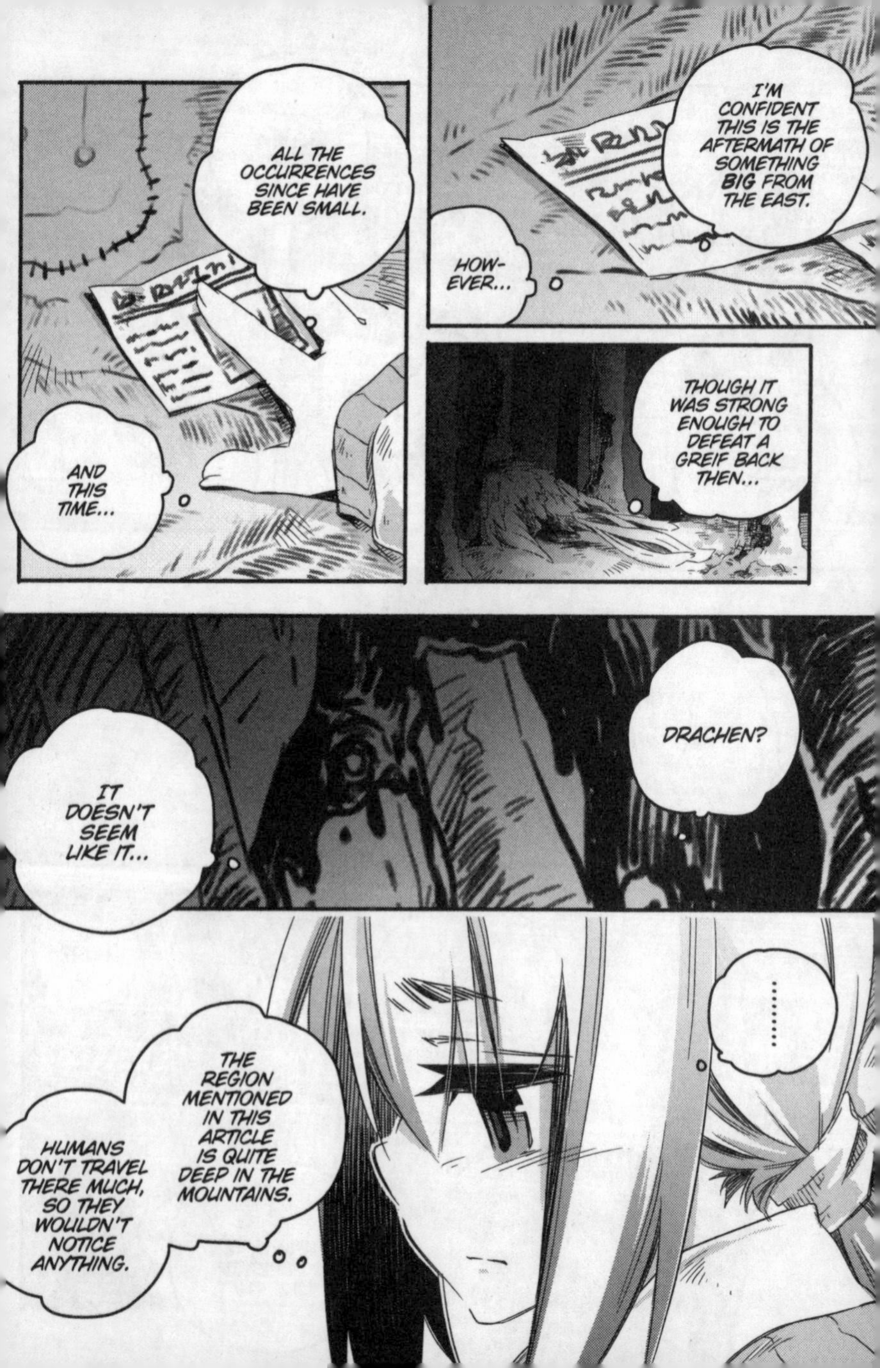
I'M CONFIDENT THIS IS THE AFTERMATH OF SOMETHING BIG FROM THE EAST.
HOW-EVER...
THOUGH IT WAS STRONG ENOUGH TO DEFEAT A GREIF BACK THEN...
ALL THE OCCURRENCES SINCE HAVE BEEN SMALL.
AND THIS TIME...
DRACHEN?
IT DOESN'T SEEM LIKE IT...
......
THE REGION MENTIONED IN THIS ARTICLE IS QUITE DEEP IN THE MOUNTAINS.
HUMANS DON'T TRAVEL THERE MUCH, SO THEY WOULDN'T NOTICE ANYTHING.

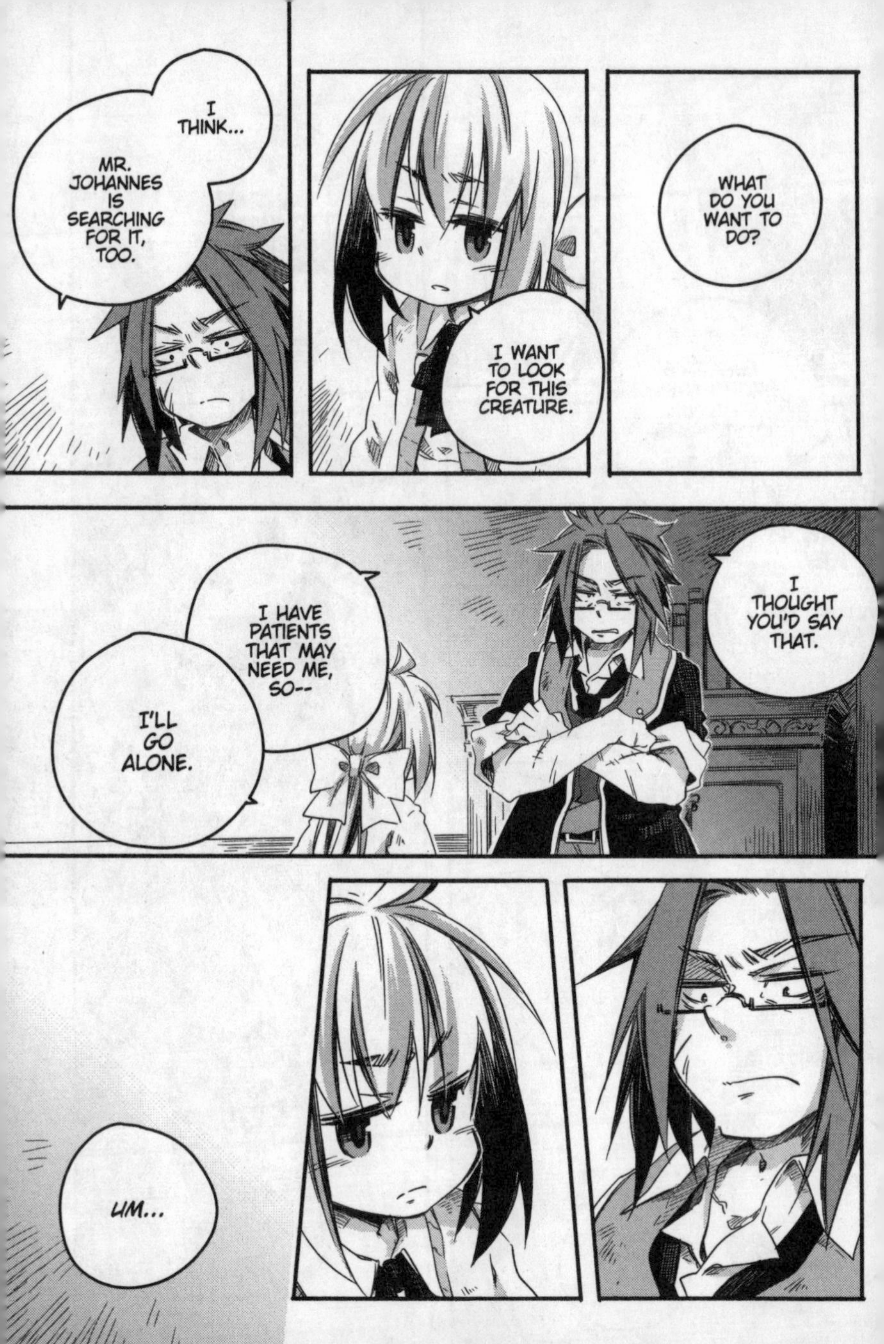
WHAT DO YOU WANT TO DO?
I WANT TO LOOK FOR THIS CREATURE.
I THINK...
MR. JOHANNES IS SEARCHING FOR IT, TOO.
I THOUGHT YOU'D SAY THAT.
I HAVE PATIENTS THAT MAY NEED ME, SO--
I'LL GO ALONE.
UM...

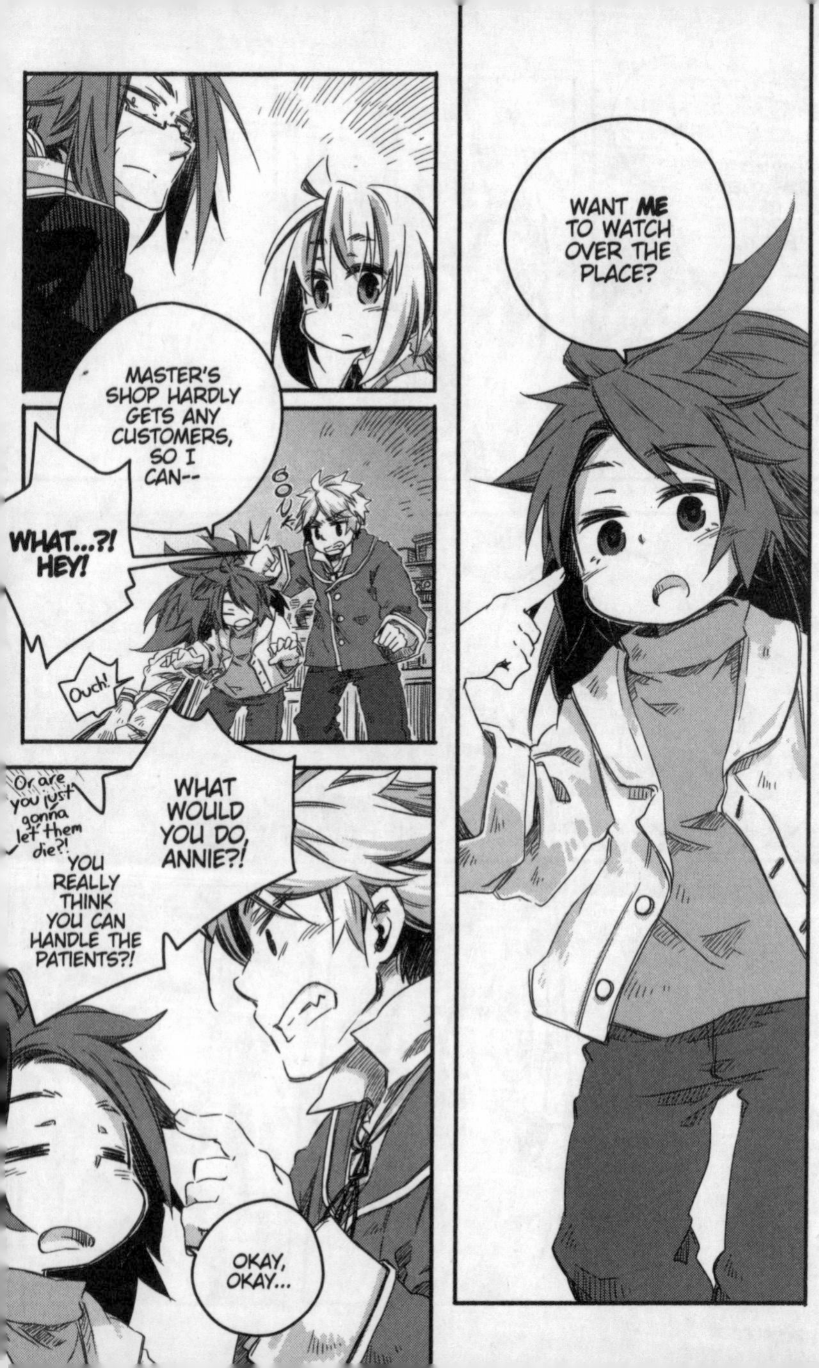
WANT **ME** TO WATCH OVER THE PLACE?
MASTER'S SHOP HARDLY GETS ANY CUSTOMERS, SO I CAN--
GONK
WHAT...?! HEY!
Ouch!
WHAT WOULD YOU DO, ANNIE?!
YOU REALLY THINK YOU CAN HANDLE THE PATIENTS?!
Or are you just gonna let them die?!
OKAY, OKAY...

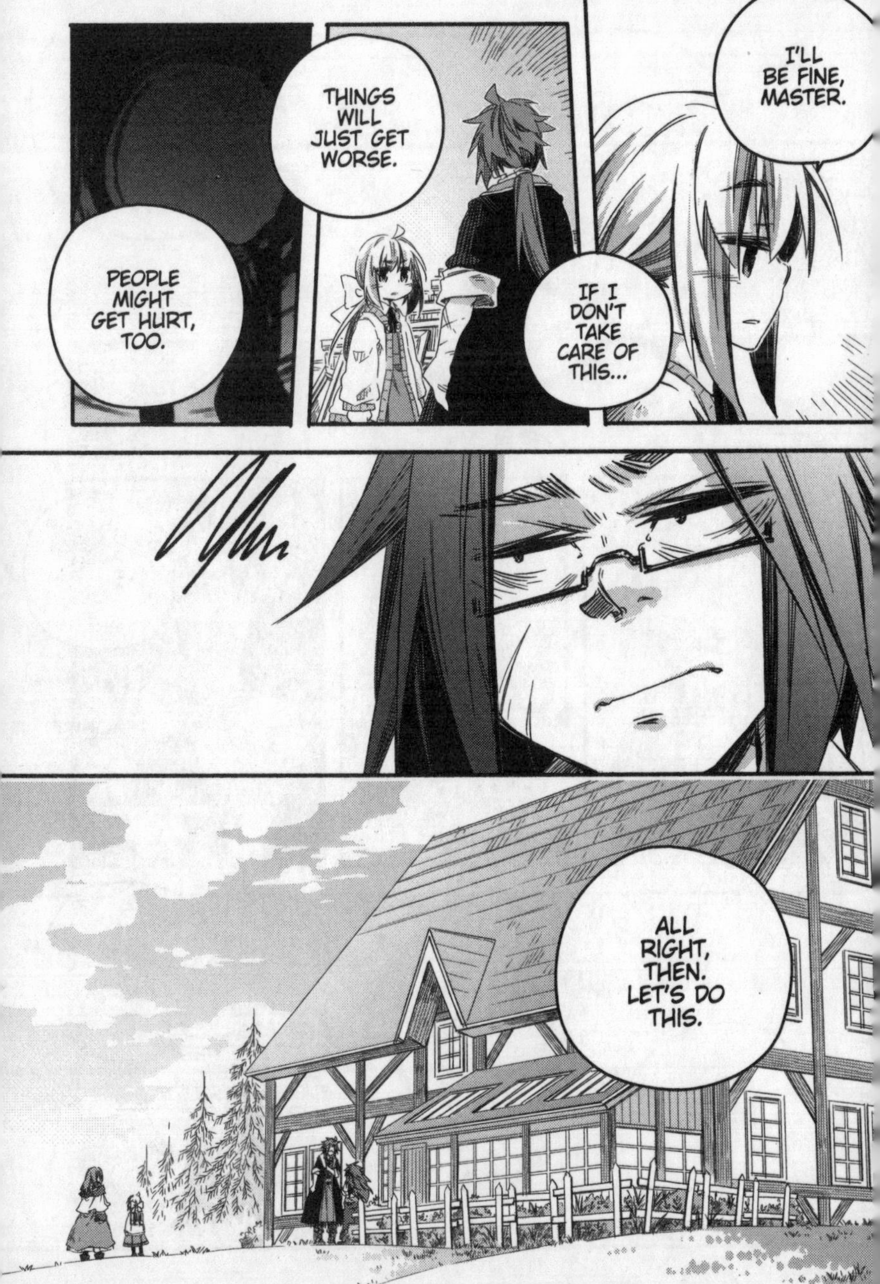
I'LL BE FINE, MASTER.
IF I DON'T TAKE CARE OF THIS...
THINGS WILL JUST GET WORSE.
PEOPLE MIGHT GET HURT, TOO.
ALL RIGHT, THEN. LET'S DO THIS.

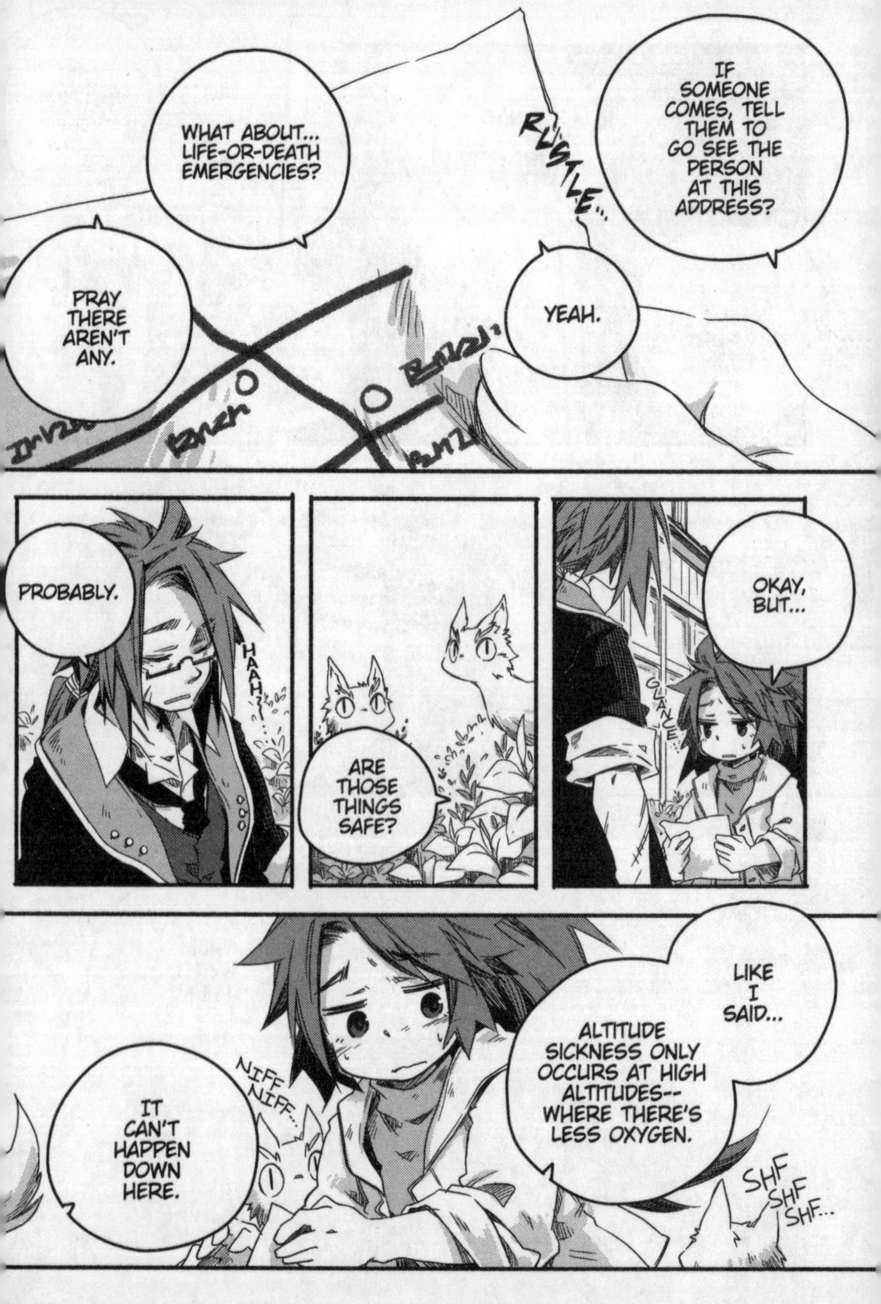
IF SOMEONE COMES, TELL THEM TO GO SEE THE PERSON AT THIS ADDRESS?
RUSTLE...
YEAH.
WHAT ABOUT... LIFE-OR-DEATH EMERGENCIES?
PRAY THERE AREN'T ANY.
OKAY, BUT...
GLANCE
ARE THOSE THINGS SAFE?
PROBABLY.
HAAH...
LIKE I SAID...
ALTITUDE SICKNESS ONLY OCCURS AT HIGH ALTITUDES-- WHERE THERE'S LESS OXYGEN.
SHF SHF SHF...
NIFF NIFF...
IT CAN'T HAPPEN DOWN HERE.

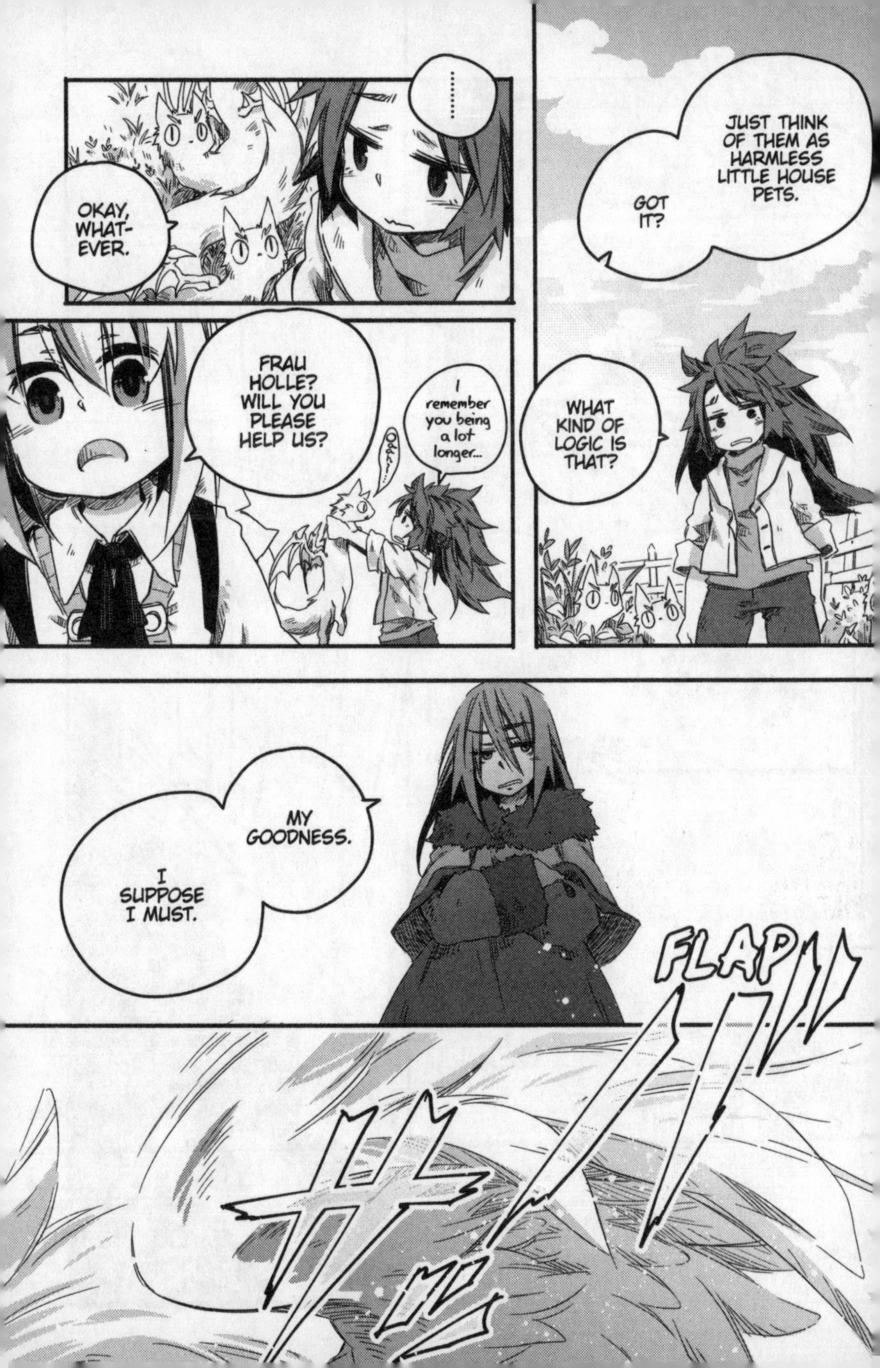
JUST THINK OF THEM AS HARMLESS LITTLE HOUSE PETS.
GOT IT?
......
OKAY, WHATEVER.
WHAT KIND OF LOGIC IS THAT?
I remember you being a lot longer...
Oddn~...
FRAU HOLLE? WILL YOU PLEASE HELP US?
MY GOODNESS.
I SUPPOSE I MUST.
FLAP

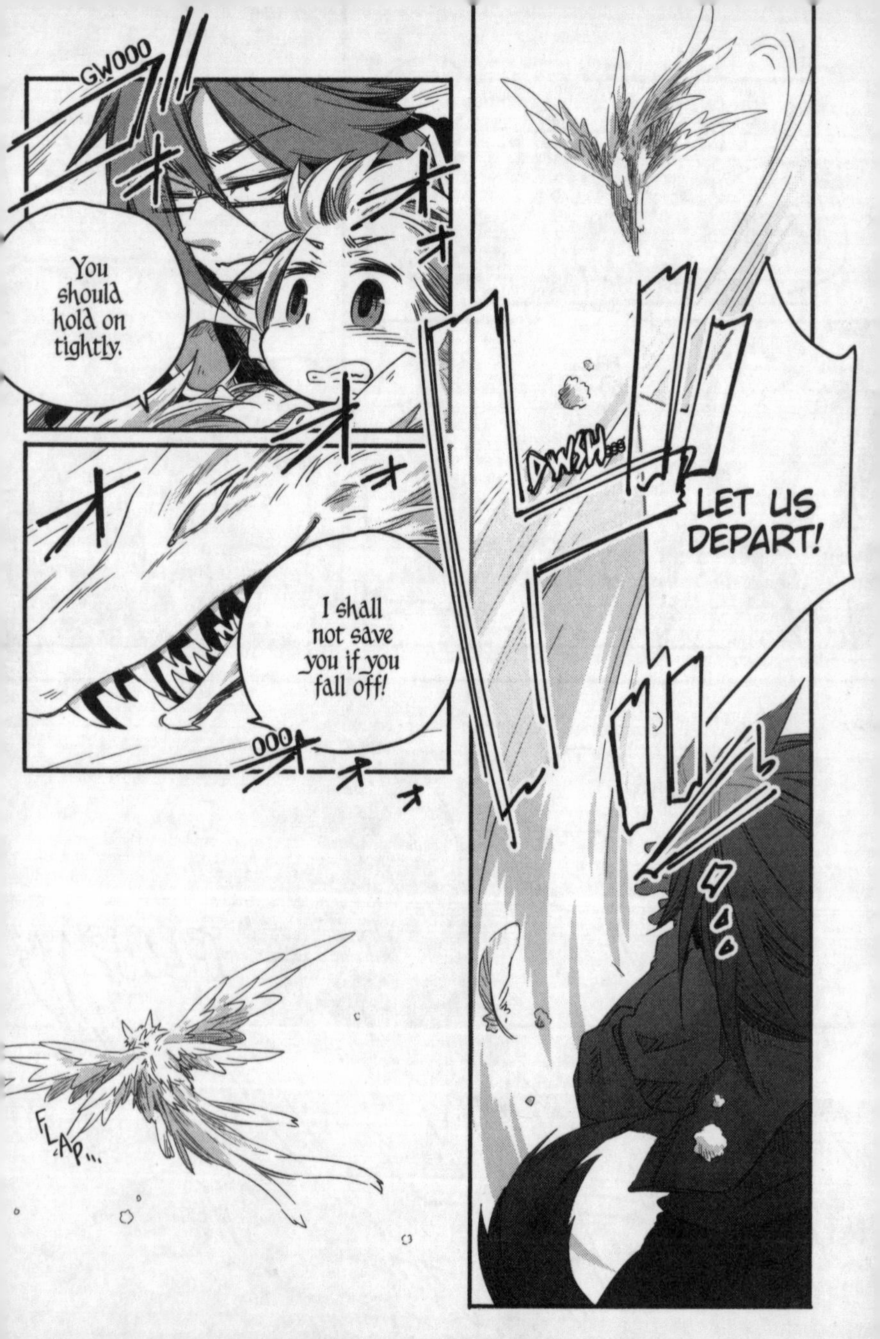
DWSH...
LET US DEPART!
GWOOO
You should hold on tightly.
I shall not save you if you fall off!
OOO
FLAP...

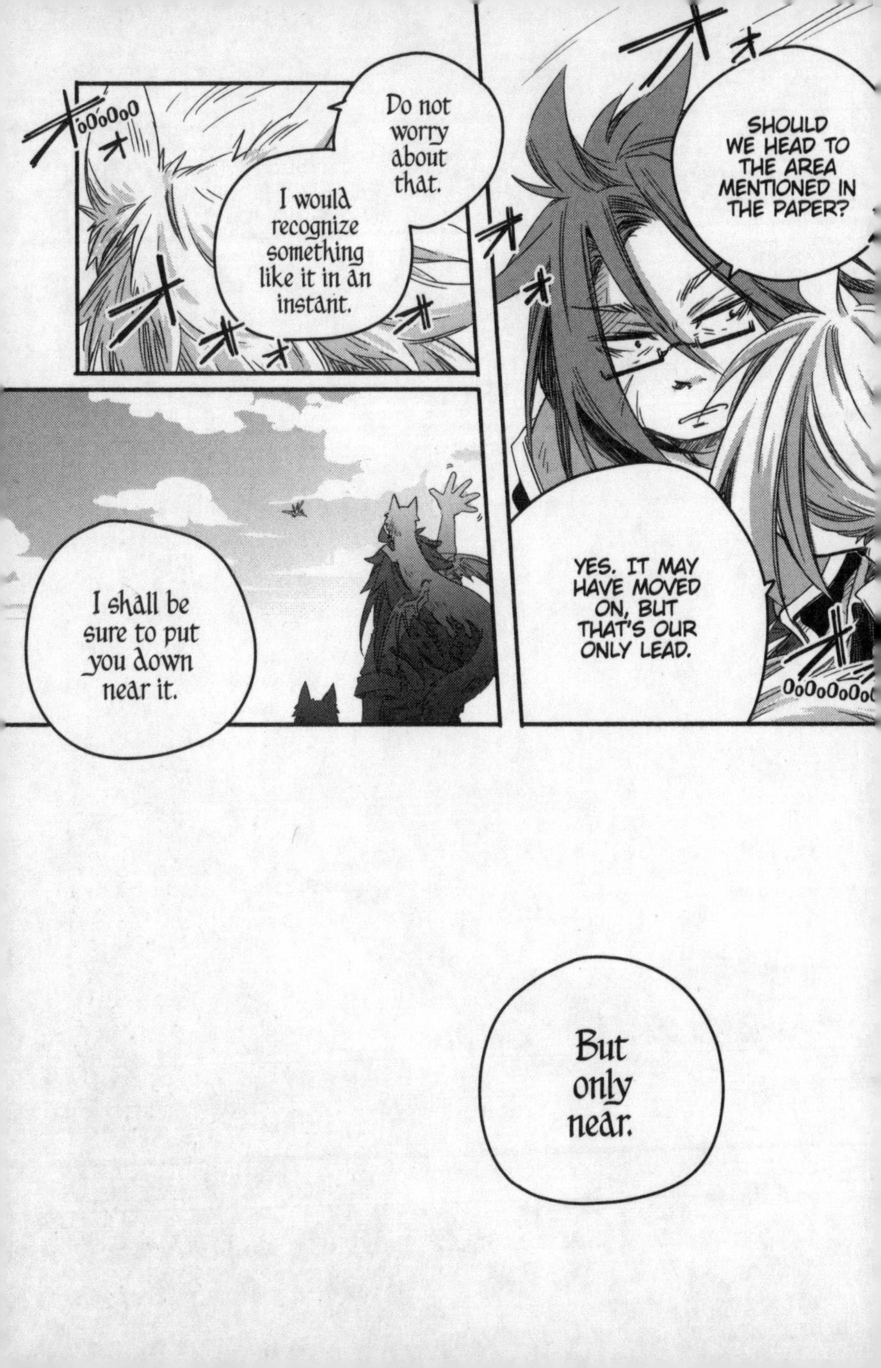
SHOULD WE HEAD TO THE AREA MENTIONED IN THE PAPER?
YES. IT MAY HAVE MOVED ON, BUT THAT'S OUR ONLY LEAD.
Do not worry about that.
I would recognize something like it in an instant.
I shall be sure to put you down near it.
But only near.

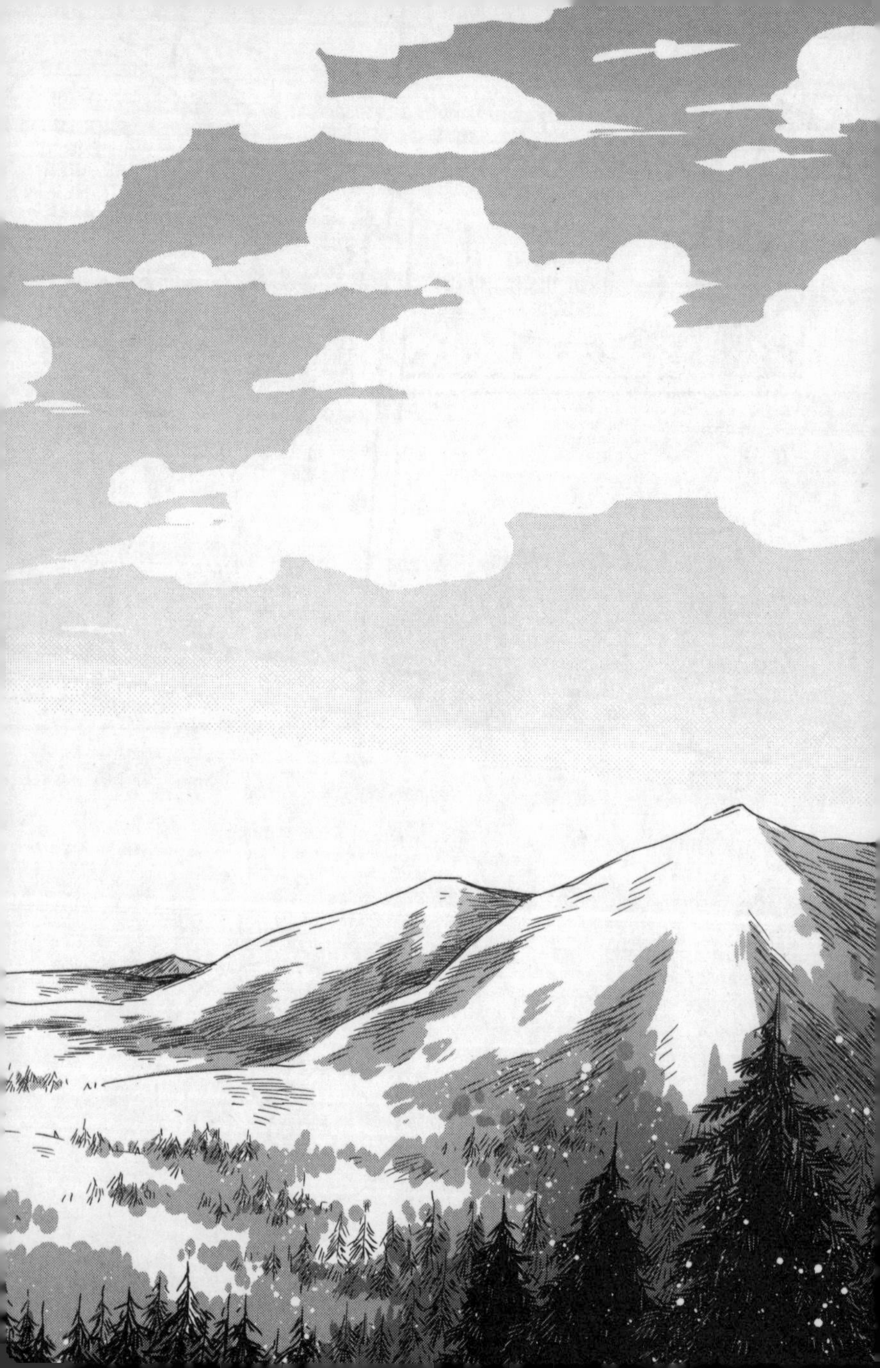

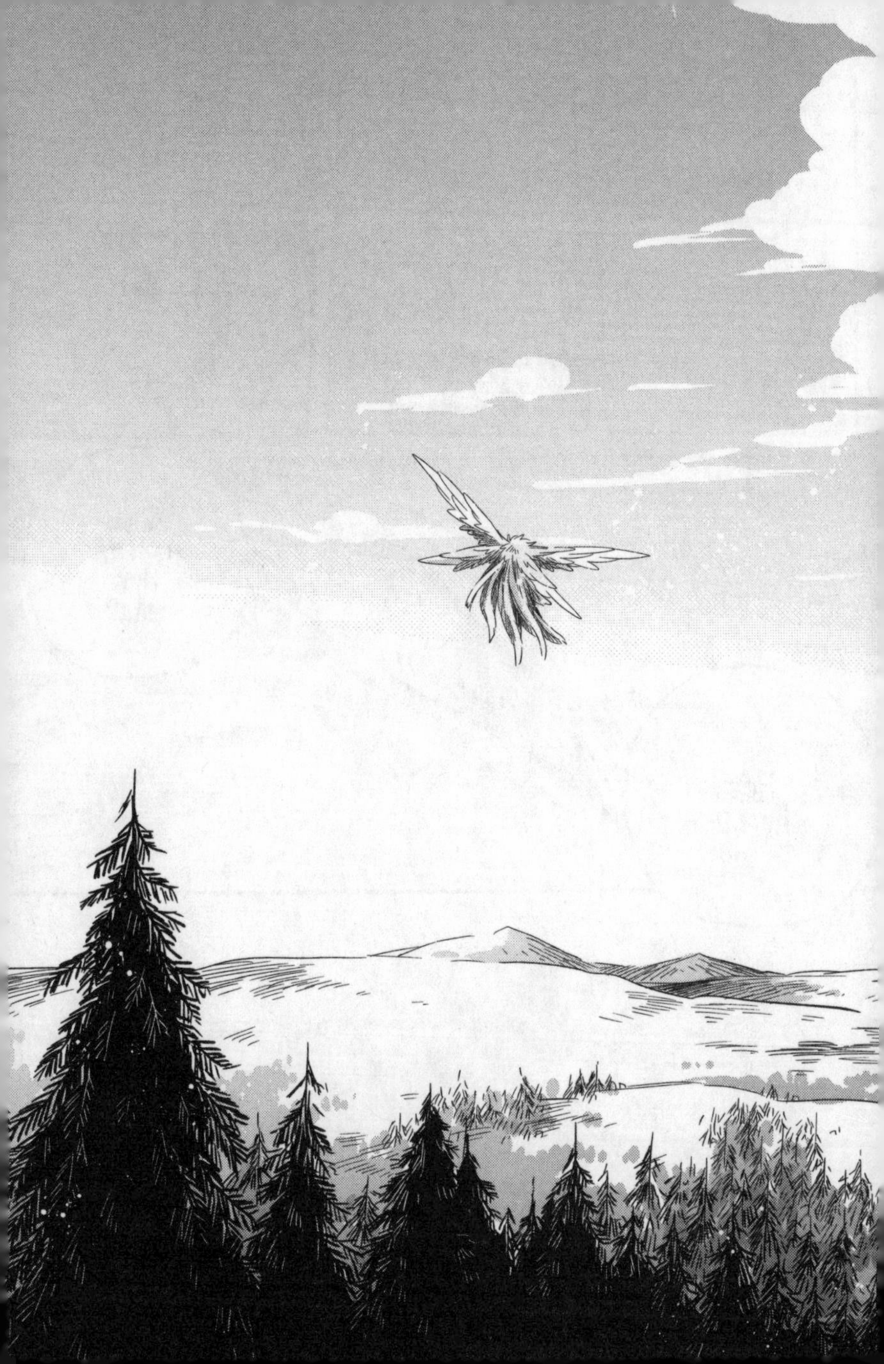

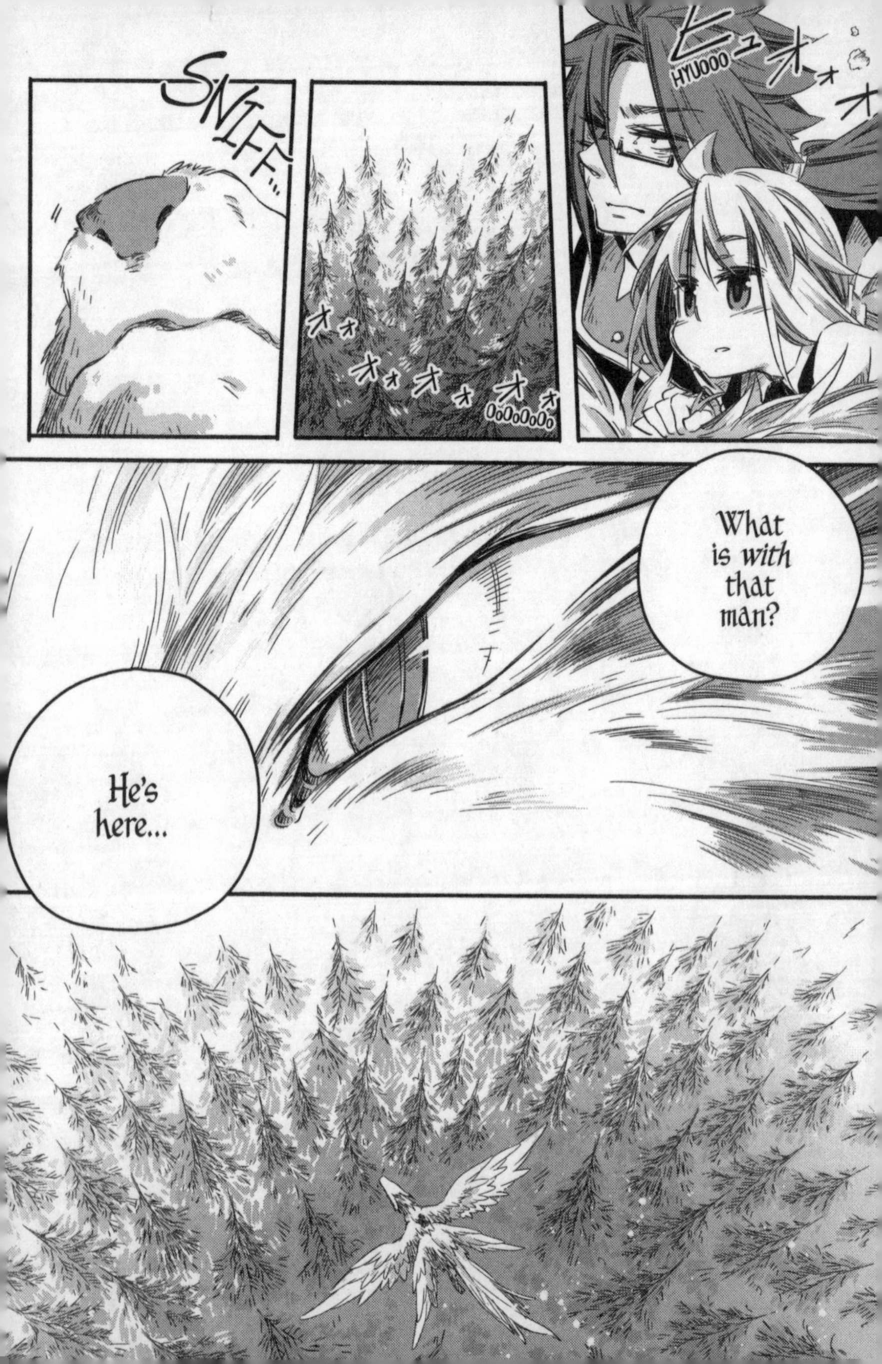
HYUOOO
OoOoOoOo
SNIFF...
What is *with* that man?
He's here...

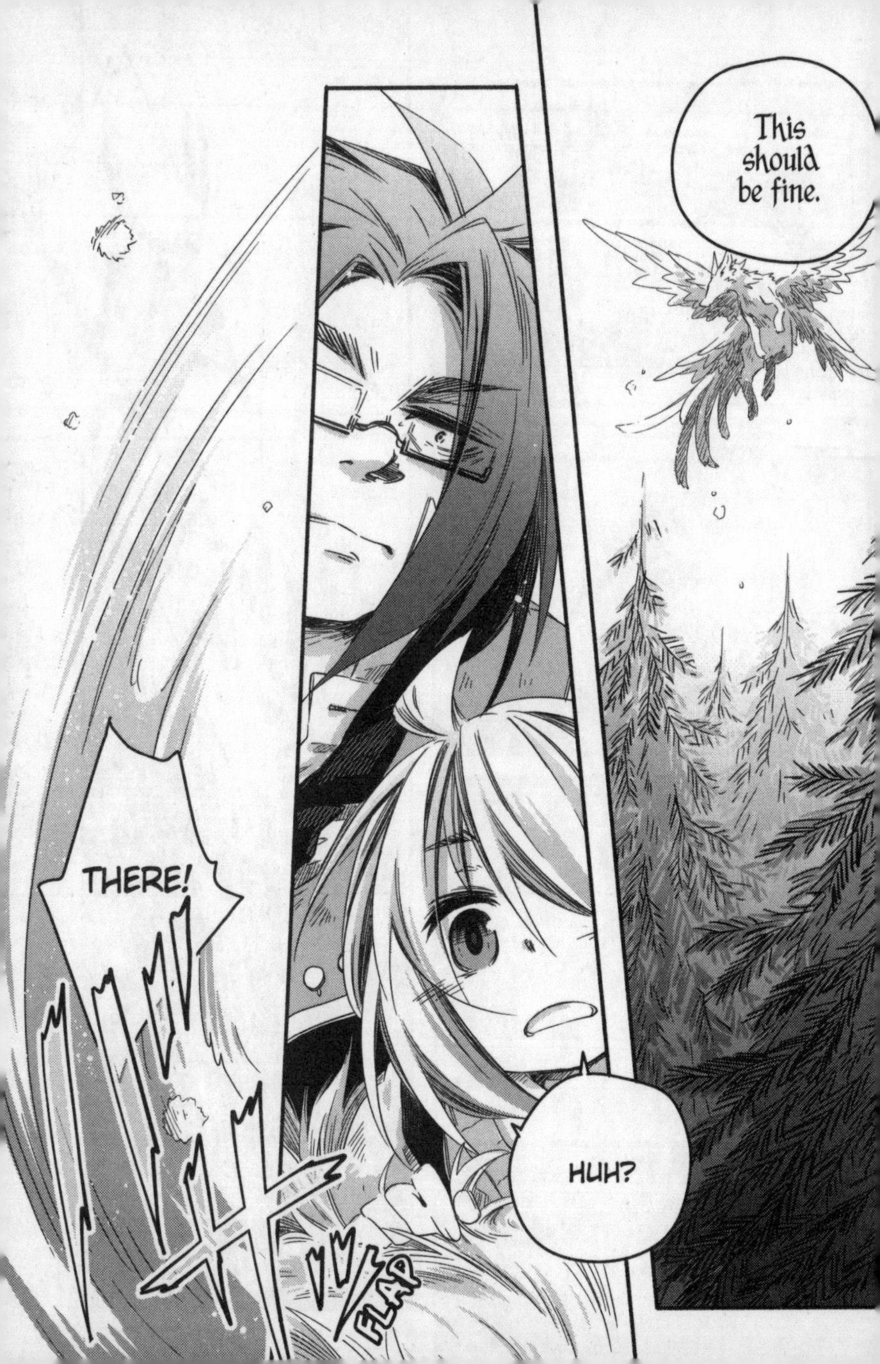
This should be fine.
HUH?
THERE!
FLAP

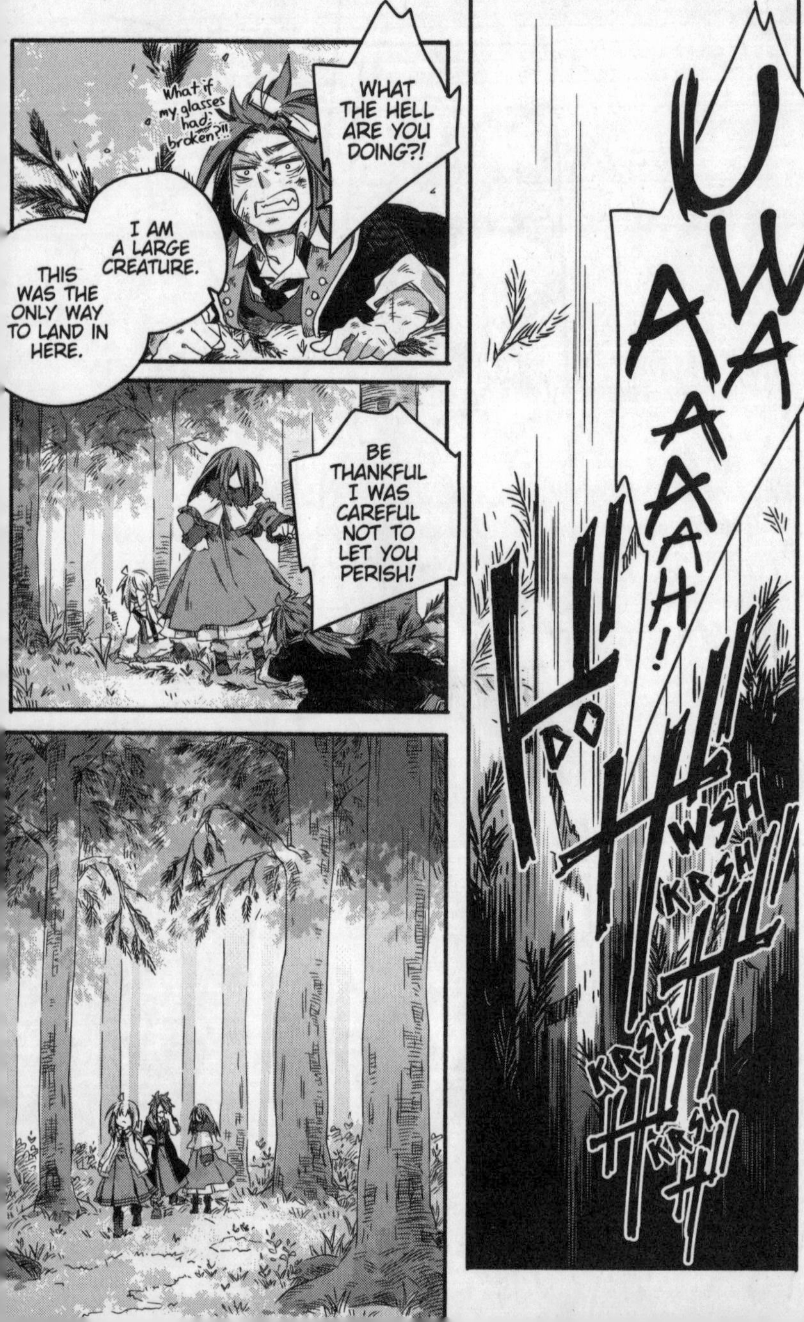

UWAAAAAH!
DO
WSH
KRSH
KRSH
KRSH
WHAT THE HELL ARE YOU DOING?!
What if my glasses had broken?!!
I AM A LARGE CREATURE.
THIS WAS THE ONLY WAY TO LAND IN HERE.
BE THANKFUL I WAS CAREFUL NOT TO LET YOU PERISH!
RUSTLE...

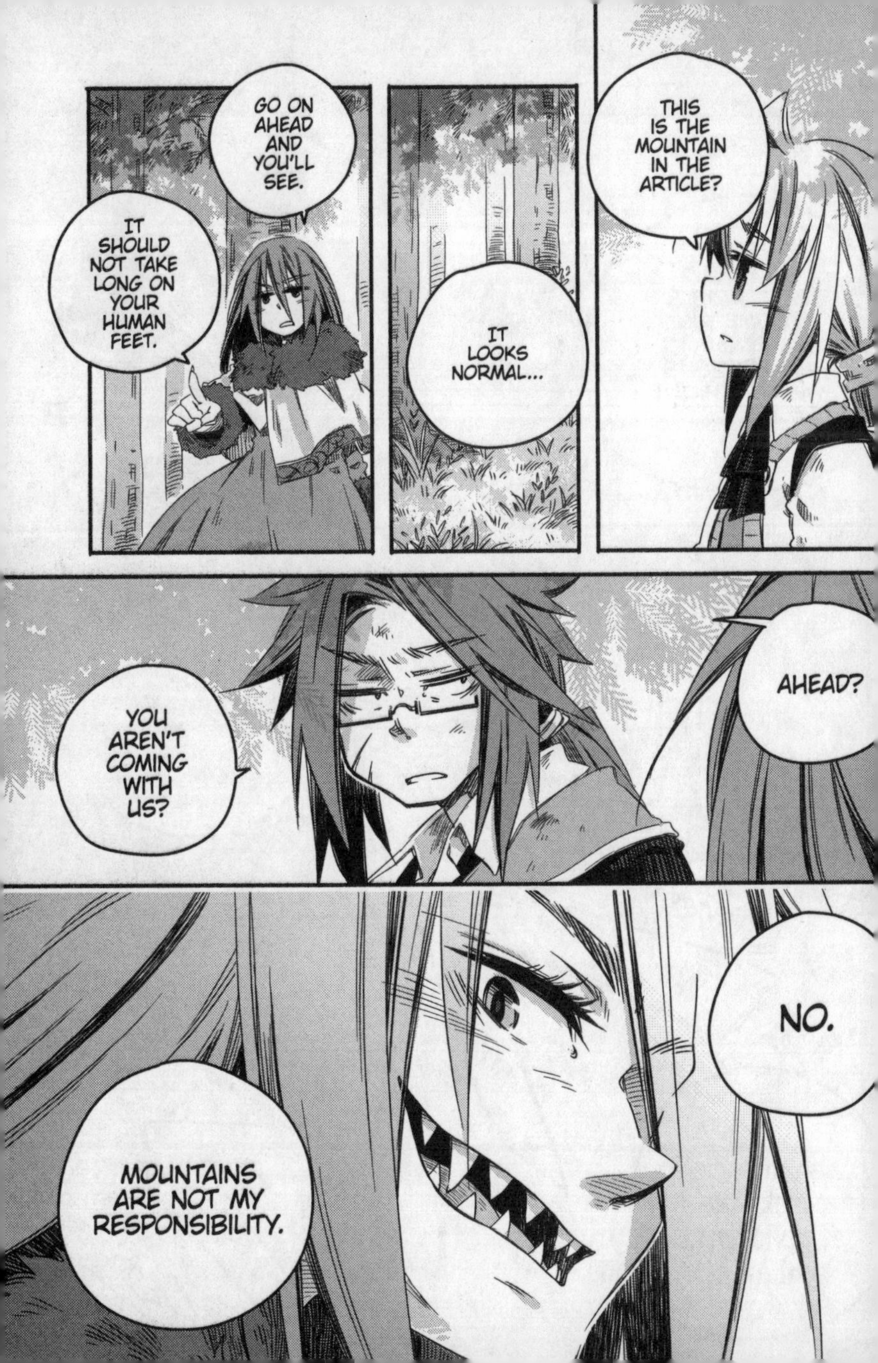
THIS IS THE MOUNTAIN IN THE ARTICLE?
IT LOOKS NORMAL...
GO ON AHEAD AND YOU'LL SEE.
IT SHOULD NOT TAKE LONG ON YOUR HUMAN FEET.
AHEAD?
YOU AREN'T COMING WITH US?
NO.
MOUNTAINS ARE NOT MY RESPONSIBILITY.

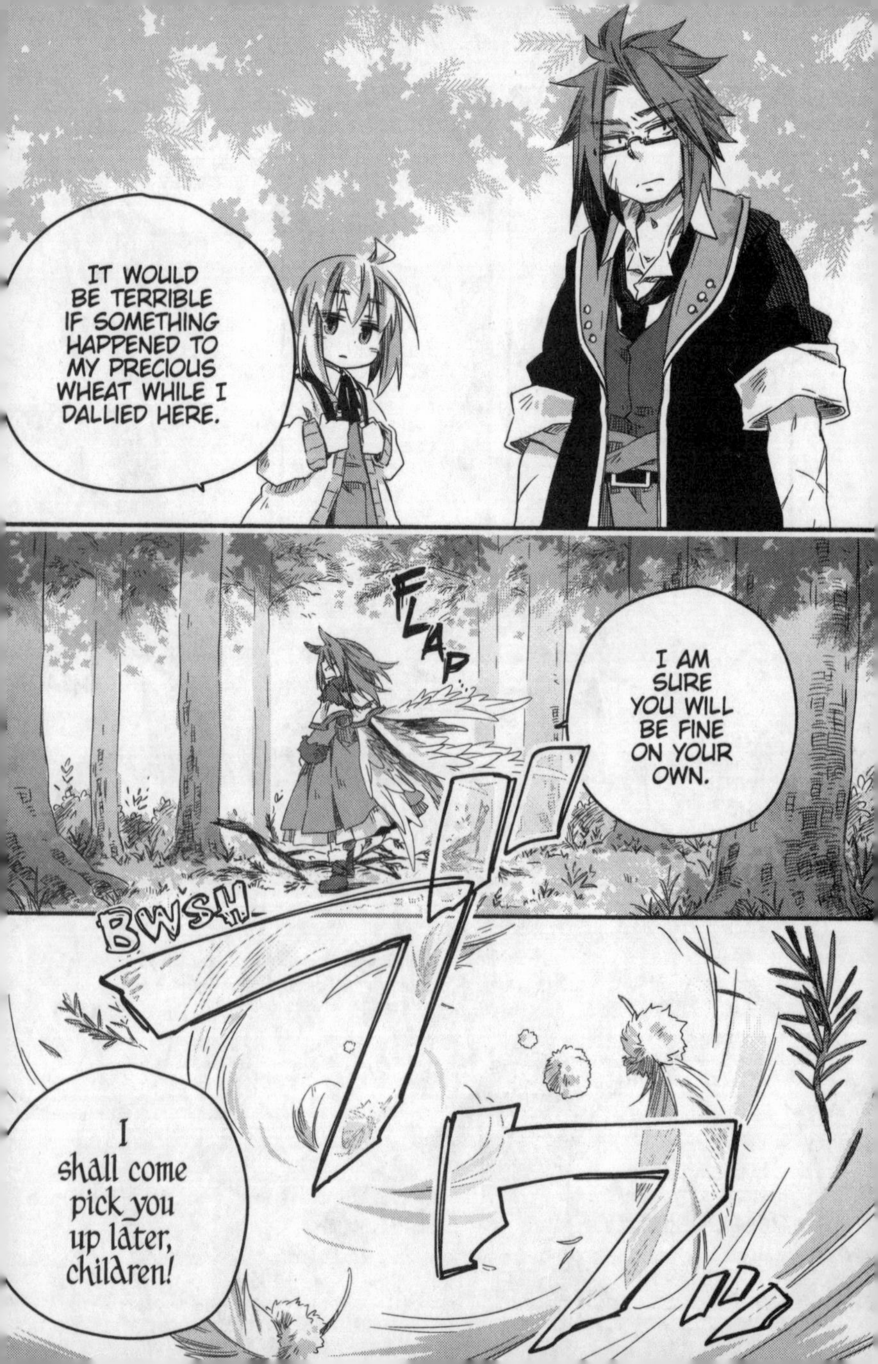
IT WOULD BE TERRIBLE IF SOMETHING HAPPENED TO MY PRECIOUS WHEAT WHILE I DALLIED HERE.
I AM SURE YOU WILL BE FINE ON YOUR OWN.
FLAP...
BWSH
I shall come pick you up later, children!

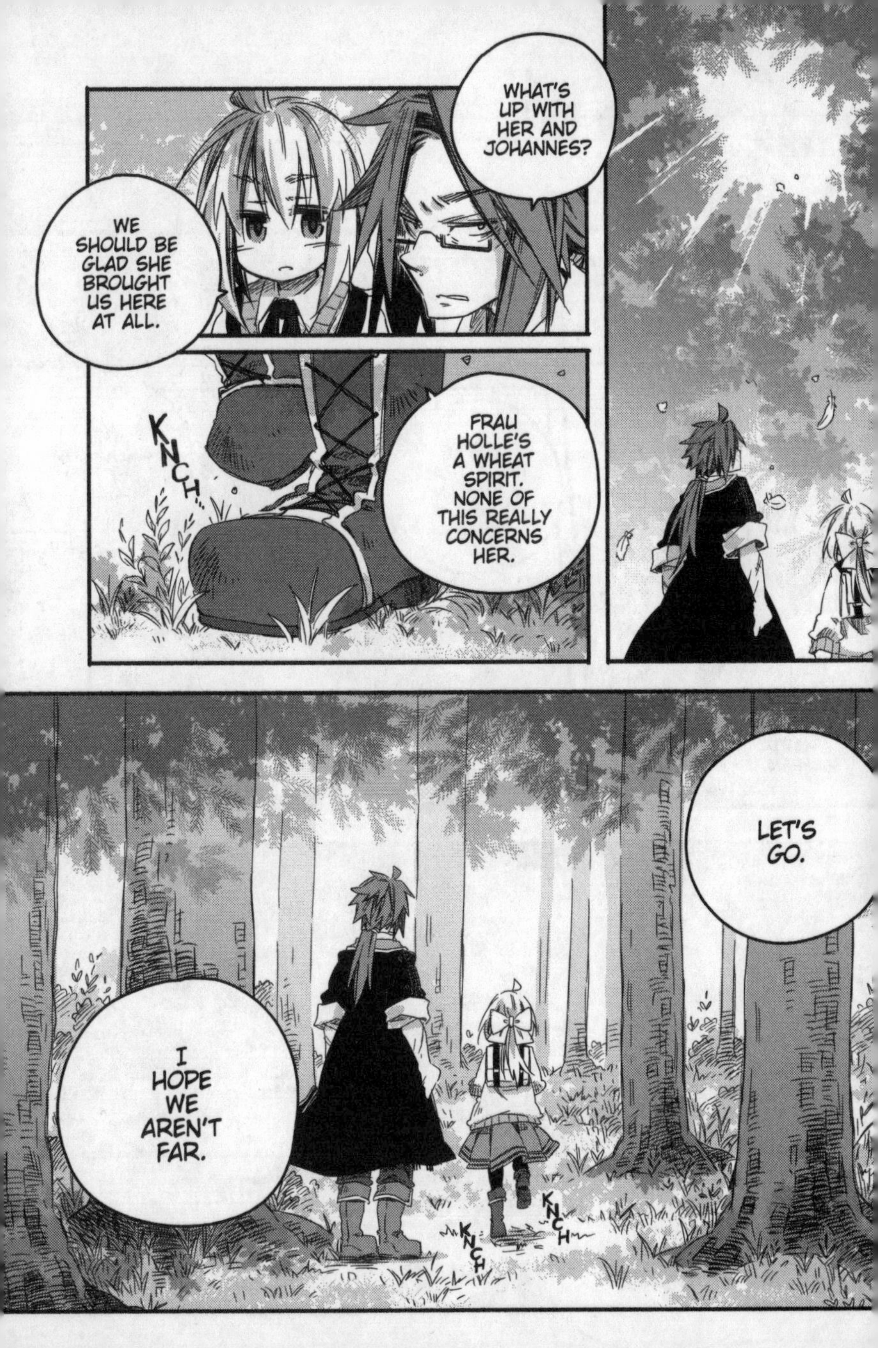
WHAT'S UP WITH HER AND JOHANNES?
WE SHOULD BE GLAD SHE BROUGHT US HERE AT ALL.
FRAU HOLLE'S A WHEAT SPIRIT. NONE OF THIS REALLY CONCERNS HER.
KNCH...
LET'S GO.
I HOPE WE AREN'T FAR.
KNCH
KNCH

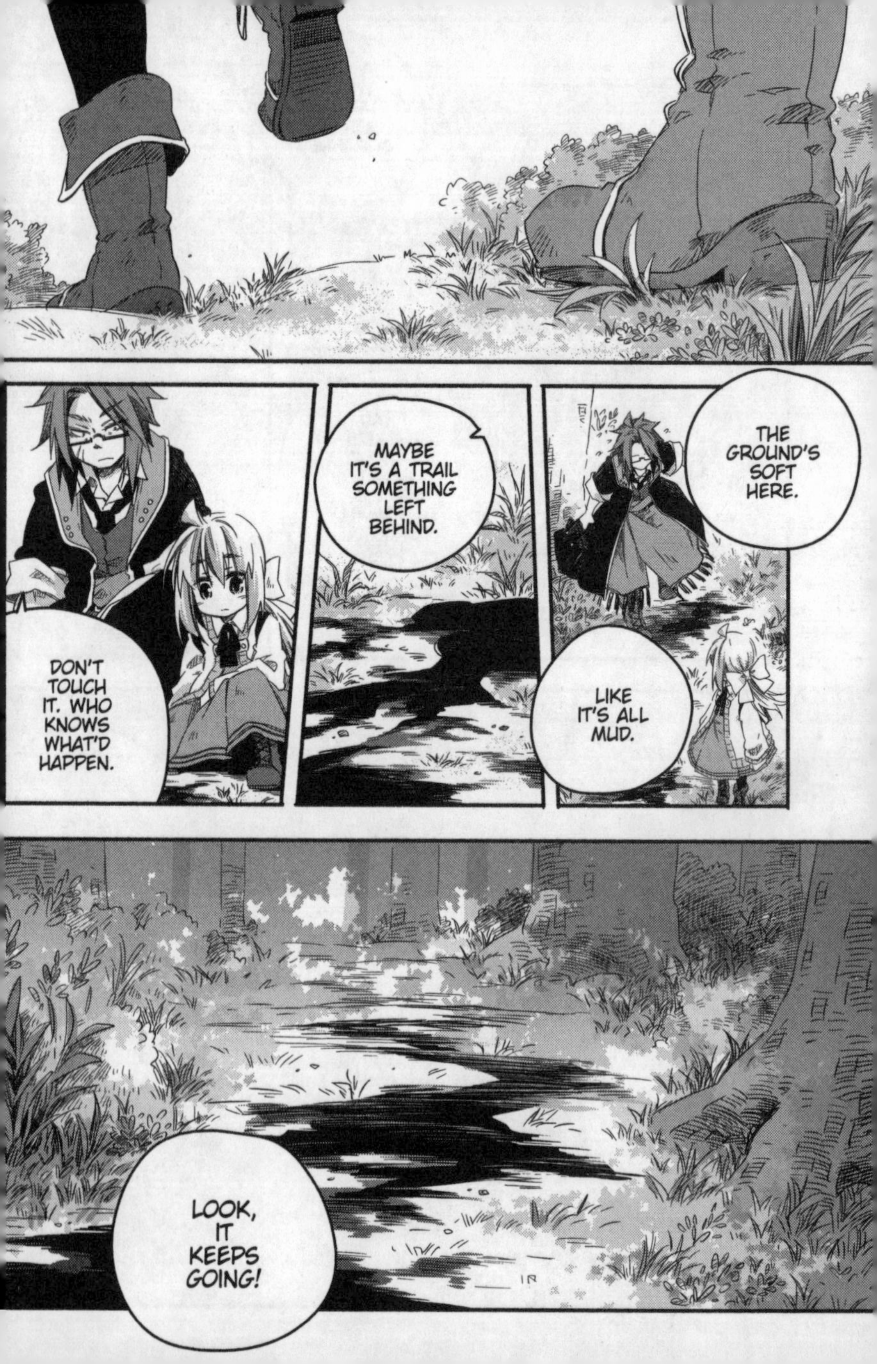
THE GROUND'S SOFT HERE.
LIKE IT'S ALL MUD.
MAYBE IT'S A TRAIL SOMETHING LEFT BEHIND.
DON'T TOUCH IT. WHO KNOWS WHAT'D HAPPEN.
LOOK, IT KEEPS GOING!

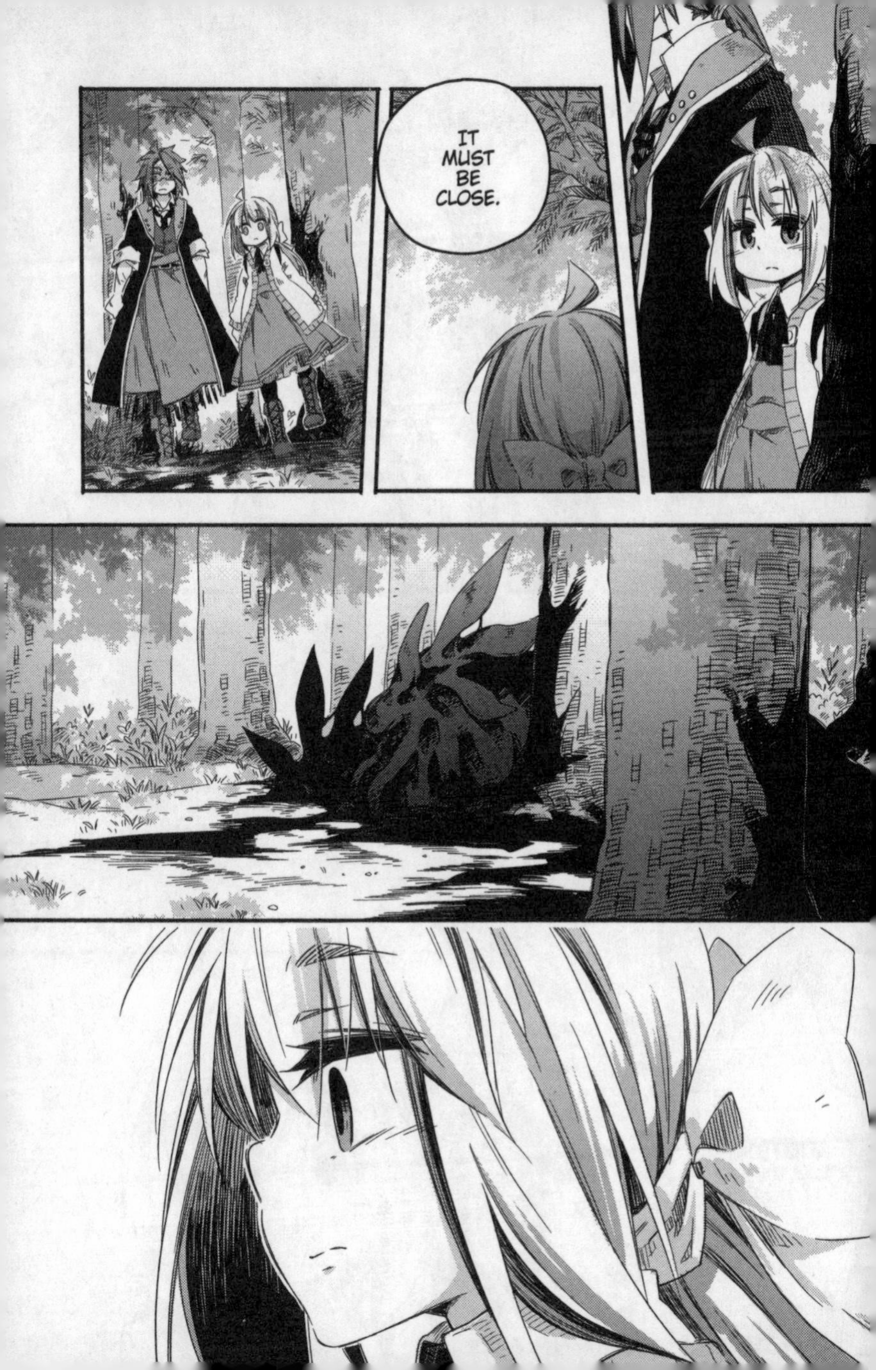
IT MUST BE CLOSE.

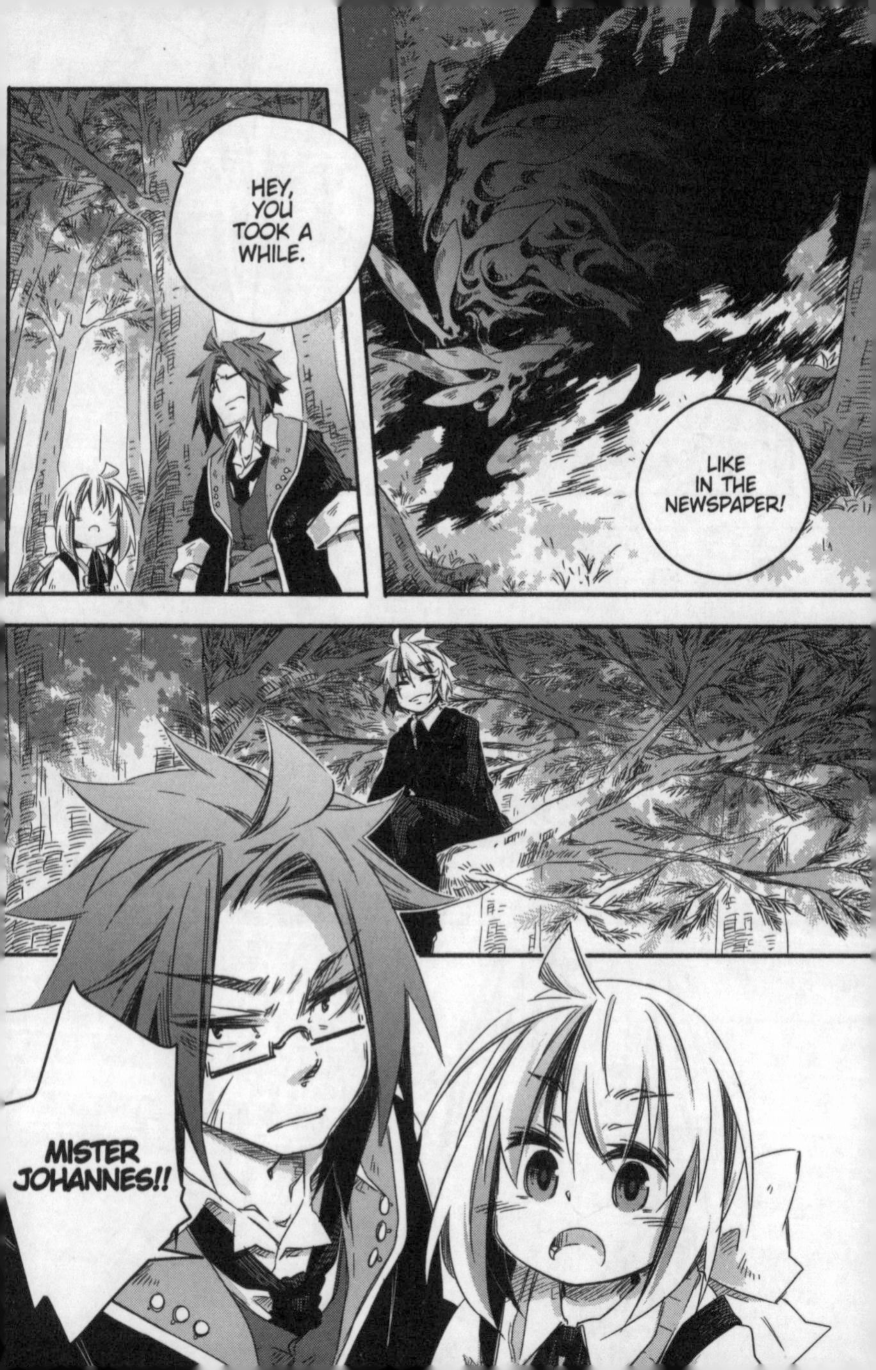
LIKE IN THE NEWSPAPER!
HEY, YOU TOOK A WHILE.
MISTER JOHANNES!!

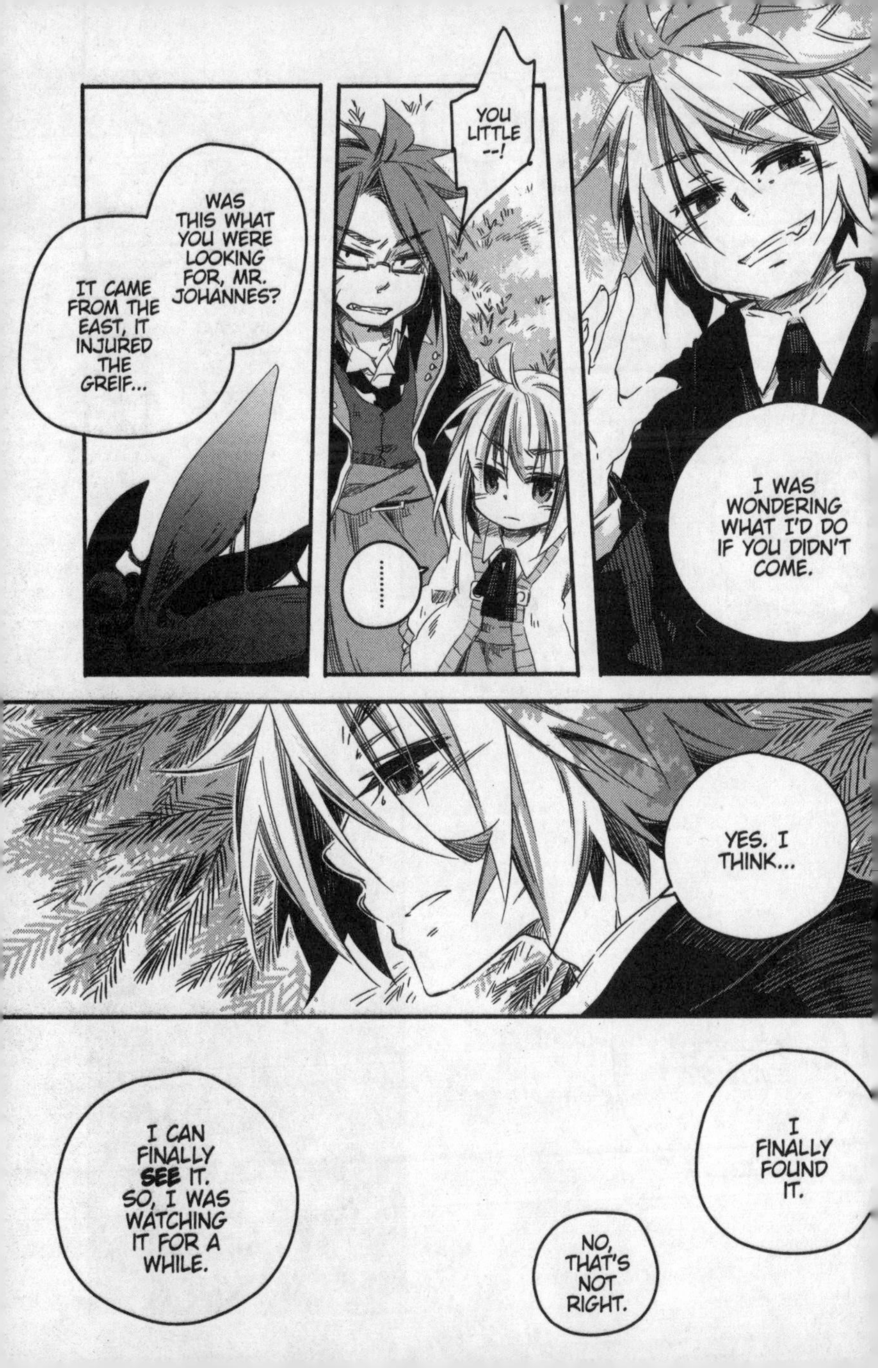
I WAS WONDERING WHAT I'D DO IF YOU DIDN'T COME.
YOU LITTLE --!
......
WAS THIS WHAT YOU WERE LOOKING FOR, MR. JOHANNES?
IT CAME FROM THE EAST, IT INJURED THE GREIF...
YES. I THINK...
I FINALLY FOUND IT.
NO, THAT'S NOT RIGHT.
I CAN FINALLY SEE IT. SO, I WAS WATCHING IT FOR A WHILE.

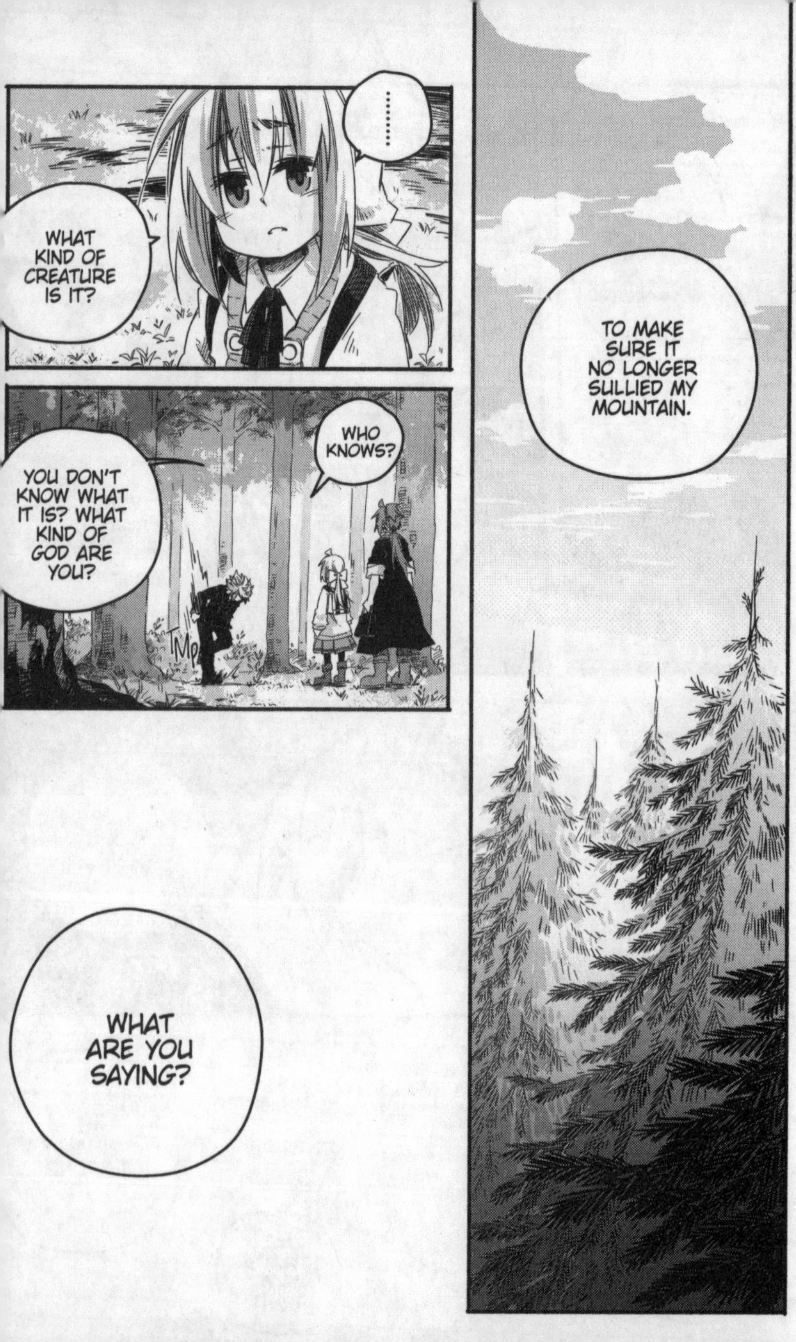
TO MAKE SURE IT NO LONGER SULLIED MY MOUNTAIN.
......
WHAT KIND OF CREATURE IS IT?
WHO KNOWS?
YOU DON'T KNOW WHAT IT IS? WHAT KIND OF GOD ARE YOU?
TMP
WHAT ARE YOU SAYING?

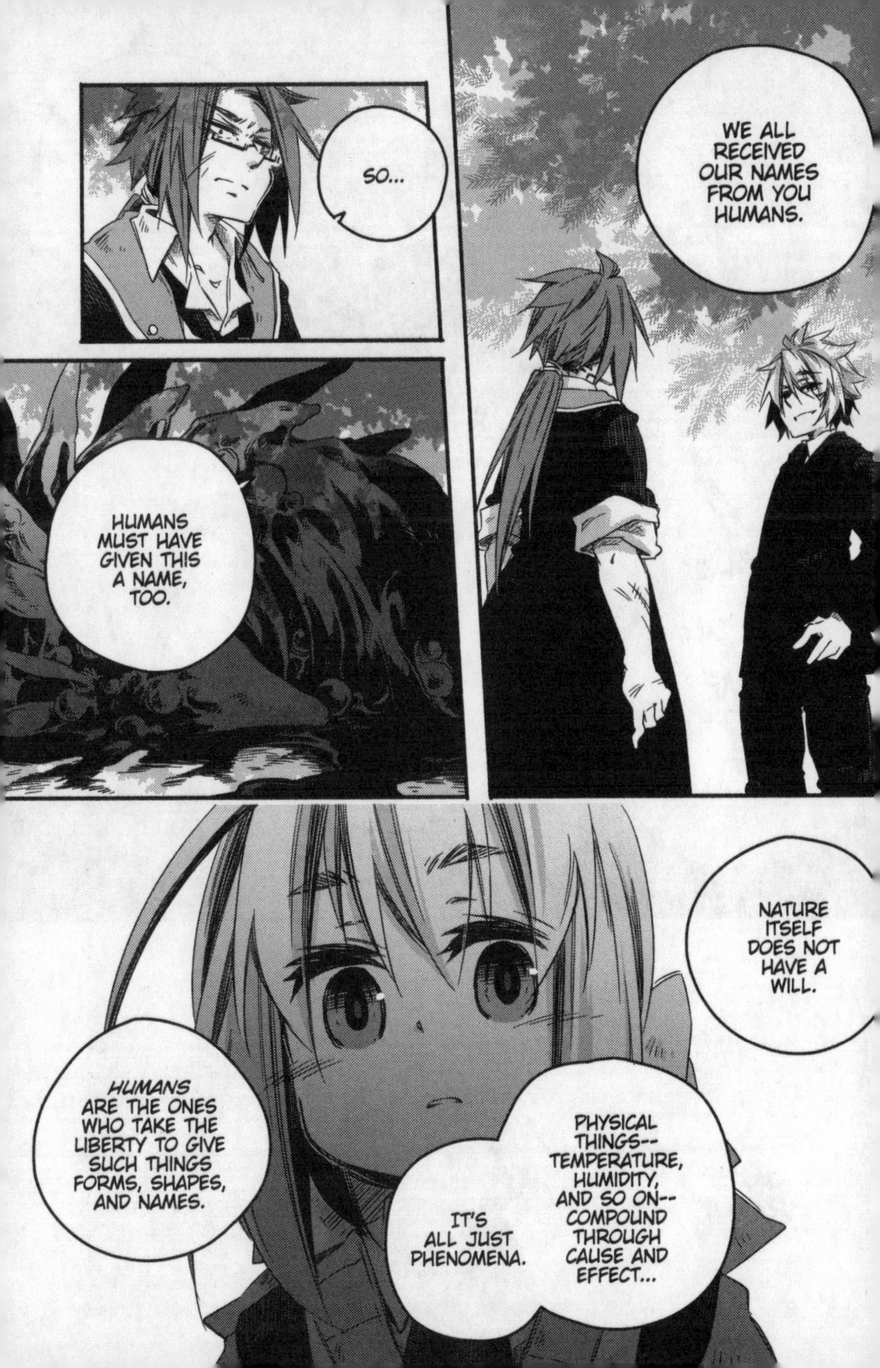
WE ALL RECEIVED OUR NAMES FROM YOU HUMANS.
SO...
HUMANS MUST HAVE GIVEN THIS A NAME, TOO.
NATURE ITSELF DOES NOT HAVE A WILL.
PHYSICAL THINGS--TEMPERATURE, HUMIDITY, AND SO ON--COMPOUND THROUGH CAUSE AND EFFECT...
IT'S ALL JUST PHENOMENA.
HUMANS ARE THE ONES WHO TAKE THE LIBERTY TO GIVE SUCH THINGS FORMS, SHAPES, AND NAMES.

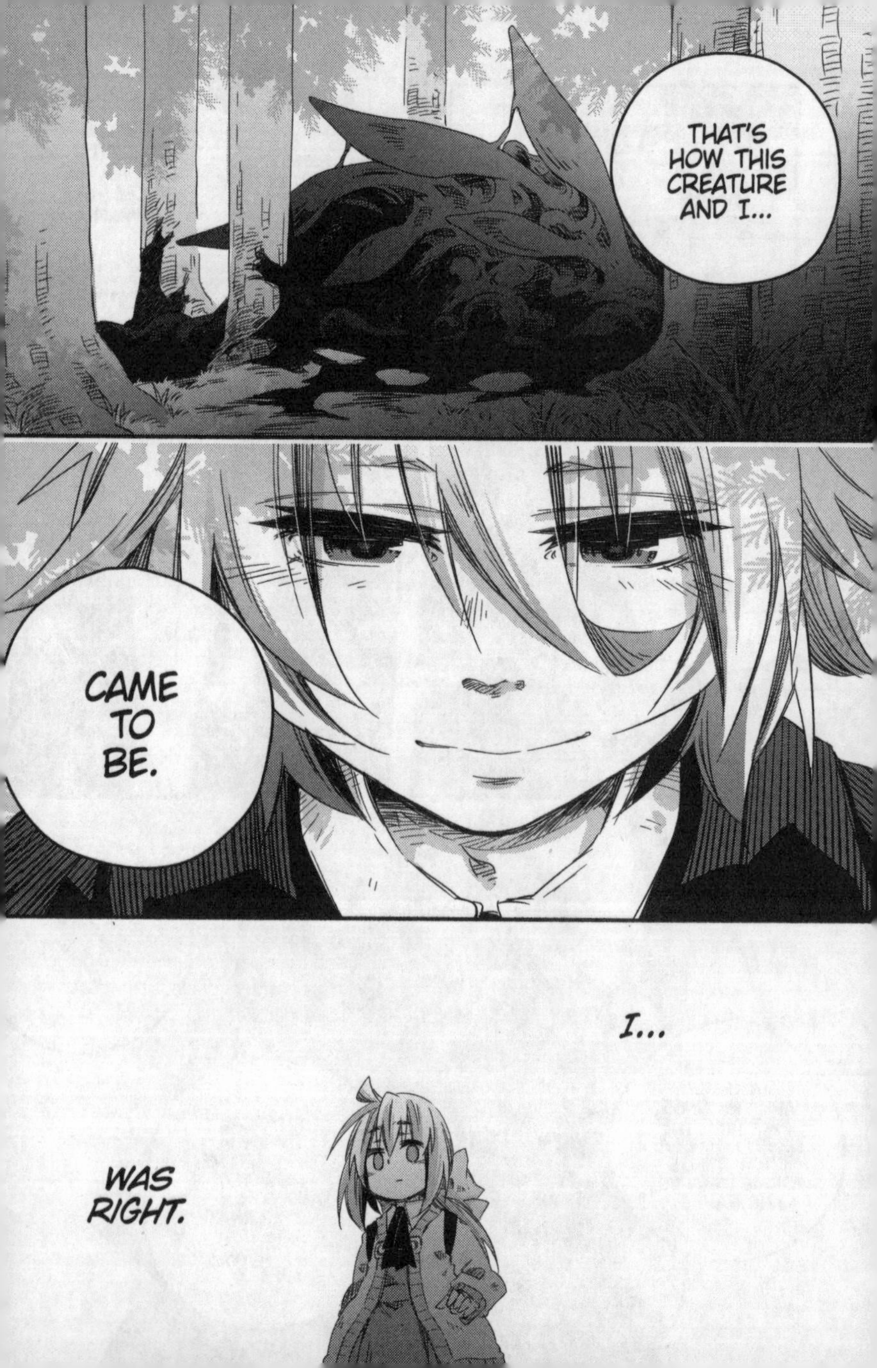
THAT'S HOW THIS CREATURE AND I...
CAME TO BE.
I...
WAS RIGHT.

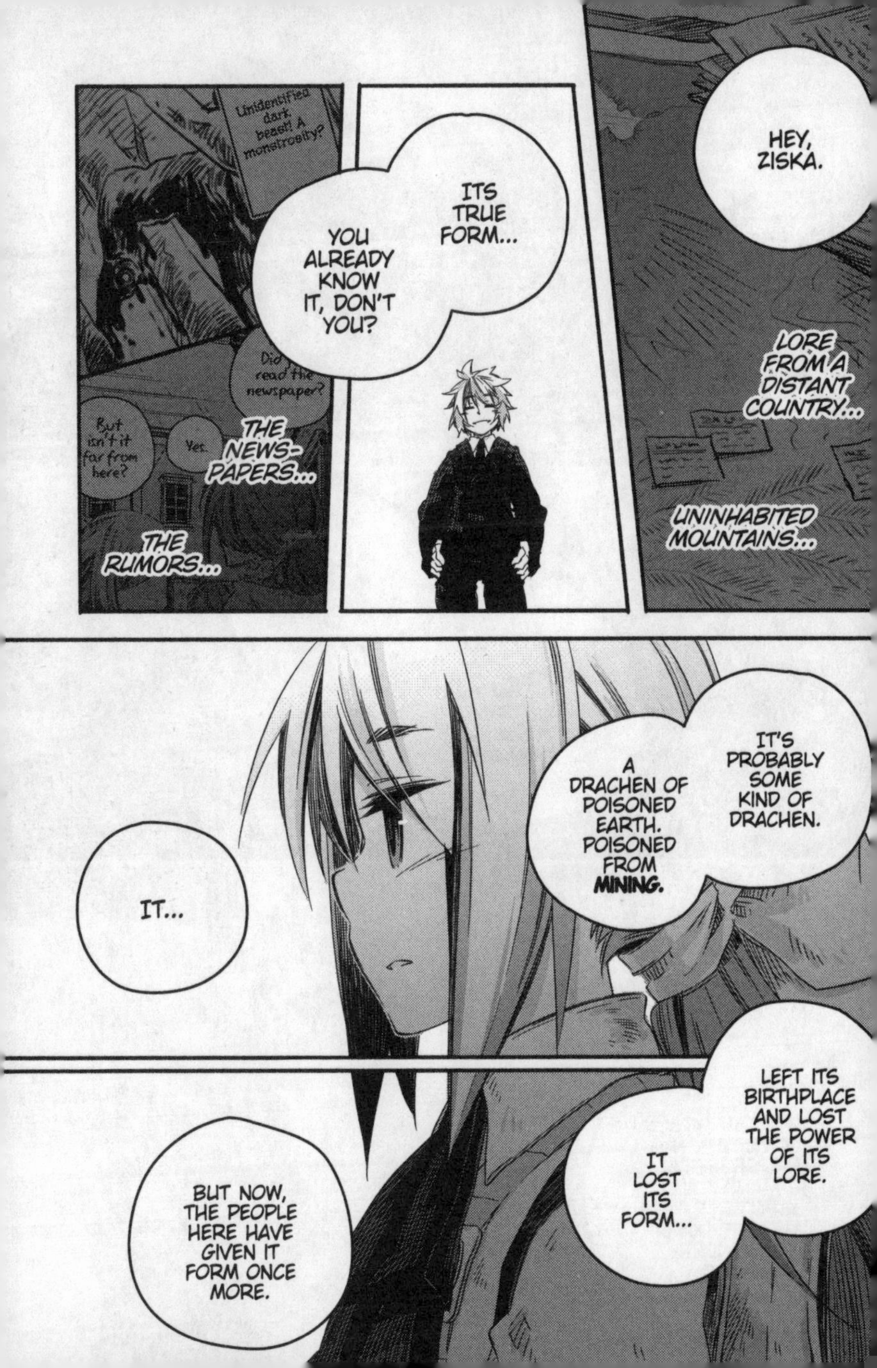
HEY, ZISKA.
LORE FROM A DISTANT COUNTRY...
UNINHABITED MOUNTAINS...
ITS TRUE FORM...
YOU ALREADY KNOW IT, DON'T YOU?
Unidentified dark beast! A monstrosity?
Did read the newspaper?
Yes.
But isn't it far from here?
THE NEWS-PAPERS...
THE RUMORS...
IT'S PROBABLY SOME KIND OF DRACHEN.
A DRACHEN OF POISONED EARTH. POISONED FROM **MINING.**
IT...
LEFT ITS BIRTHPLACE AND LOST THE POWER OF ITS LORE.
IT LOST ITS FORM...
BUT NOW, THE PEOPLE HERE HAVE GIVEN IT FORM ONCE MORE.

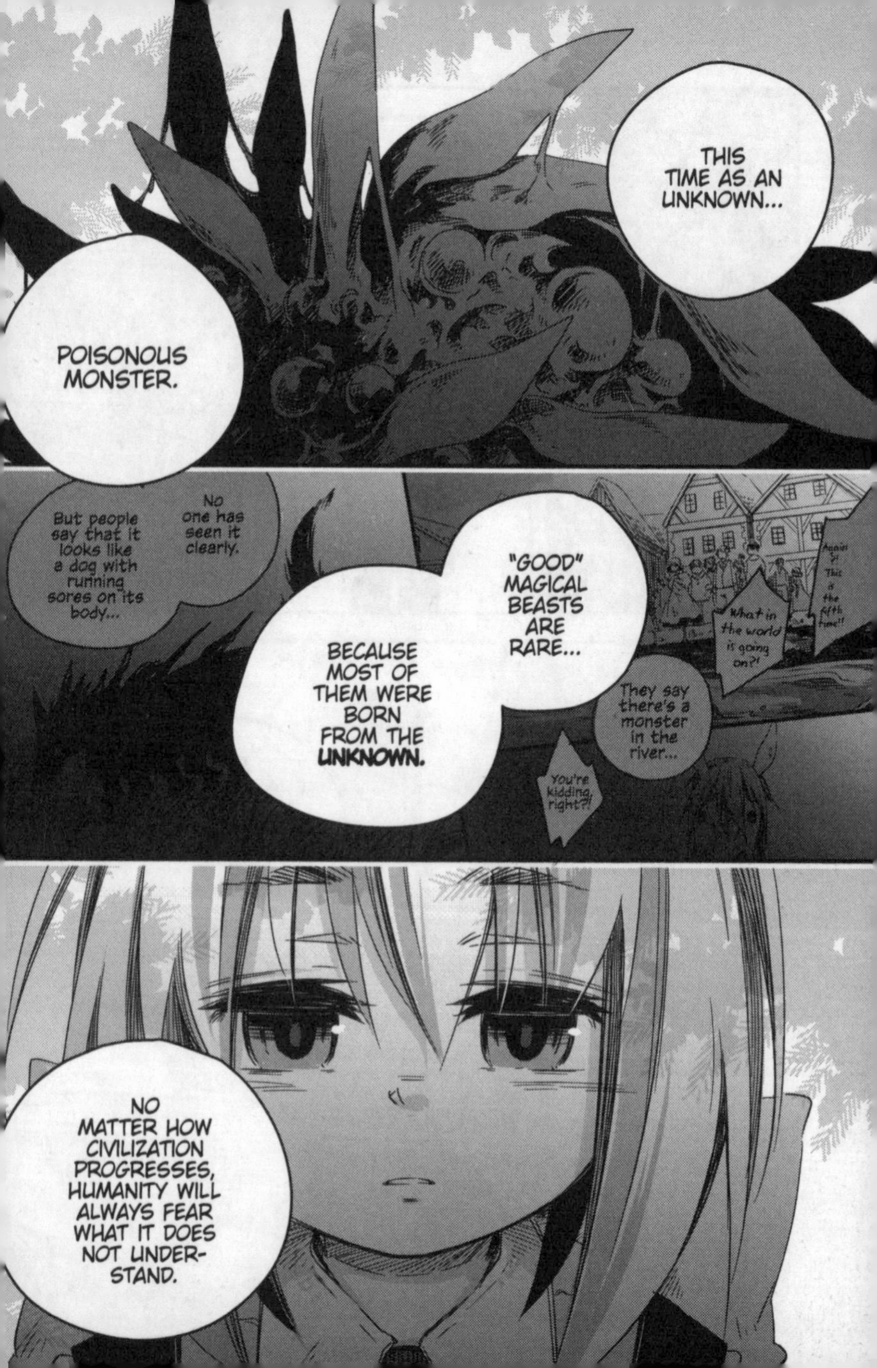
THIS TIME AS AN UNKNOWN...
POISONOUS MONSTER.
Again?! This is the fifth time!!
What in the world is going on?!
They say there's a monster in the river...
You're kidding, right?!
"GOOD" MAGICAL BEASTS ARE RARE...
BECAUSE MOST OF THEM WERE BORN FROM THE **UNKNOWN.**
No one has seen it clearly.
But people say that it looks like a dog with running sores on its body...
NO MATTER HOW CIVILIZATION PROGRESSES, HUMANITY WILL ALWAYS FEAR WHAT IT DOES NOT UNDER-STAND.

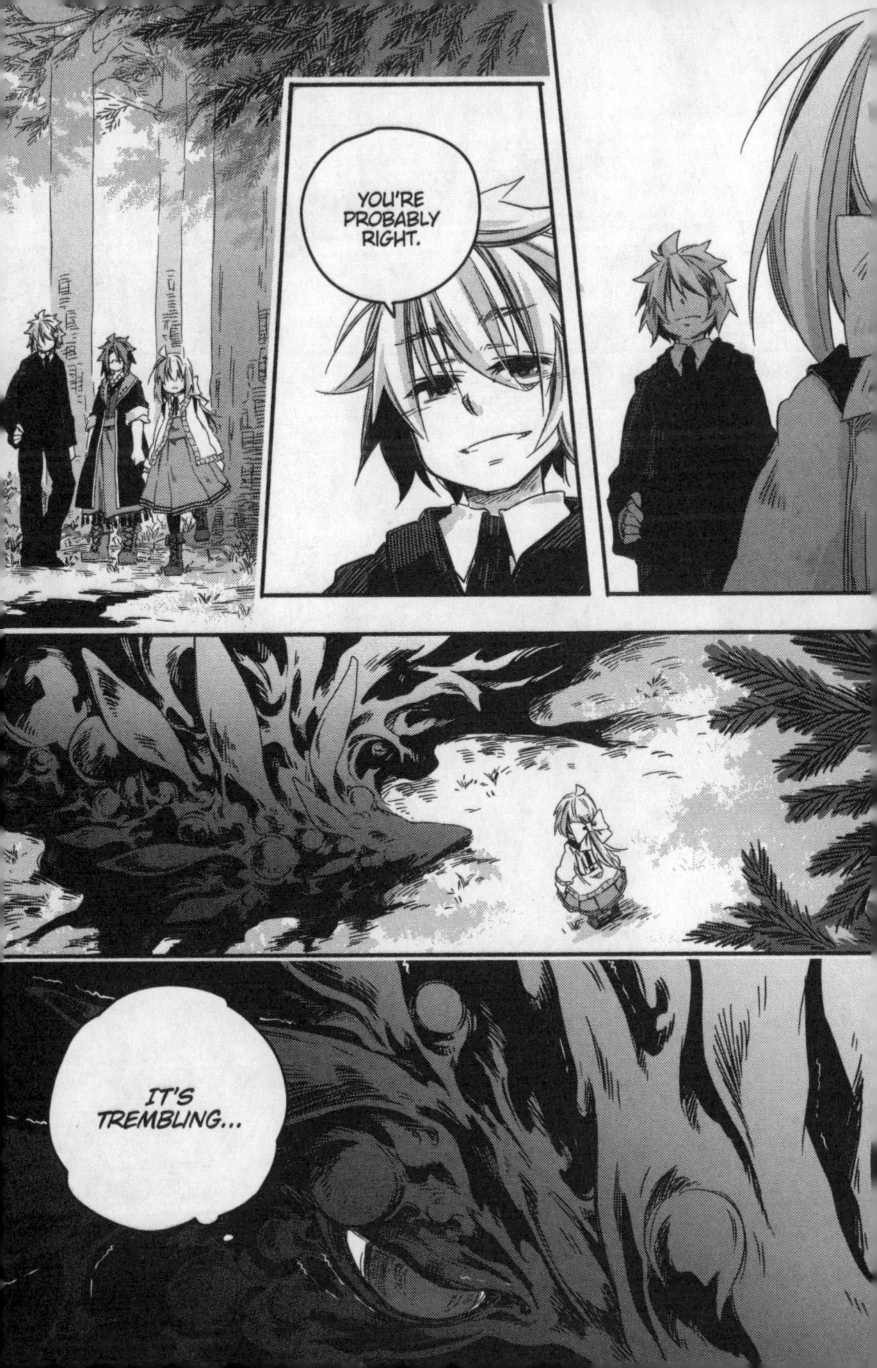
YOU'RE PROBABLY RIGHT.
IT'S TREMBLING...

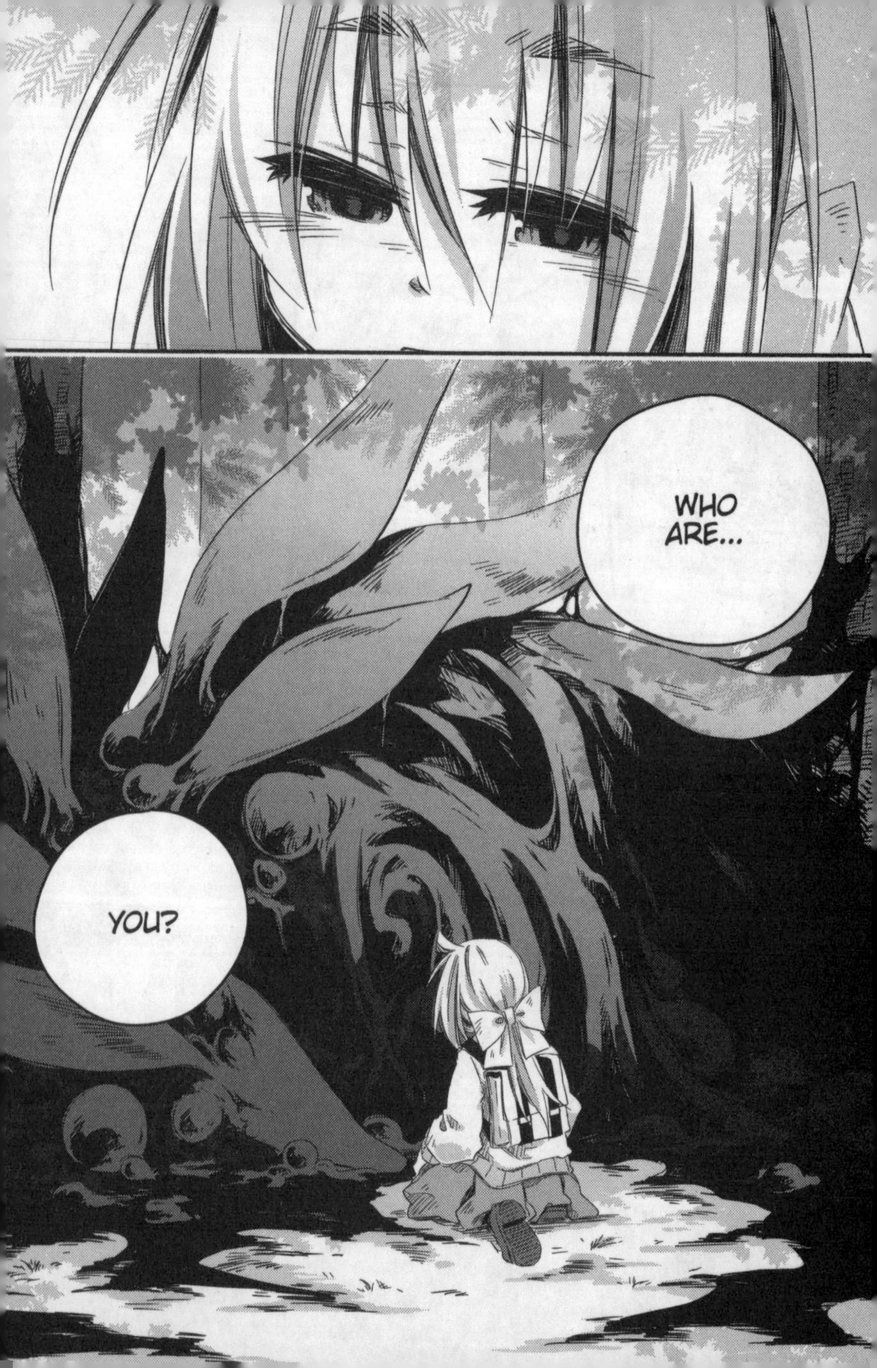
WHO ARE...
YOU?

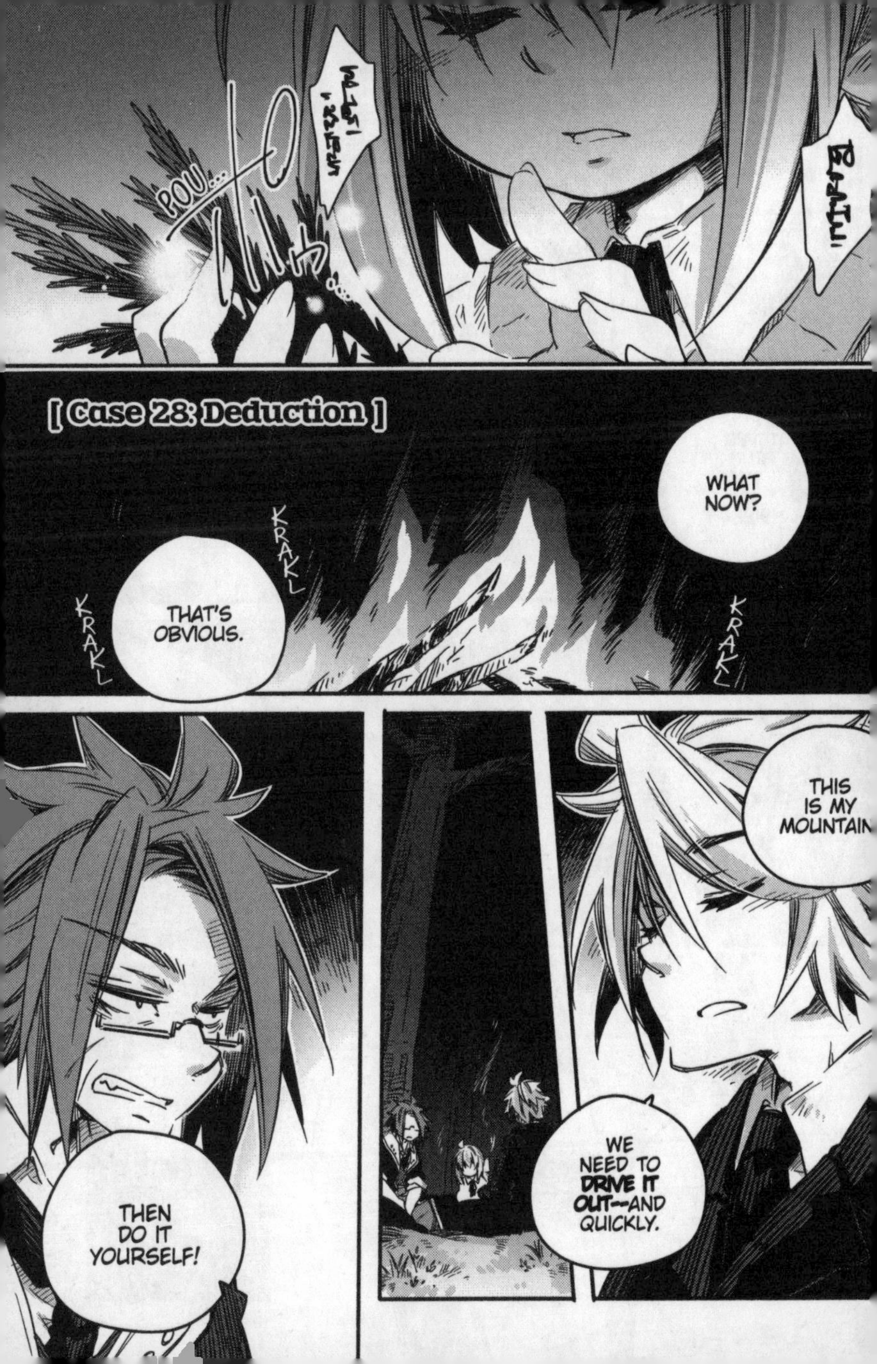
POU...
[Case 28: Deduction]
WHAT NOW?
KRAKL
THAT'S OBVIOUS.
KRAKL
KRAKL
THIS IS MY MOUNTAIN
WE NEED TO DRIVE IT OUT--AND QUICKLY.
THEN DO IT YOURSELF!

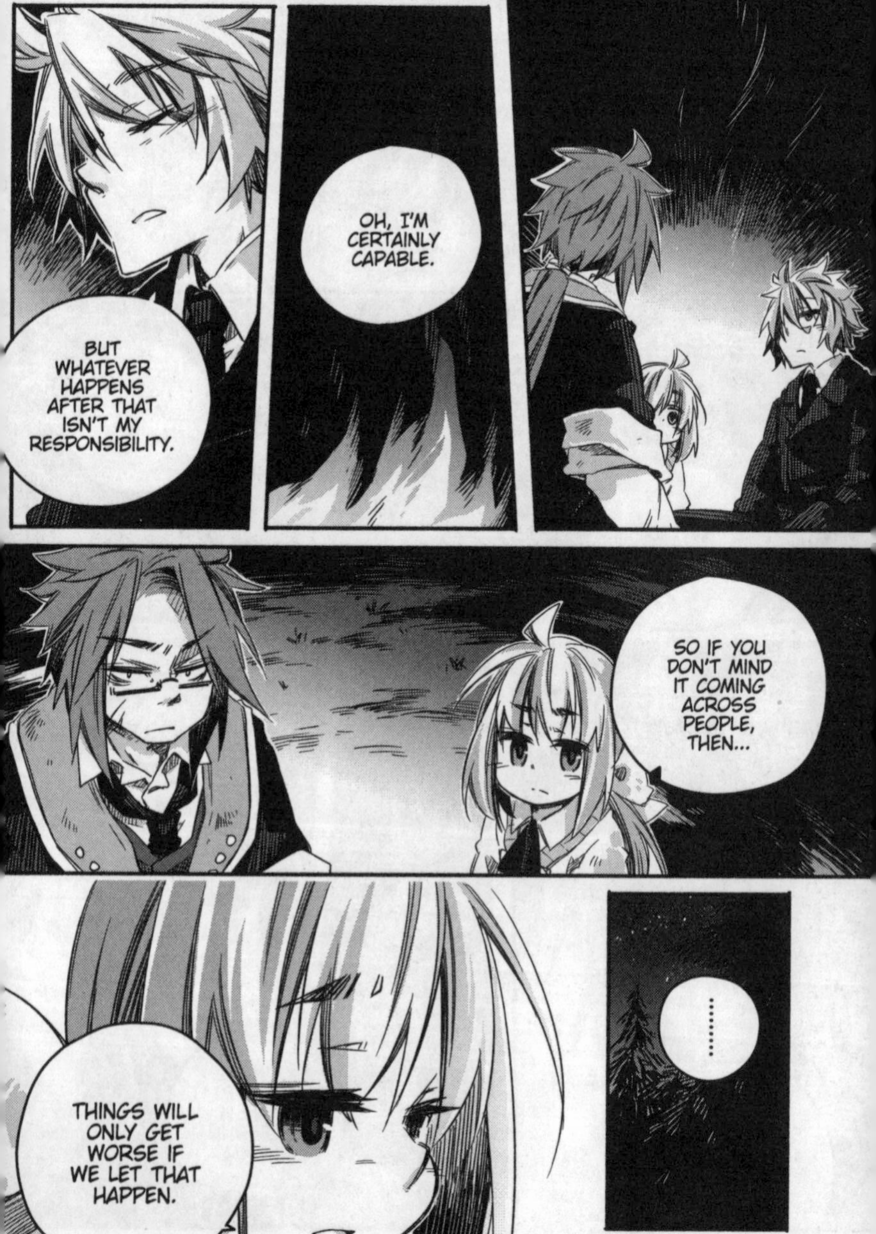
OH, I'M CERTAINLY CAPABLE.
BUT WHATEVER HAPPENS AFTER THAT ISN'T MY RESPONSIBILITY.
SO IF YOU DON'T MIND IT COMING ACROSS PEOPLE, THEN...
....
THINGS WILL ONLY GET WORSE IF WE LET THAT HAPPEN.

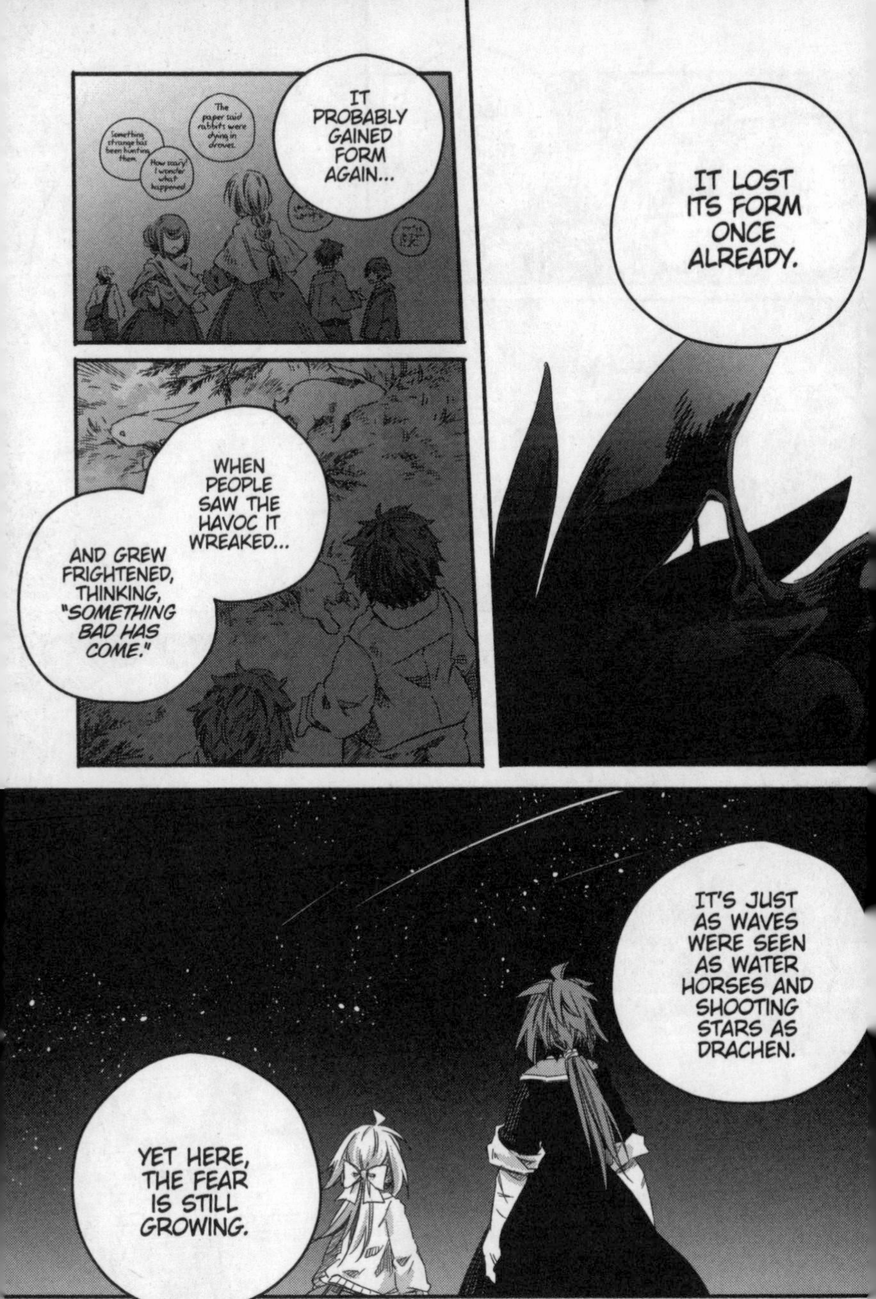
IT LOST ITS FORM ONCE ALREADY.
IT PROBABLY GAINED FORM AGAIN...
The paper said rabbits were dying in droves.
Something strange has been hunting them.
How scary! I wonder what happened.
WHEN PEOPLE SAW THE HAVOC IT WREAKED...
AND GREW FRIGHTENED, THINKING, "SOMETHING BAD HAS COME."
IT'S JUST AS WAVES WERE SEEN AS WATER HORSES AND SHOOTING STARS AS DRACHEN.
YET HERE, THE FEAR IS STILL GROWING.

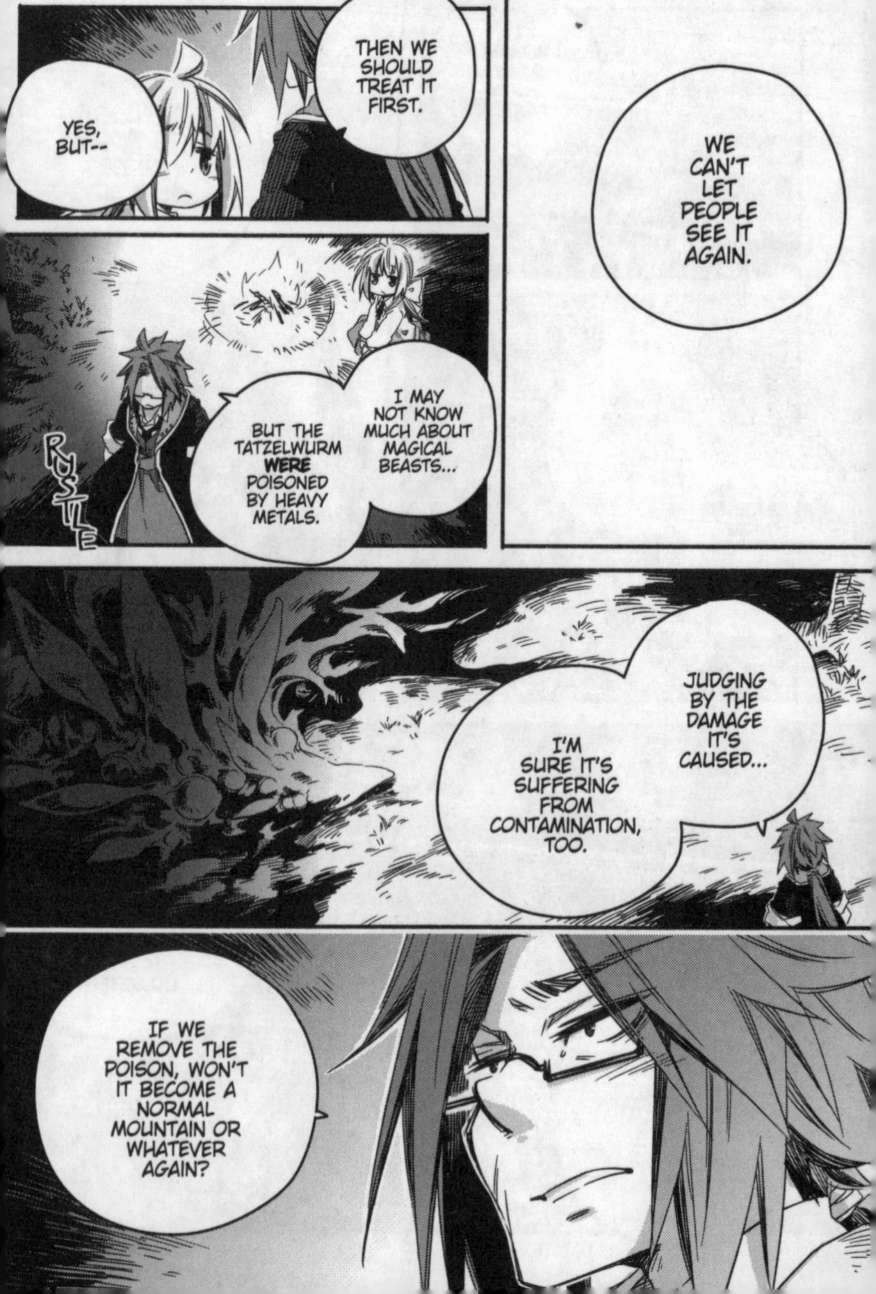
WE CAN'T LET PEOPLE SEE IT AGAIN.
THEN WE SHOULD TREAT IT FIRST.
YES, BUT--
I MAY NOT KNOW MUCH ABOUT MAGICAL BEASTS...
BUT THE TATZELWURM **WERE** POISONED BY HEAVY METALS.
RUSTLE
JUDGING BY THE DAMAGE IT'S CAUSED...
I'M SURE IT'S SUFFERING FROM CONTAMINATION, TOO.
IF WE REMOVE THE POISON, WON'T IT BECOME A NORMAL MOUNTAIN OR WHATEVER AGAIN?

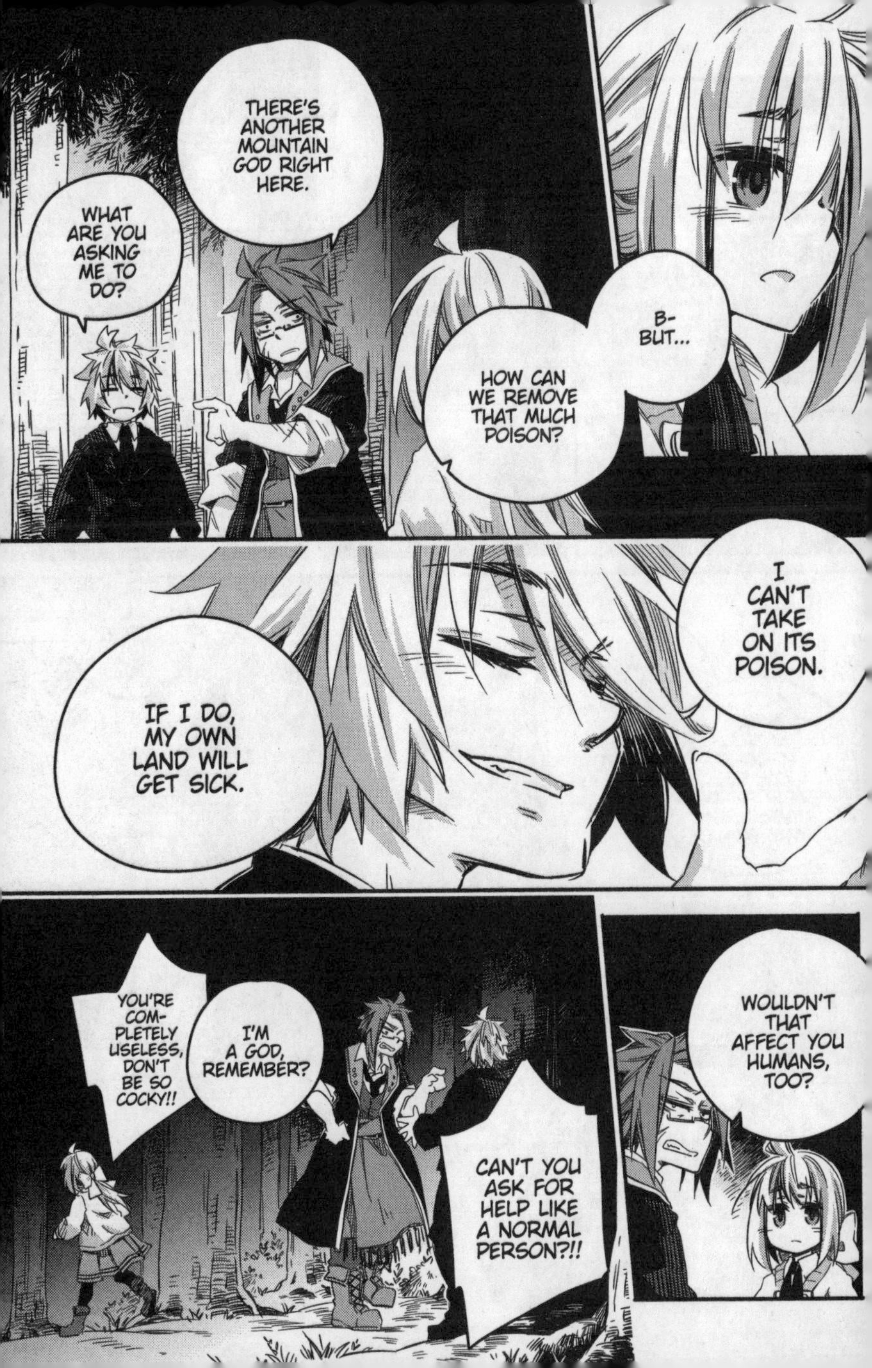
B-BUT...
HOW CAN WE REMOVE THAT MUCH POISON?
THERE'S ANOTHER MOUNTAIN GOD RIGHT HERE.
WHAT ARE YOU ASKING ME TO DO?
I CAN'T TAKE ON ITS POISON.
IF I DO, MY OWN LAND WILL GET SICK.
WOULDN'T THAT AFFECT YOU HUMANS, TOO?
CAN'T YOU ASK FOR HELP LIKE A NORMAL PERSON?!!
I'M A GOD, REMEMBER?
YOU'RE COM-PLETELY USELESS, DON'T BE SO COCKY!!

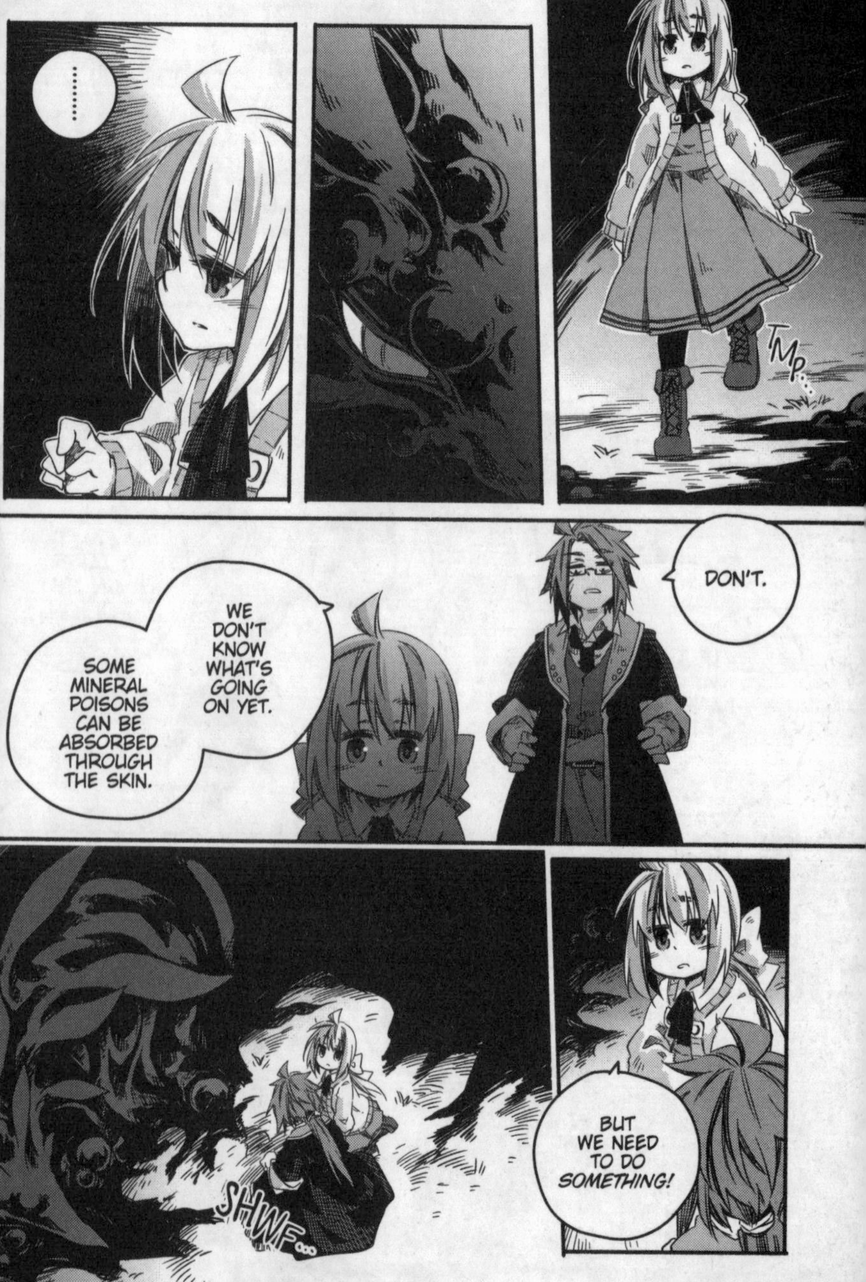
TMP...
......
DON'T.
WE DON'T KNOW WHAT'S GOING ON YET.
SOME MINERAL POISONS CAN BE ABSORBED THROUGH THE SKIN.
BUT WE NEED TO DO SOMETHING!
SHWF...

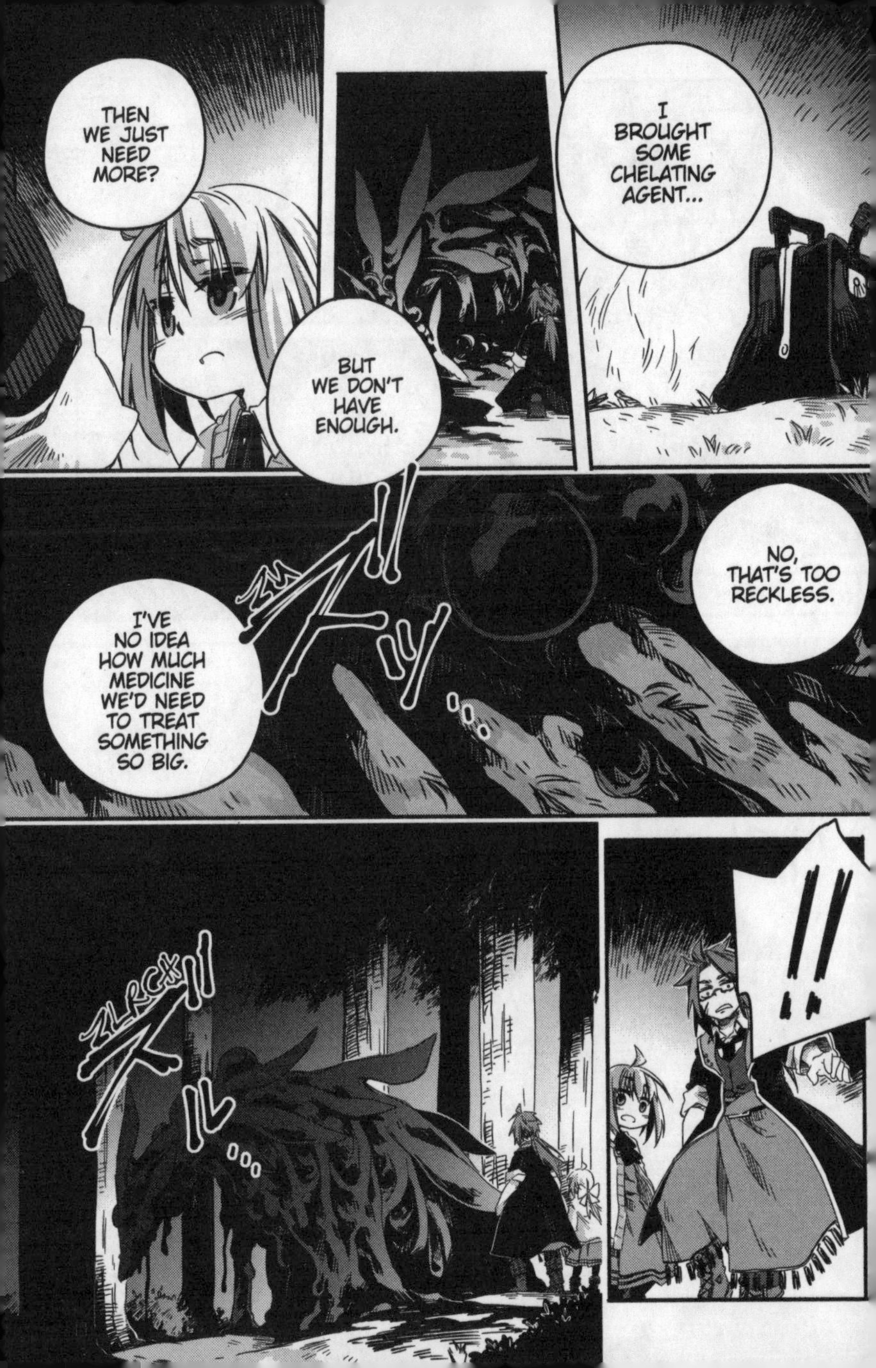
I BROUGHT SOME CHELATING AGENT...
THEN WE JUST NEED MORE?
BUT WE DON'T HAVE ENOUGH.
NO, THAT'S TOO RECKLESS.
ZM
I'VE NO IDEA HOW MUCH MEDICINE WE'D NEED TO TREAT SOMETHING SO BIG.
!!
ZLRCK!!

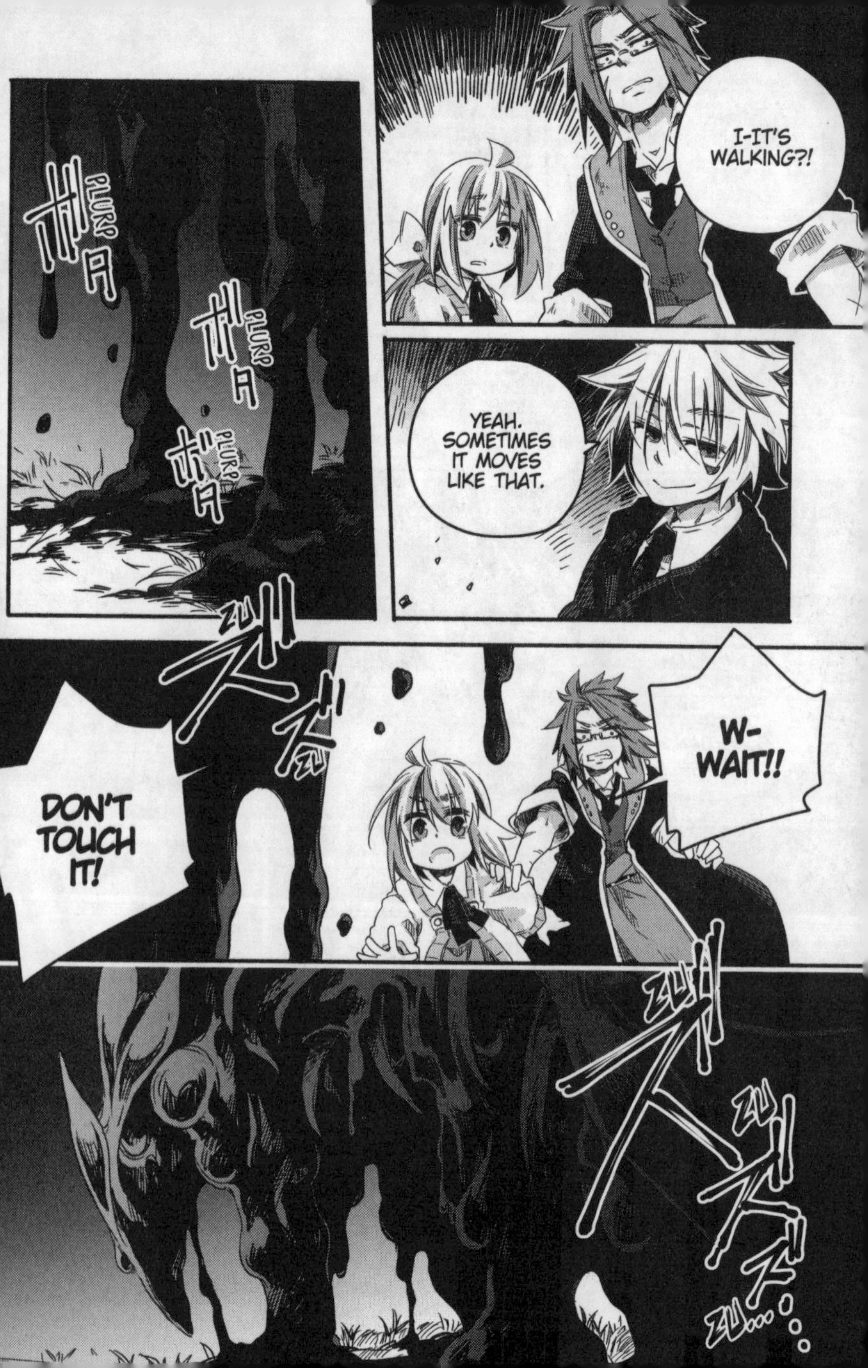
I-IT'S WALKING?!
YEAH. SOMETIMES IT MOVES LIKE THAT.
PLURP
PLURP
PLURP
ZU
W-WAIT!!
DON'T TOUCH IT!
ZU
ZU
ZU...

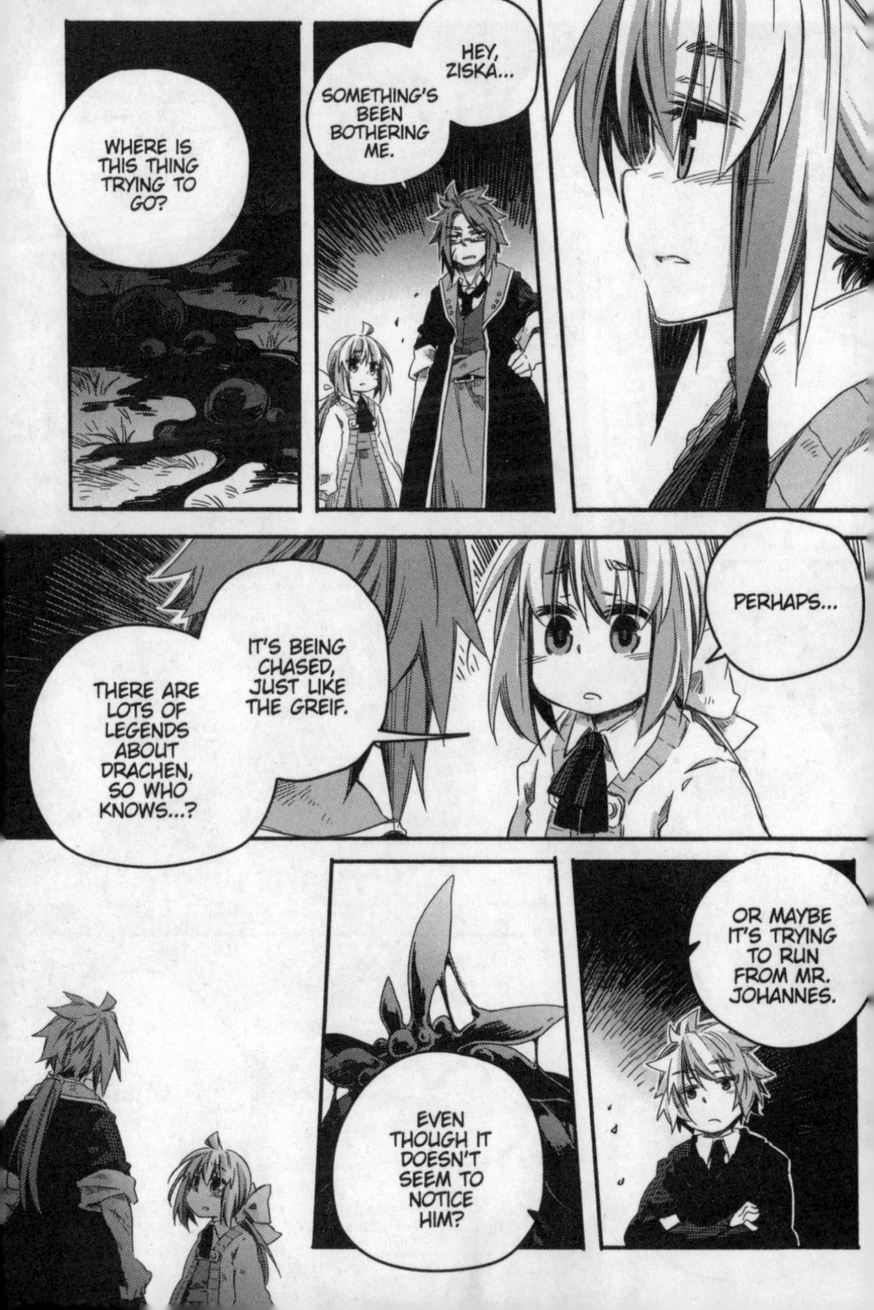
HEY, ZISKA...
SOMETHING'S BEEN BOTHERING ME.
WHERE IS THIS THING TRYING TO GO?
PERHAPS...
IT'S BEING CHASED, JUST LIKE THE GREIF.
THERE ARE LOTS OF LEGENDS ABOUT DRACHEN, SO WHO KNOWS...?
OR MAYBE IT'S TRYING TO RUN FROM MR. JOHANNES.
EVEN THOUGH IT DOESN'T SEEM TO NOTICE HIM?

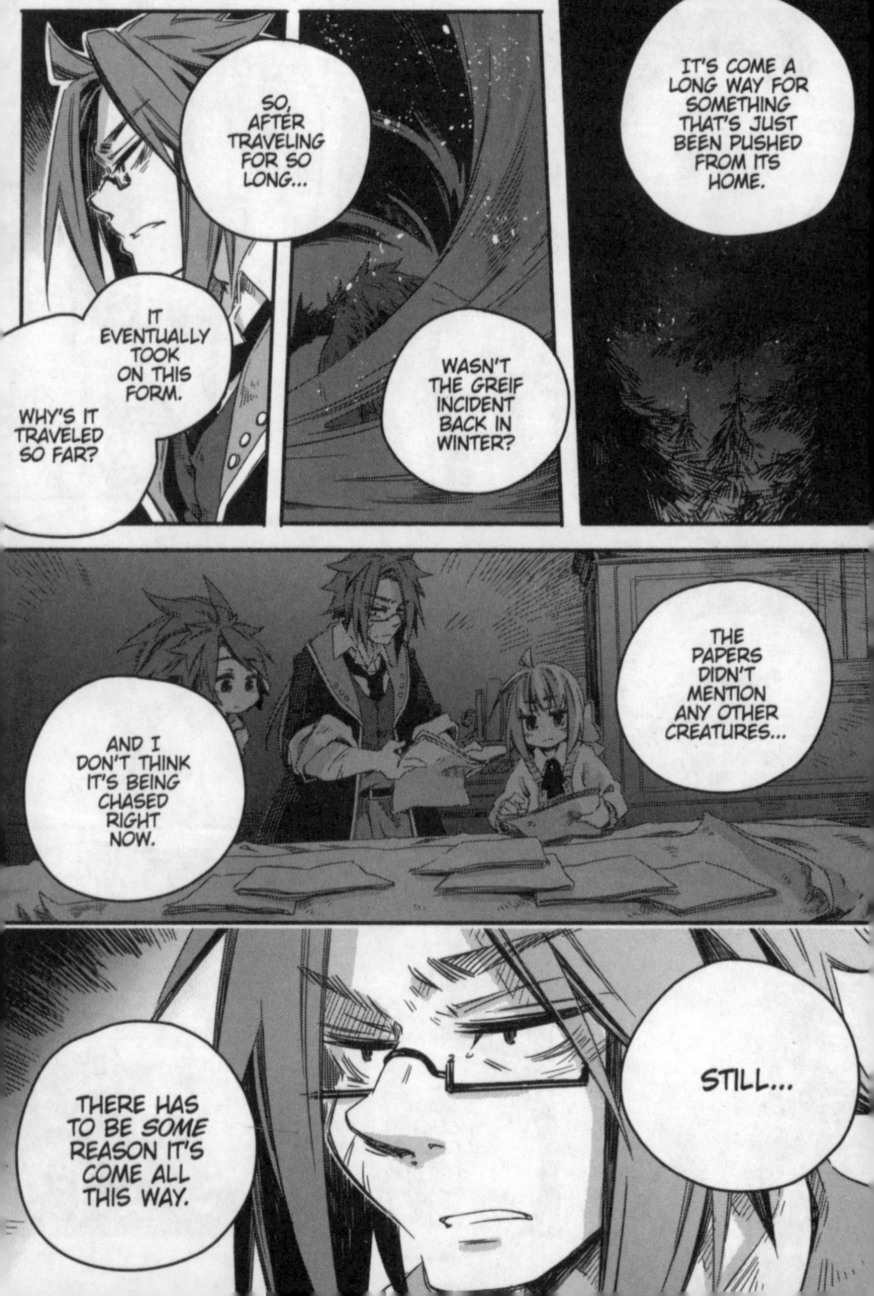
IT'S COME A LONG WAY FOR SOMETHING THAT'S JUST BEEN PUSHED FROM ITS HOME.
WASN'T THE GREIF INCIDENT BACK IN WINTER?
SO, AFTER TRAVELING FOR SO LONG...
IT EVENTUALLY TOOK ON THIS FORM.
WHY'S IT TRAVELED SO FAR?
THE PAPERS DIDN'T MENTION ANY OTHER CREATURES...
AND I DON'T THINK IT'S BEING CHASED RIGHT NOW.
STILL...
THERE HAS TO BE *SOME* REASON IT'S COME ALL THIS WAY.

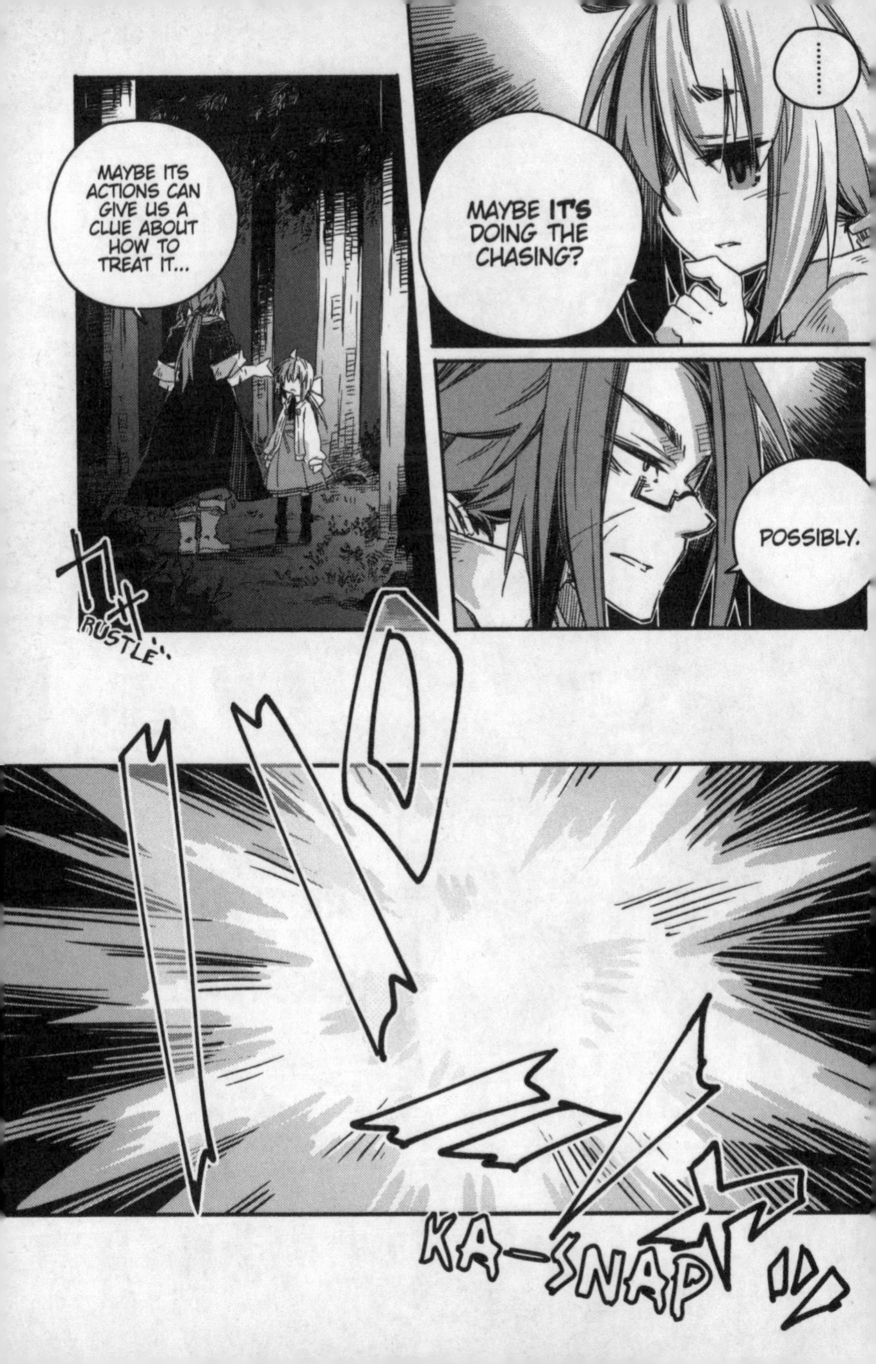
......
MAYBE IT'S DOING THE CHASING?
POSSIBLY.
MAYBE ITS ACTIONS CAN GIVE US A CLUE ABOUT HOW TO TREAT IT...
RUSTLE...
KA-SNAP!!

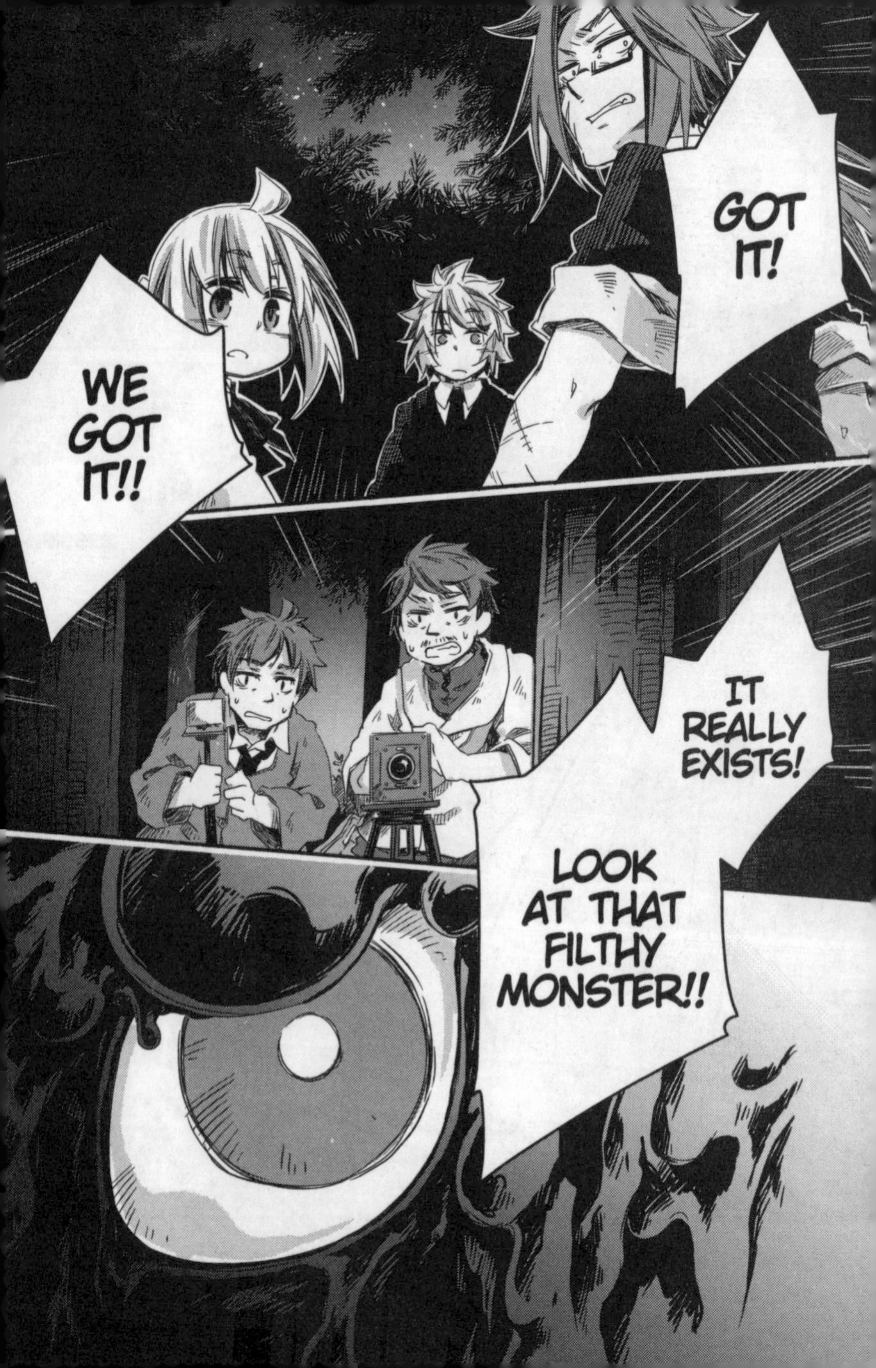
GOT IT!
WE GOT IT!!
IT REALLY EXISTS!
LOOK AT THAT FILTHY MONSTER!!

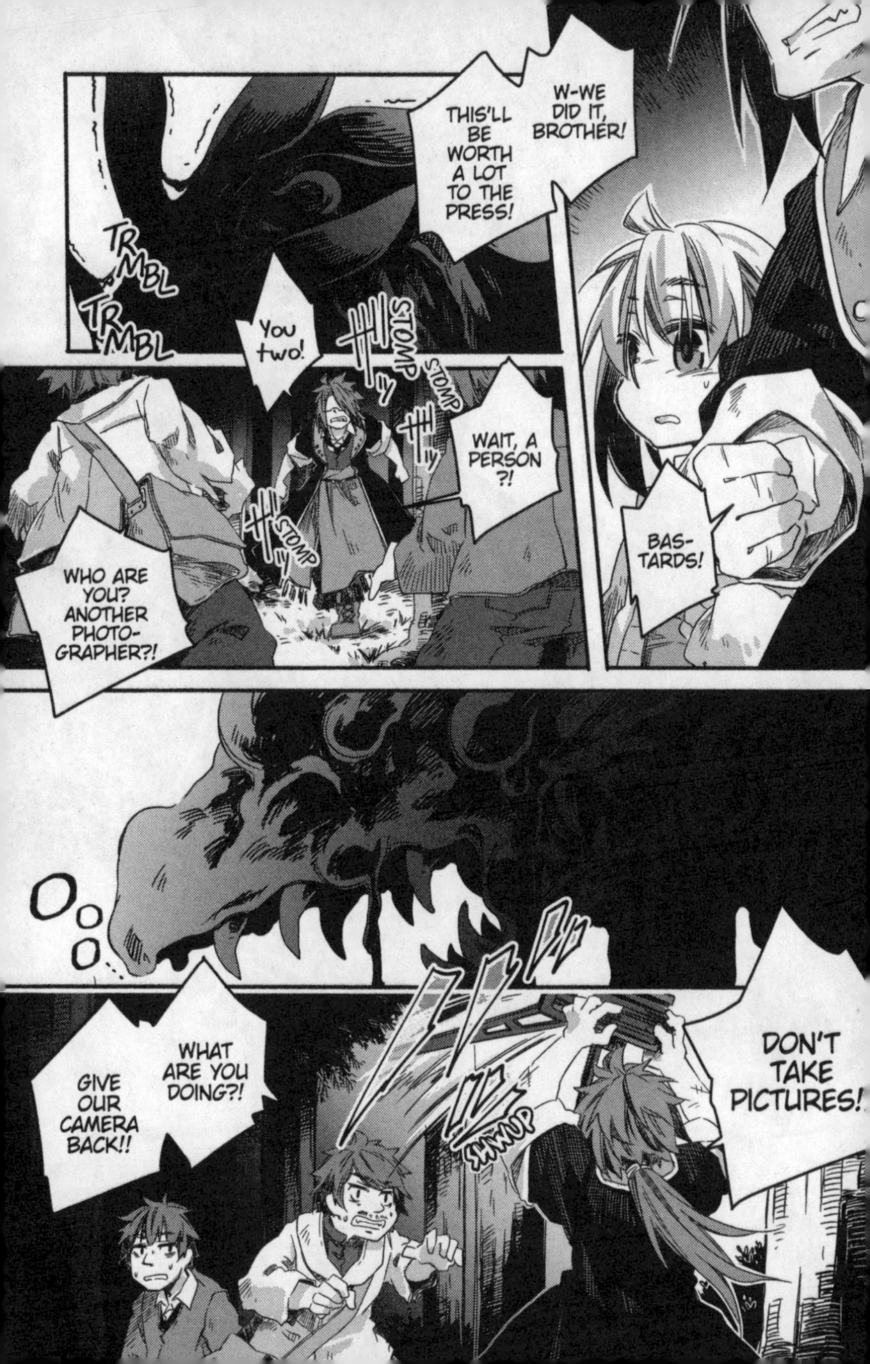
W-WE DID IT, BROTHER!
THIS'LL BE WORTH A LOT TO THE PRESS!
BASTARDS!
TRMBL
TRMBL
You two!
STOMP
STOMP
STOMP
WAIT, A PERSON?!
WHO ARE YOU? ANOTHER PHOTO-GRAPHER?!
OOO
DON'T TAKE PICTURES!
SHWUP
WHAT ARE YOU DOING?!
GIVE OUR CAMERA BACK!!

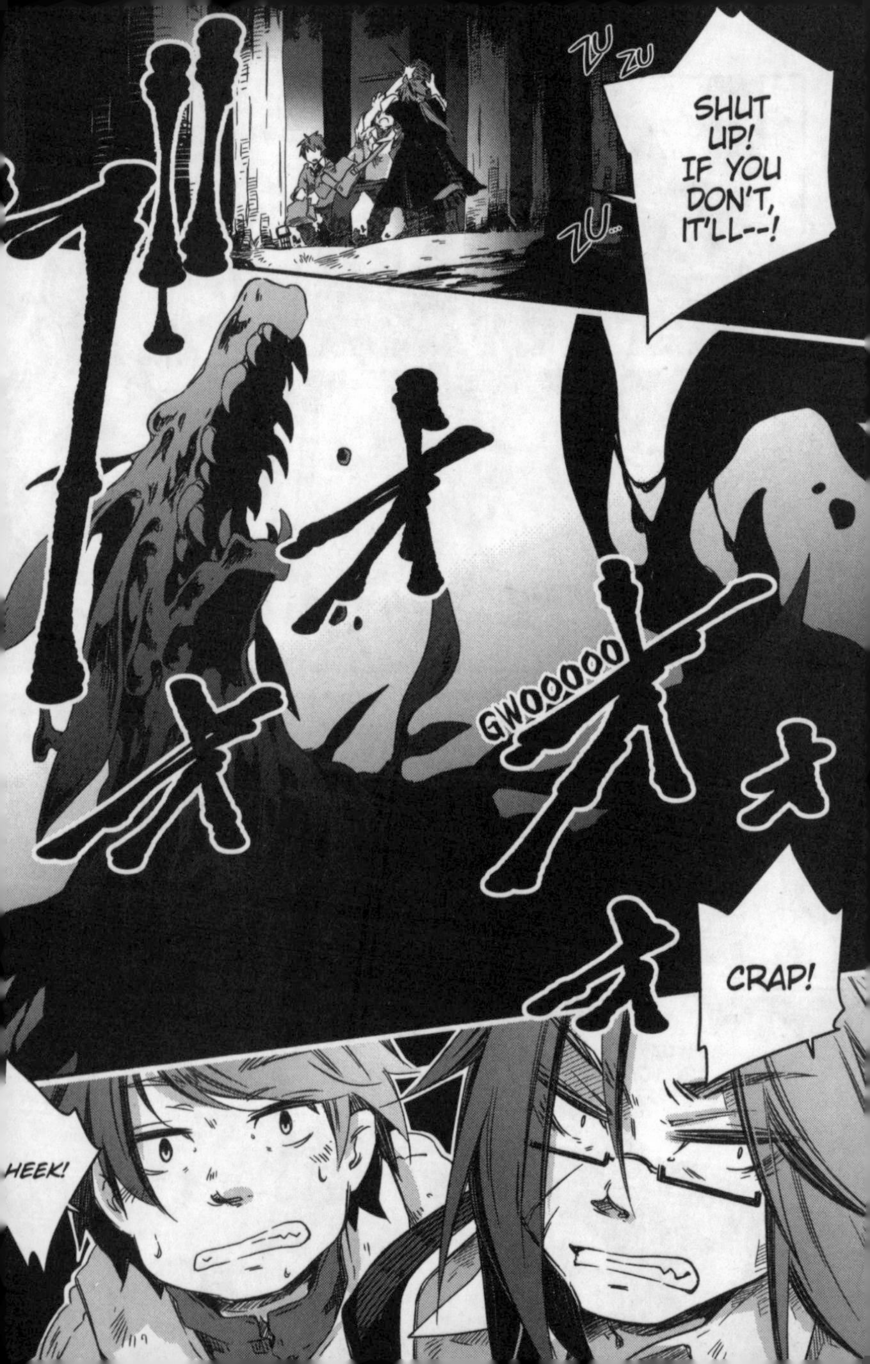
SHUT UP! IF YOU DON'T, IT'LL--!
ZU ZU
ZU...
GWOOOOOO
CRAP!
HEEK!

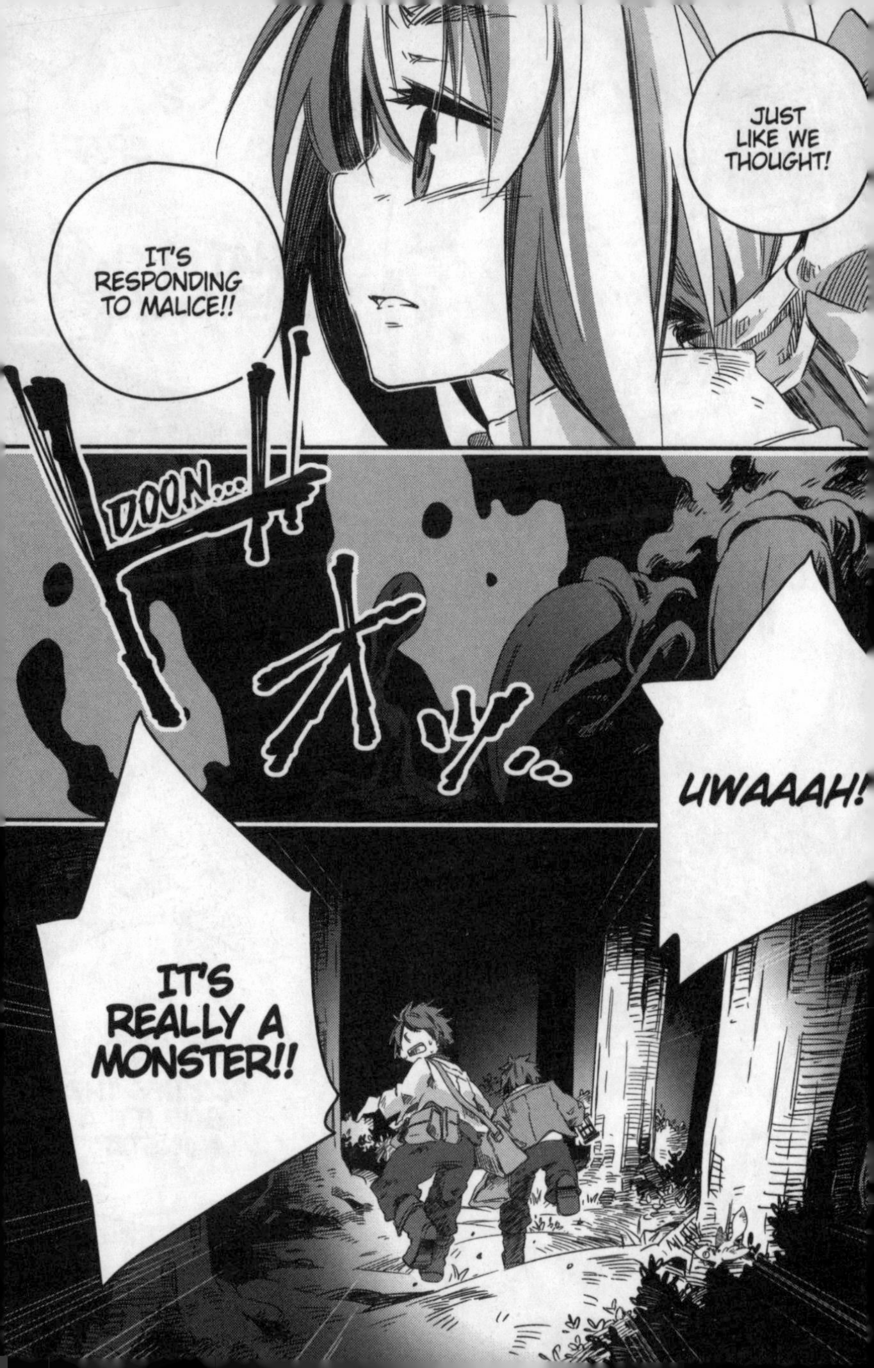
JUST LIKE WE THOUGHT!
IT'S RESPONDING TO MALICE!!
DOON...
オッ..
UWAAAH!
IT'S REALLY A MONSTER!!

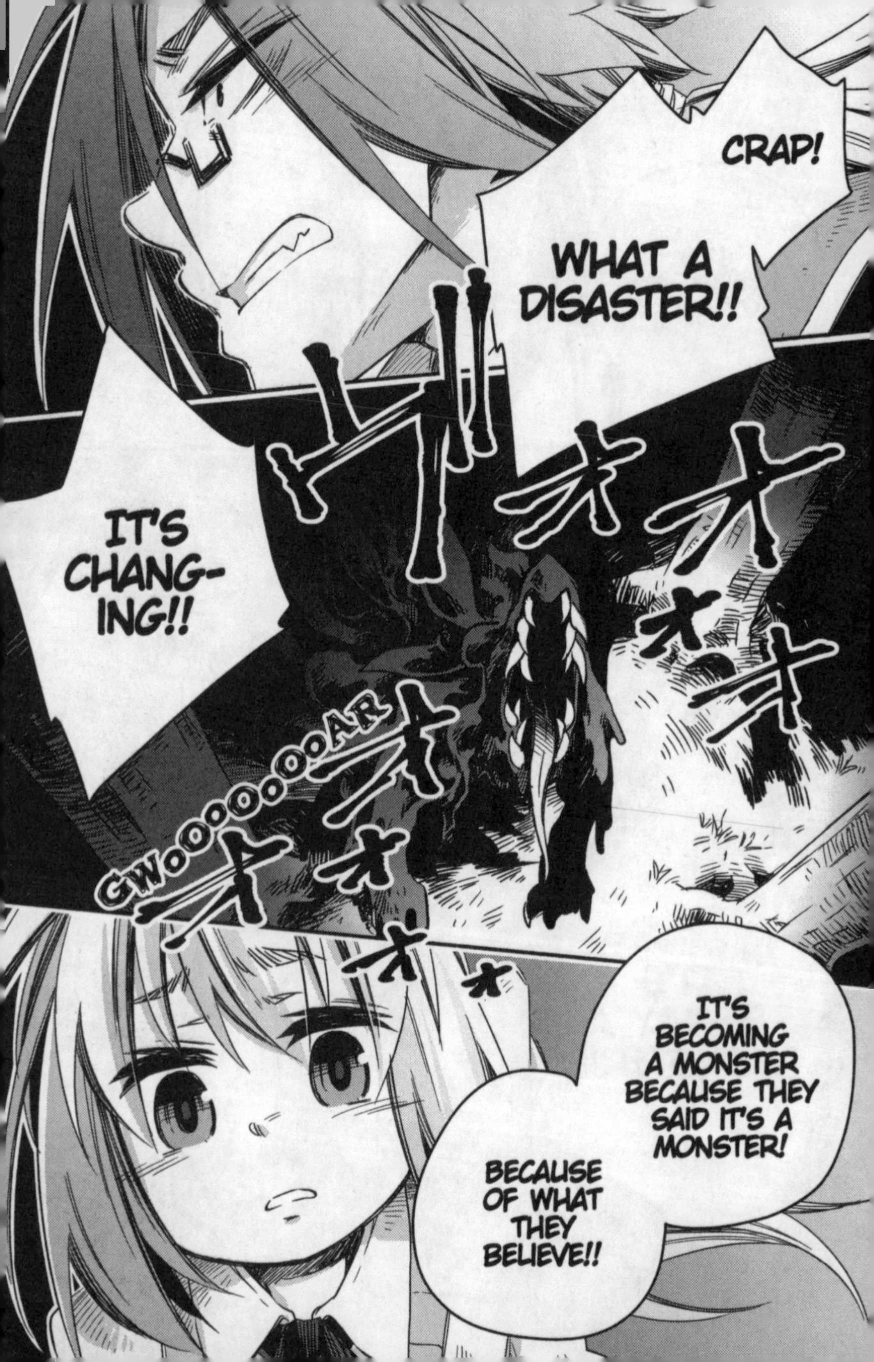
CRAP!
WHAT A DISASTER!!
IT'S CHANG-ING!!
GW·O·O·O·O·O·AR
IT'S BECOMING A MONSTER BECAUSE THEY SAID IT'S A MONSTER!
BECAUSE OF WHAT THEY BELIEVE!!

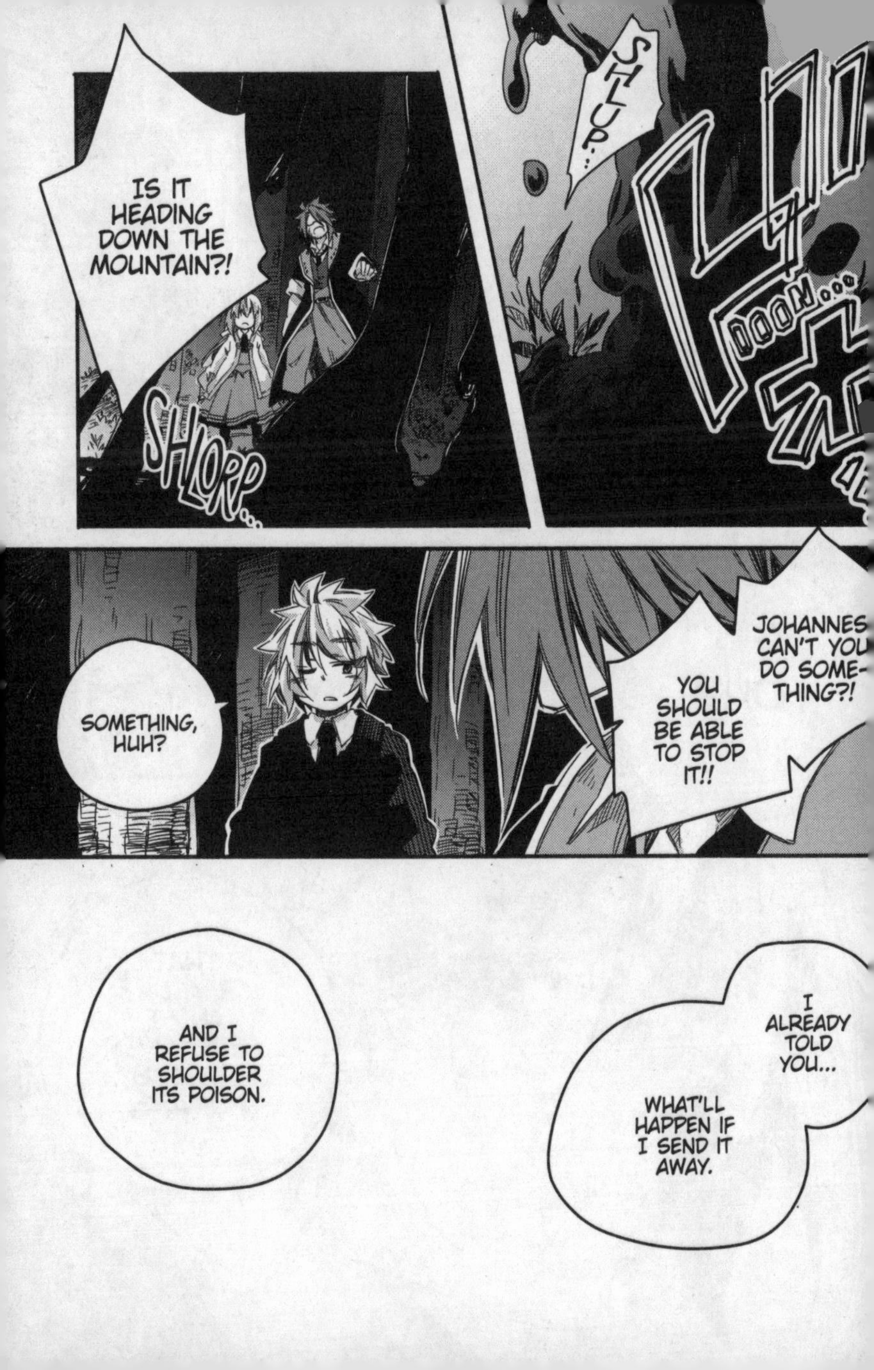
SHLUP...
DOOM...
IS IT HEADING DOWN THE MOUNTAIN?!
SHLORP...
JOHANNES, CAN'T YOU DO SOMETHING?!
YOU SHOULD BE ABLE TO STOP IT!!
SOMETHING, HUH?
I ALREADY TOLD YOU...
WHAT'LL HAPPEN IF I SEND IT AWAY.
AND I REFUSE TO SHOULDER ITS POISON.

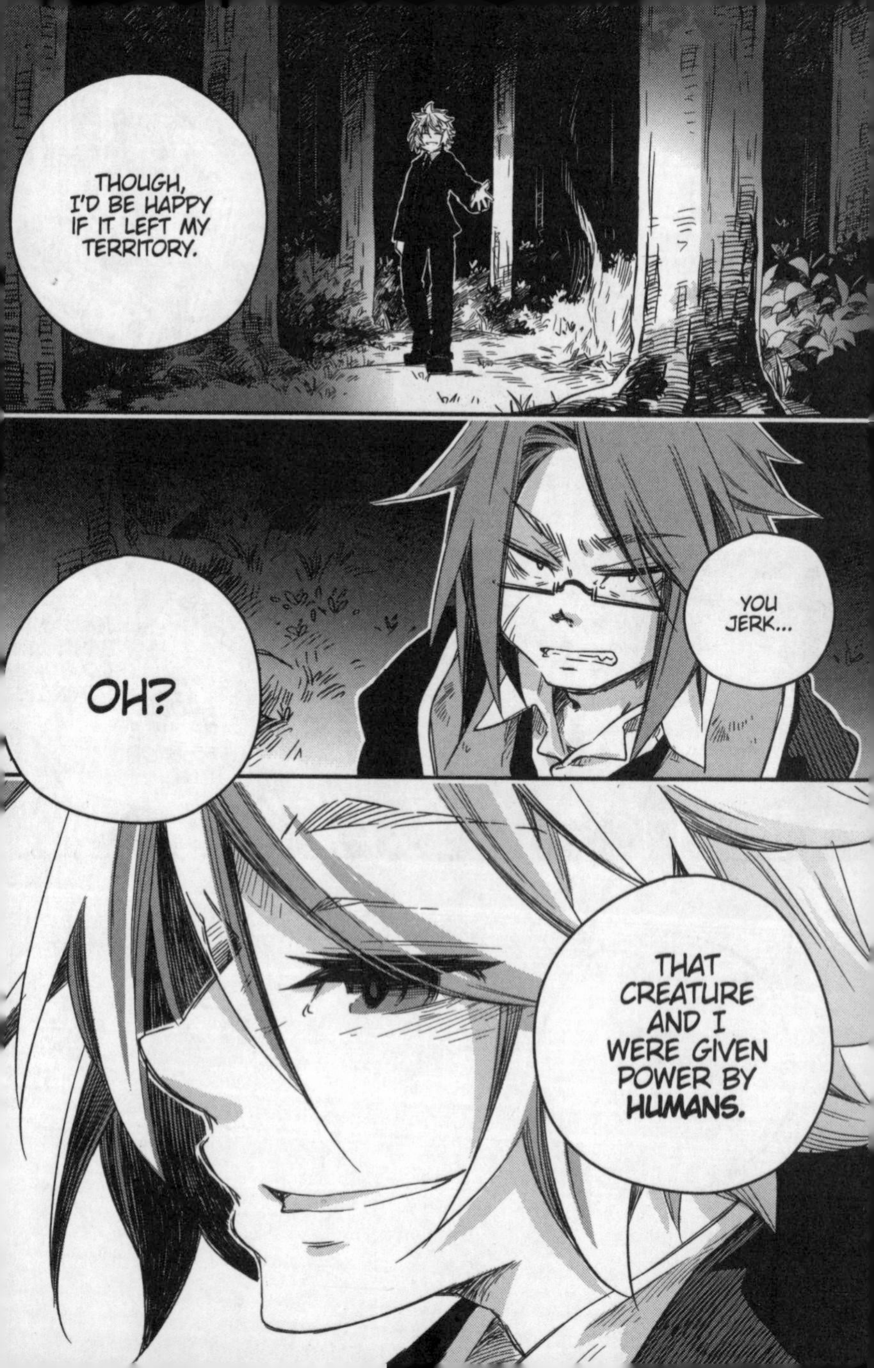
THOUGH, I'D BE HAPPY IF IT LEFT MY TERRITORY.
YOU JERK...
OH?
THAT CREATURE AND I WERE GIVEN POWER BY HUMANS.

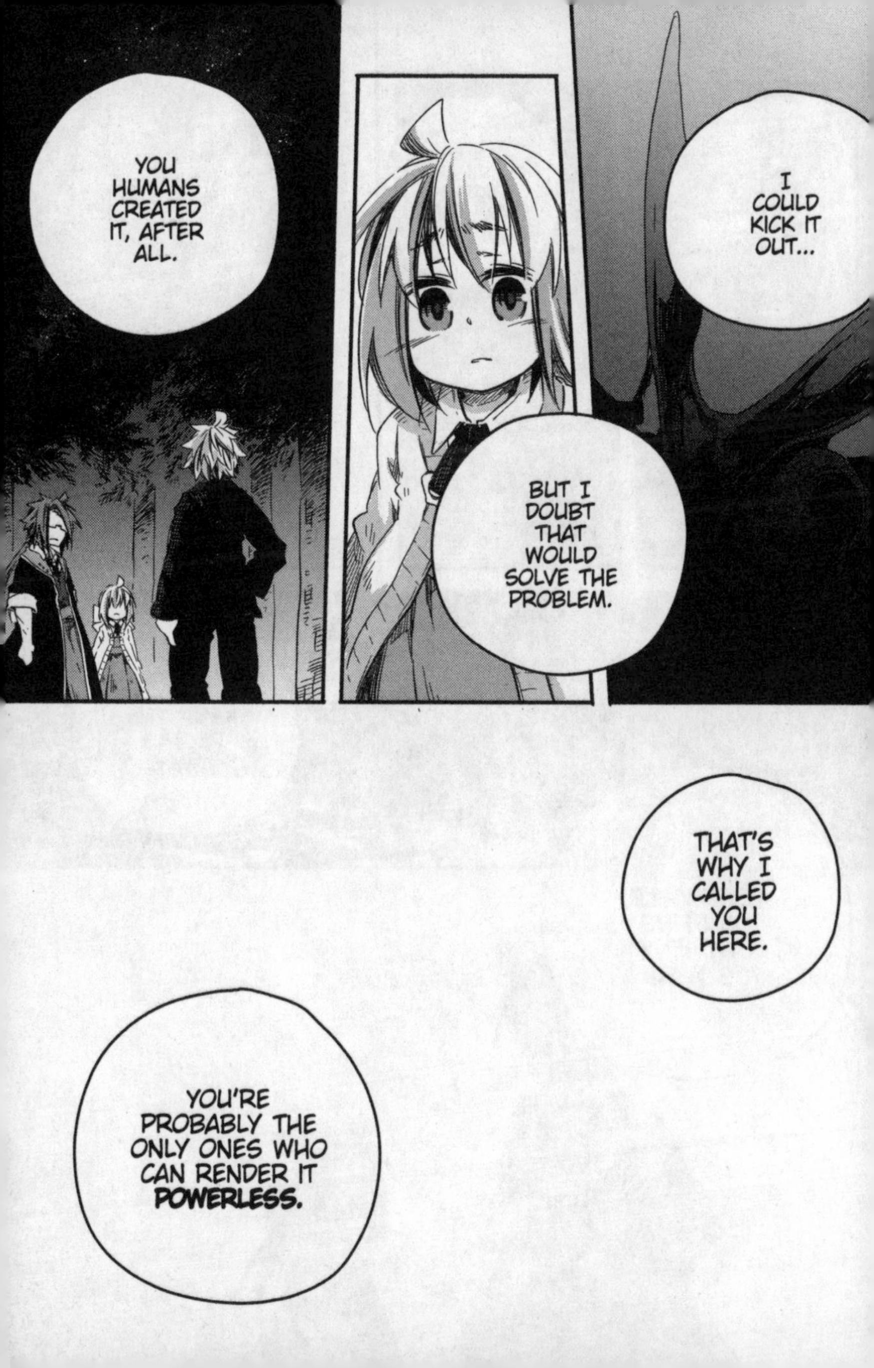
I COULD KICK IT OUT...
BUT I DOUBT THAT WOULD SOLVE THE PROBLEM.
YOU HUMANS CREATED IT, AFTER ALL.
THAT'S WHY I CALLED YOU HERE.
YOU'RE PROBABLY THE ONLY ONES WHO CAN RENDER IT **POWERLESS.**

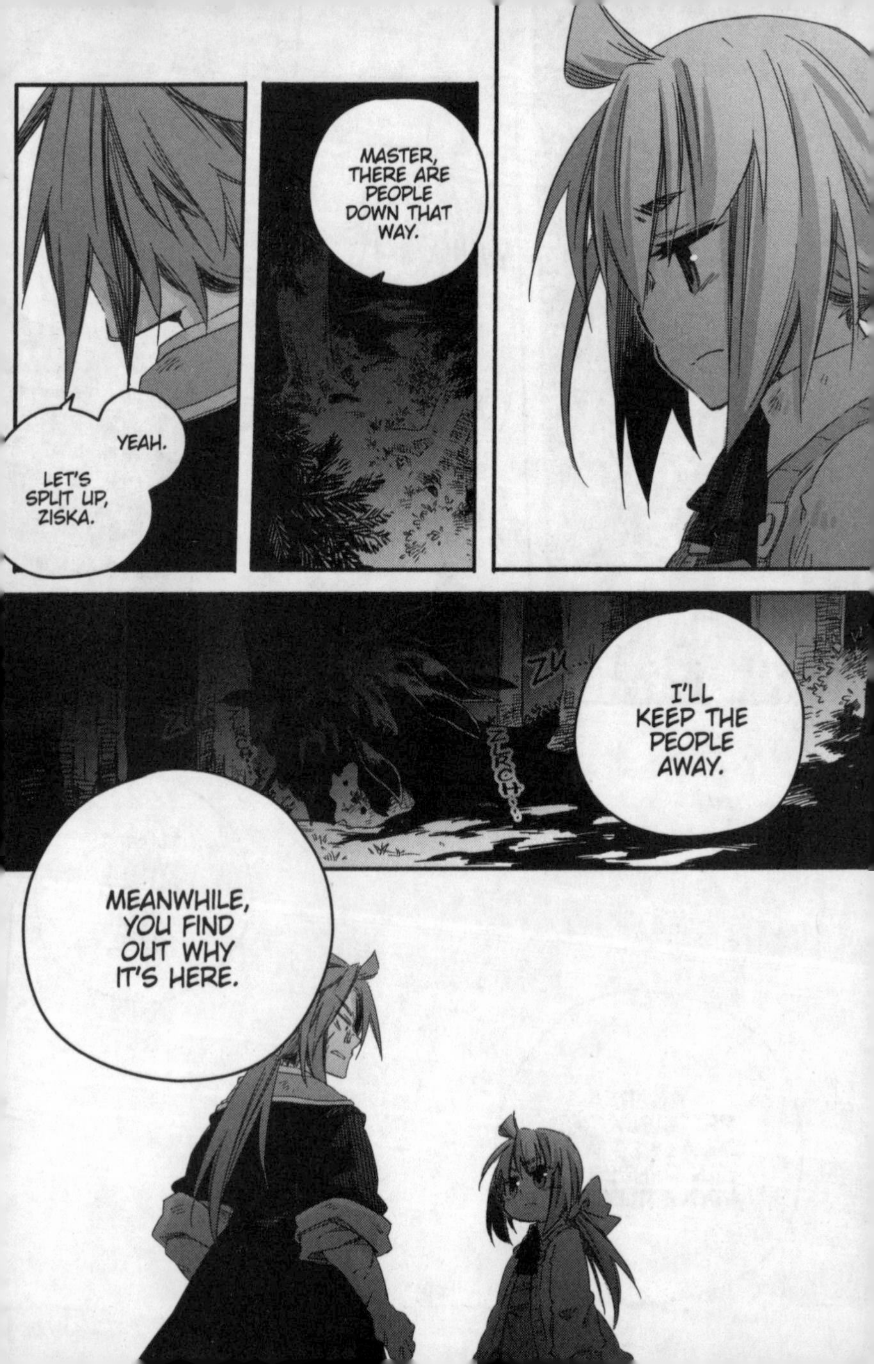
MASTER, THERE ARE PEOPLE DOWN THAT WAY.
YEAH.
LET'S SPLIT UP, ZISKA.
ZU...
I'LL KEEP THE PEOPLE AWAY.
ZLRCH...
MEANWHILE, YOU FIND OUT WHY IT'S HERE.

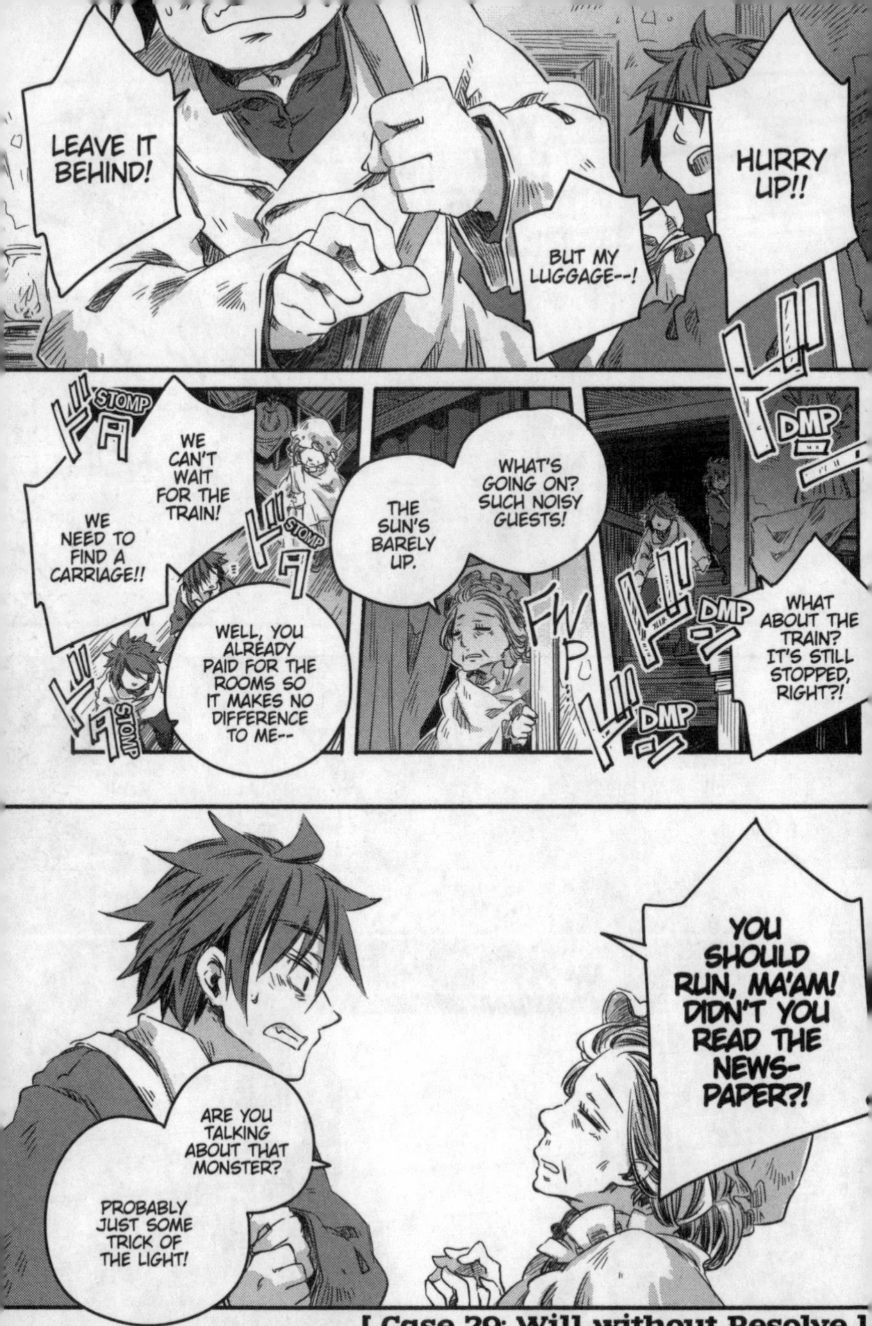
HURRY UP!!
BUT MY LUGGAGE--!
LEAVE IT BEHIND!
DMP
WHAT ABOUT THE TRAIN? IT'S STILL STOPPED, RIGHT?!
DMP
DMP
WHAT'S GOING ON? SUCH NOISY GUESTS!
THE SUN'S BARELY UP.
FWP
STOMP
WE CAN'T WAIT FOR THE TRAIN!
WE NEED TO FIND A CARRIAGE!!
STOMP
WELL, YOU ALREADY PAID FOR THE ROOMS SO IT MAKES NO DIFFERENCE TO ME--
STOMP
YOU SHOULD RUN, MA'AM! DIDN'T YOU READ THE NEWS-PAPER?!
ARE YOU TALKING ABOUT THAT MONSTER?
PROBABLY JUST SOME TRICK OF THE LIGHT!

[Case 29: Will without Resolve]

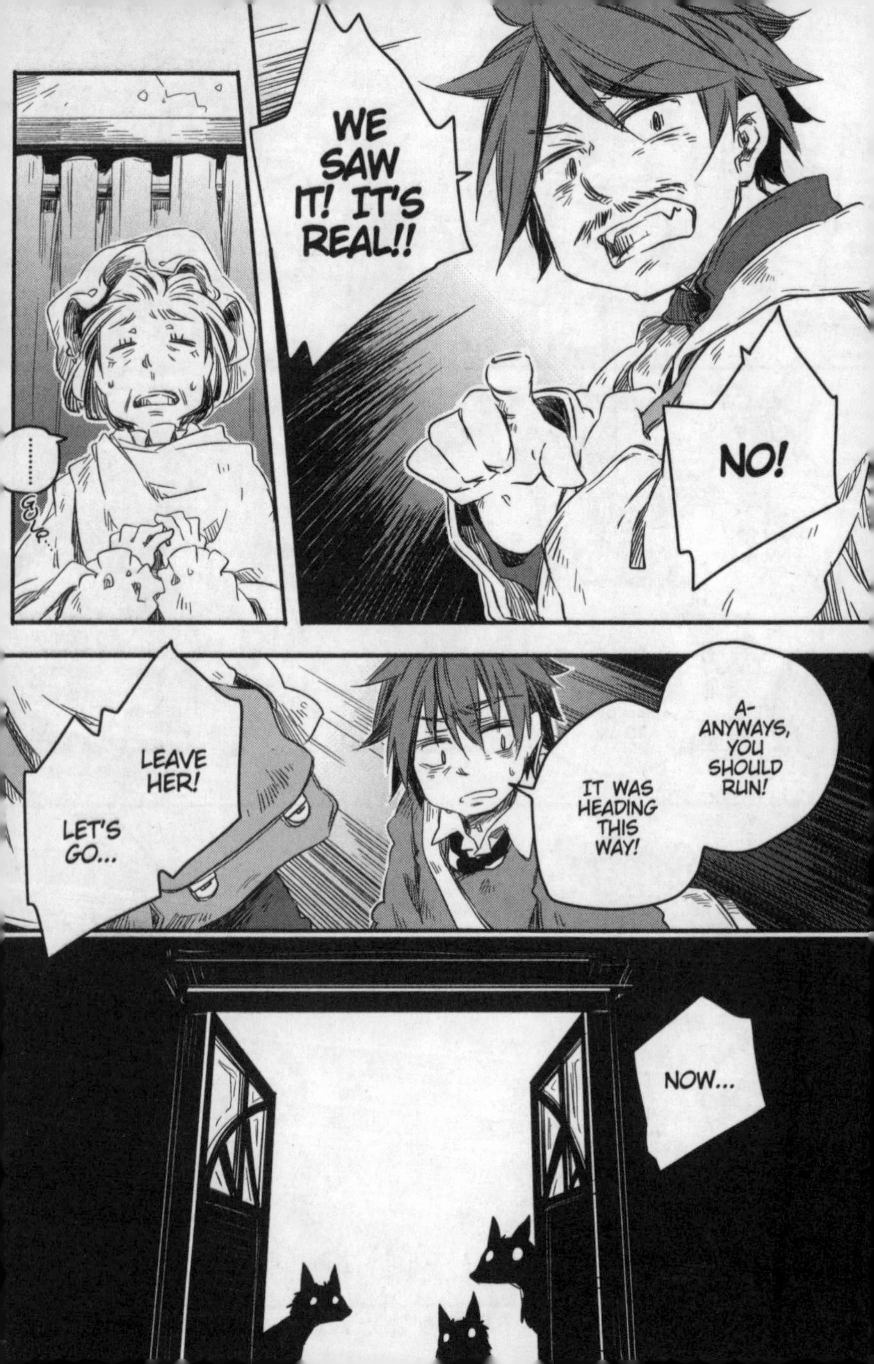
WE SAW IT! IT'S REAL!!
NO!
......
GULP...
A- ANYWAYS, YOU SHOULD RUN!
IT WAS HEADING THIS WAY!
LEAVE HER!
LET'S GO...
NOW...

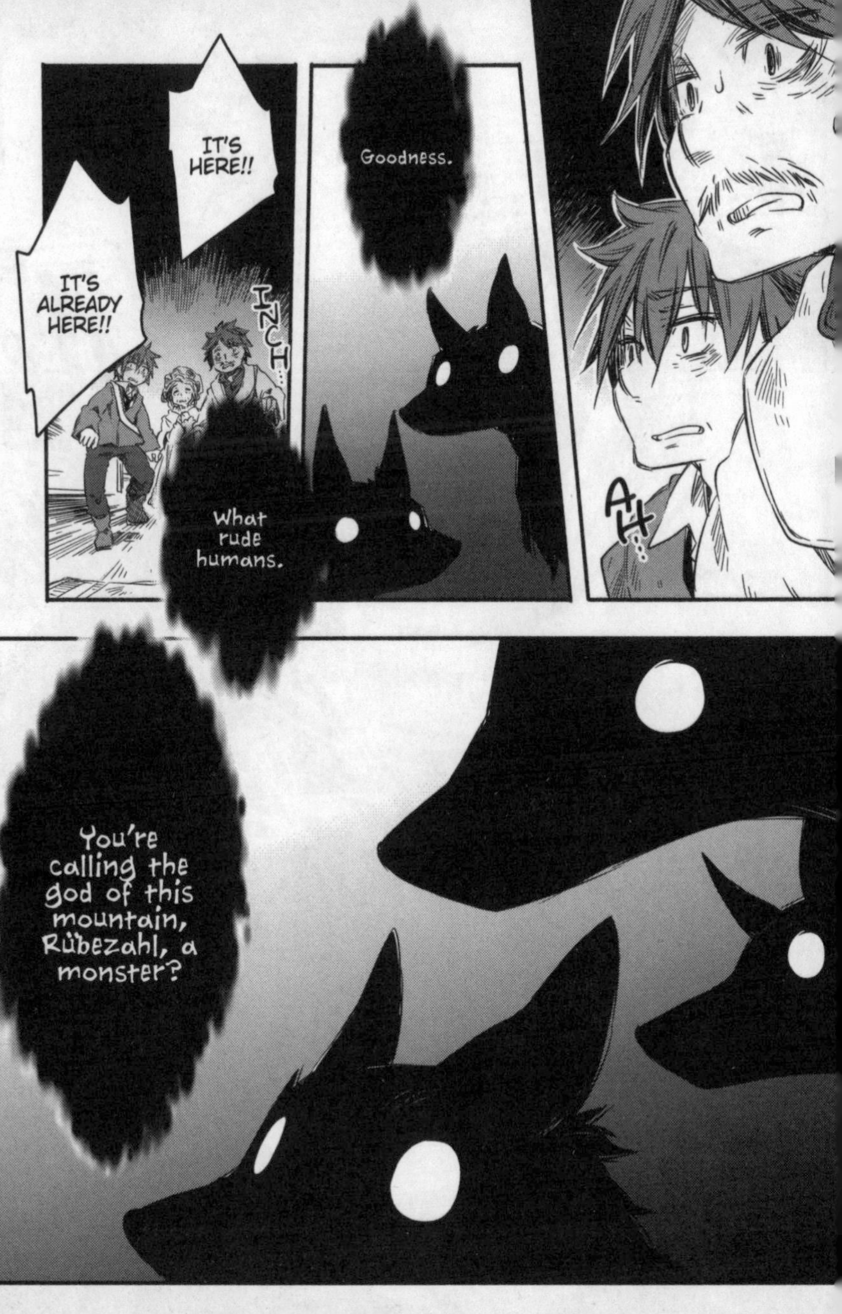
AH...
Goodness.
What rude humans.
IT'S HERE!!
IT'S ALREADY HERE!!
INCH...
You're calling the god of this mountain, Rübezahl, a monster?

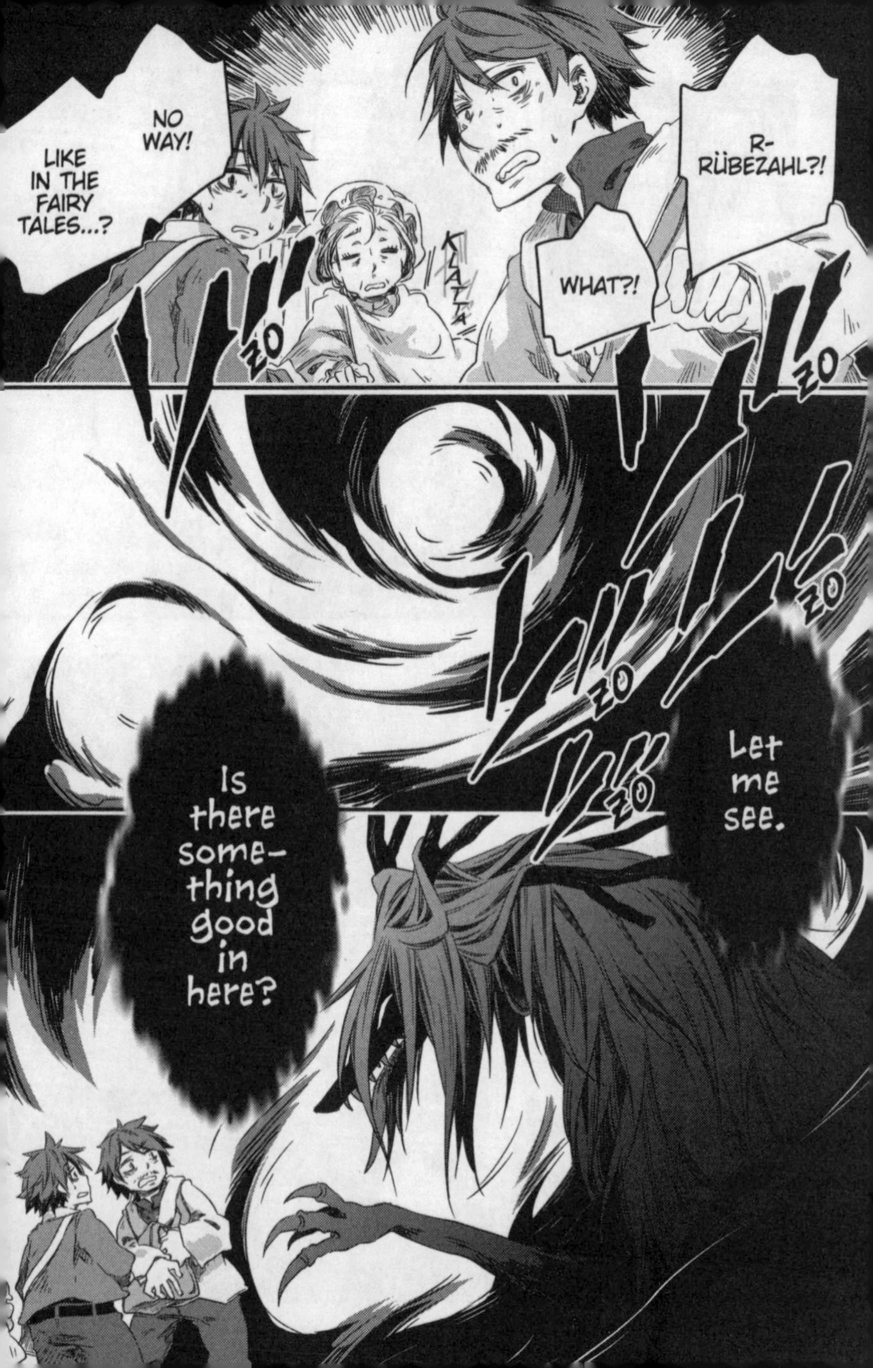
R-RÜBEZAHL?!
WHAT?!
NO WAY!
LIKE IN THE FAIRY TALES...?
KLATTA
ZO
ZO
ZO
ZO
ZO
Let me see.
Is there some-thing good in here?

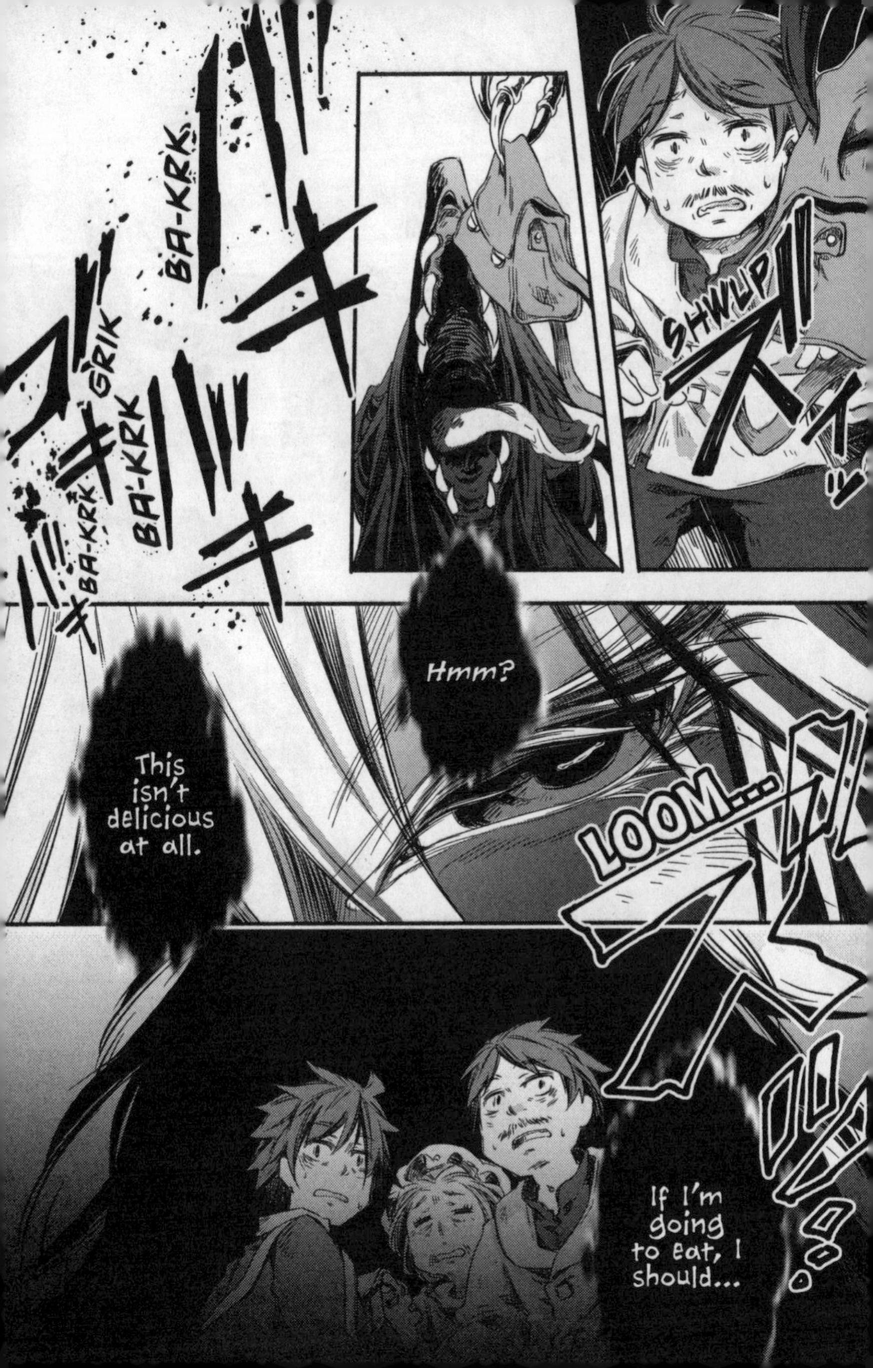
SHWLP
BA-KRK
GRIK
BA-KRK
BA-KRK
LOOM...
Hmm?
This isn't delicious at all.
If I'm going to eat, I should...

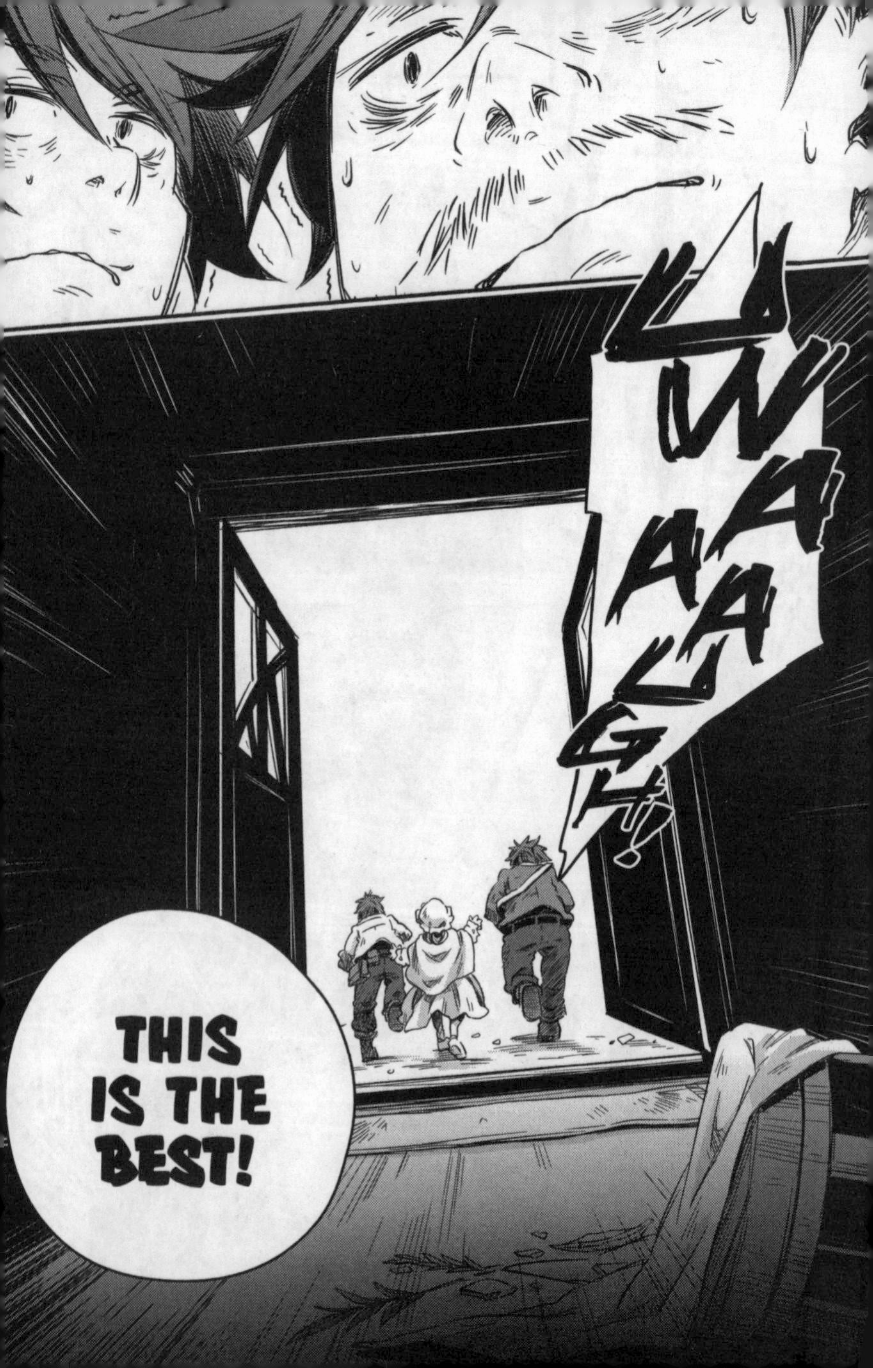
WAAAAUGH!
THIS IS THE BEST!

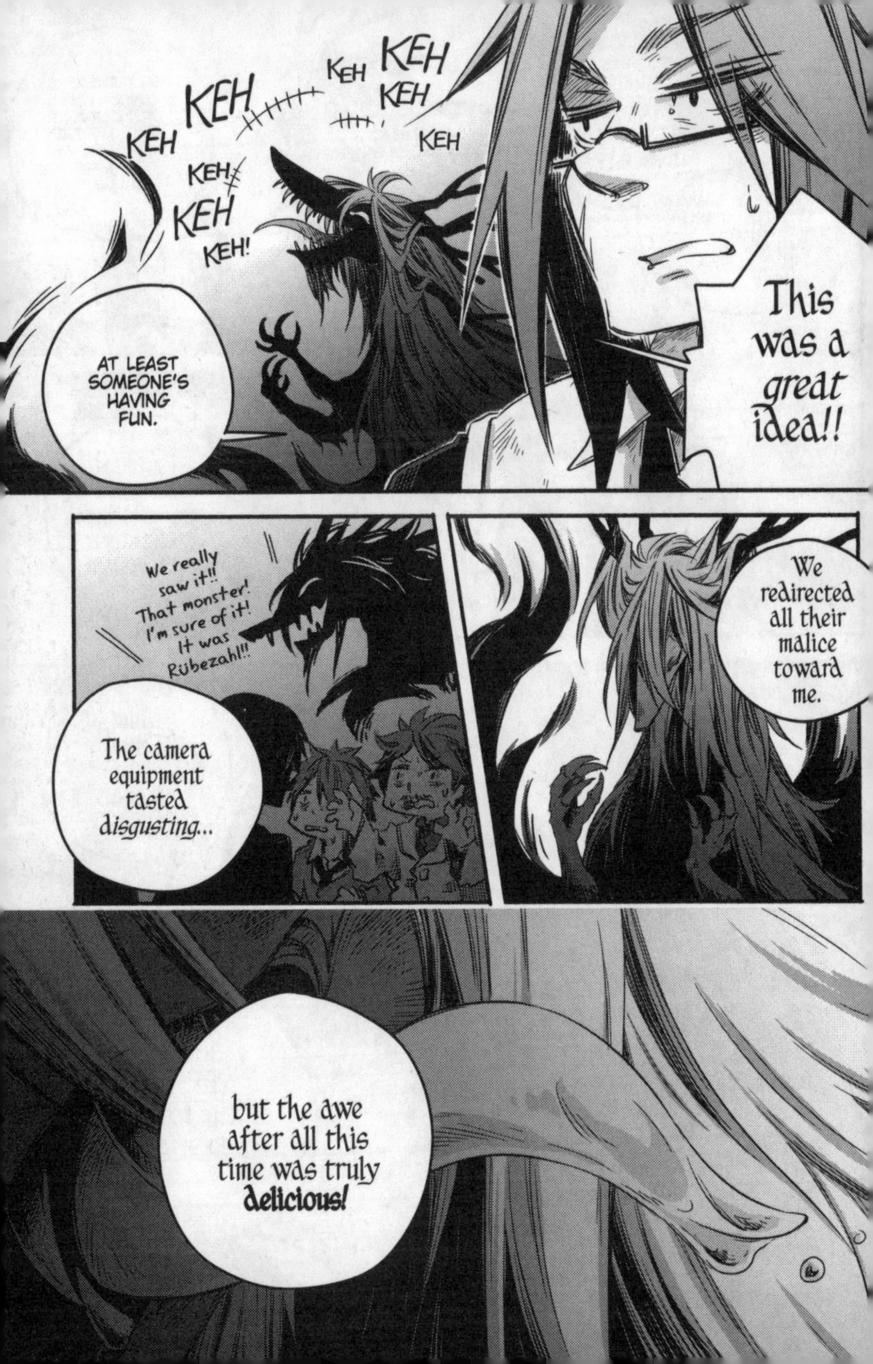
This was a *great* idea!!
KEH KEH KEH KEH KEH KEH KEH KEH KEH!
AT LEAST SOMEONE'S HAVING FUN.
We redirected all their malice toward me.
We really saw it!! That monster! I'm sure of it! It was Rübezahl!!
The camera equipment tasted di*sgusting*...
but the awe after all this time was truly **delicious!**

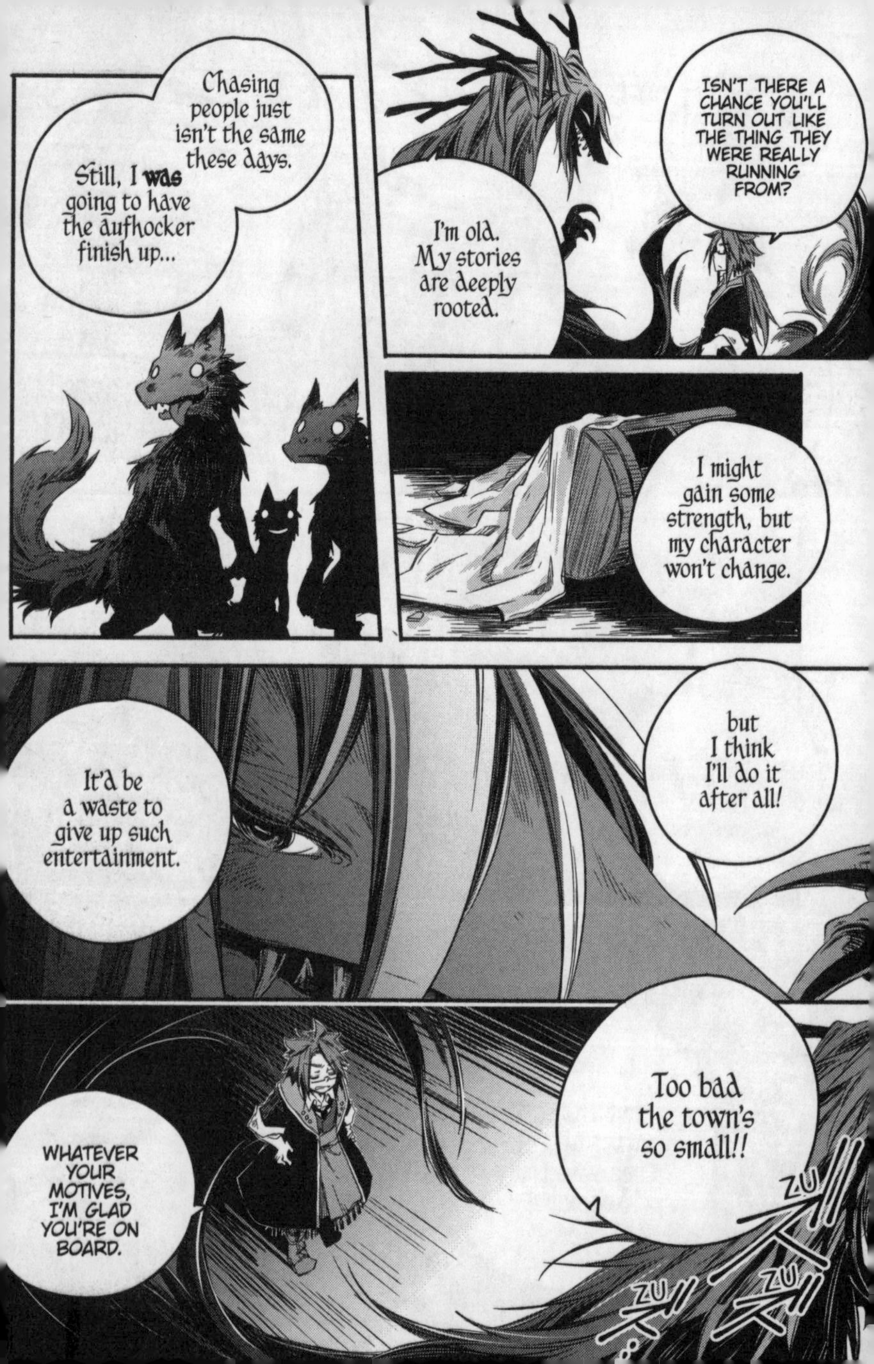
ISN'T THERE A CHANCE YOU'LL TURN OUT LIKE THE THING THEY WERE REALLY RUNNING FROM?
I'm old. My stories are deeply rooted.
I might gain some strength, but my character won't change.
Chasing people just isn't the same these days.
Still, I **was** going to have the aufhocker finish up...
but I think I'll do it after all!
It'd be a waste to give up such entertainment.
Too bad the town's so small!!
ZU
ZU
ZU
WHATEVER YOUR MOTIVES, I'M GLAD YOU'RE ON BOARD.

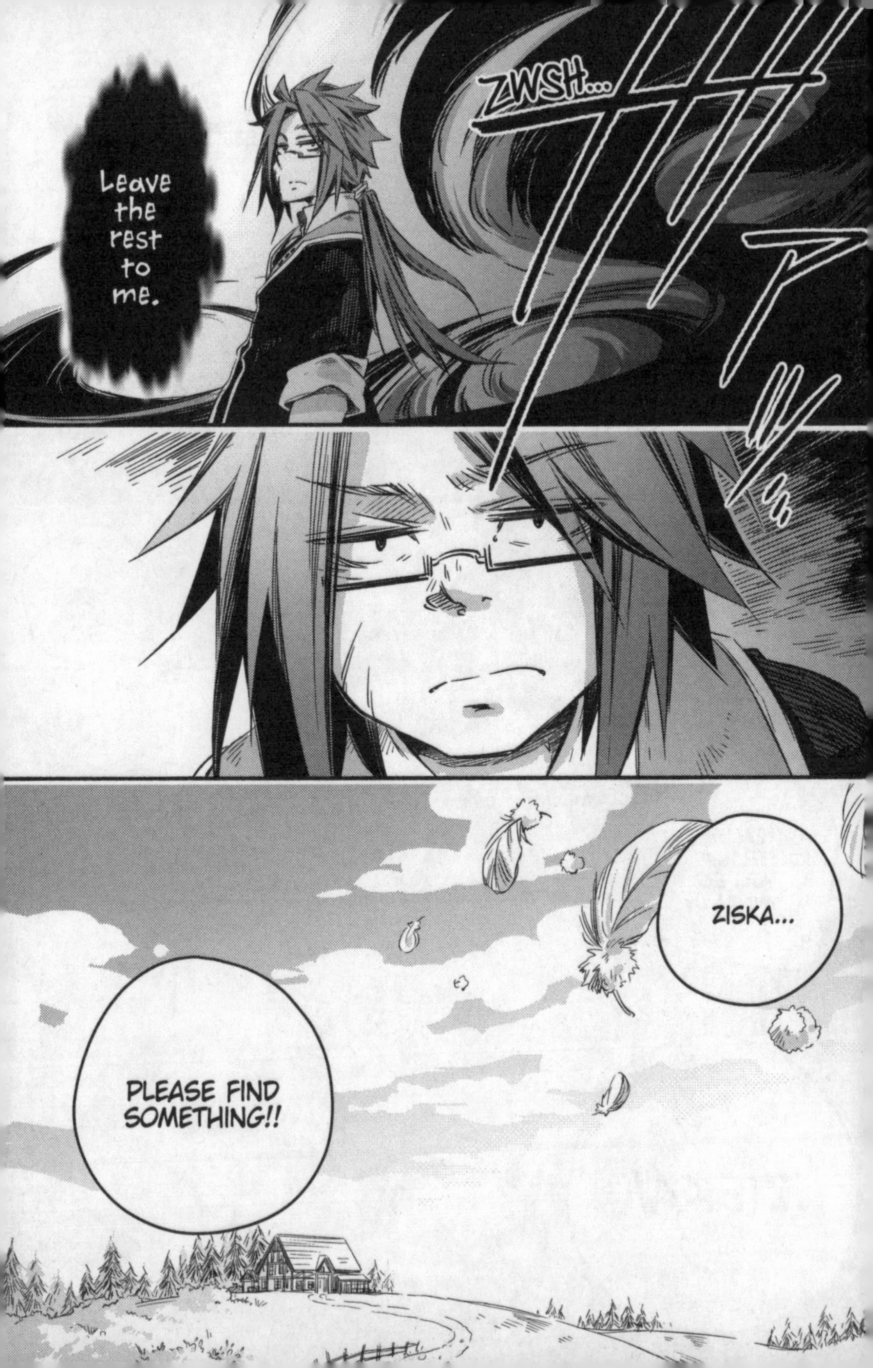
ZWSH...
Leave the rest to me.
ZISKA...
PLEASE FIND SOMETHING!!

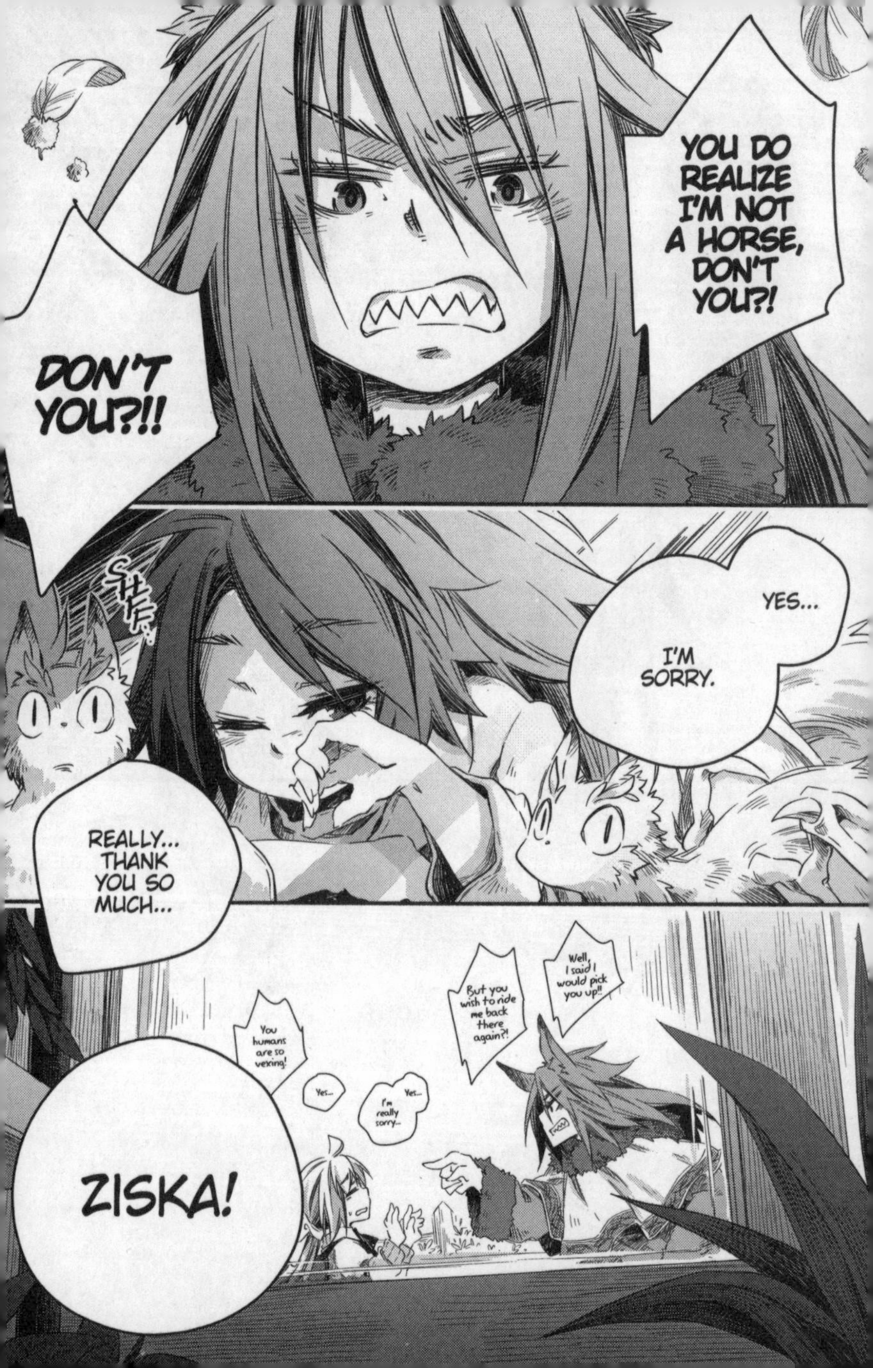
YOU DO REALIZE I'M NOT A HORSE, DON'T YOU?!
DON'T YOU?!!
YES...
I'M SORRY.
SHFF...
REALLY... THANK YOU SO MUCH...
Well, I said I would pick you up!!
But you wish to ride me back there again?!
Yes...
I'm really sorry...
You humans are so vexing!
Yes...
ZISKA!

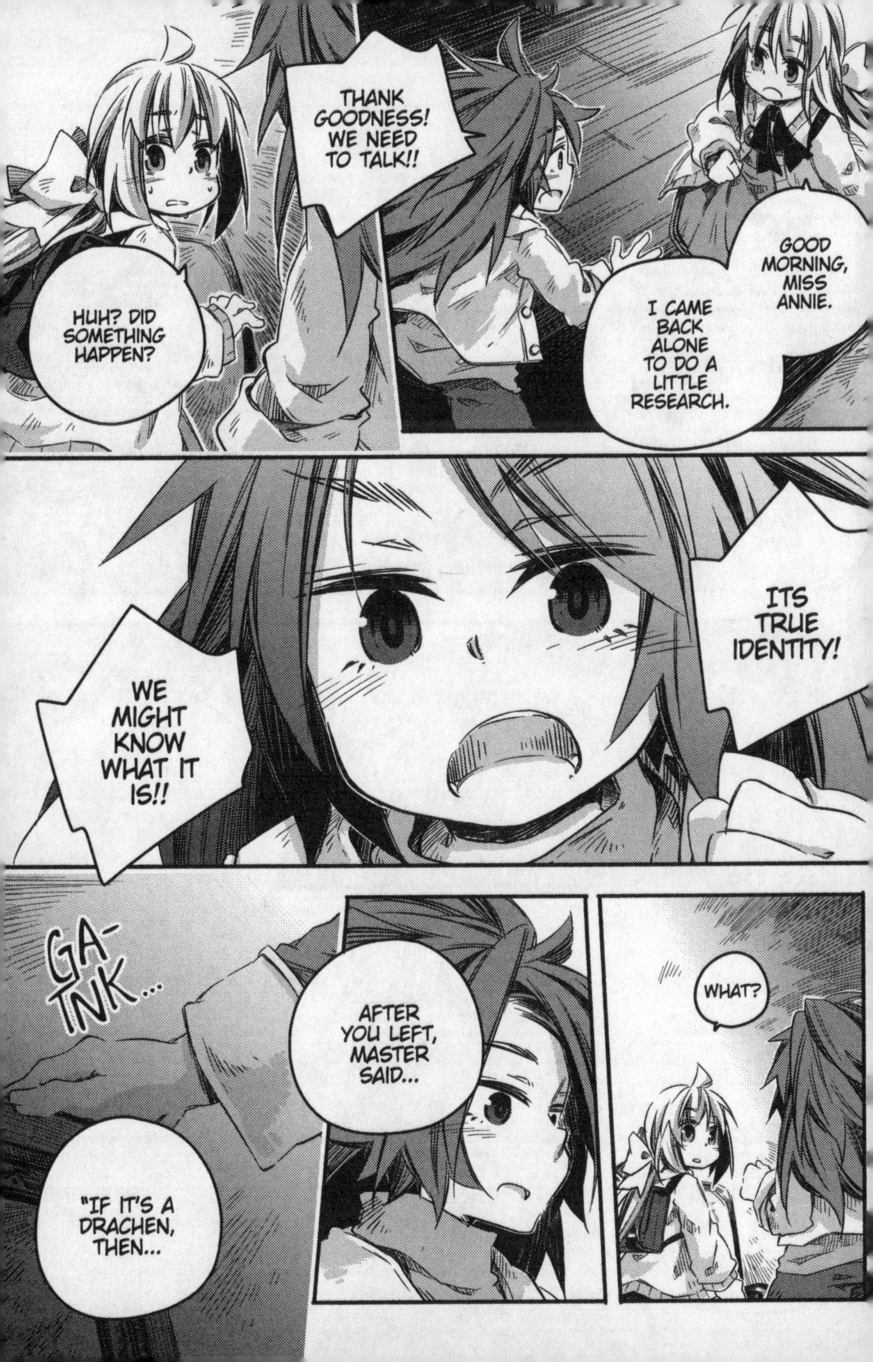
GOOD MORNING, MISS ANNIE.
I CAME BACK ALONE TO DO A LITTLE RESEARCH.
THANK GOODNESS! WE NEED TO TALK!!
HUH? DID SOMETHING HAPPEN?
ITS TRUE IDENTITY!
WE MIGHT KNOW WHAT IT IS!!
WHAT?
AFTER YOU LEFT, MASTER SAID...
GA-TNK...
"IF IT'S A DRACHEN, THEN...

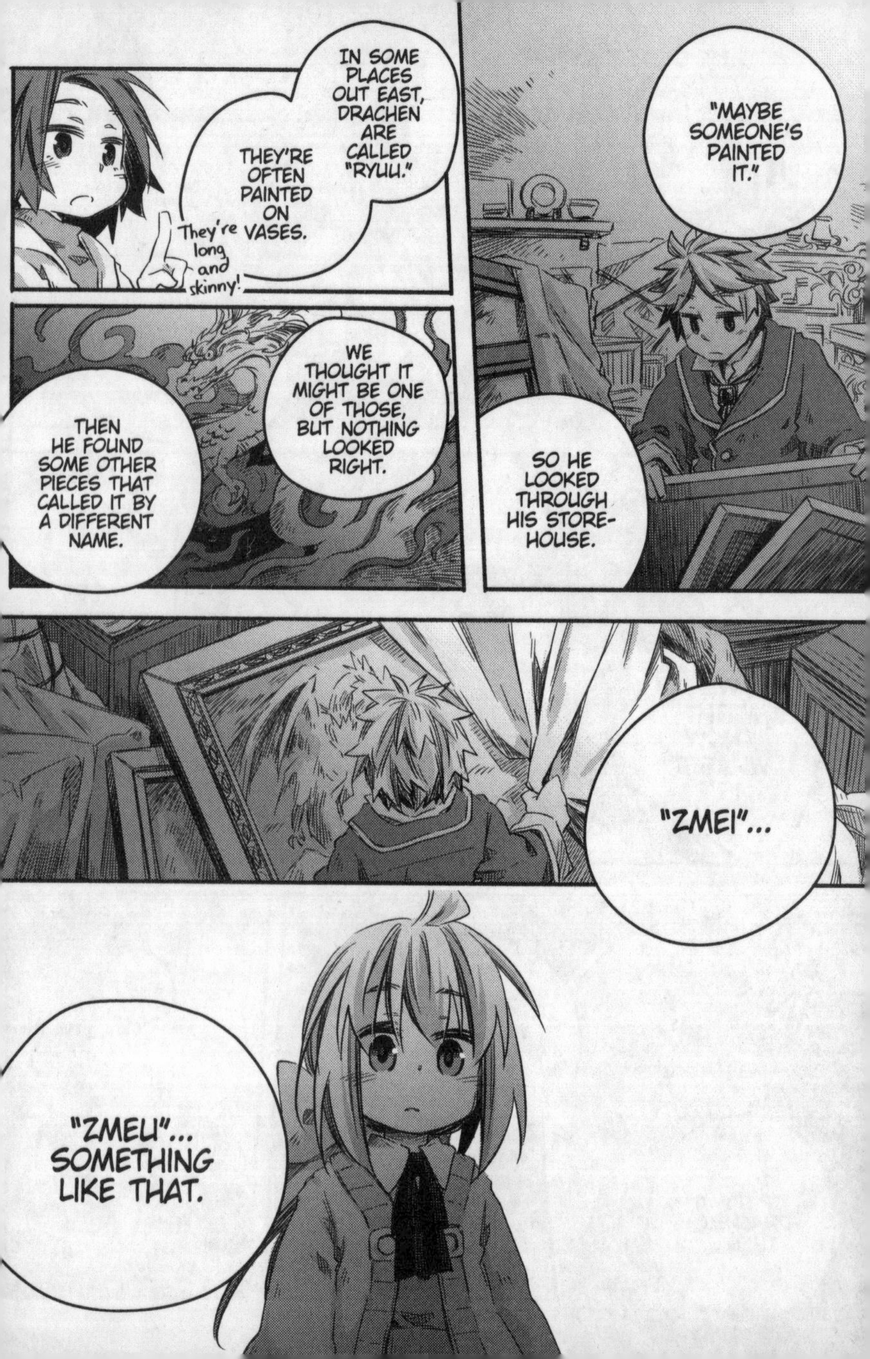
"MAYBE SOMEONE'S PAINTED IT."
IN SOME PLACES OUT EAST, DRACHEN ARE CALLED "RYUU."
THEY'RE OFTEN PAINTED ON VASES.
They're long and skinny!
SO HE LOOKED THROUGH HIS STORE-HOUSE.
WE THOUGHT IT MIGHT BE ONE OF THOSE, BUT NOTHING LOOKED RIGHT.
THEN HE FOUND SOME OTHER PIECES THAT CALLED IT BY A DIFFERENT NAME.
"ZMEI"...
"ZMEU"... SOMETHING LIKE THAT.

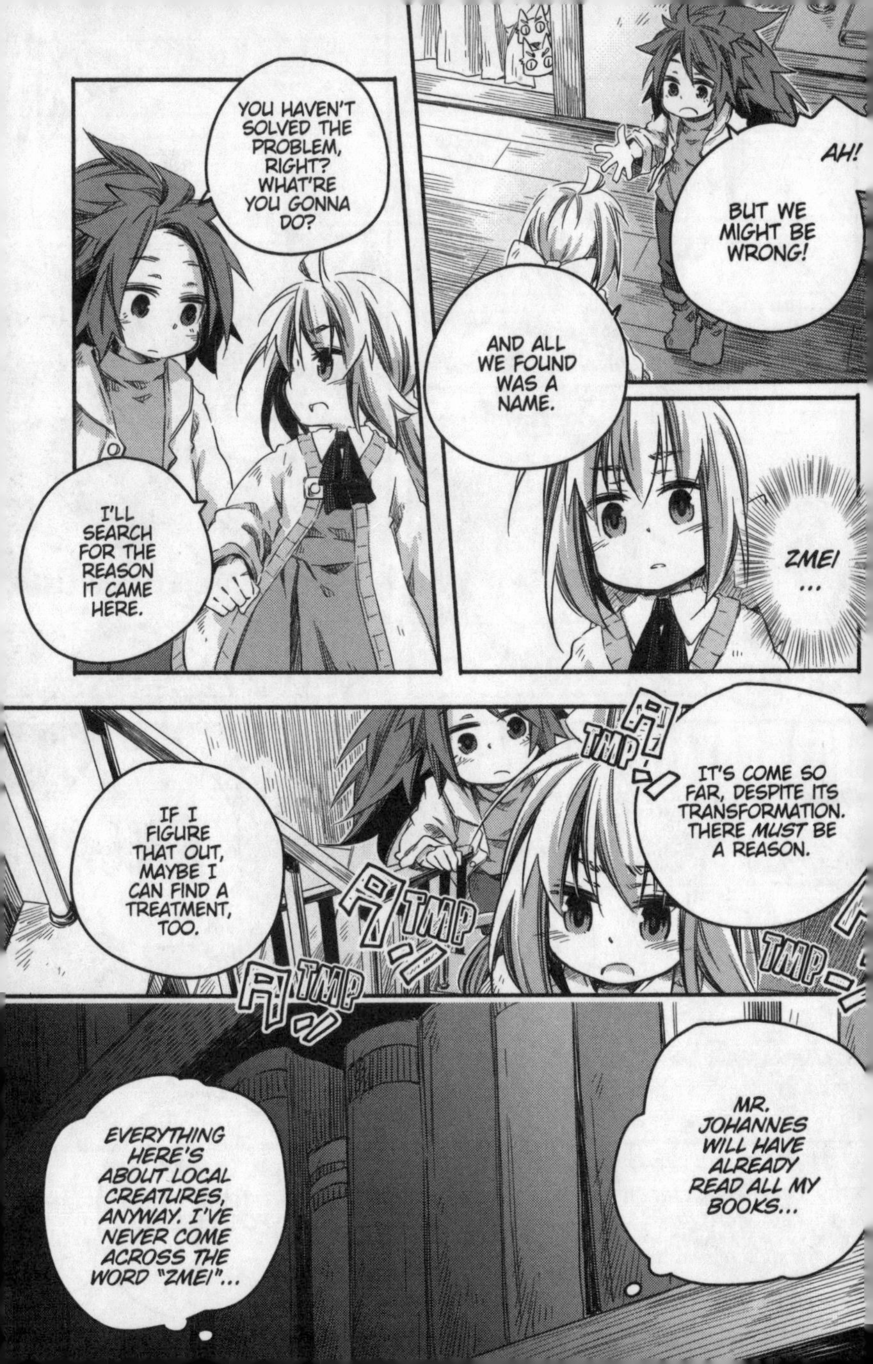
AH!
BUT WE MIGHT BE WRONG!
AND ALL WE FOUND WAS A NAME.
ZMEI ...
YOU HAVEN'T SOLVED THE PROBLEM, RIGHT? WHAT'RE YOU GONNA DO?
I'LL SEARCH FOR THE REASON IT CAME HERE.
IT'S COME SO FAR, DESPITE ITS TRANSFORMATION. THERE *MUST* BE A REASON.
TMP
TMP
TMP
IF I FIGURE THAT OUT, MAYBE I CAN FIND A TREATMENT, TOO.
TMP
MR. JOHANNES WILL HAVE ALREADY READ ALL MY BOOKS...
EVERYTHING HERE'S ABOUT LOCAL CREATURES, ANYWAY. I'VE NEVER COME ACROSS THE WORD "ZMEI"...

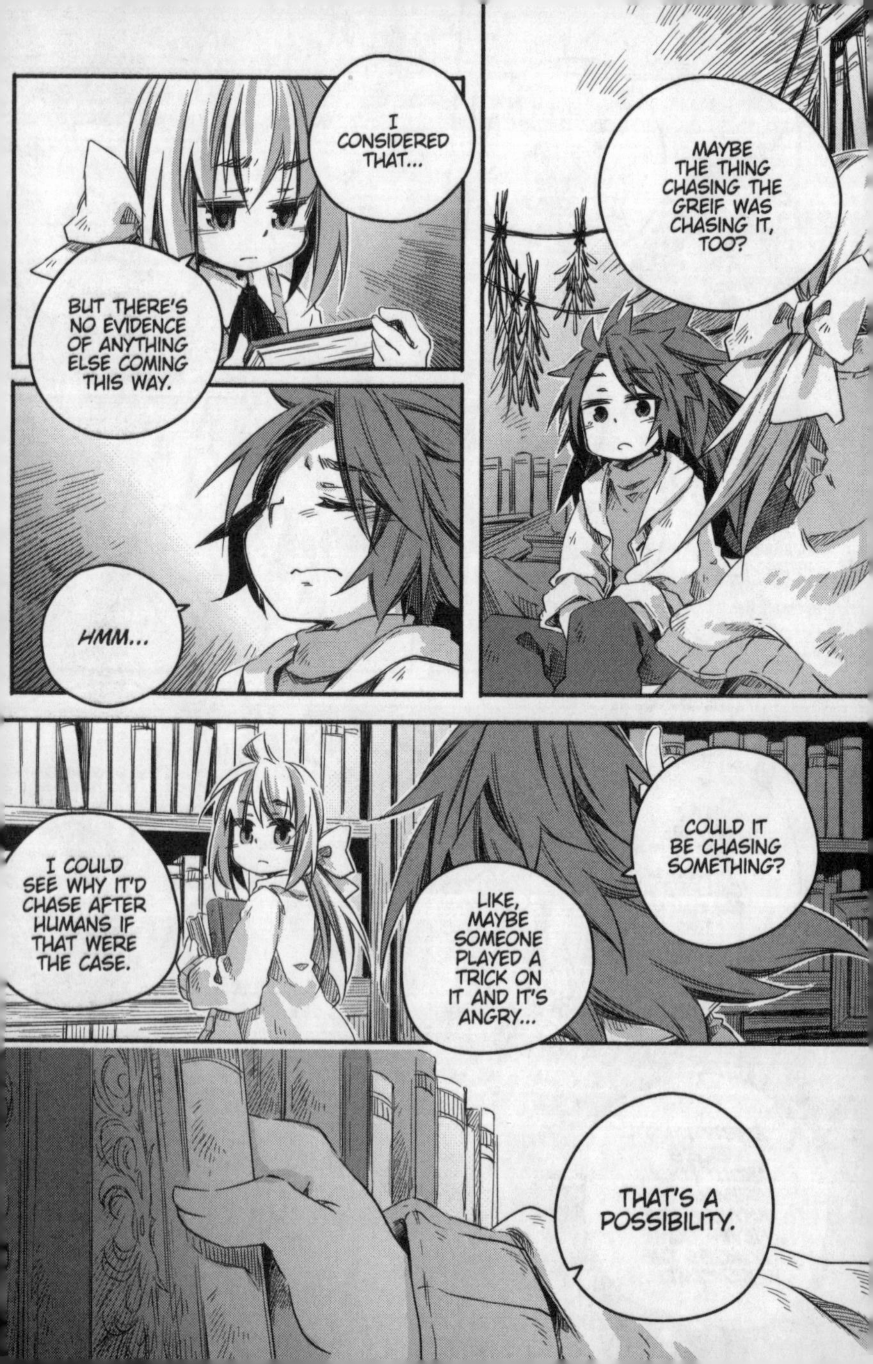
MAYBE THE THING CHASING THE GREIF WAS CHASING IT, TOO?
I CONSIDERED THAT...
BUT THERE'S NO EVIDENCE OF ANYTHING ELSE COMING THIS WAY.
HMM...
COULD IT BE CHASING SOMETHING?
LIKE, MAYBE SOMEONE PLAYED A TRICK ON IT AND IT'S ANGRY...
I COULD SEE WHY IT'D CHASE AFTER HUMANS IF THAT WERE THE CASE.
THAT'S A POSSIBILITY.

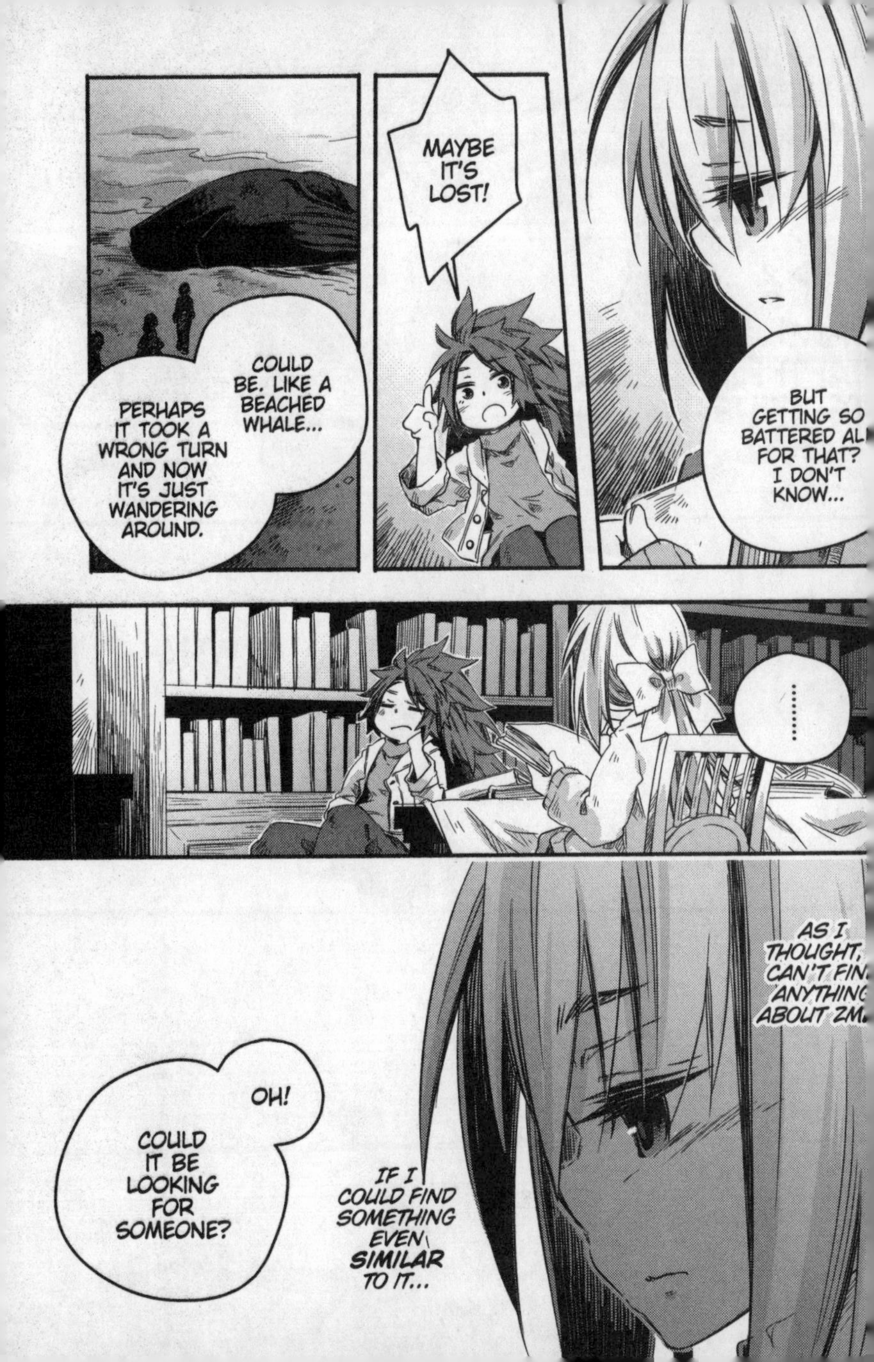
BUT GETTING SO BATTERED AL FOR THAT? I DON'T KNOW...
MAYBE IT'S LOST!
COULD BE. LIKE A BEACHED WHALE...
PERHAPS IT TOOK A WRONG TURN AND NOW IT'S JUST WANDERING AROUND.
......
AS I THOUGHT, CAN'T FIN ANYTHIN ABOUT ZM.
IF I COULD FIND SOMETHING EVEN SIMILAR TO IT...
OH!
COULD IT BE LOOKING FOR SOMEONE?

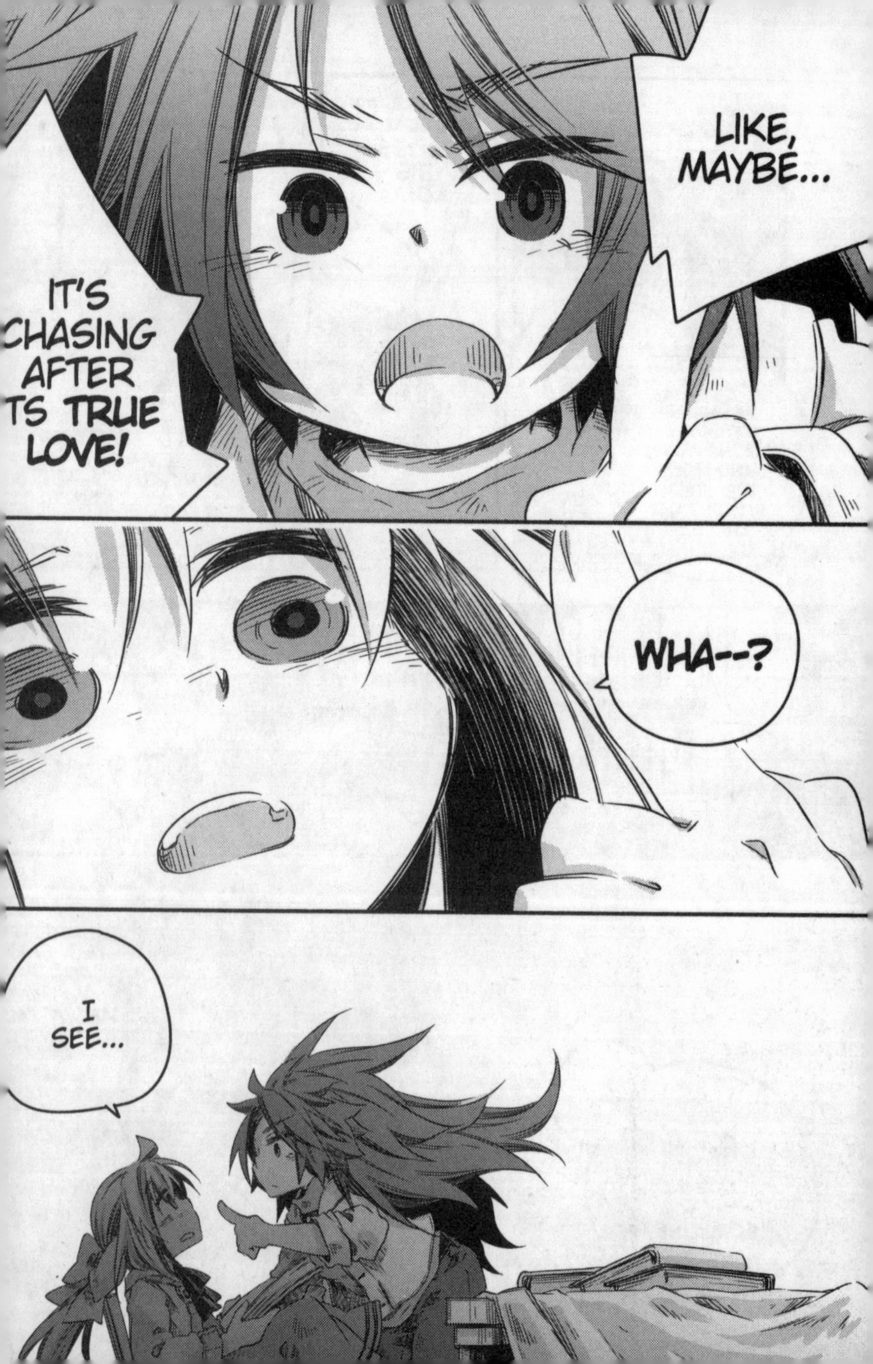
LIKE, MAYBE...
IT'S CHASING AFTER TS TRUE LOVE!
WHA--?
I SEE...

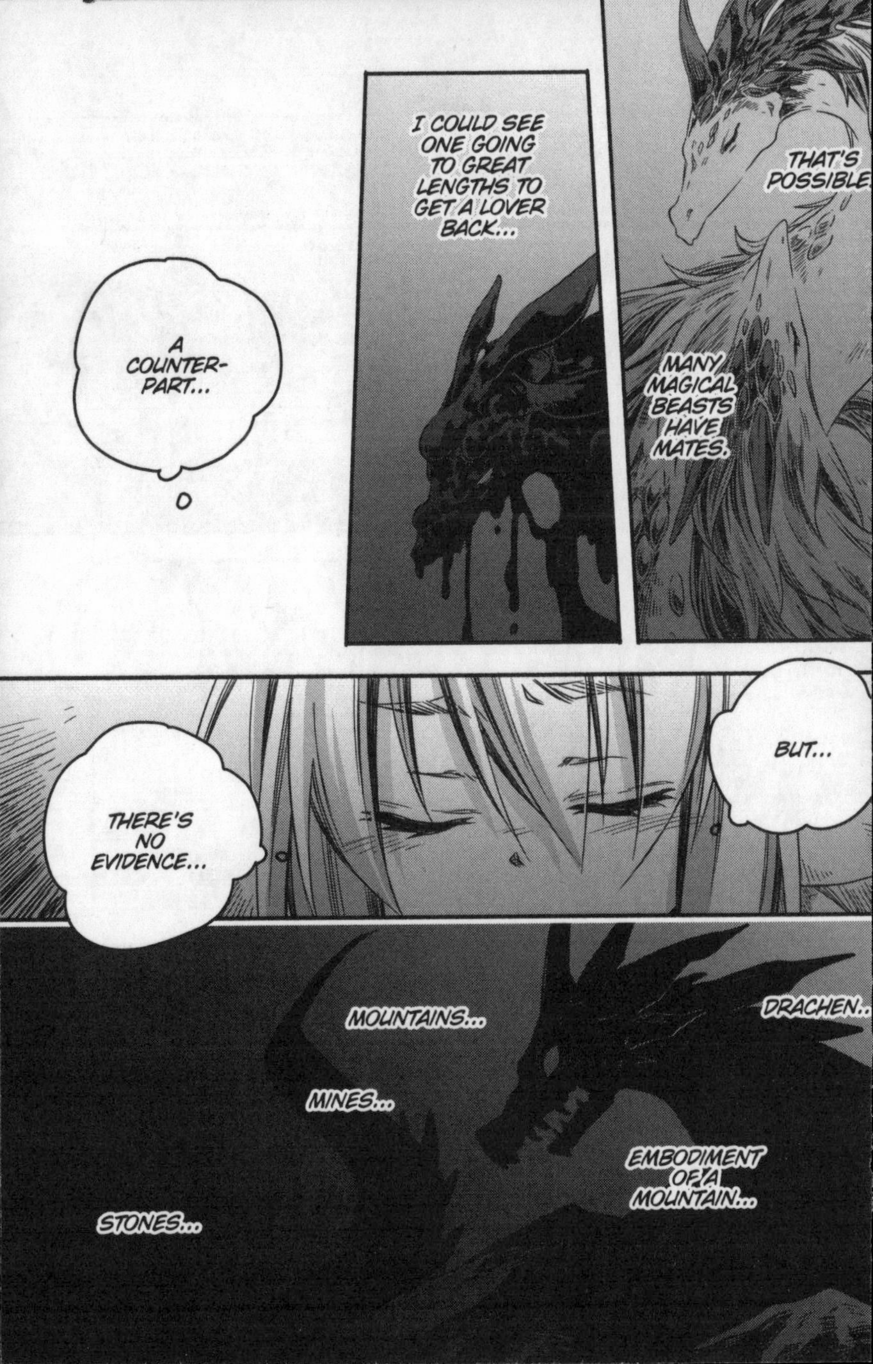
THAT'S POSSIBLE.
MANY MAGICAL BEASTS HAVE MATES.
I COULD SEE ONE GOING TO GREAT LENGTHS TO GET A LOVER BACK...
A COUNTER-PART...
BUT...
THERE'S NO EVIDENCE...
DRACHEN...
MOUNTAINS...
MINES...
EMBODIMENT OF A MOUNTAIN...
STONES...

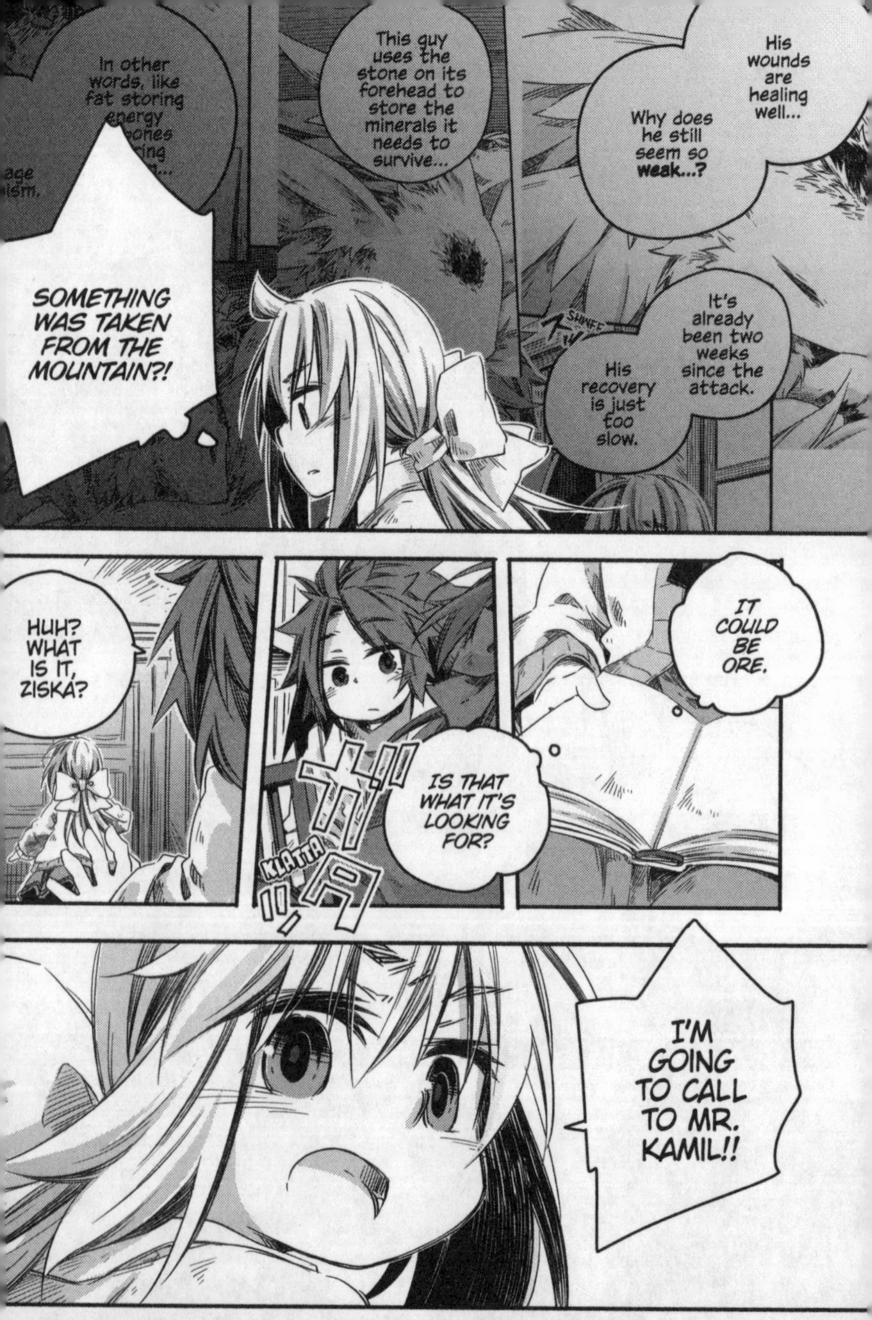
His wounds are healing well...
Why does he still seem so **weak...?**
It's already been two weeks since the attack.
His recovery is just too slow.
This guy uses the stone on its forehead to store the minerals it needs to survive...
In other words, like fat storing energy
SOMETHING WAS TAKEN FROM THE MOUNTAIN?!
IT COULD BE ORE.
IS THAT WHAT IT'S LOOKING FOR?
KLATTA
HUH? WHAT IS IT, ZISKA?
I'M GOING TO CALL TO MR. KAMIL!!

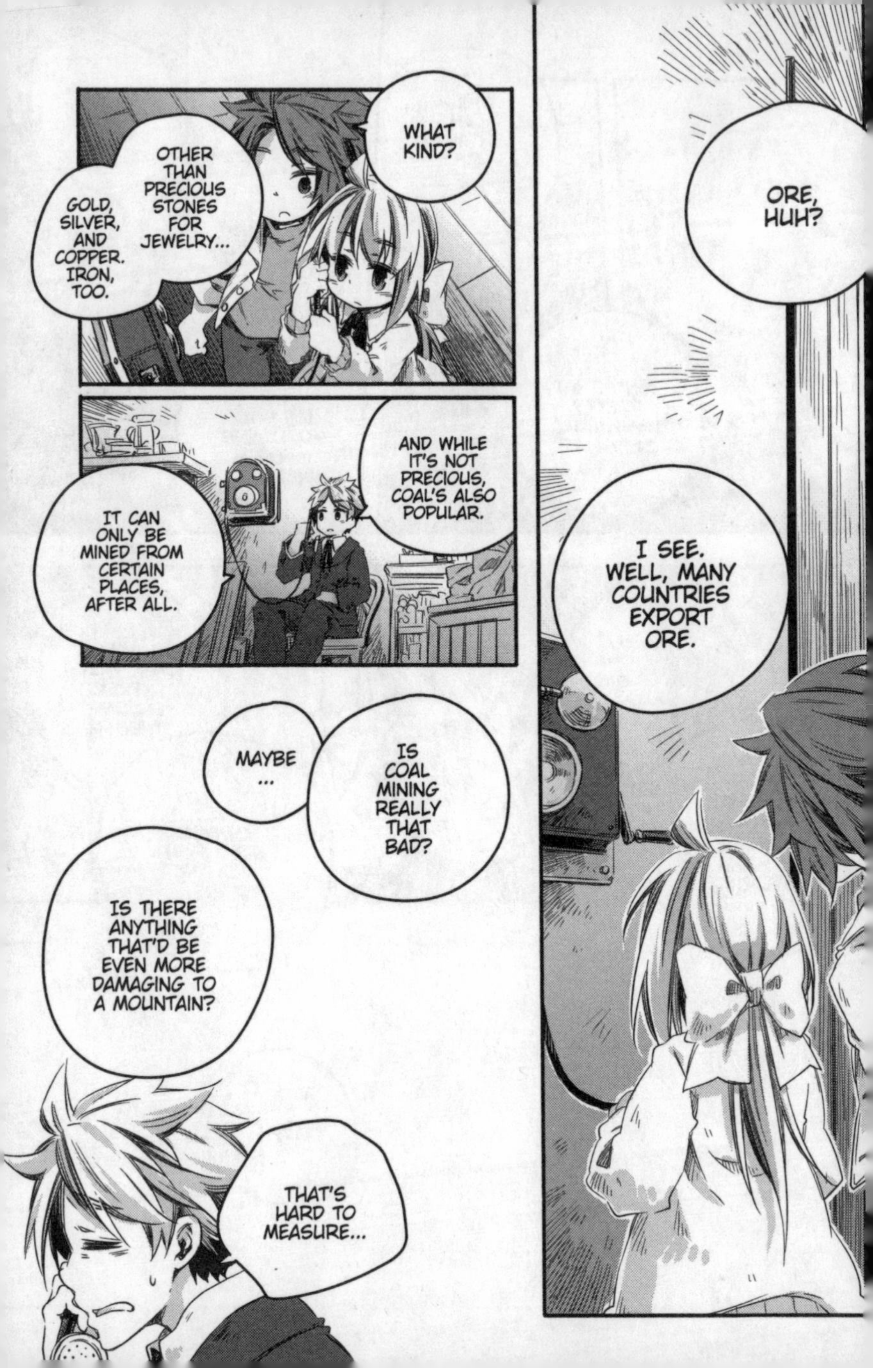
ORE, HUH?
I SEE. WELL, MANY COUNTRIES EXPORT ORE.
WHAT KIND?
OTHER THAN PRECIOUS STONES FOR JEWELRY...
GOLD, SILVER, AND COPPER. IRON, TOO.
AND WHILE IT'S NOT PRECIOUS, COAL'S ALSO POPULAR.
IT CAN ONLY BE MINED FROM CERTAIN PLACES, AFTER ALL.
IS COAL MINING REALLY THAT BAD?
MAYBE...
IS THERE ANYTHING THAT'D BE EVEN MORE DAMAGING TO A MOUNTAIN?
THAT'S HARD TO MEASURE...

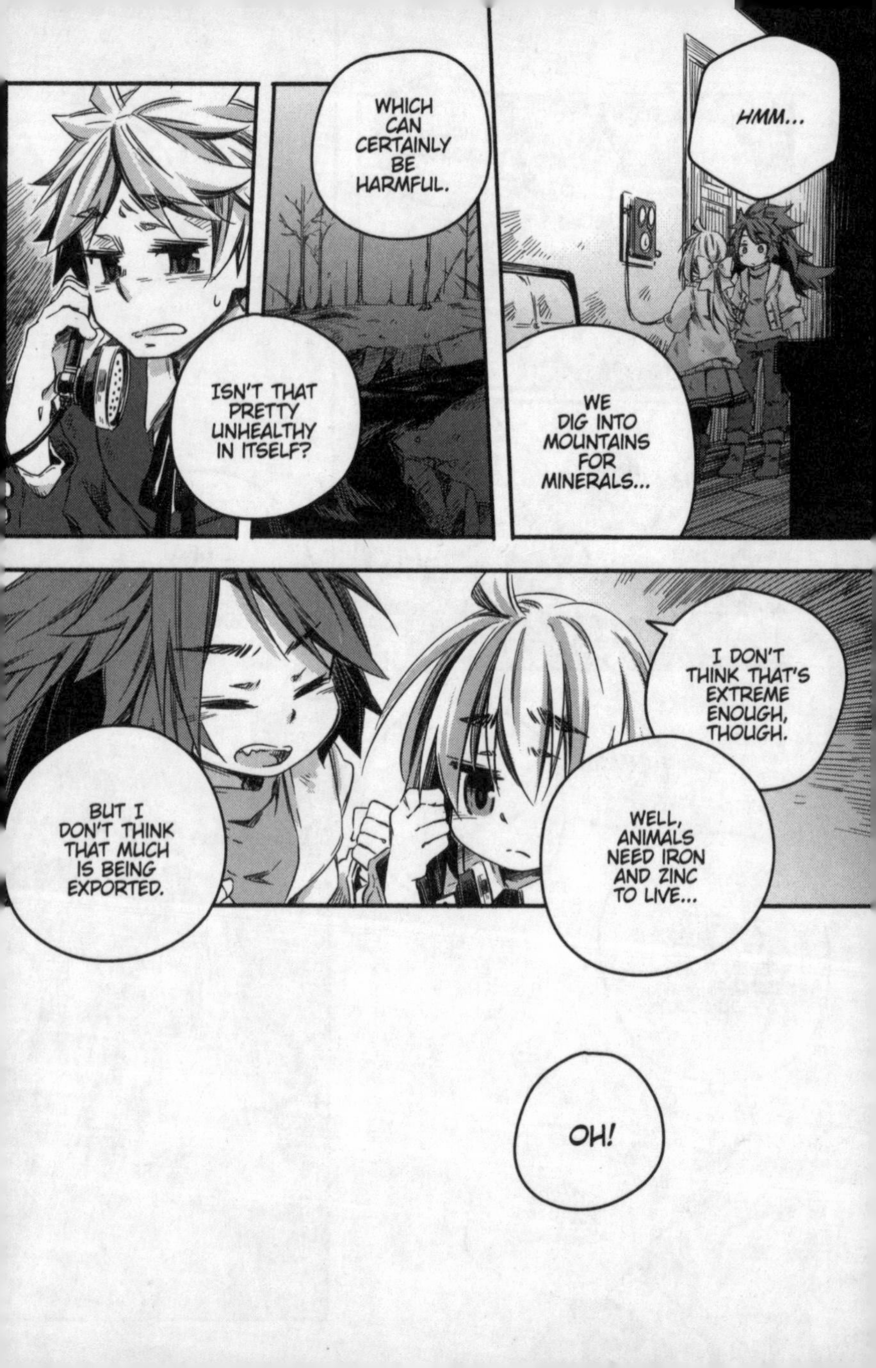
HMM...
WE DIG INTO MOUNTAINS FOR MINERALS...
WHICH CAN CERTAINLY BE HARMFUL.
ISN'T THAT PRETTY UNHEALTHY IN ITSELF?
I DON'T THINK THAT'S EXTREME ENOUGH, THOUGH.
WELL, ANIMALS NEED IRON AND ZINC TO LIVE...
BUT I DON'T THINK THAT MUCH IS BEING EXPORTED.
OH!

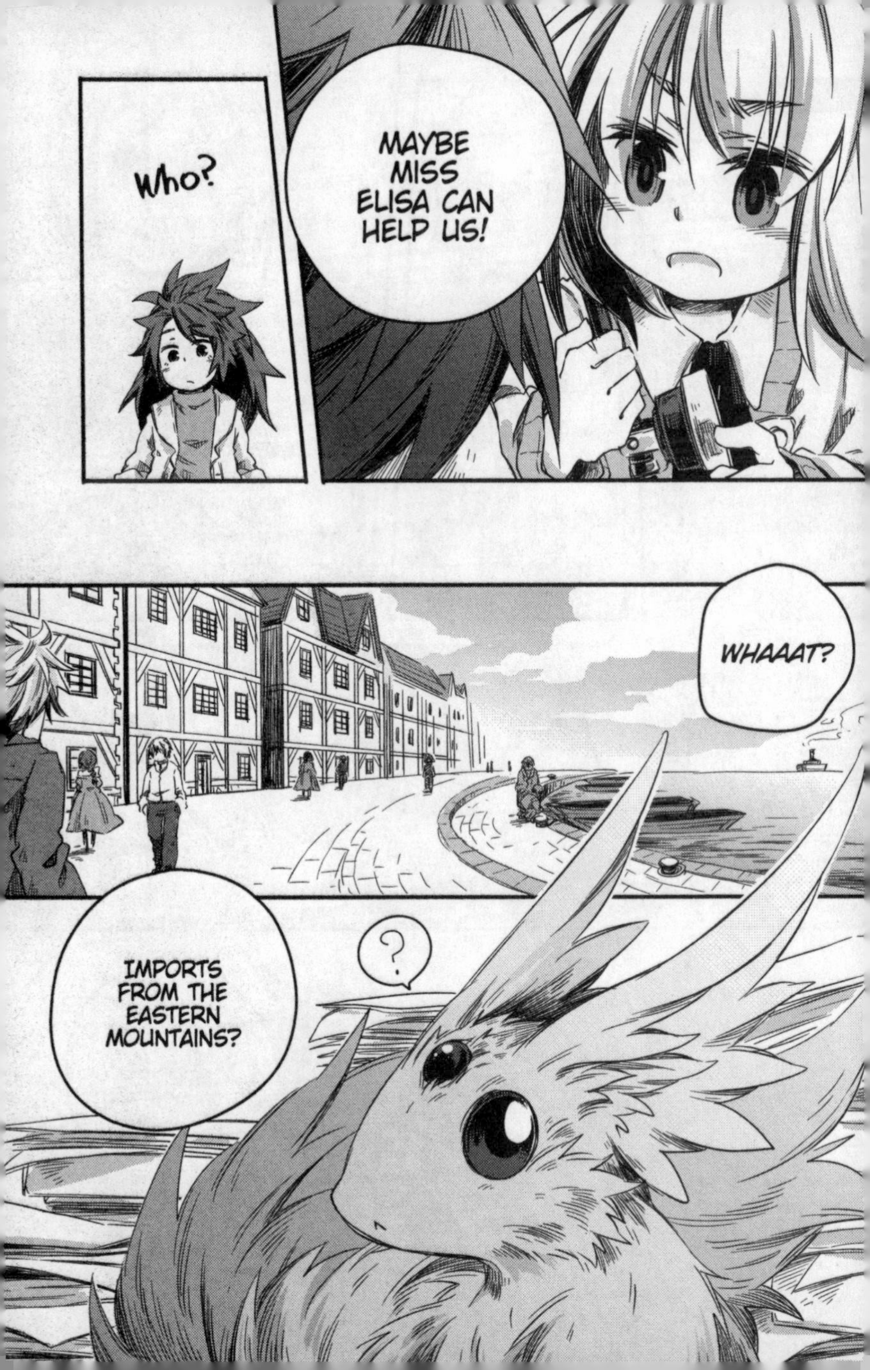
MAYBE MISS ELISA CAN HELP US!
Who?
WHAAAT?
IMPORTS FROM THE EASTERN MOUNTAINS?
?

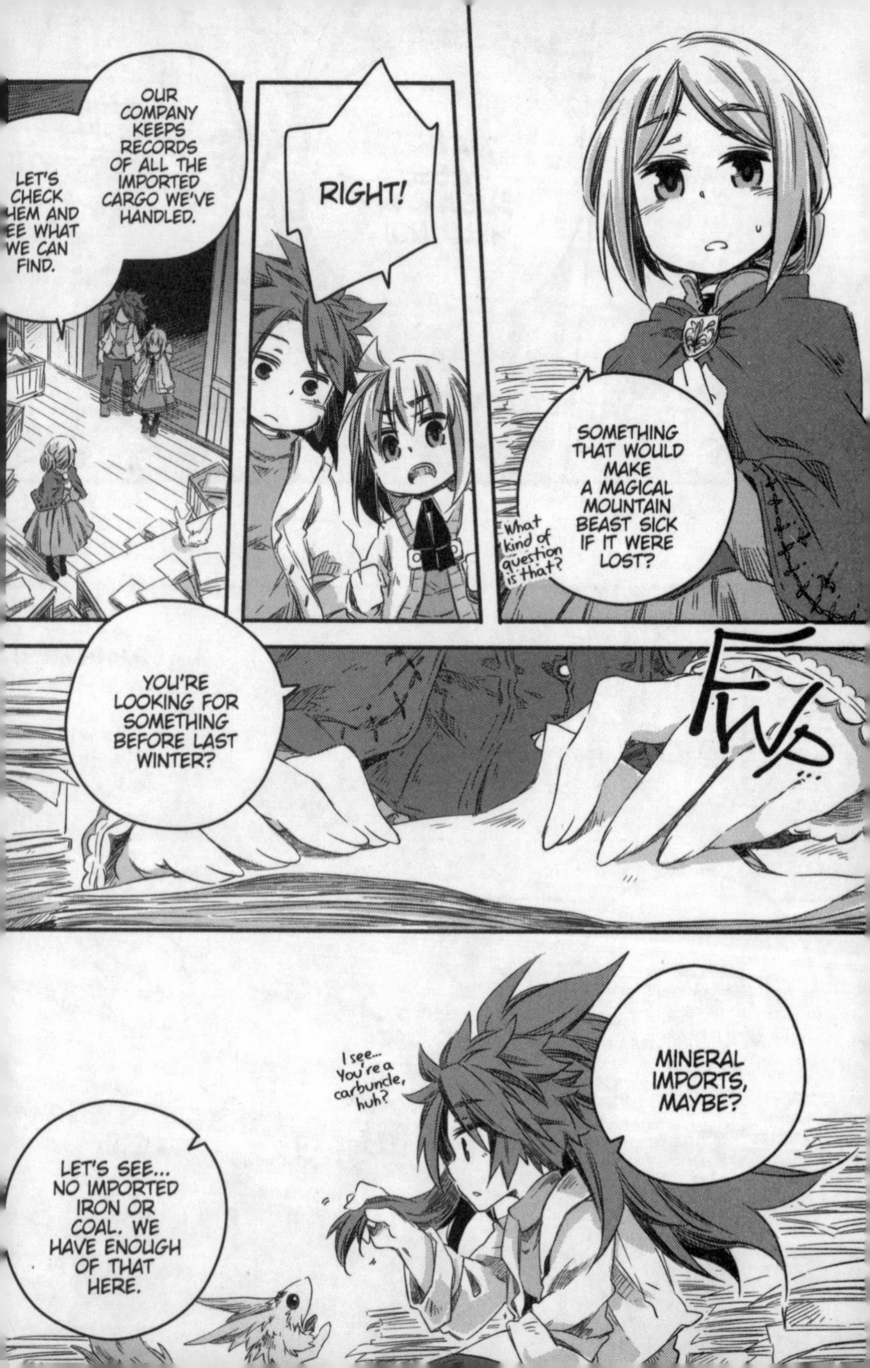
SOMETHING THAT WOULD MAKE A MAGICAL MOUNTAIN BEAST SICK IF IT WERE LOST?
What kind of question is that?
RIGHT!
OUR COMPANY KEEPS RECORDS OF ALL THE IMPORTED CARGO WE'VE HANDLED.
LET'S CHECK HEM AND EE WHAT WE CAN FIND.
FWP
YOU'RE LOOKING FOR SOMETHING BEFORE LAST WINTER?
MINERAL IMPORTS, MAYBE?
I see... You're a carbuncle, huh?
LET'S SEE... NO IMPORTED IRON OR COAL. WE HAVE ENOUGH OF THAT HERE.

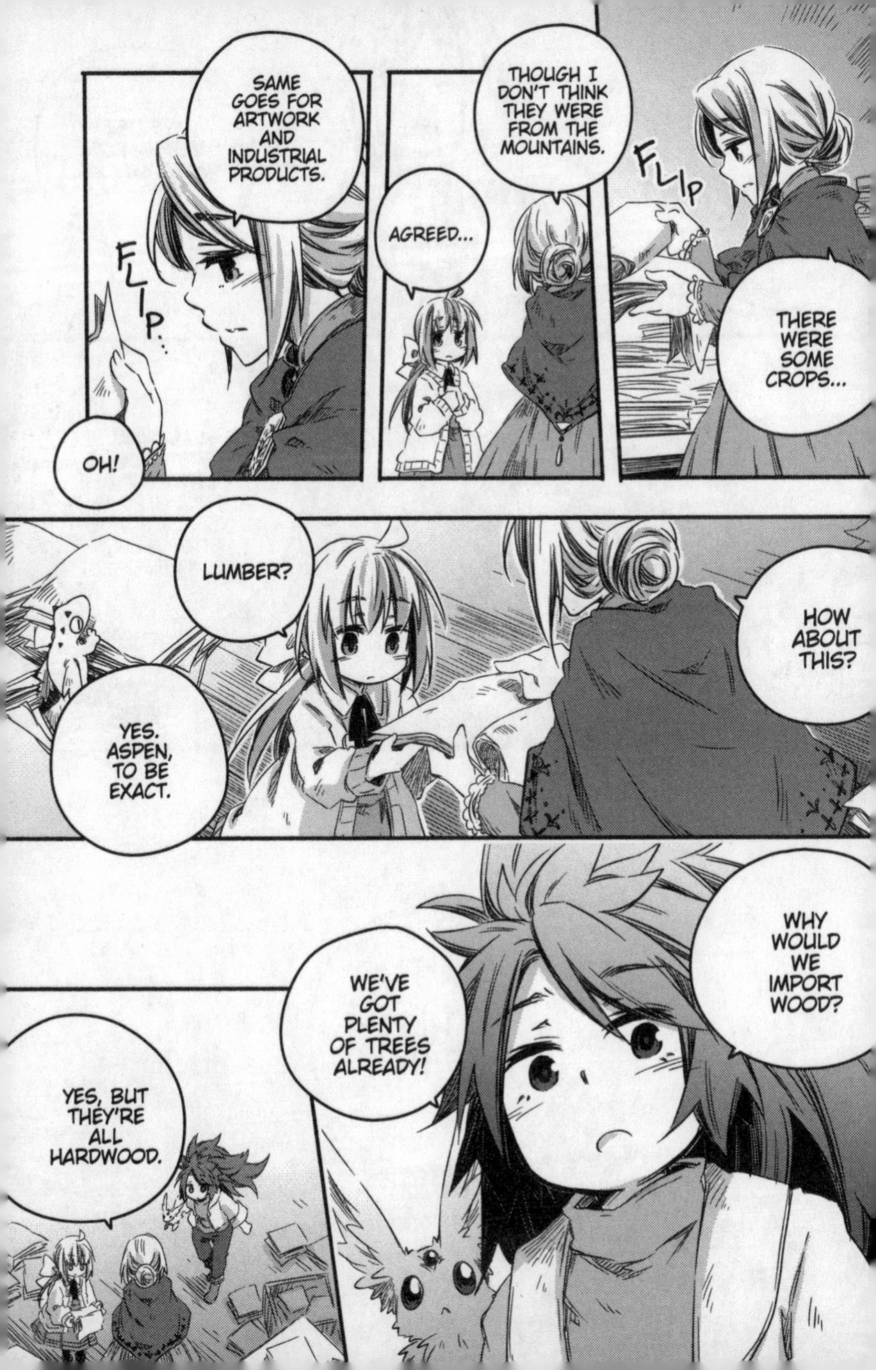
FLIP
THERE WERE SOME CROPS...
THOUGH I DON'T THINK THEY WERE FROM THE MOUNTAINS.
AGREED...
SAME GOES FOR ARTWORK AND INDUSTRIAL PRODUCTS.
FLIP...
OH!
HOW ABOUT THIS?
LUMBER?
YES. ASPEN, TO BE EXACT.
WHY WOULD WE IMPORT WOOD?
WE'VE GOT PLENTY OF TREES ALREADY!
YES, BUT THEY'RE ALL HARDWOOD.

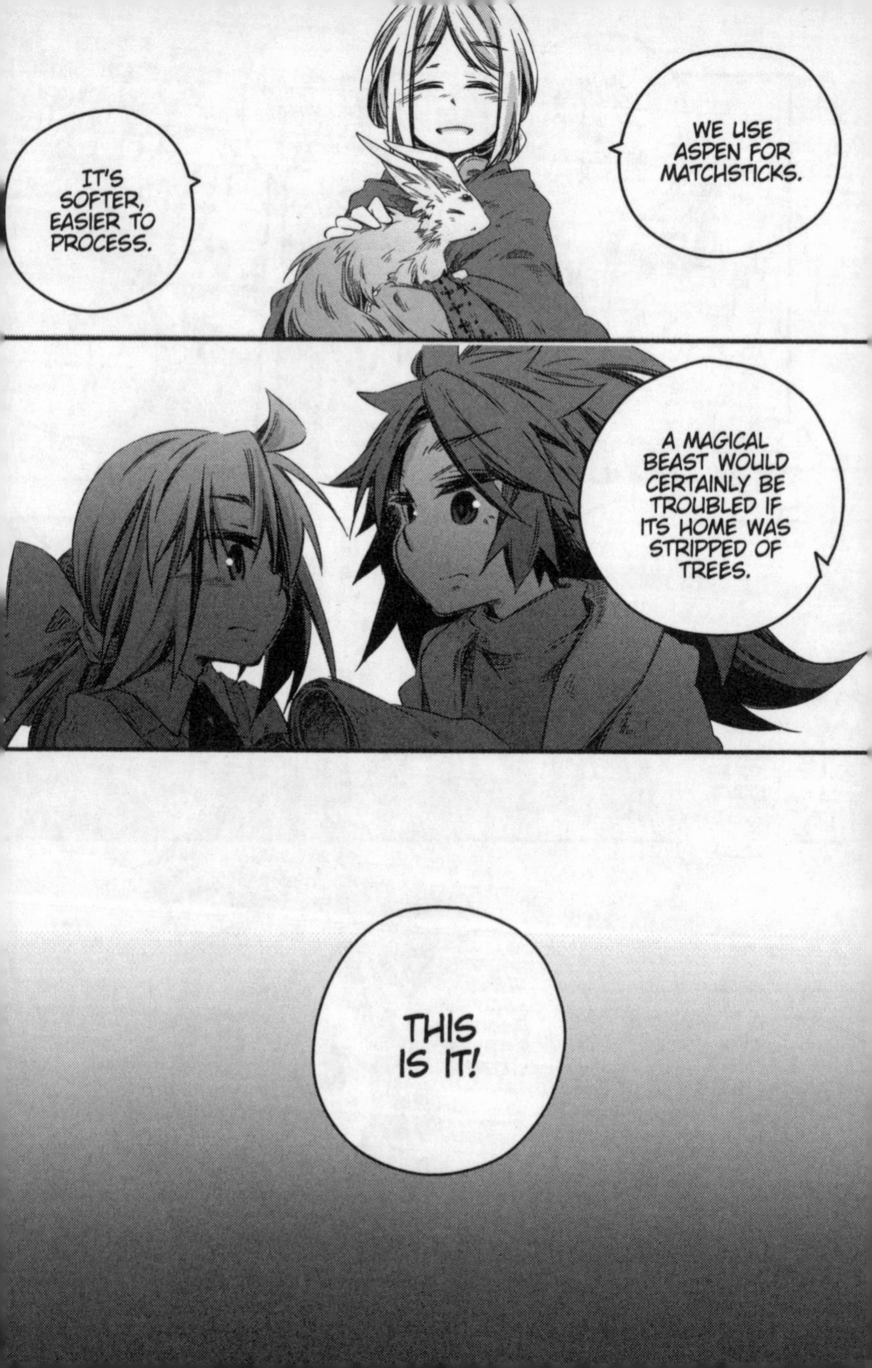
WE USE ASPEN FOR MATCHSTICKS.
IT'S SOFTER, EASIER TO PROCESS.
A MAGICAL BEAST WOULD CERTAINLY BE TROUBLED IF ITS HOME WAS STRIPPED OF TREES.
THIS IS IT!

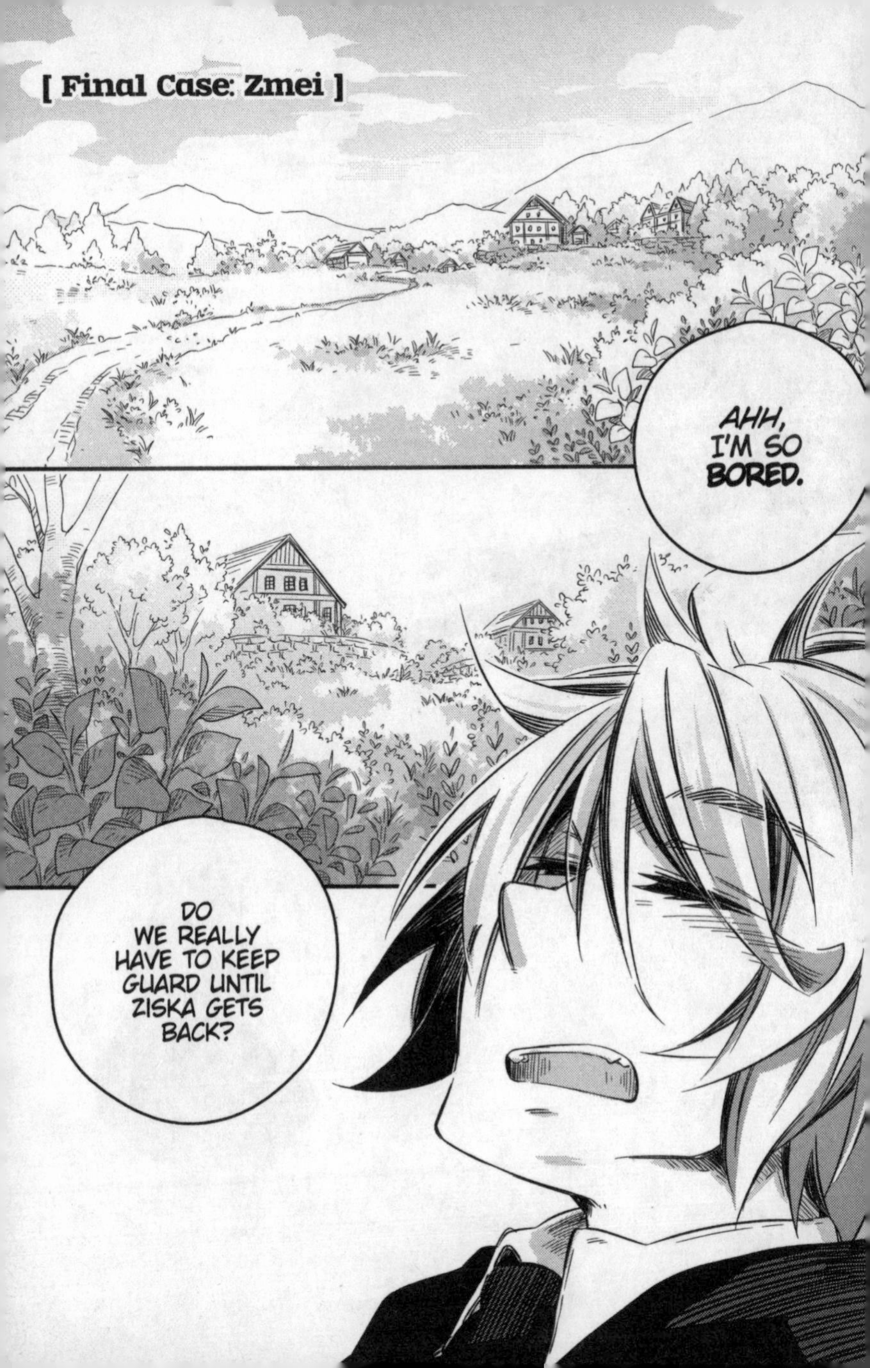
[Final Case: Zmei]
AHH, I'M SO BORED.
DO WE REALLY HAVE TO KEEP GUARD UNTIL ZISKA GETS BACK?

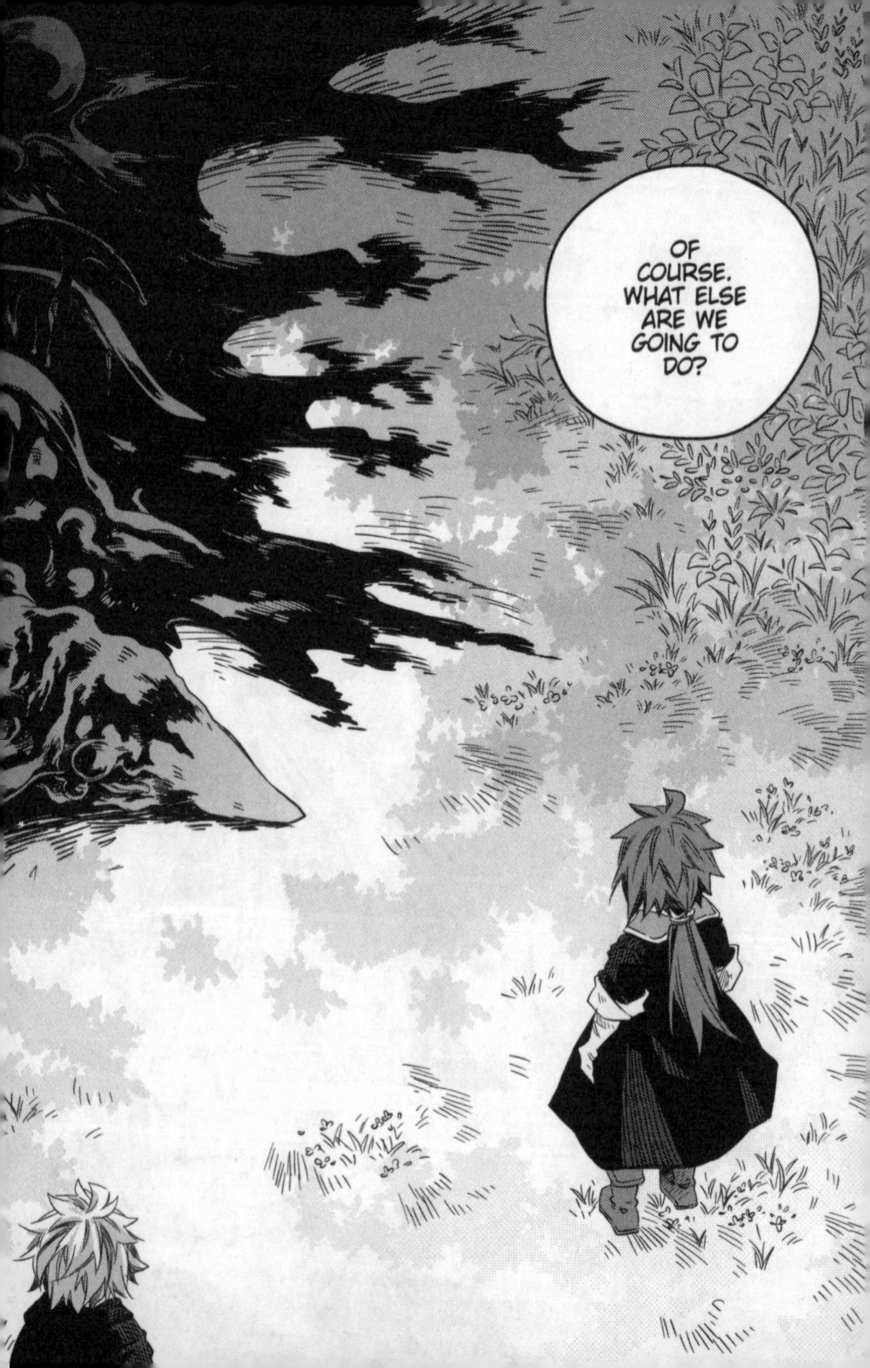
OF COURSE. WHAT ELSE ARE WE GOING TO DO?

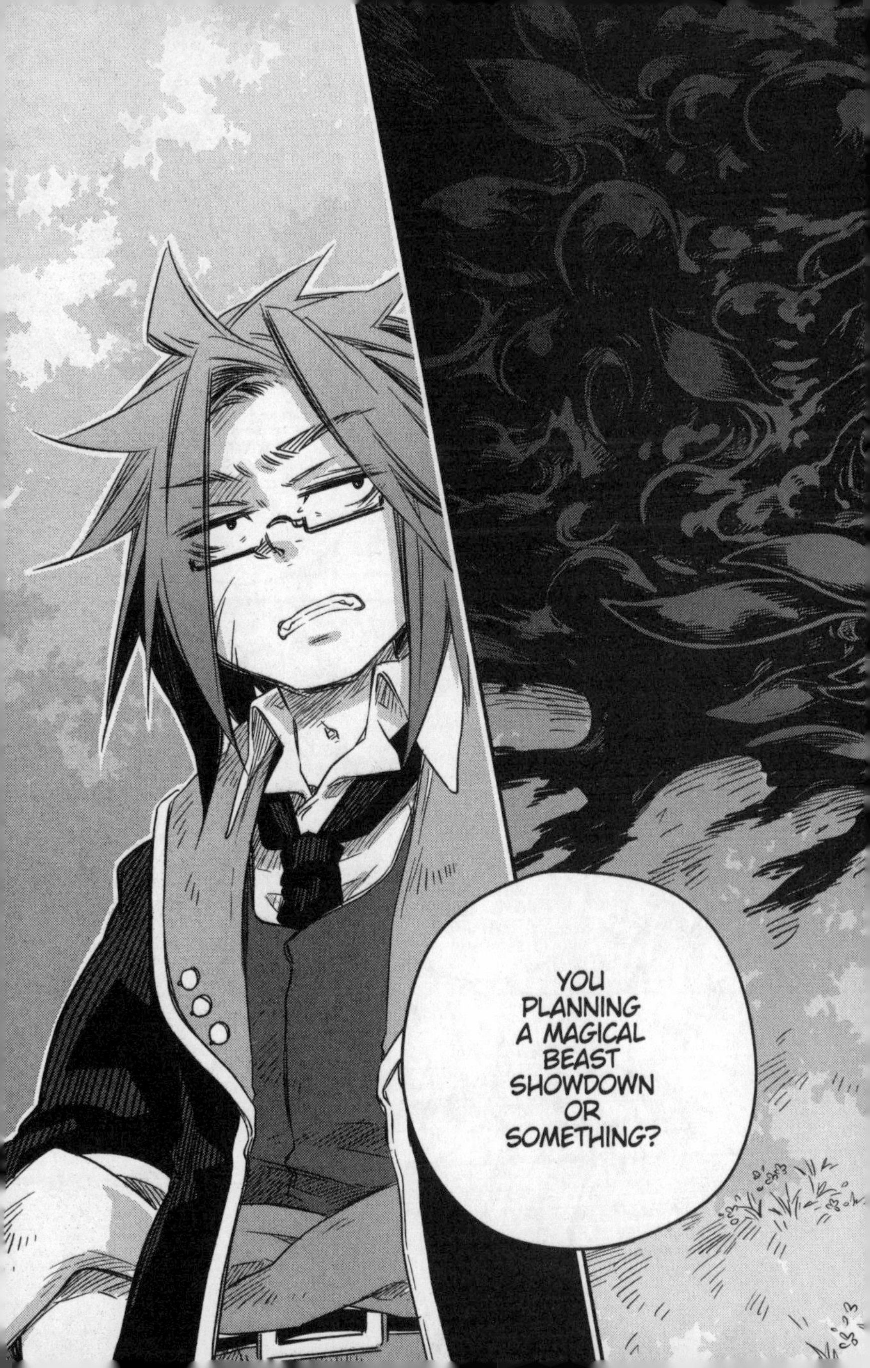
YOU PLANNING A MAGICAL BEAST SHOWDOWN OR SOMETHING?

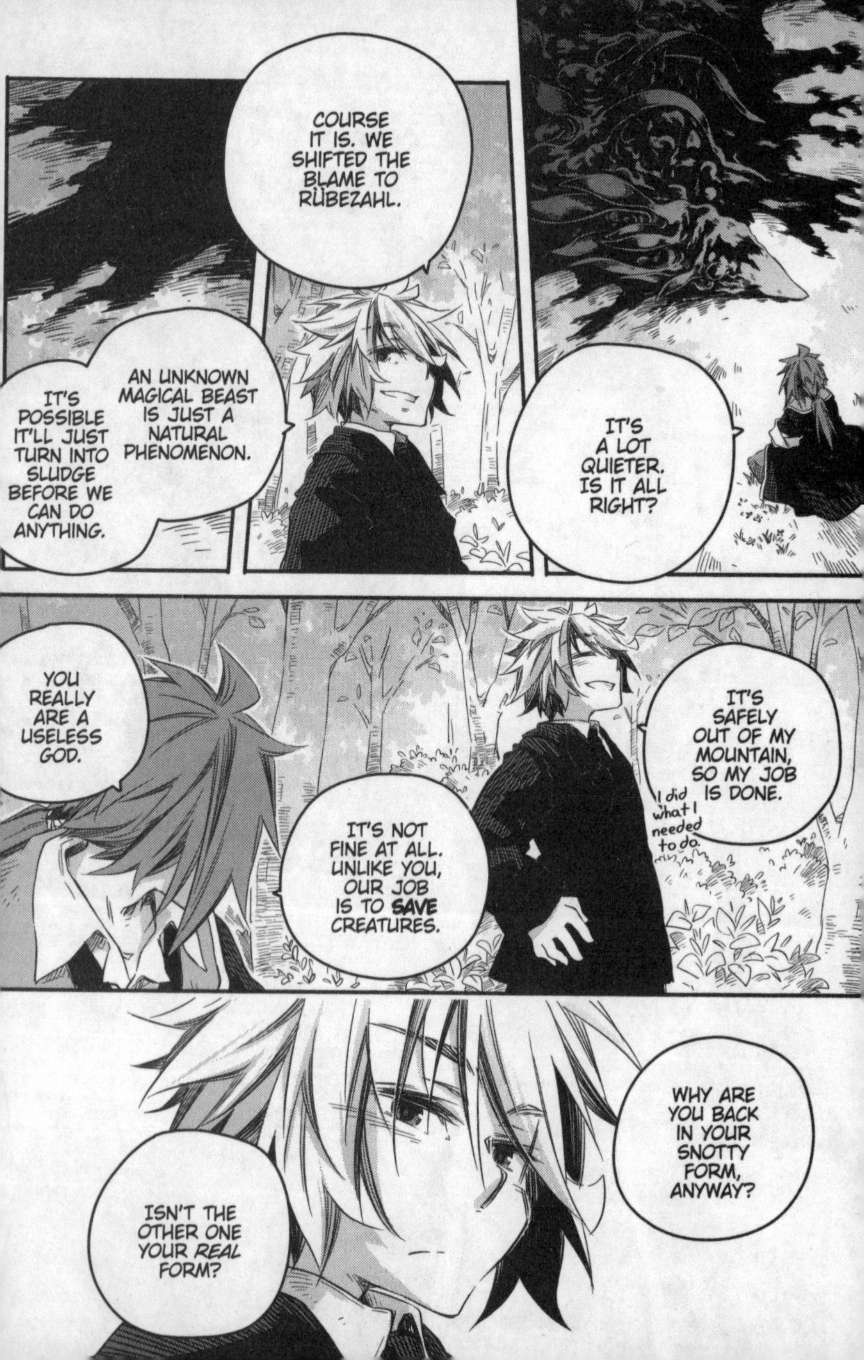
IT'S A LOT QUIETER. IS IT ALL RIGHT?
COURSE IT IS. WE SHIFTED THE BLAME TO RÜBEZAHL.
AN UNKNOWN MAGICAL BEAST IS JUST A NATURAL PHENOMENON.
IT'S POSSIBLE IT'LL JUST TURN INTO SLUDGE BEFORE WE CAN DO ANYTHING.
IT'S SAFELY OUT OF MY MOUNTAIN, SO MY JOB IS DONE.
I did what I needed to do.
IT'S NOT FINE AT ALL. UNLIKE YOU, OUR JOB IS TO **SAVE** CREATURES.
YOU REALLY ARE A USELESS GOD.
WHY ARE YOU BACK IN YOUR SNOTTY FORM, ANYWAY?
ISN'T THE OTHER ONE YOUR *REAL* FORM?

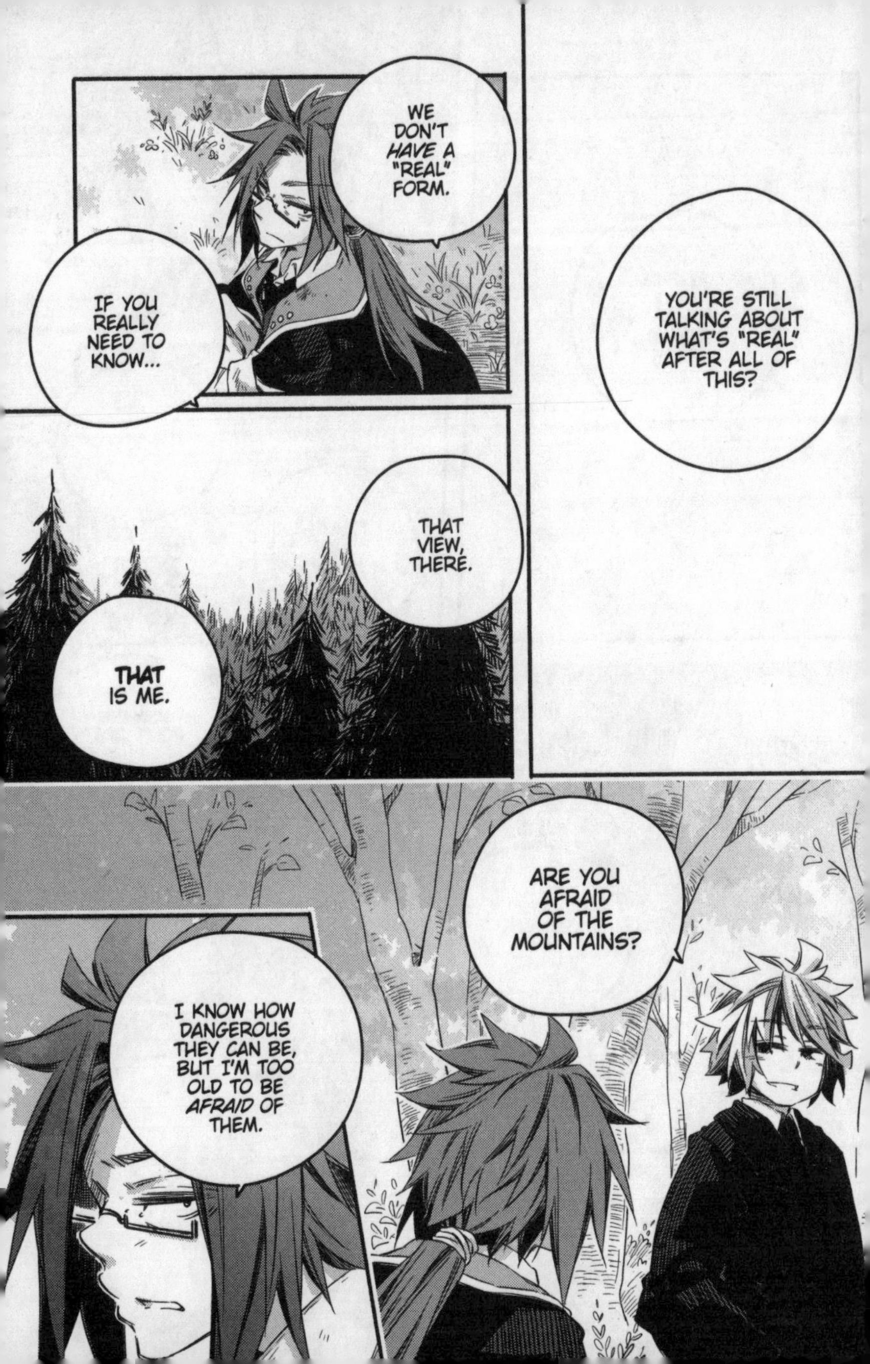
YOU'RE STILL TALKING ABOUT WHAT'S "REAL" AFTER ALL OF THIS?
WE DON'T HAVE A "REAL" FORM.
IF YOU REALLY NEED TO KNOW...
THAT VIEW, THERE.
THAT IS ME.
ARE YOU AFRAID OF THE MOUNTAINS?
I KNOW HOW DANGEROUS THEY CAN BE, BUT I'M TOO OLD TO BE AFRAID OF THEM.

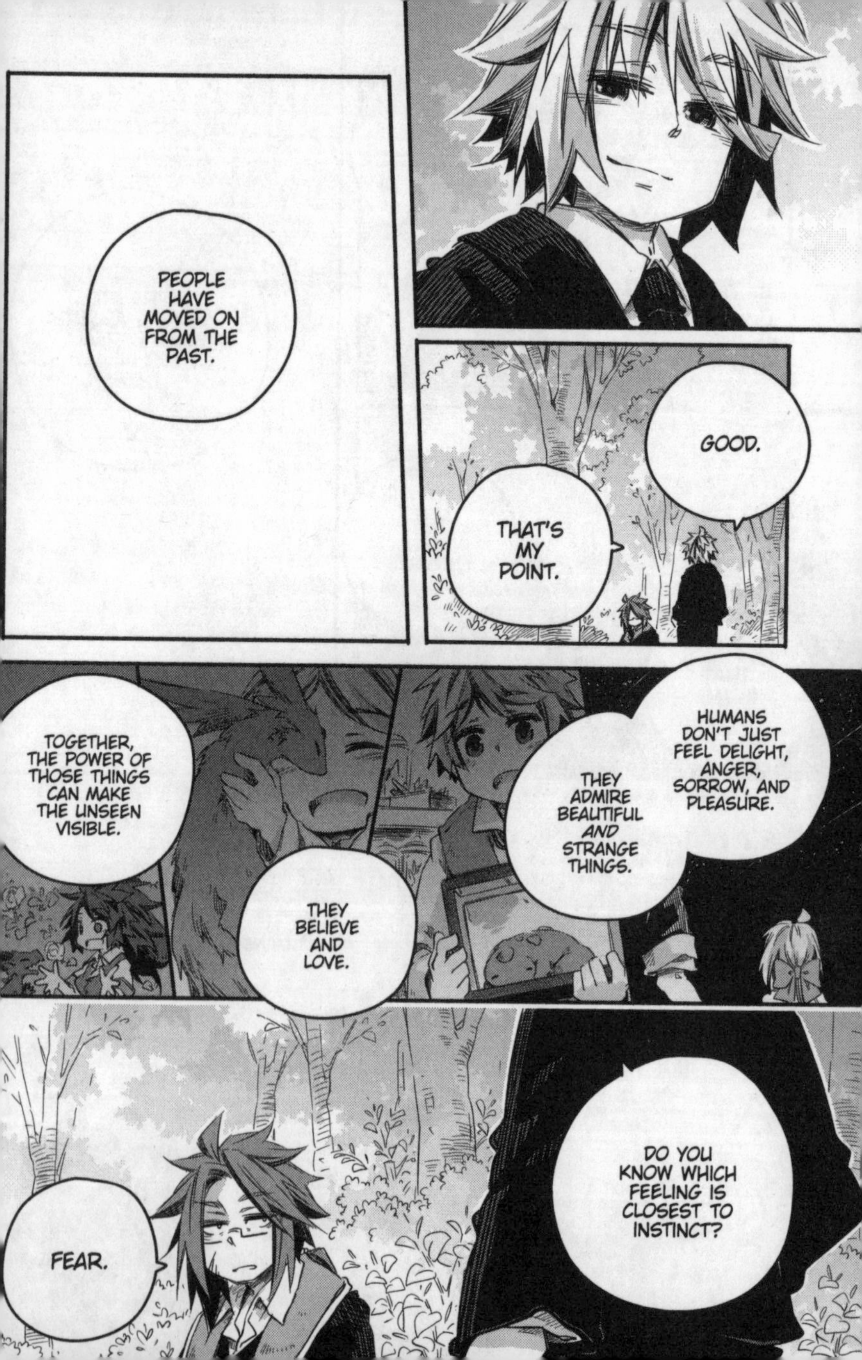
GOOD.
THAT'S MY POINT.
PEOPLE HAVE MOVED ON FROM THE PAST.
HUMANS DON'T JUST FEEL DELIGHT, ANGER, SORROW, AND PLEASURE.
THEY ADMIRE BEAUTIFUL *AND* STRANGE THINGS.
THEY BELIEVE AND LOVE.
TOGETHER, THE POWER OF THOSE THINGS CAN MAKE THE UNSEEN VISIBLE.
DO YOU KNOW WHICH FEELING IS CLOSEST TO INSTINCT?
FEAR.

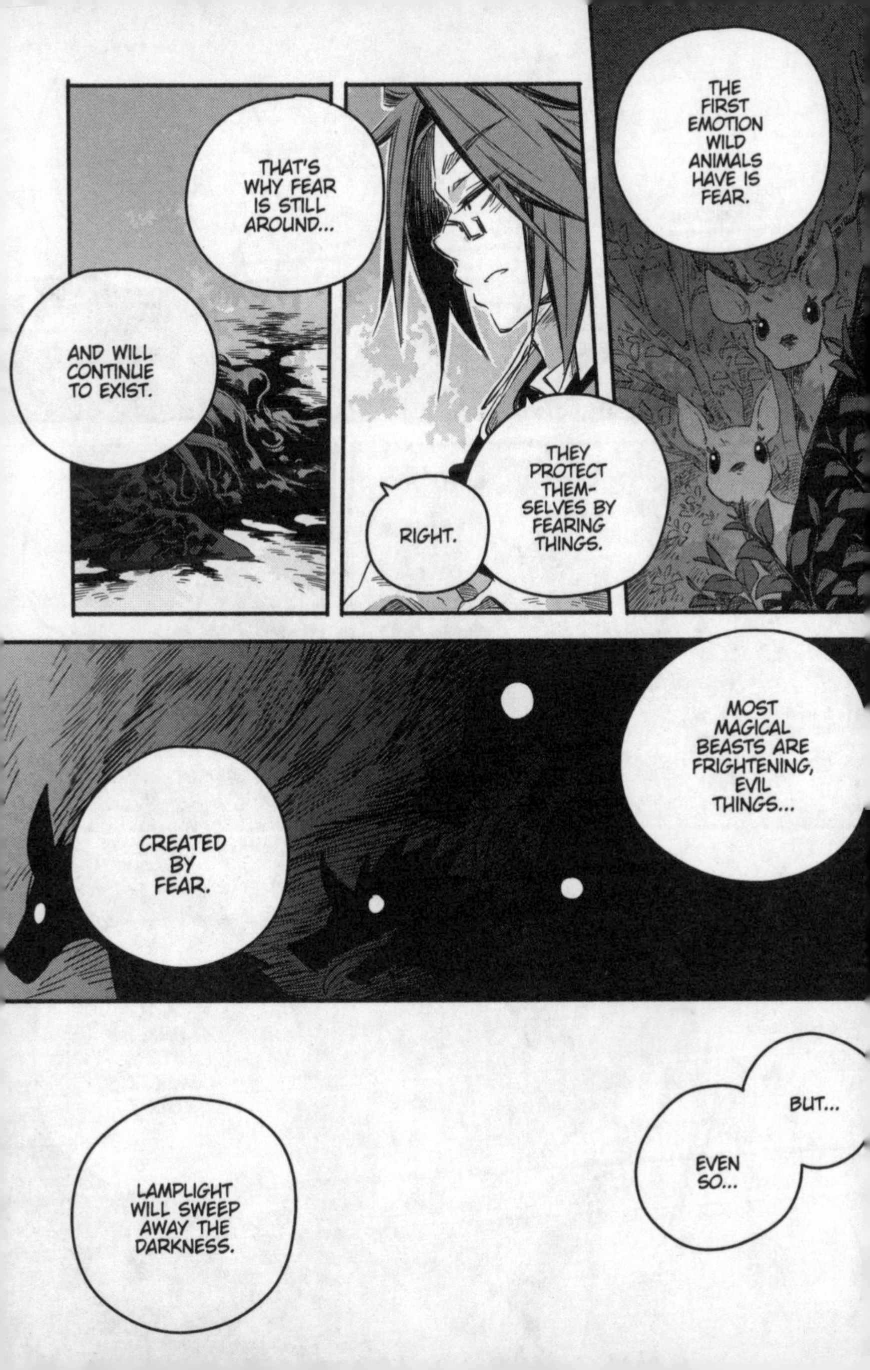
THE FIRST EMOTION WILD ANIMALS HAVE IS FEAR.
THEY PROTECT THEM-SELVES BY FEARING THINGS.
RIGHT.
THAT'S WHY FEAR IS STILL AROUND...
AND WILL CONTINUE TO EXIST.
MOST MAGICAL BEASTS ARE FRIGHTENING, EVIL THINGS...
CREATED BY FEAR.
BUT...
EVEN SO...
LAMPLIGHT WILL SWEEP AWAY THE DARKNESS.

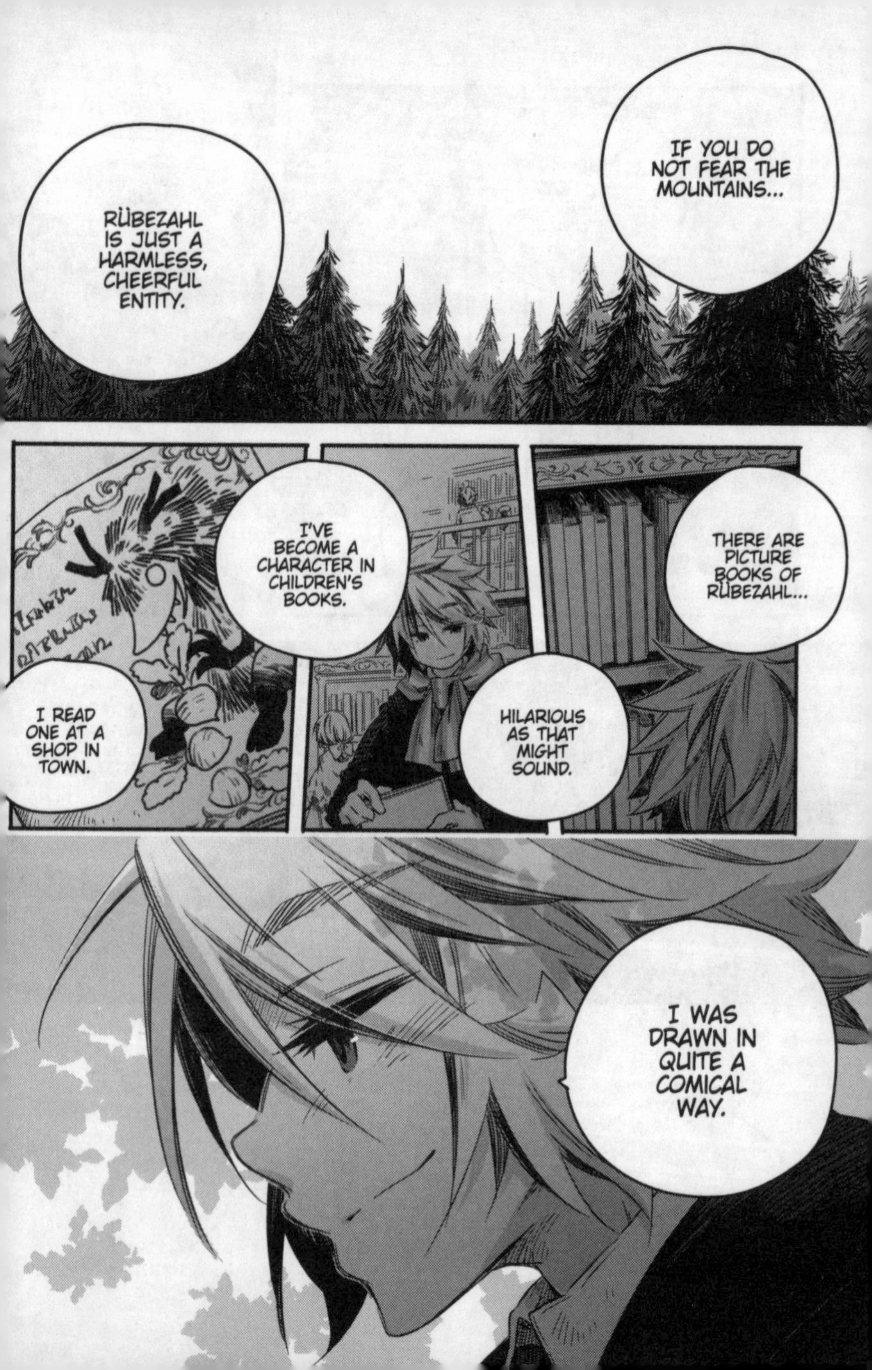
IF YOU DO NOT FEAR THE MOUNTAINS...
RÜBEZAHL IS JUST A HARMLESS, CHEERFUL ENTITY.
THERE ARE PICTURE BOOKS OF RÜBEZAHL...
HILARIOUS AS THAT MIGHT SOUND.
I'VE BECOME A CHARACTER IN CHILDREN'S BOOKS.
I READ ONE AT A SHOP IN TOWN.
I WAS DRAWN IN QUITE A COMICAL WAY.

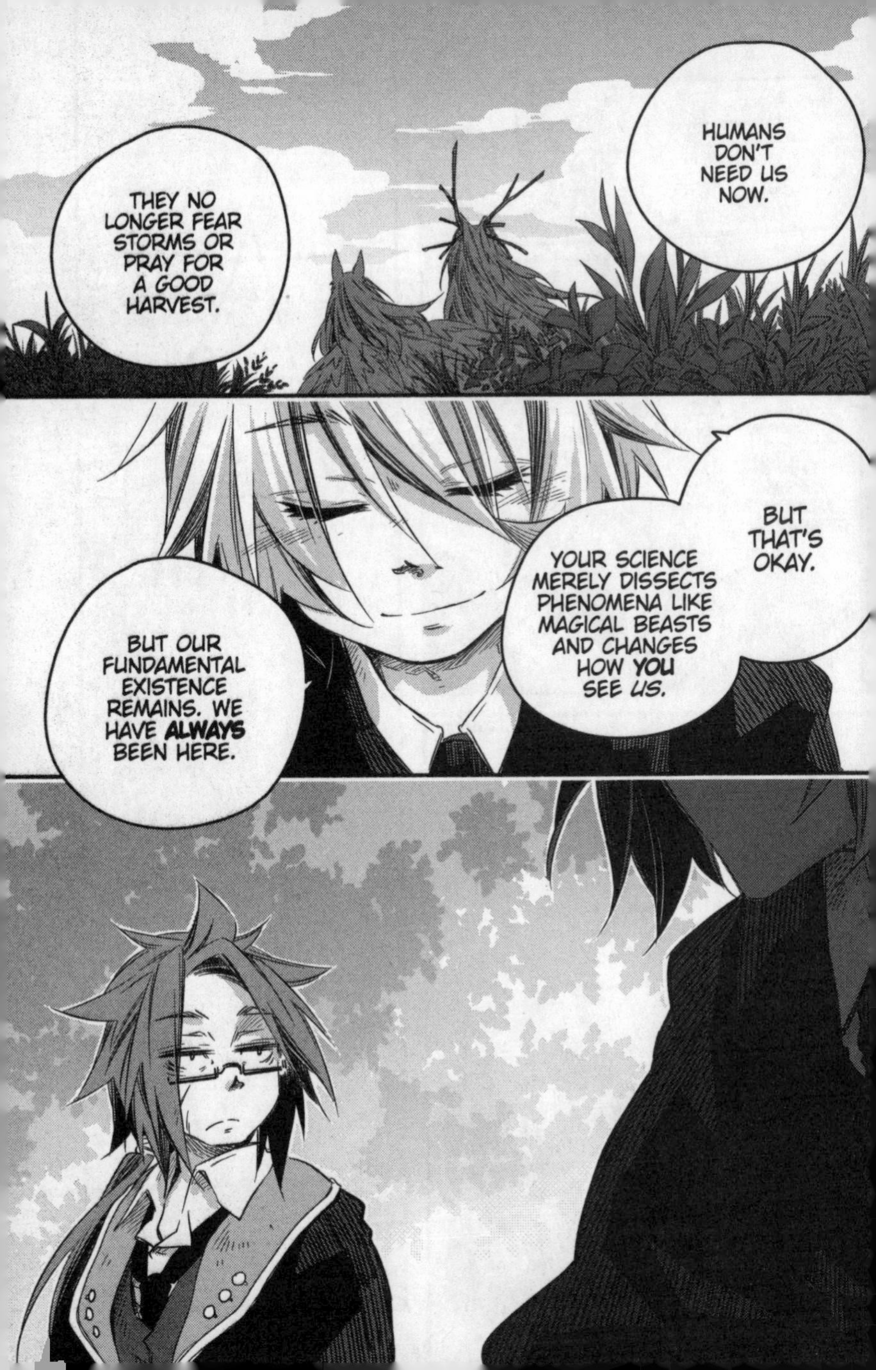
HUMANS DON'T NEED US NOW.
THEY NO LONGER FEAR STORMS OR PRAY FOR A GOOD HARVEST.
BUT THAT'S OKAY.
YOUR SCIENCE MERELY DISSECTS PHENOMENA LIKE MAGICAL BEASTS AND CHANGES HOW YOU SEE US.
BUT OUR FUNDAMENTAL EXISTENCE REMAINS. WE HAVE ALWAYS BEEN HERE.

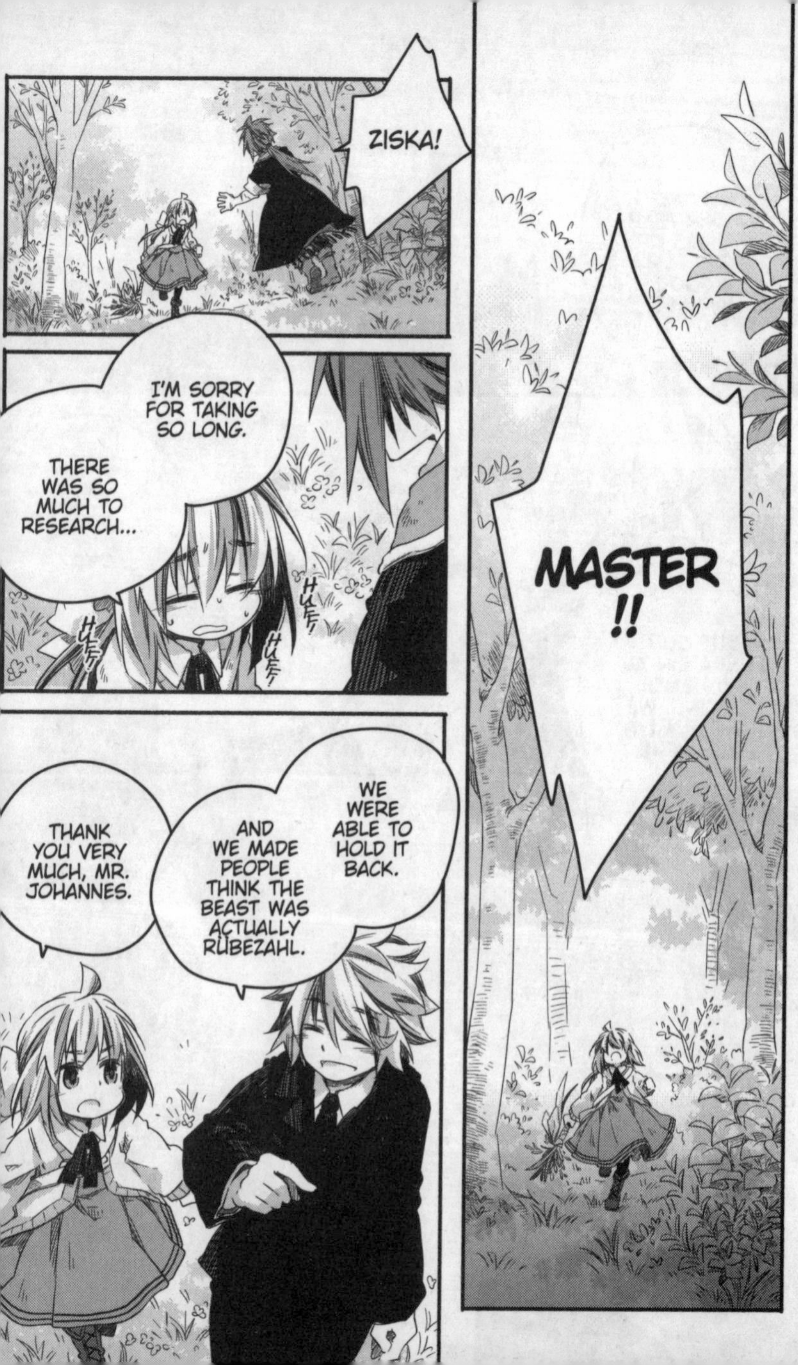
MASTER !!
ZISKA!
I'M SORRY FOR TAKING SO LONG.
THERE WAS SO MUCH TO RESEARCH...
HUFF!
HUFF!
HUFF!
WE WERE ABLE TO HOLD IT BACK.
AND WE MADE PEOPLE THINK THE BEAST WAS ACTUALLY RÜBEZAHL.
THANK YOU VERY MUCH, MR. JOHANNES.

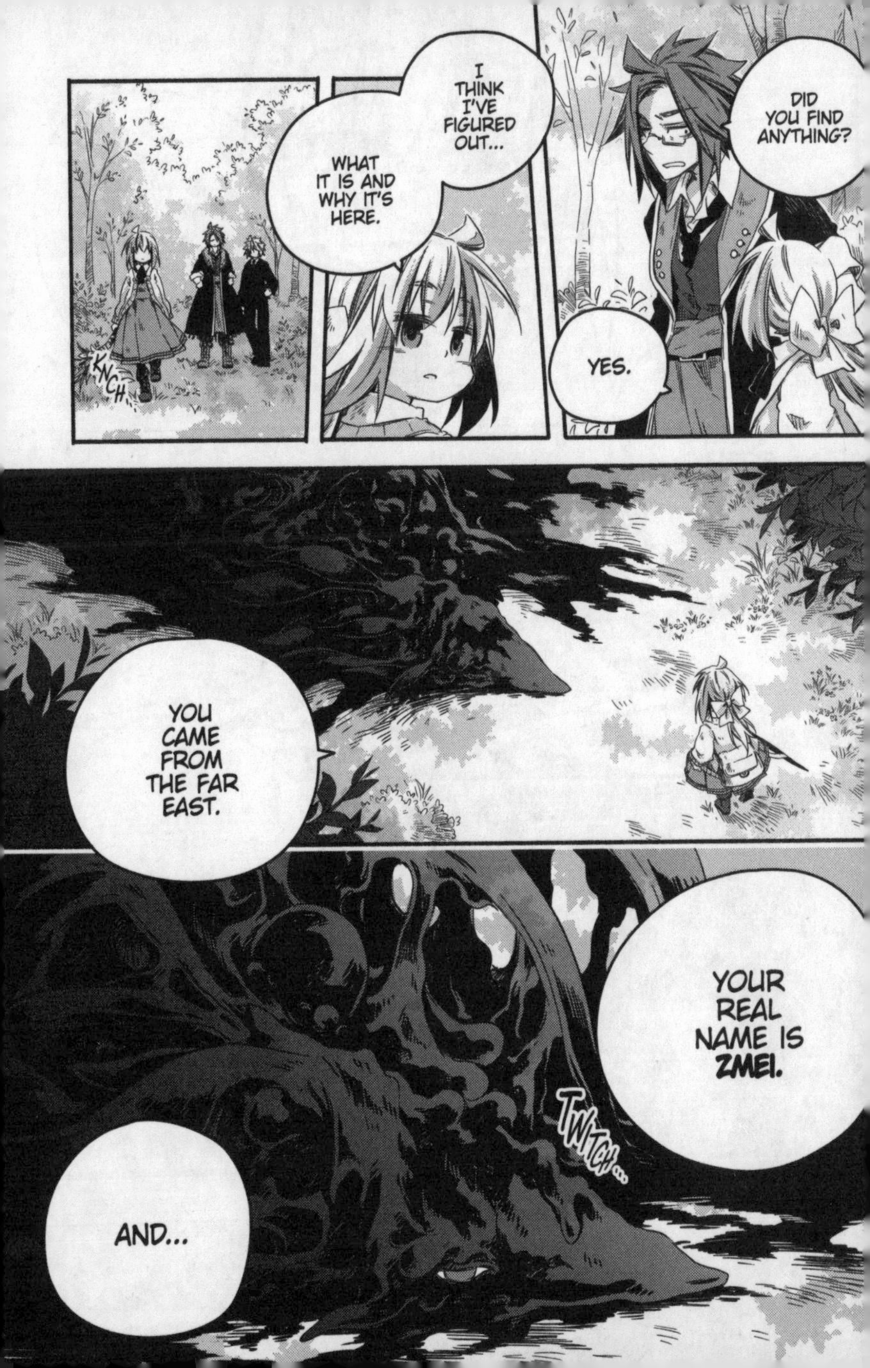
DID YOU FIND ANYTHING?
YES.
I THINK I'VE FIGURED OUT...
WHAT IT IS AND WHY IT'S HERE.
KNCH...
YOU CAME FROM THE FAR EAST.
YOUR REAL NAME IS **ZMEI.**
TWITCH...
AND...

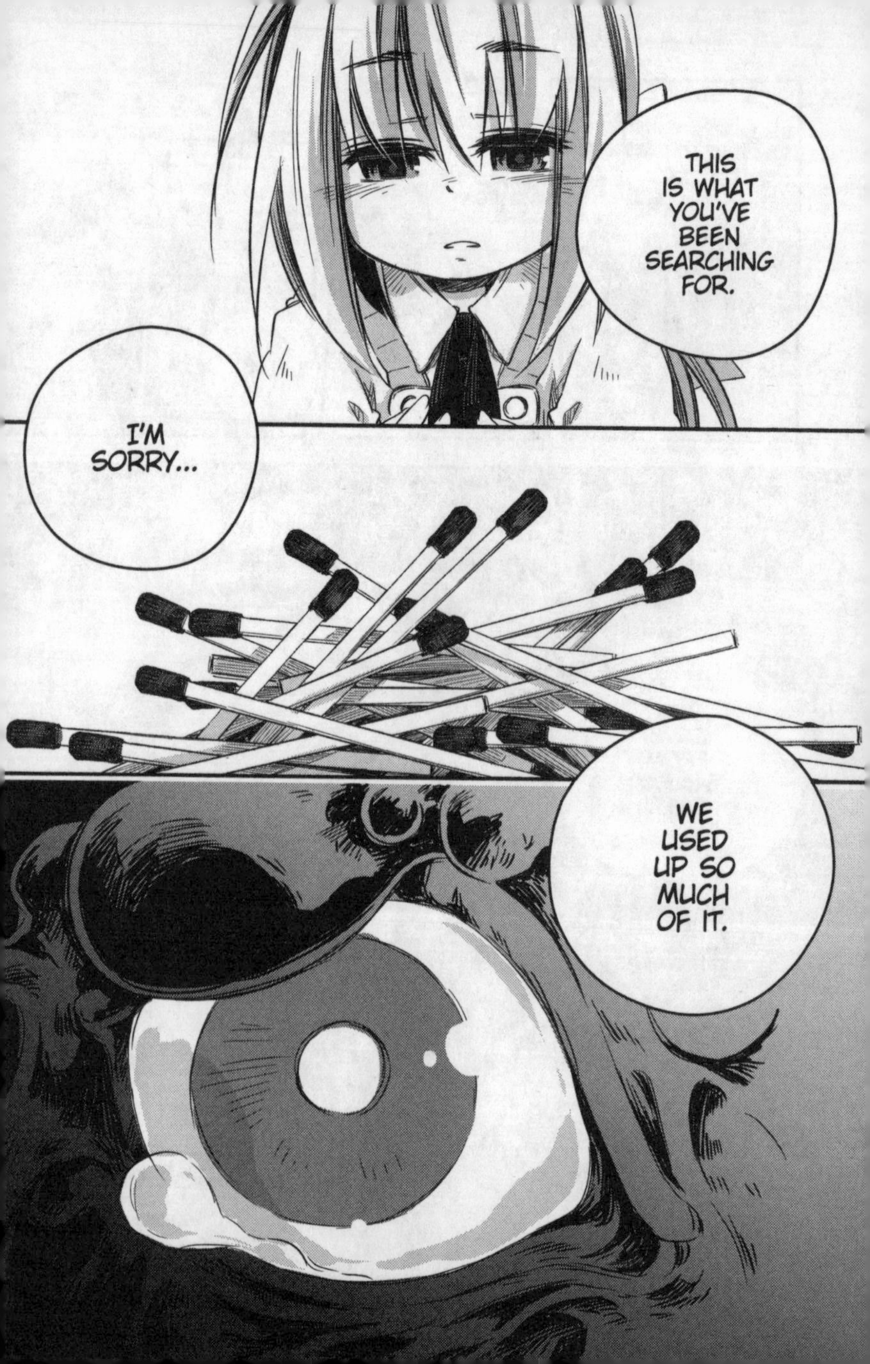
THIS IS WHAT YOU'VE BEEN SEARCHING FOR.
I'M SORRY...
WE USED UP SO MUCH OF IT.

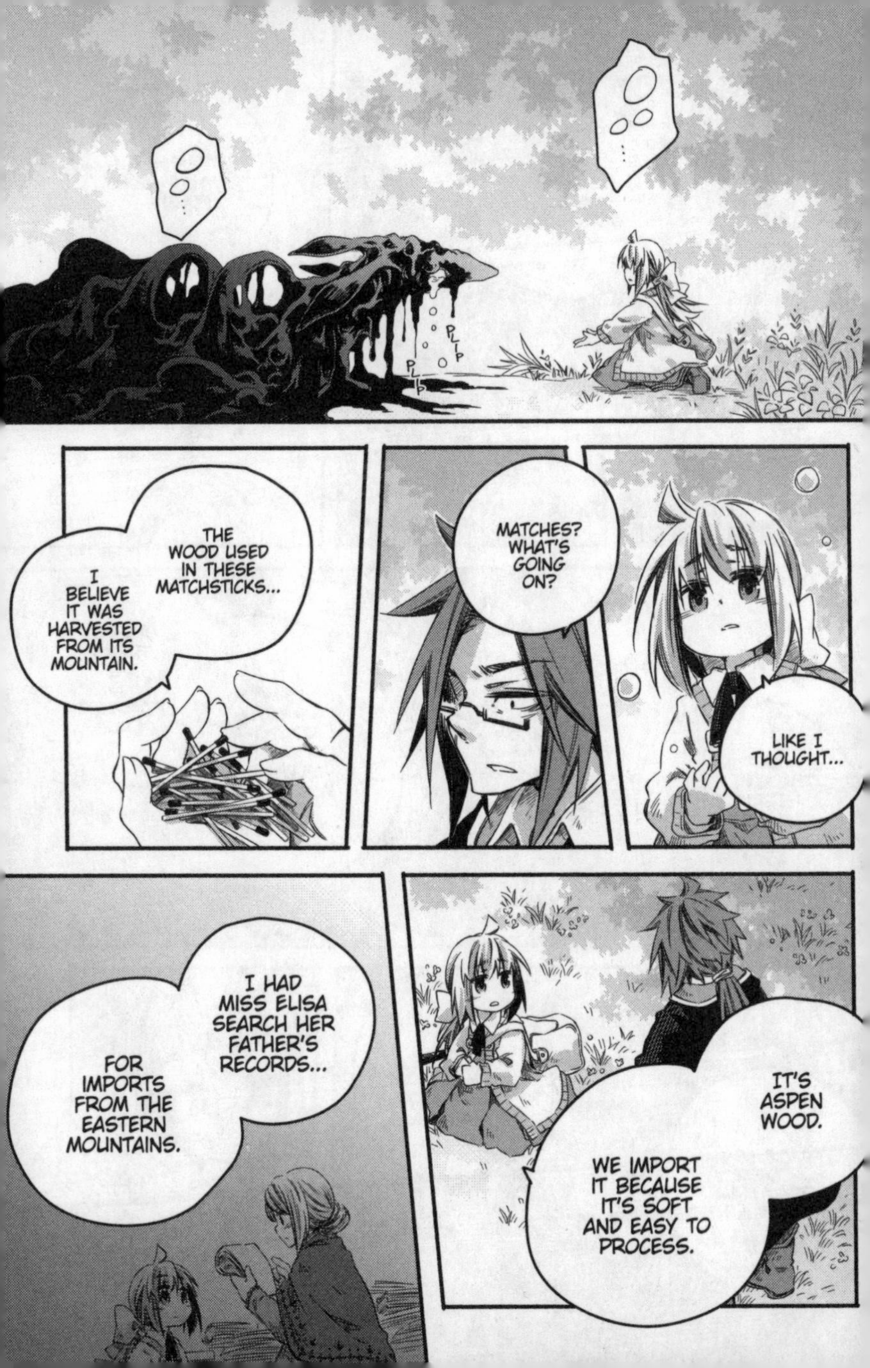
...
...
PLIP
PLIP
LIKE I THOUGHT...
MATCHES? WHAT'S GOING ON?
THE WOOD USED IN THESE MATCHSTICKS...
I BELIEVE IT WAS HARVESTED FROM ITS MOUNTAIN.
IT'S ASPEN WOOD.
WE IMPORT IT BECAUSE IT'S SOFT AND EASY TO PROCESS.
I HAD MISS ELISA SEARCH HER FATHER'S RECORDS...
FOR IMPORTS FROM THE EASTERN MOUNTAINS.

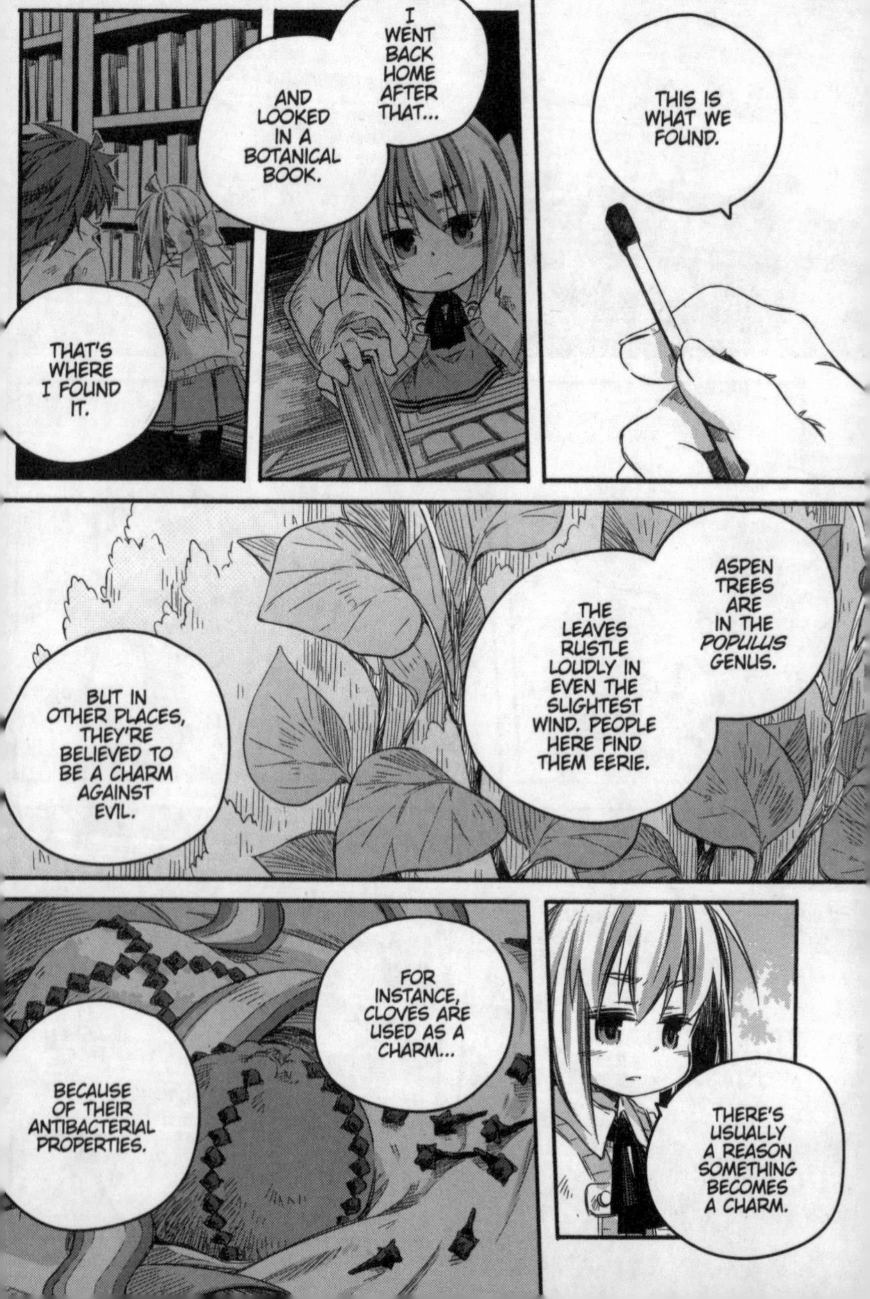
THIS IS WHAT WE FOUND.
I WENT BACK HOME AFTER THAT...
AND LOOKED IN A BOTANICAL BOOK.
THAT'S WHERE I FOUND IT.
ASPEN TREES ARE IN THE *POPULUS* GENUS.
THE LEAVES RUSTLE LOUDLY IN EVEN THE SLIGHTEST WIND. PEOPLE HERE FIND THEM EERIE.
BUT IN OTHER PLACES, THEY'RE BELIEVED TO BE A CHARM AGAINST EVIL.
THERE'S USUALLY A REASON SOMETHING BECOMES A CHARM.
FOR INSTANCE, CLOVES ARE USED AS A CHARM...
BECAUSE OF THEIR ANTIBACTERIAL PROPERTIES.

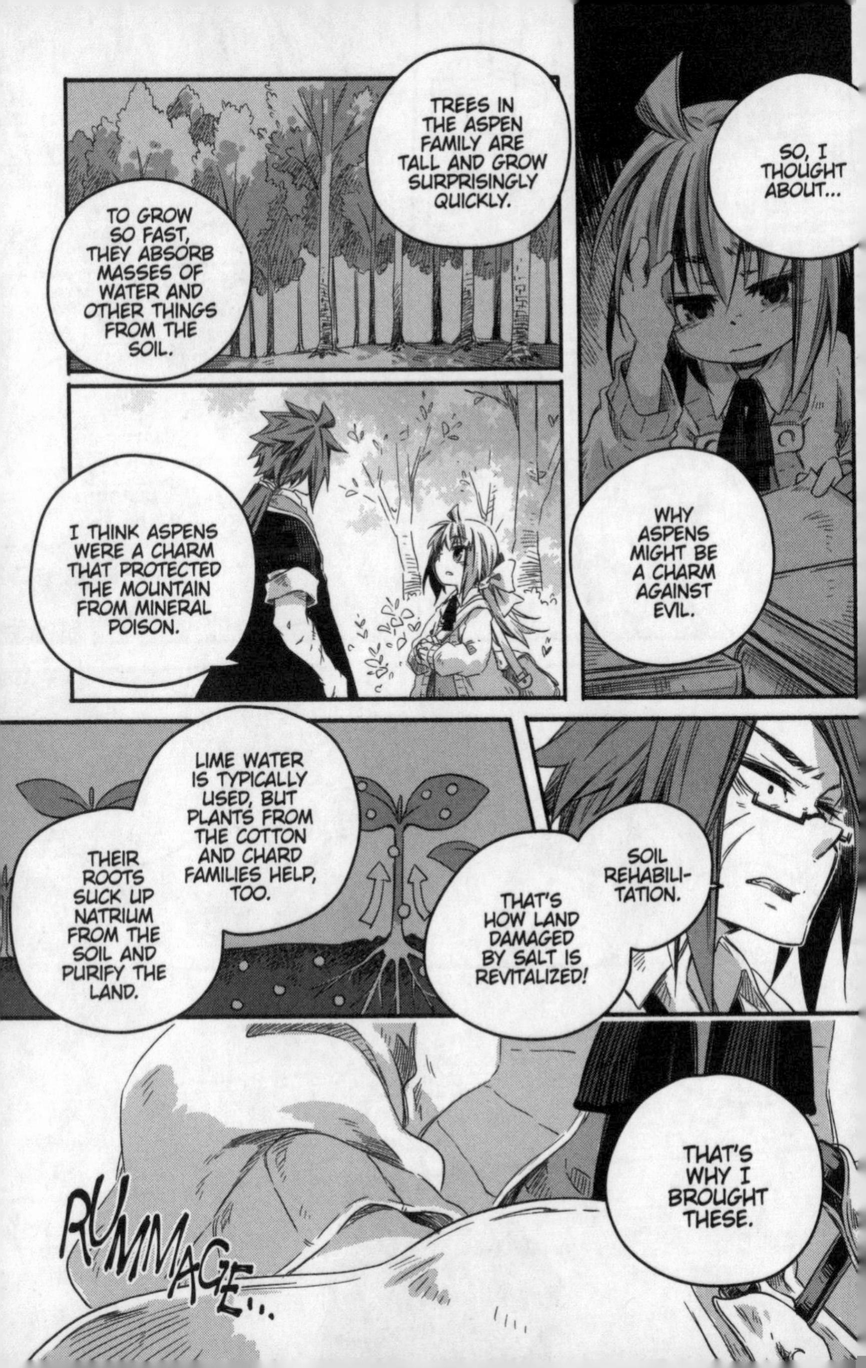
SO, I THOUGHT ABOUT...
WHY ASPENS MIGHT BE A CHARM AGAINST EVIL.
TREES IN THE ASPEN FAMILY ARE TALL AND GROW SURPRISINGLY QUICKLY.
TO GROW SO FAST, THEY ABSORB MASSES OF WATER AND OTHER THINGS FROM THE SOIL.
I THINK ASPENS WERE A CHARM THAT PROTECTED THE MOUNTAIN FROM MINERAL POISON.
SOIL REHABILITATION.
THAT'S HOW LAND DAMAGED BY SALT IS REVITALIZED!
LIME WATER IS TYPICALLY USED, BUT PLANTS FROM THE COTTON AND CHARD FAMILIES HELP, TOO.
THEIR ROOTS SUCK UP NATRIUM FROM THE SOIL AND PURIFY THE LAND.
THAT'S WHY I BROUGHT THESE.
RUMMAGE...

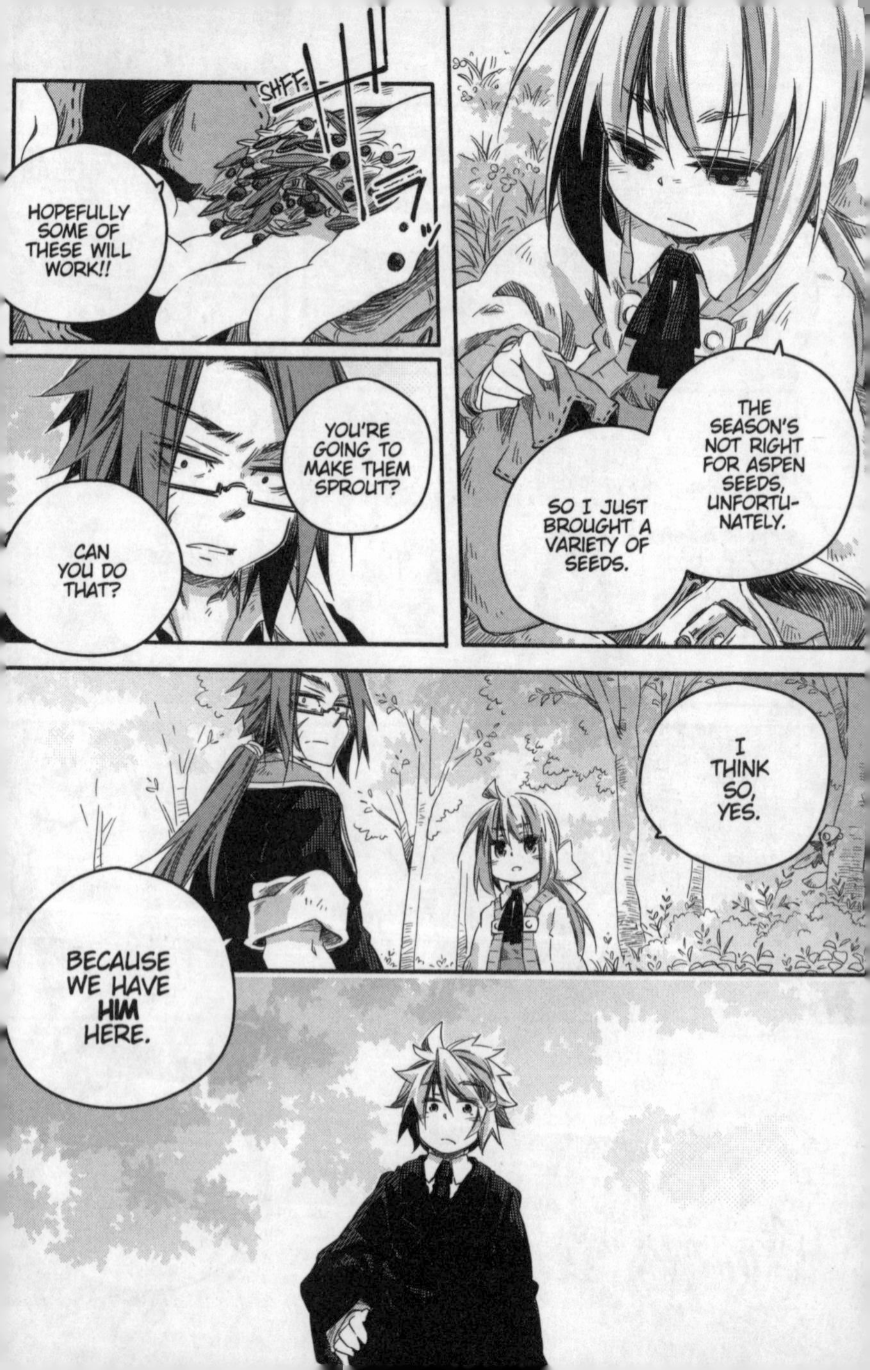
THE SEASON'S NOT RIGHT FOR ASPEN SEEDS, UNFORTUNATELY.
SO I JUST BROUGHT A VARIETY OF SEEDS.
SHFF
HOPEFULLY SOME OF THESE WILL WORK!!
YOU'RE GOING TO MAKE THEM SPROUT?
CAN YOU DO THAT?
I THINK SO, YES.
BECAUSE WE HAVE **HIM** HERE.

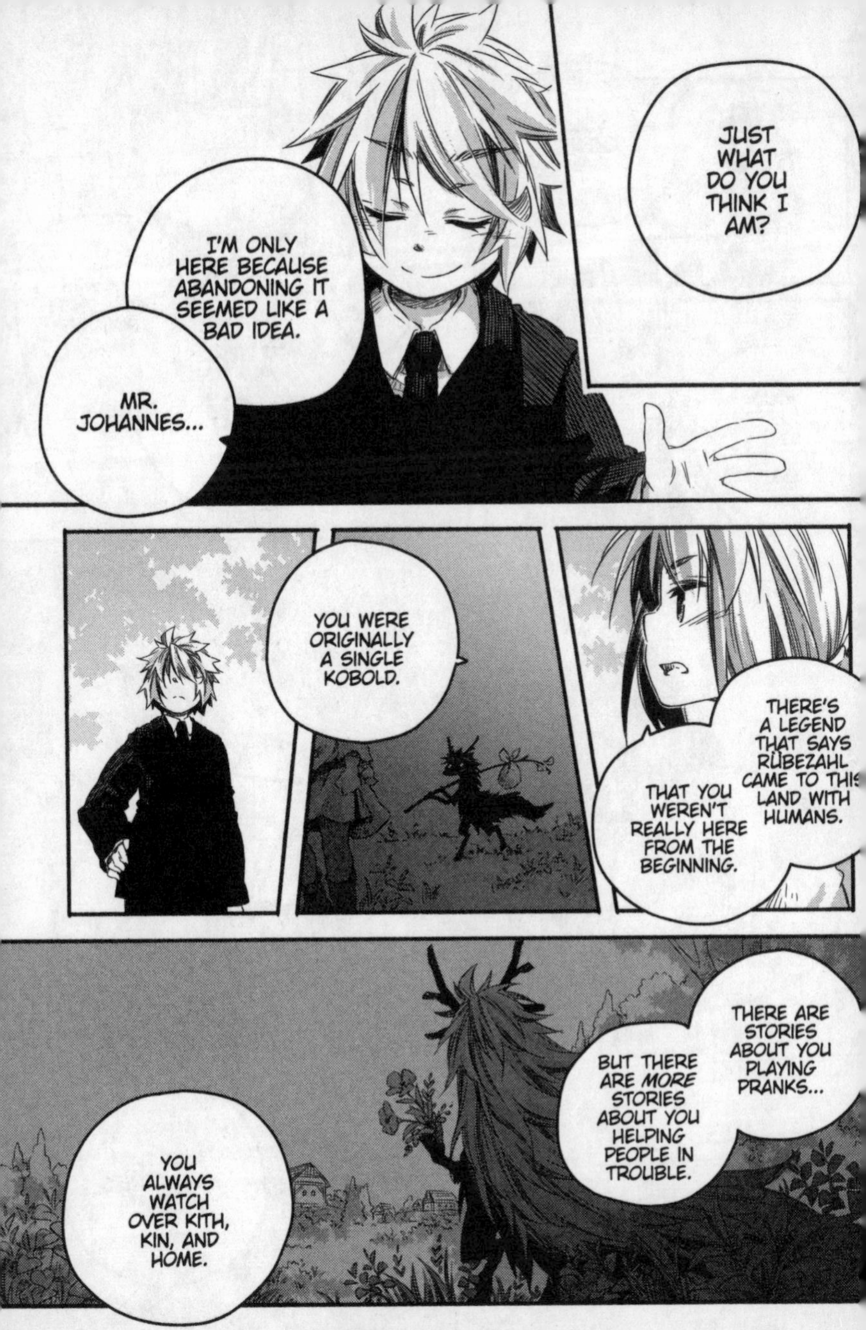
JUST WHAT DO YOU THINK I AM?
I'M ONLY HERE BECAUSE ABANDONING IT SEEMED LIKE A BAD IDEA.
MR. JOHANNES...
THERE'S A LEGEND THAT SAYS RÜBEZAHL CAME TO THIS LAND WITH HUMANS.
THAT YOU WEREN'T REALLY HERE FROM THE BEGINNING.
YOU WERE ORIGINALLY A SINGLE KOBOLD.
THERE ARE STORIES ABOUT YOU PLAYING PRANKS...
BUT THERE ARE *MORE* STORIES ABOUT YOU HELPING PEOPLE IN TROUBLE.
YOU ALWAYS WATCH OVER KITH, KIN, AND HOME.

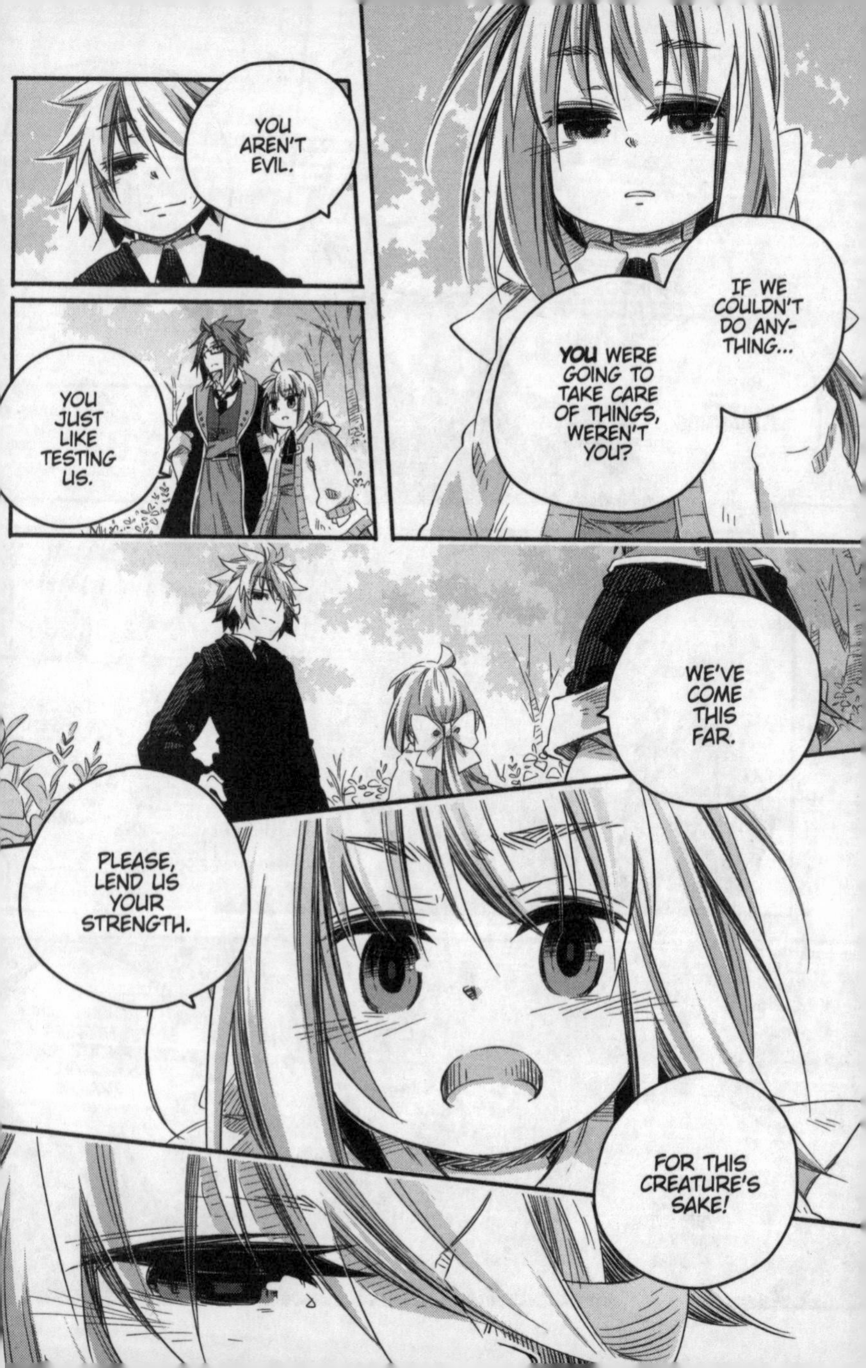
IF WE COULDN'T DO ANY-THING...
YOU WERE GOING TO TAKE CARE OF THINGS, WEREN'T YOU?
YOU AREN'T EVIL.
YOU JUST LIKE TESTING US.
WE'VE COME THIS FAR.
PLEASE, LEND US YOUR STRENGTH.
FOR THIS CREATURE'S SAKE!

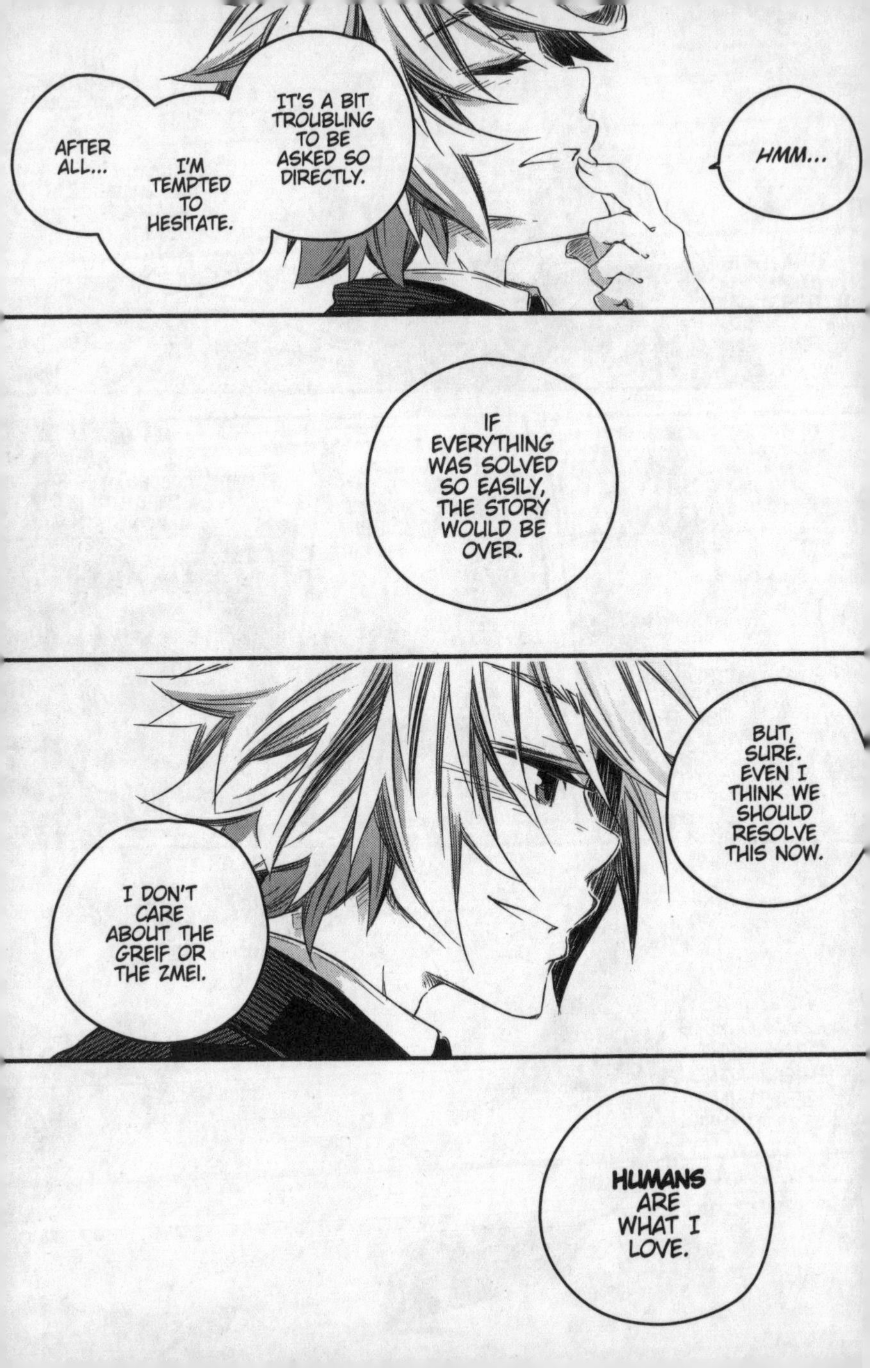
HMM...
IT'S A BIT TROUBLING TO BE ASKED SO DIRECTLY.
I'M TEMPTED TO HESITATE.
AFTER ALL...
IF EVERYTHING WAS SOLVED SO EASILY, THE STORY WOULD BE OVER.
BUT, SURE. EVEN I THINK WE SHOULD RESOLVE THIS NOW.
I DON'T CARE ABOUT THE GREIF OR THE ZMEI.
HUMANS ARE WHAT I LOVE.

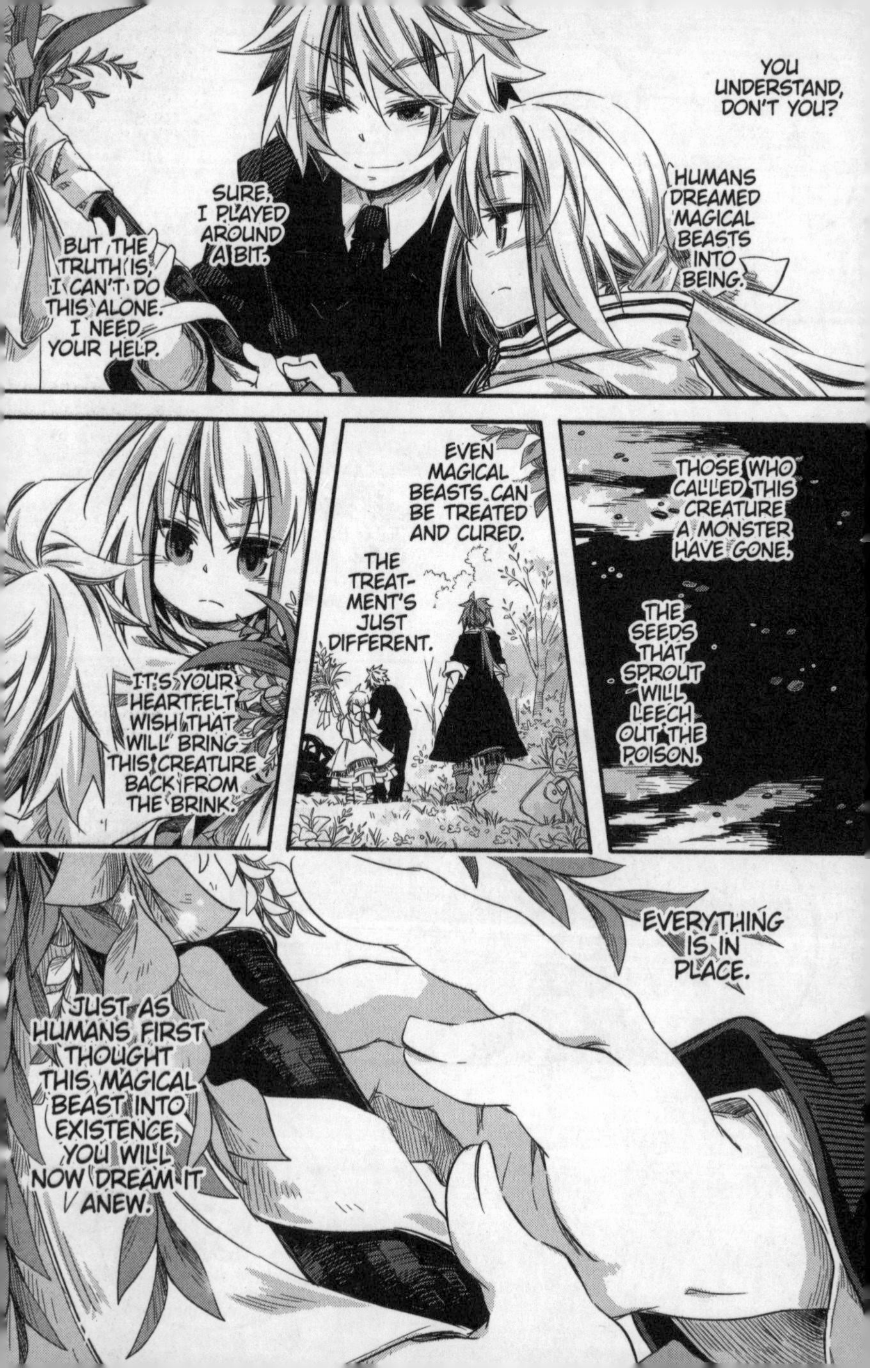
YOU UNDERSTAND, DON'T YOU?
HUMANS DREAMED MAGICAL BEASTS INTO BEING.
SURE, I PLAYED AROUND A BIT.
BUT THE TRUTH IS, I CAN'T DO THIS ALONE. I NEED YOUR HELP.
THOSE WHO CALLED THIS CREATURE A MONSTER HAVE GONE.
THE SEEDS THAT SPROUT WILL LEECH OUT THE POISON.
EVEN MAGICAL BEASTS CAN BE TREATED AND CURED.
THE TREATMENT'S JUST DIFFERENT.
IT'S YOUR HEARTFELT WISH THAT WILL BRING THIS CREATURE BACK FROM THE BRINK.
EVERYTHING IS IN PLACE.
JUST AS HUMANS FIRST THOUGHT THIS MAGICAL BEAST INTO EXISTENCE, YOU WILL NOW DREAM IT ANEW.

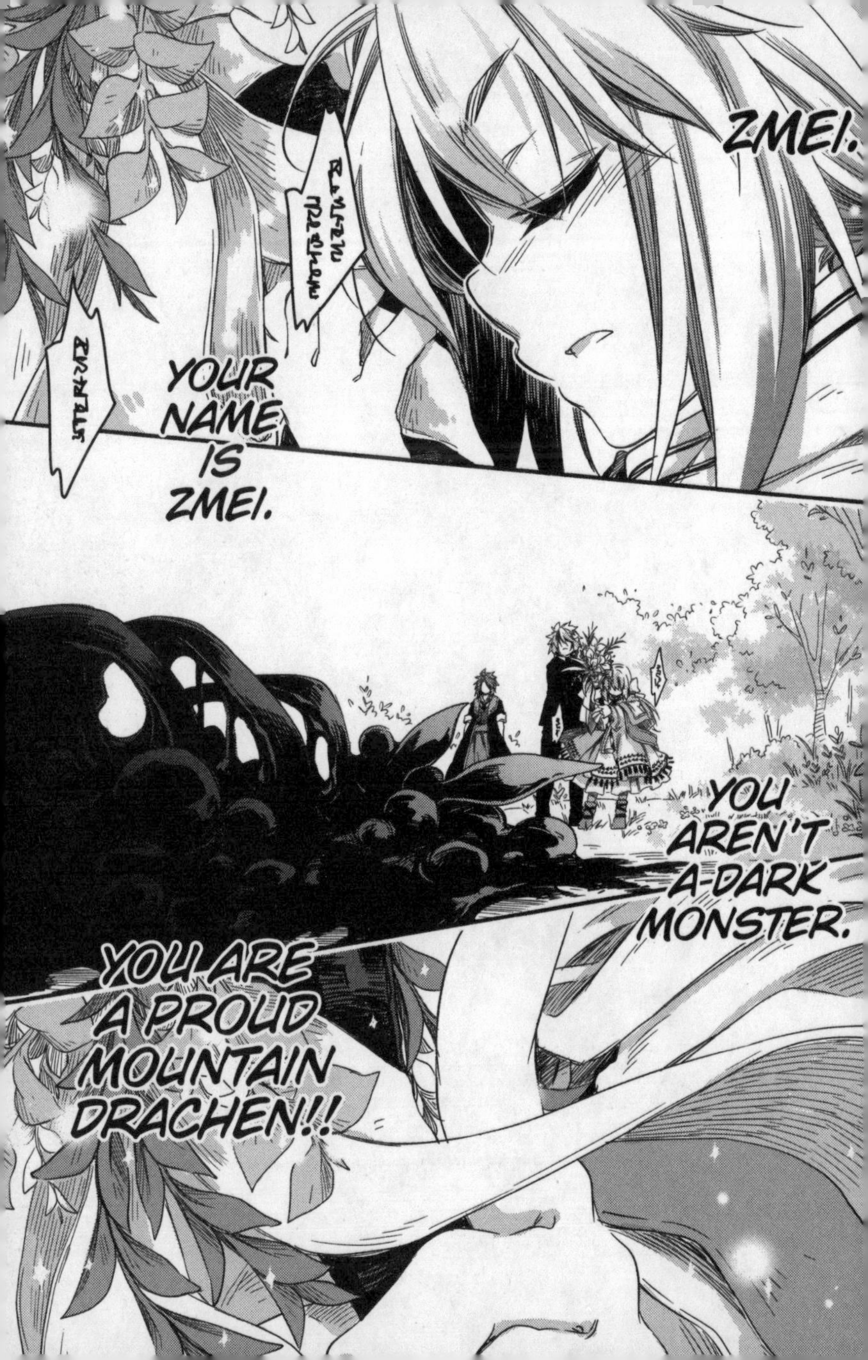
ZMEI.
YOUR NAME IS ZMEI.
YOU AREN'T A DARK MONSTER.
YOU ARE A PROUD MOUNTAIN DRACHEN!!

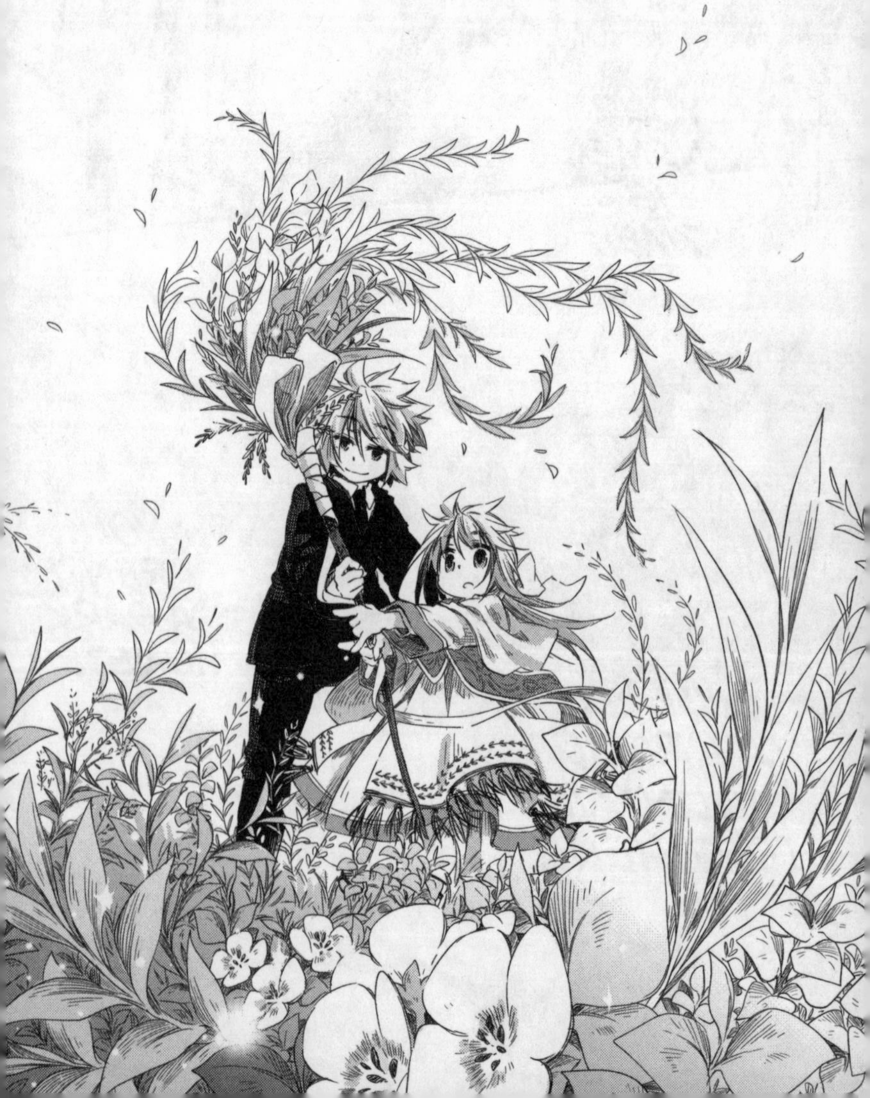

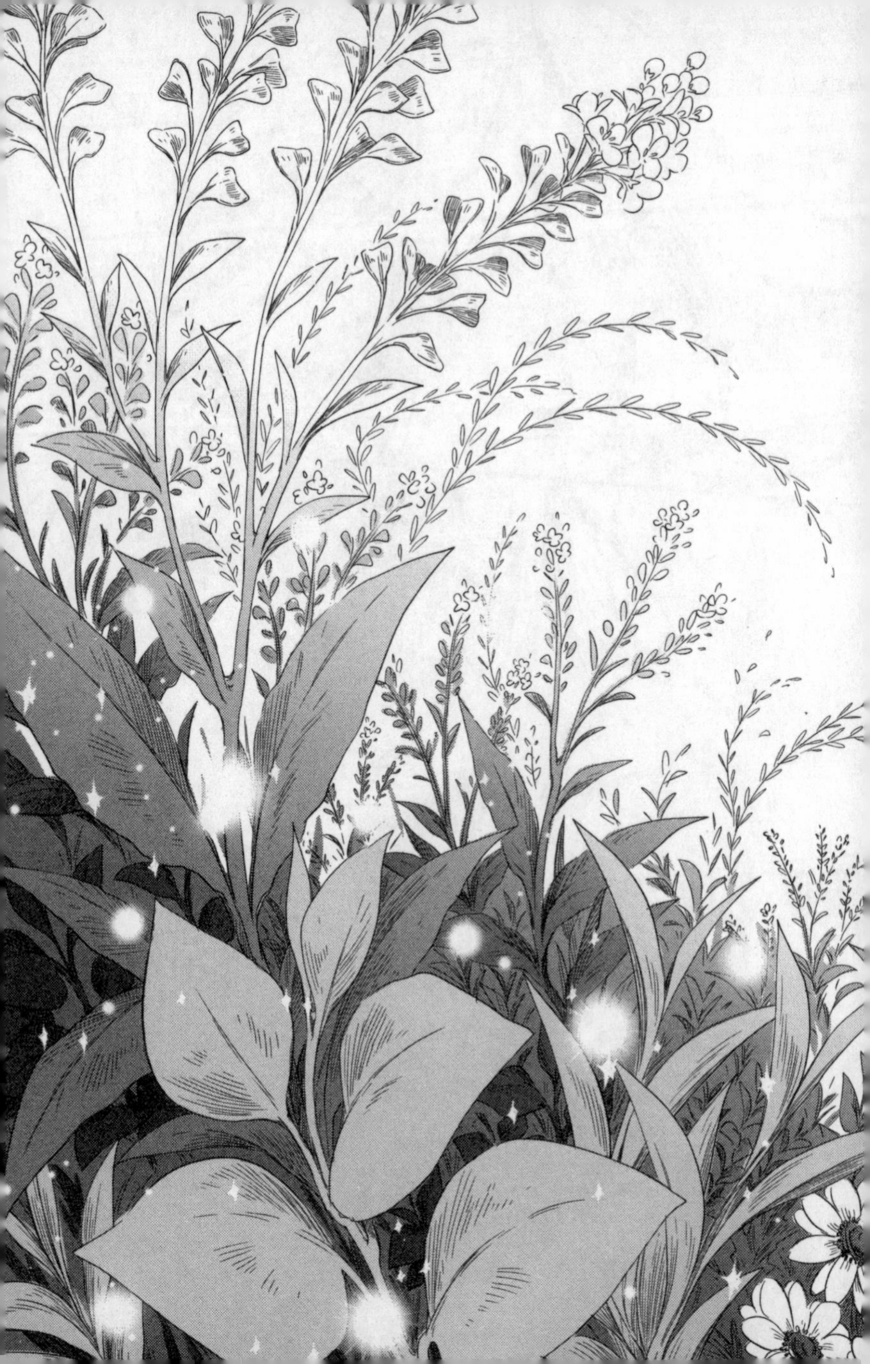

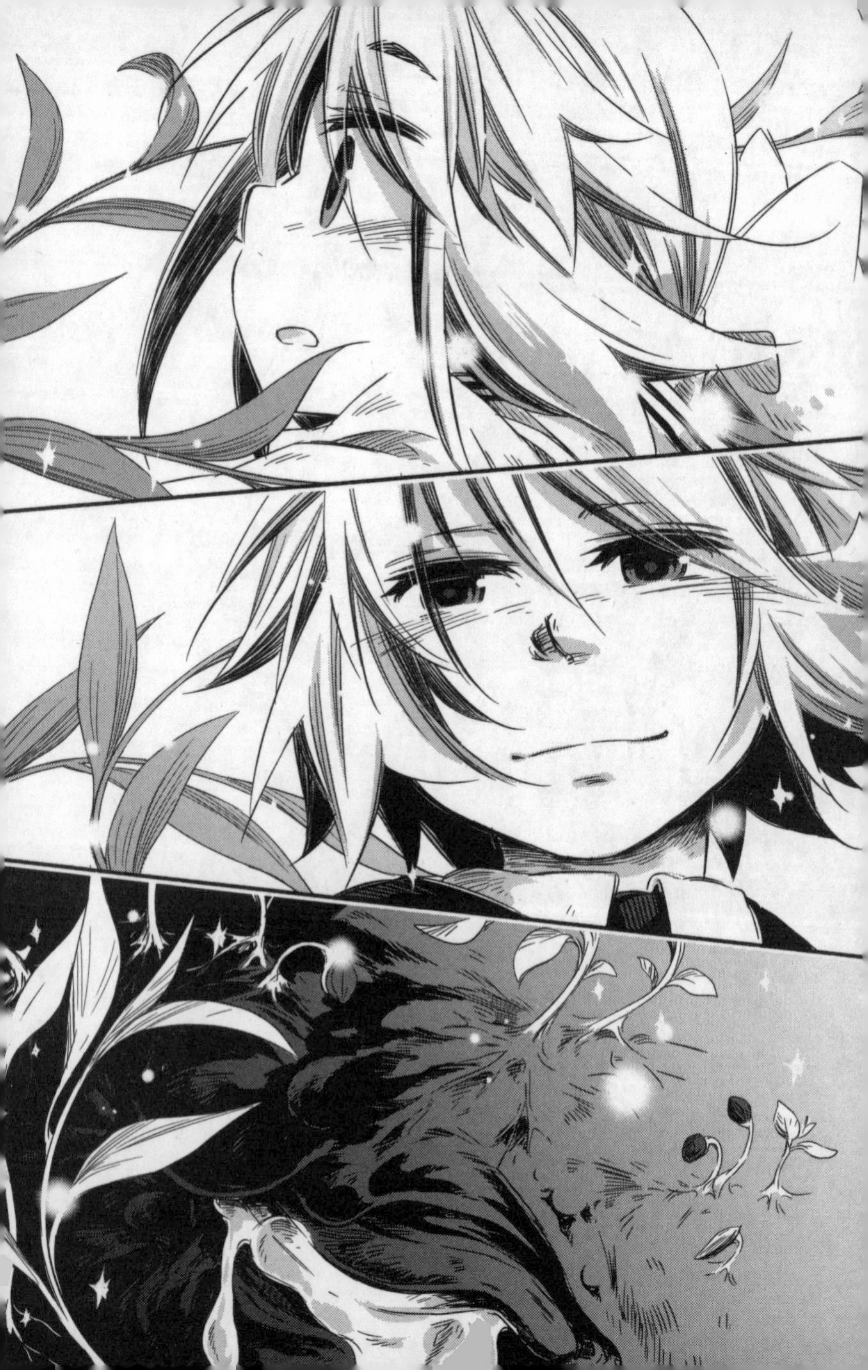

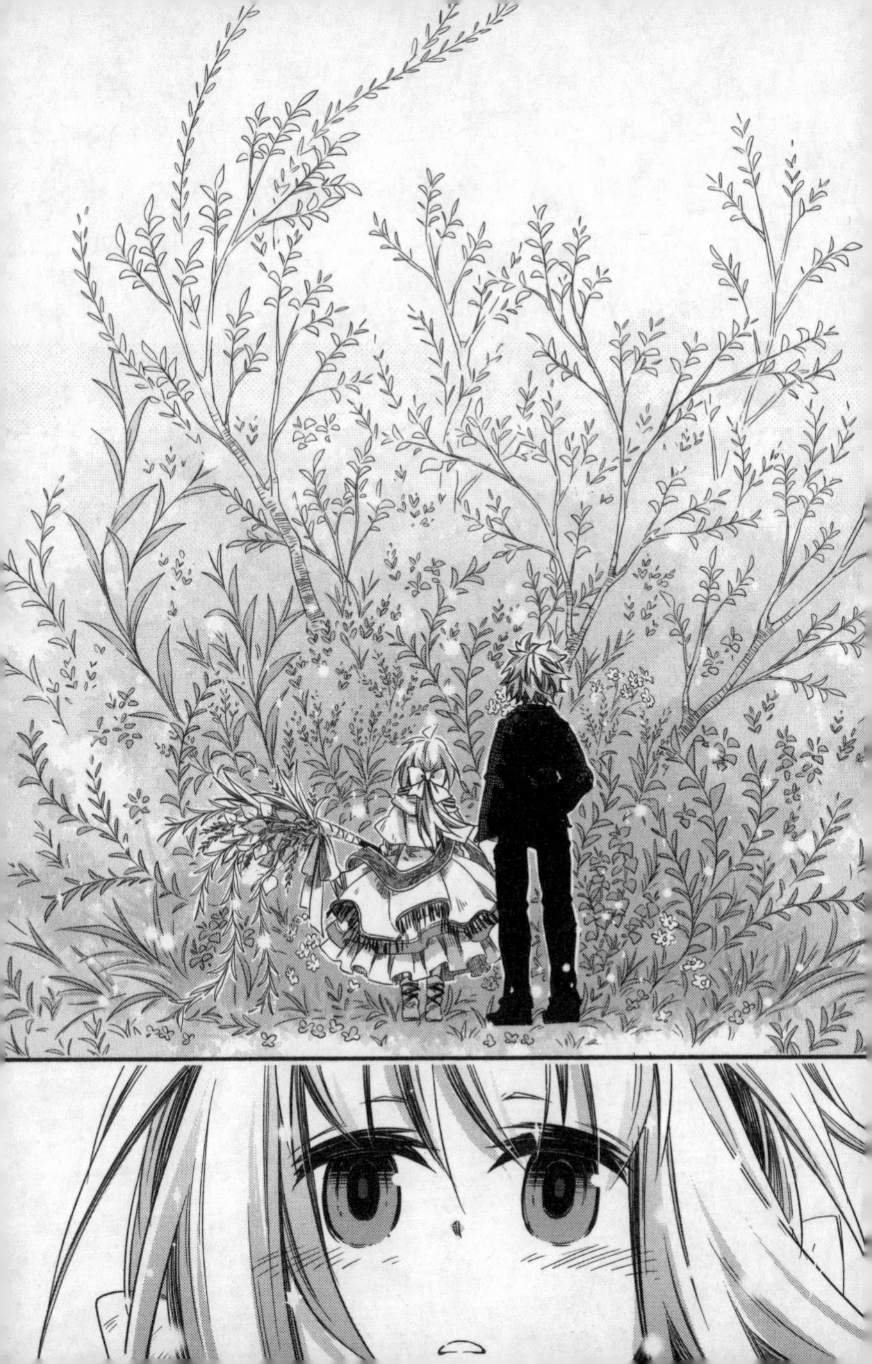

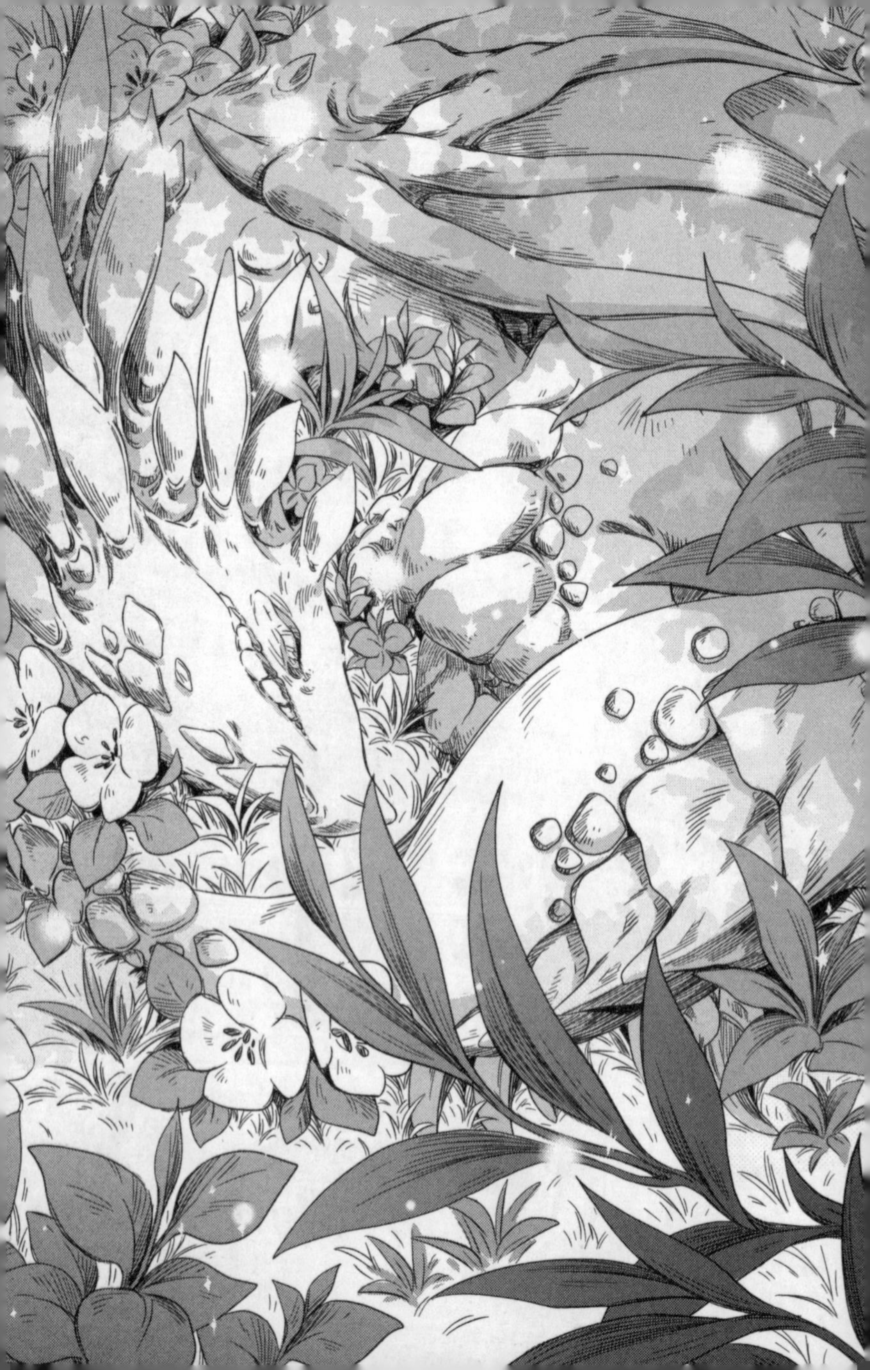

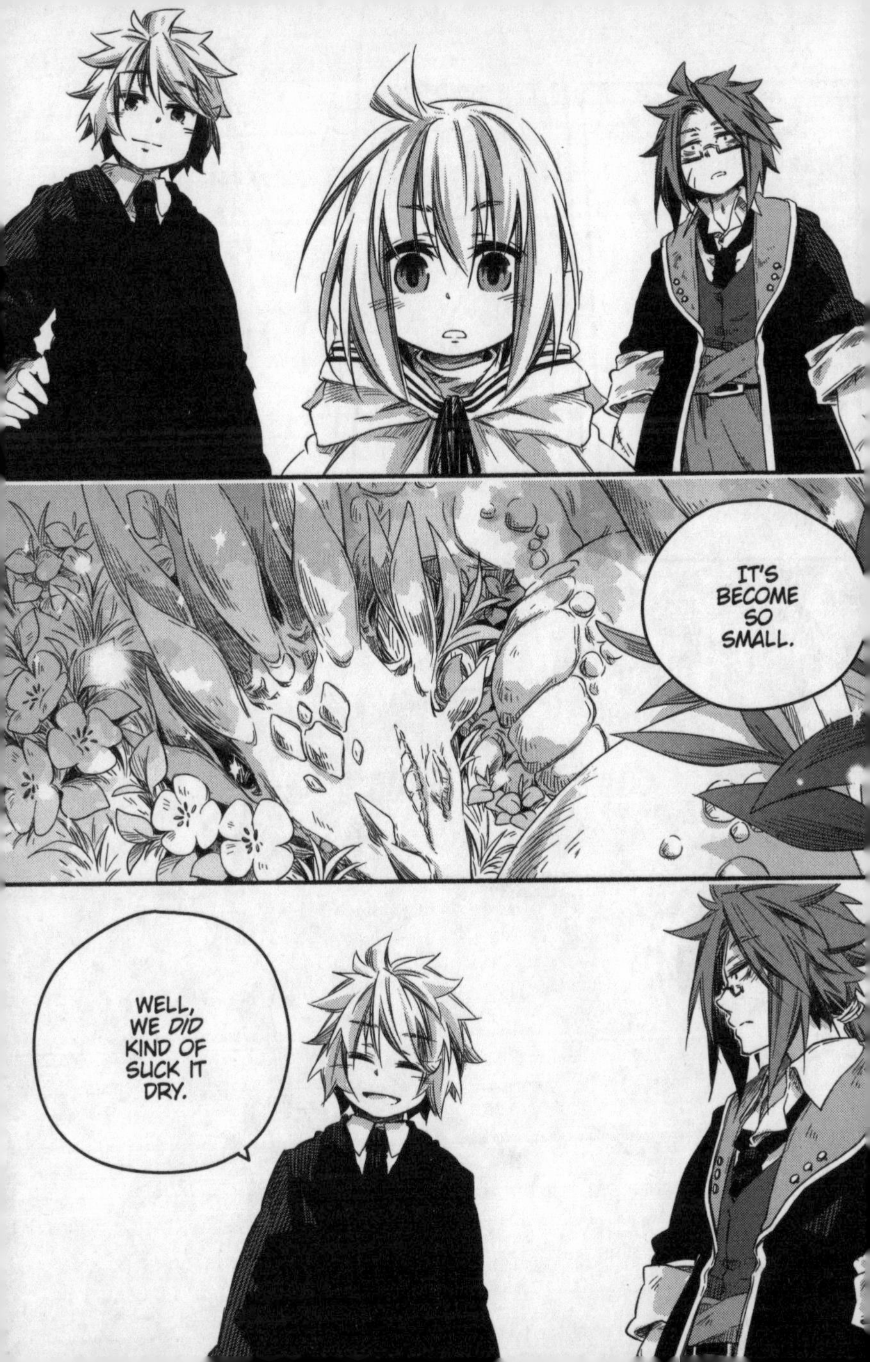
IT'S BECOME SO SMALL.
WELL, WE *DID* KIND OF SUCK IT DRY.

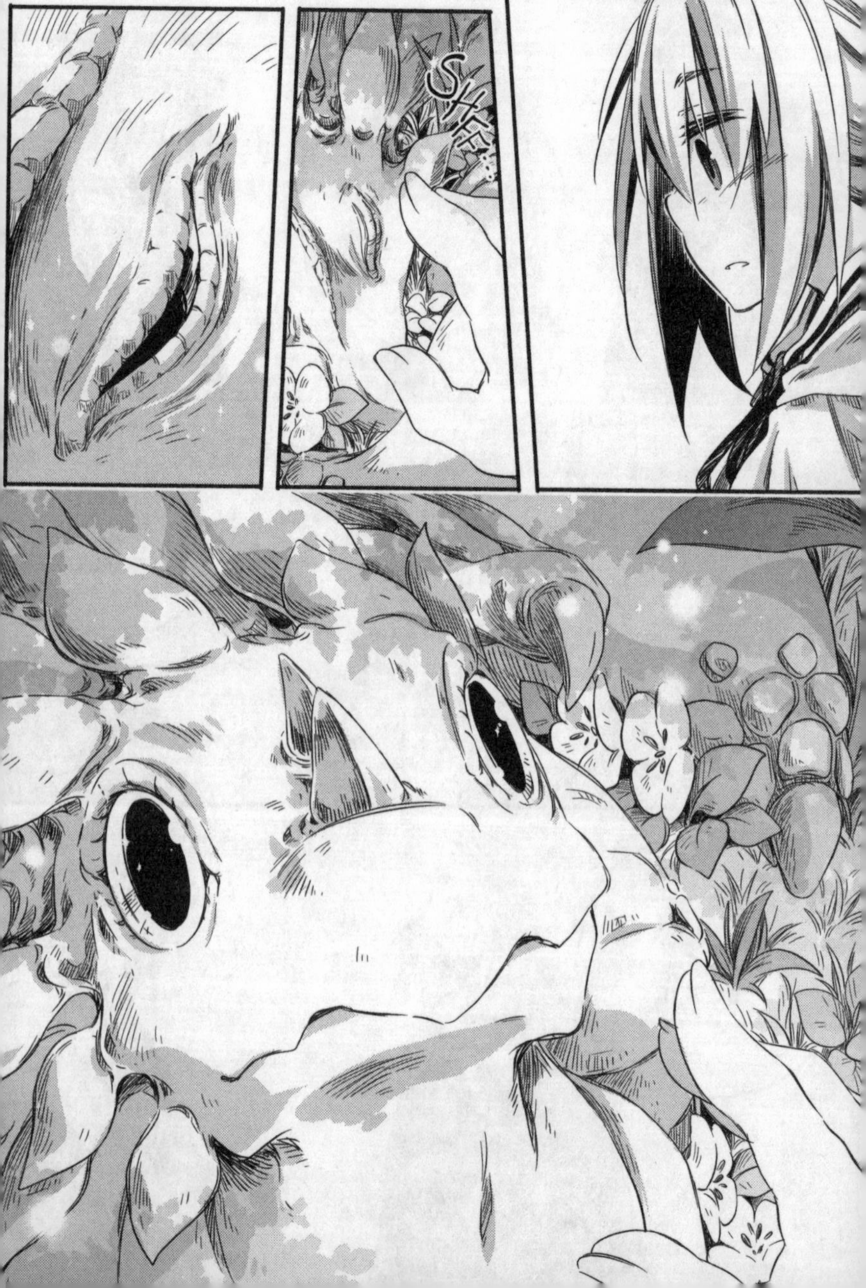
SHFF...

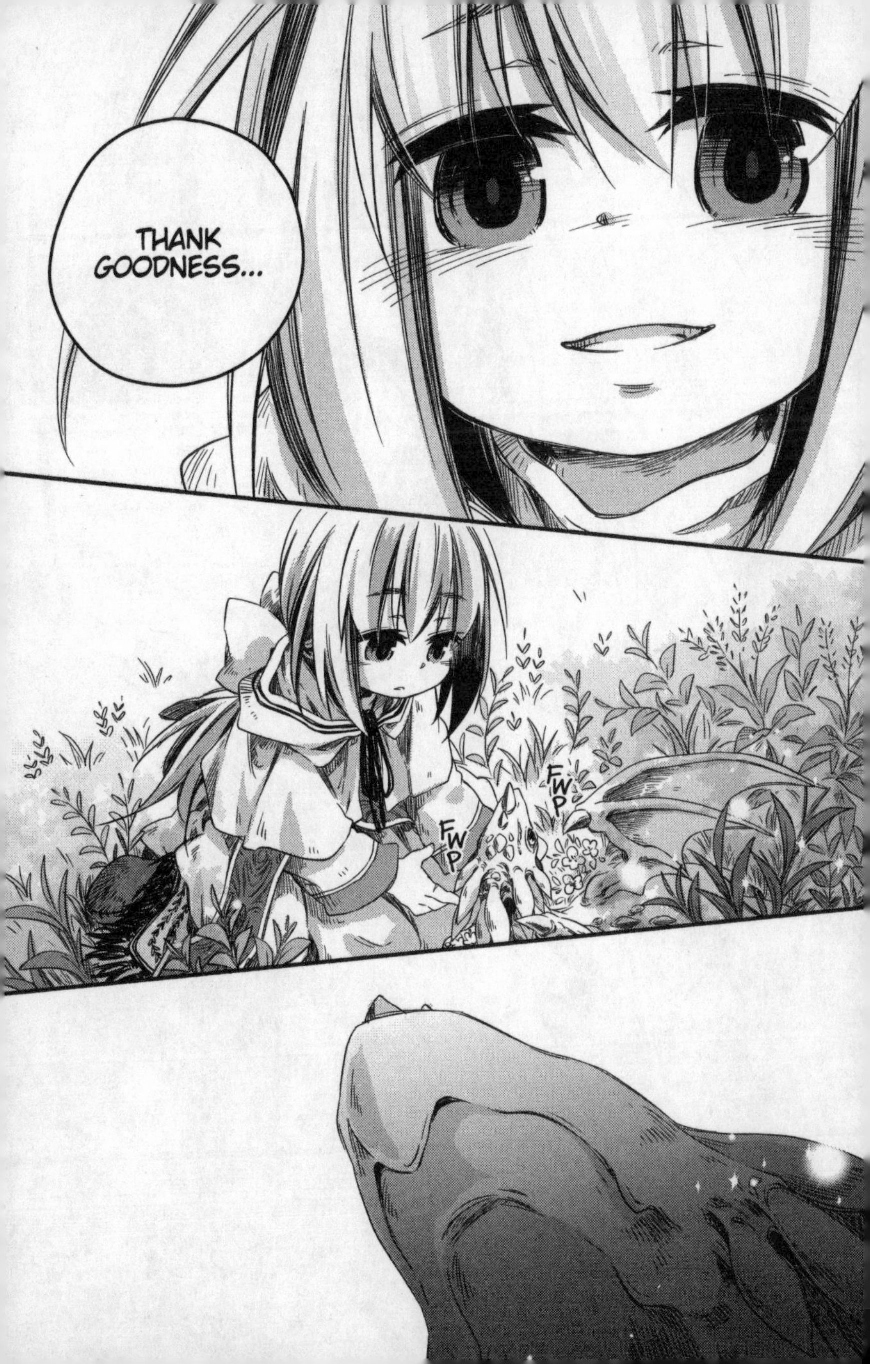
THANK GOODNESS...
FWP
FWP

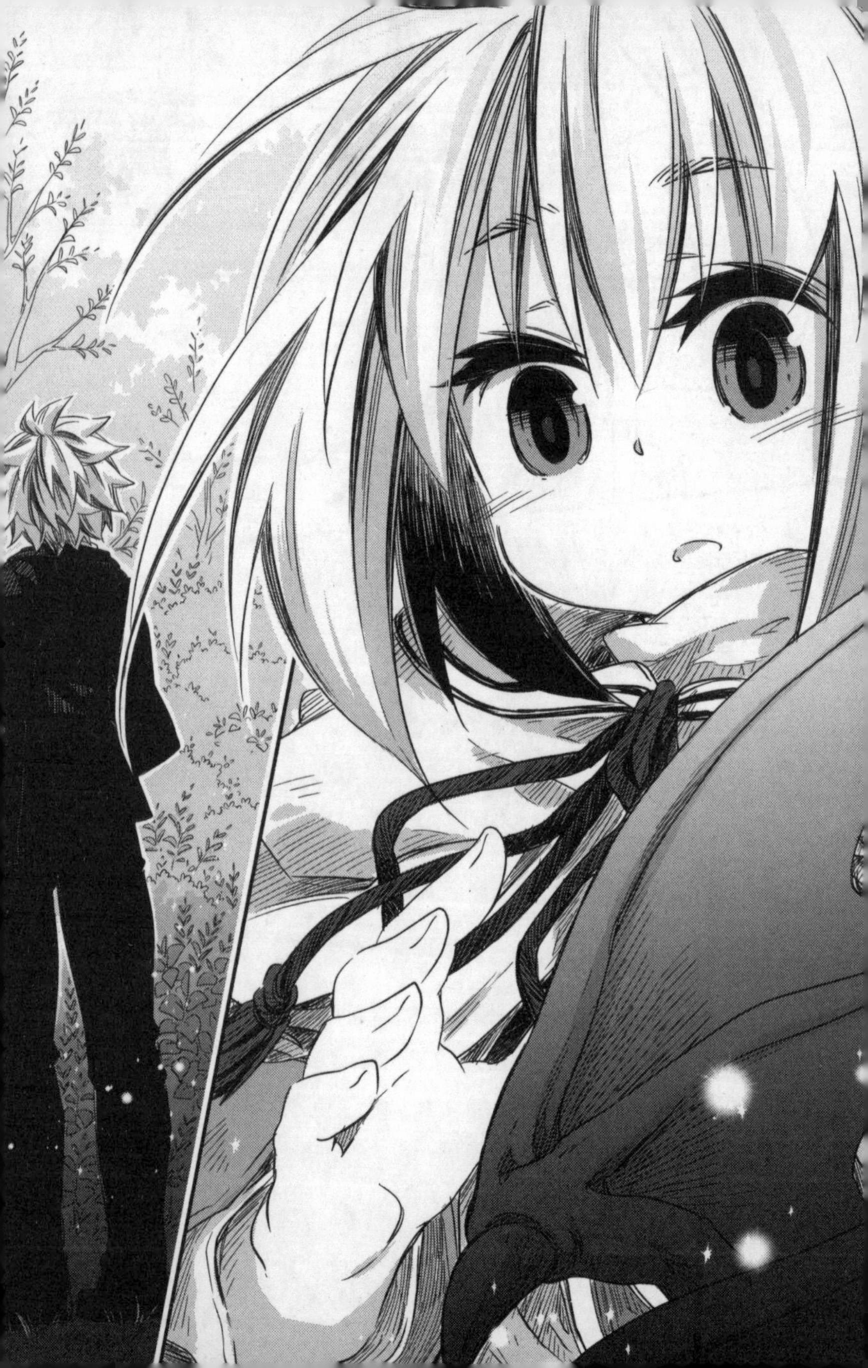

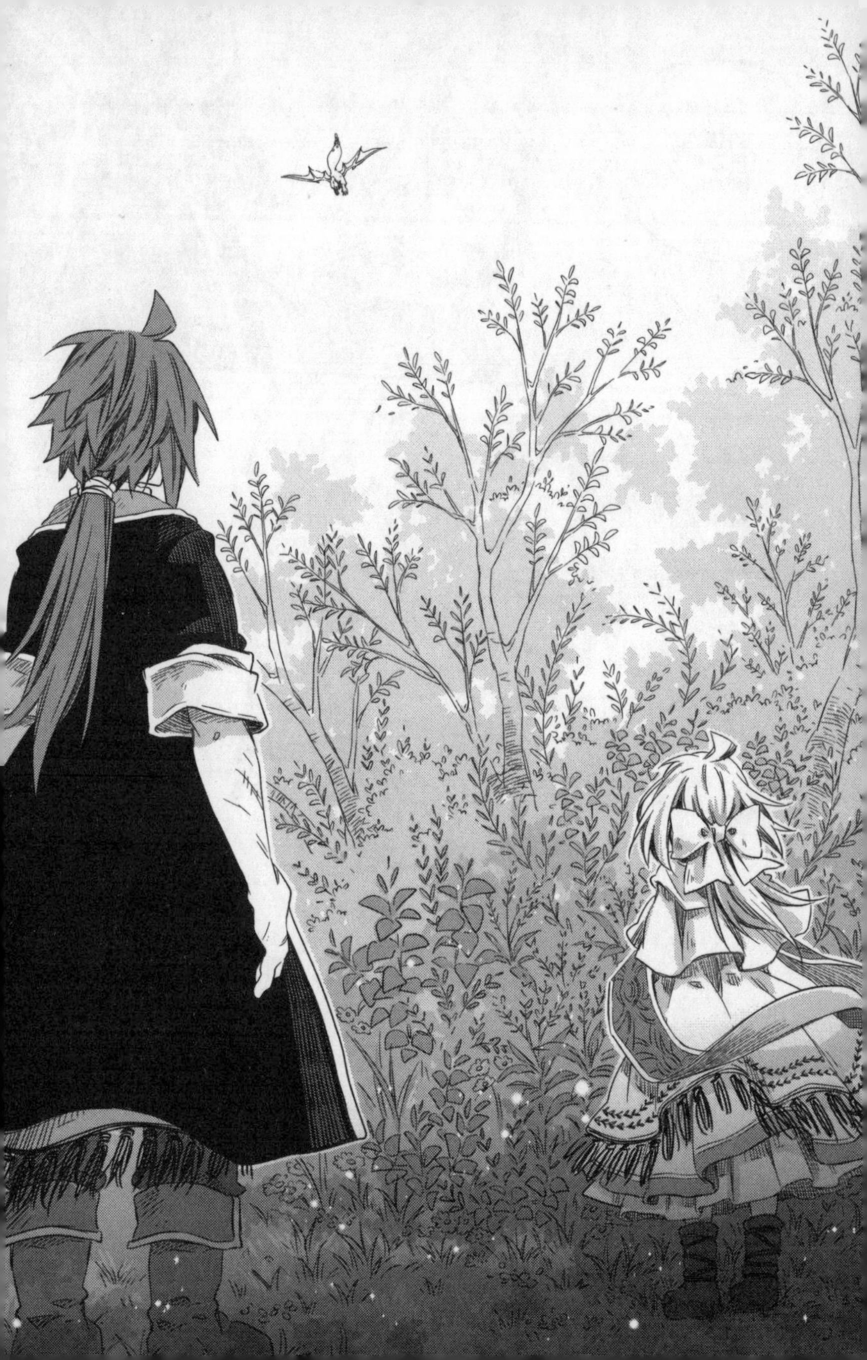

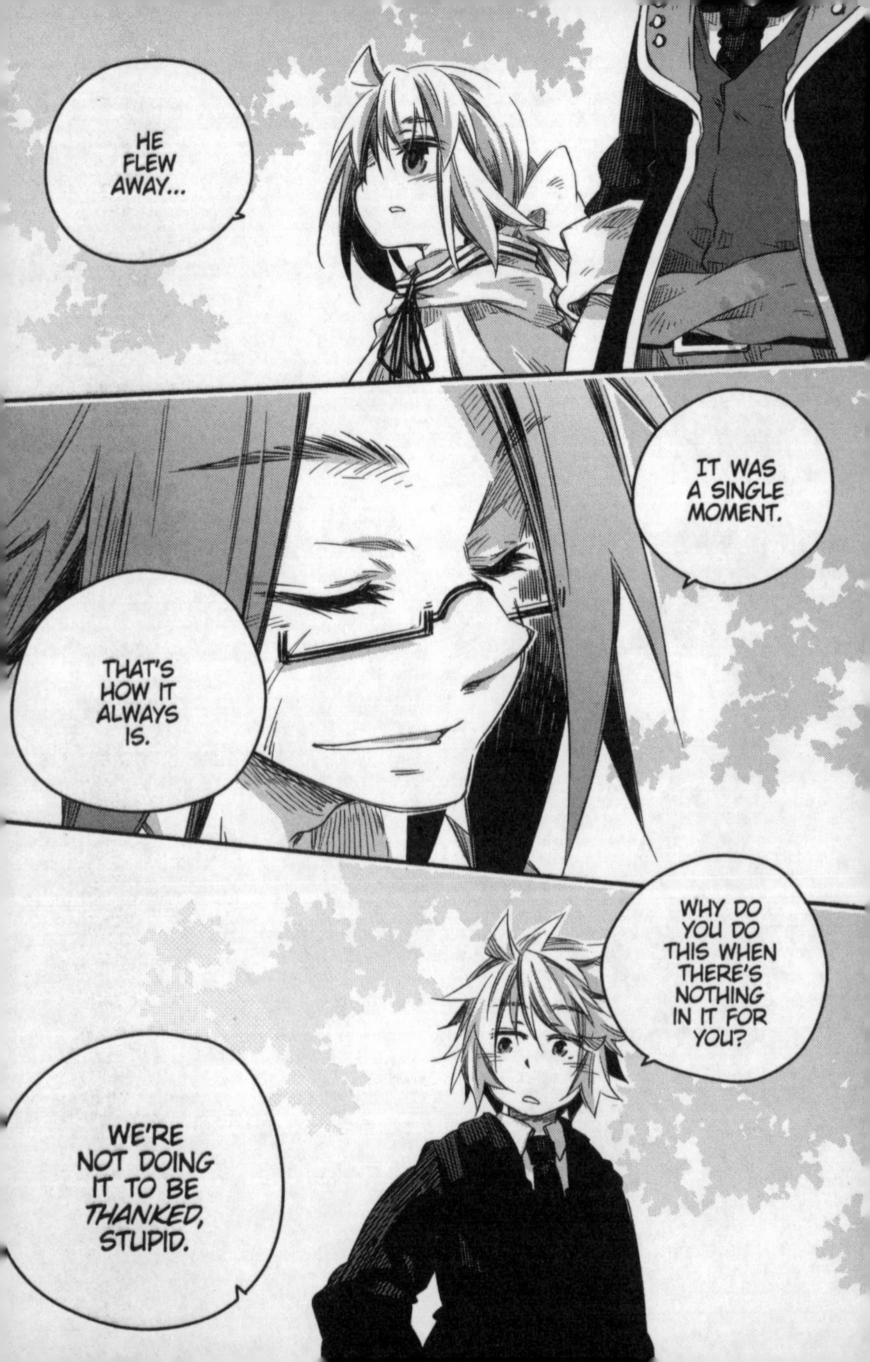
HE FLEW AWAY...
IT WAS A SINGLE MOMENT.
THAT'S HOW IT ALWAYS IS.
WHY DO YOU DO THIS WHEN THERE'S NOTHING IN IT FOR YOU?
WE'RE NOT DOING IT TO BE THANKED, STUPID.

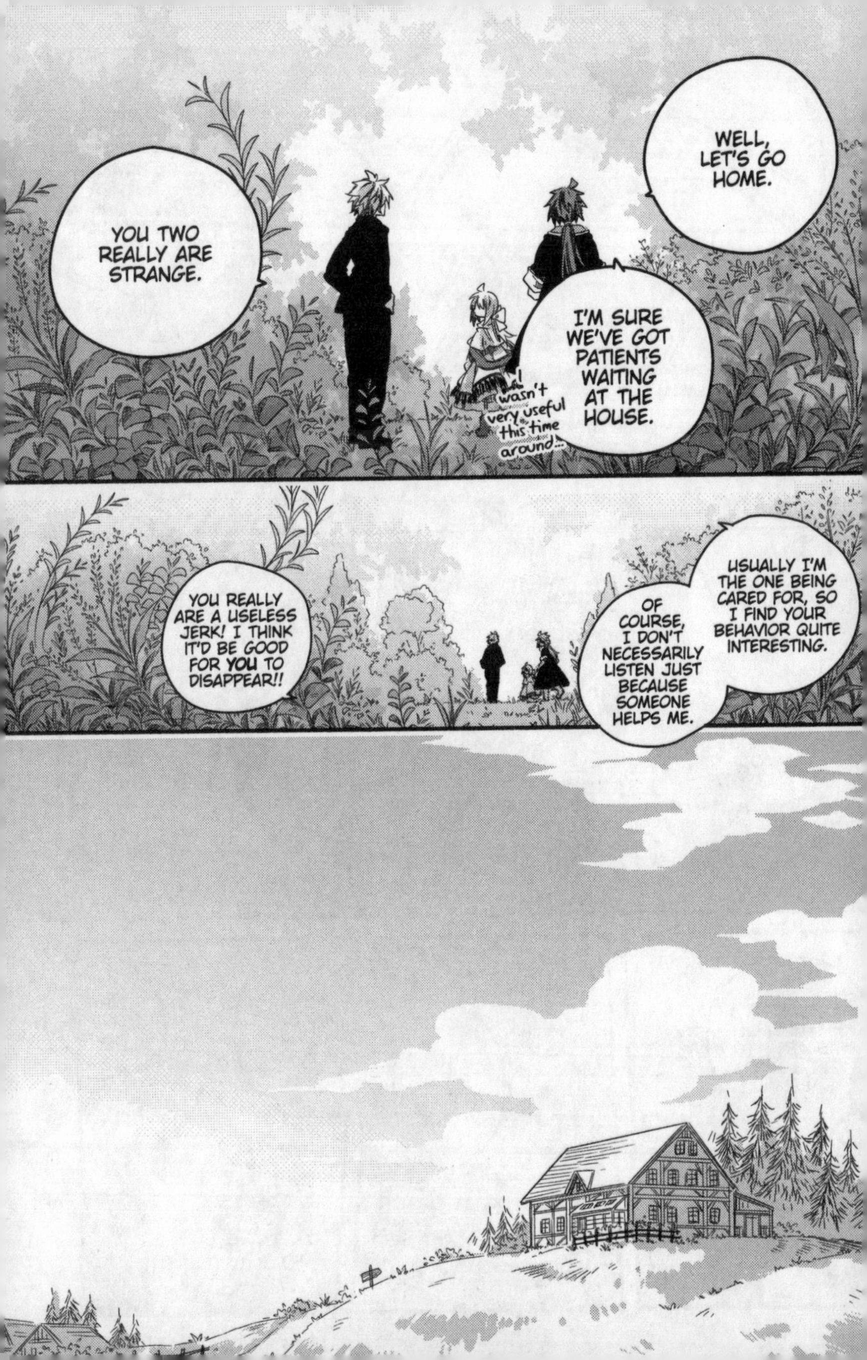
WELL, LET'S GO HOME.
I'M SURE WE'VE GOT PATIENTS WAITING AT THE HOUSE.
I wasn't very useful this time around...
YOU TWO REALLY ARE STRANGE.
USUALLY I'M THE ONE BEING CARED FOR, SO I FIND YOUR BEHAVIOR QUITE INTERESTING.
OF COURSE, I DON'T NECESSARILY LISTEN JUST BECAUSE SOMEONE HELPS ME.
YOU REALLY ARE A USELESS JERK! I THINK IT'D BE GOOD FOR **YOU** TO DISAPPEAR!!

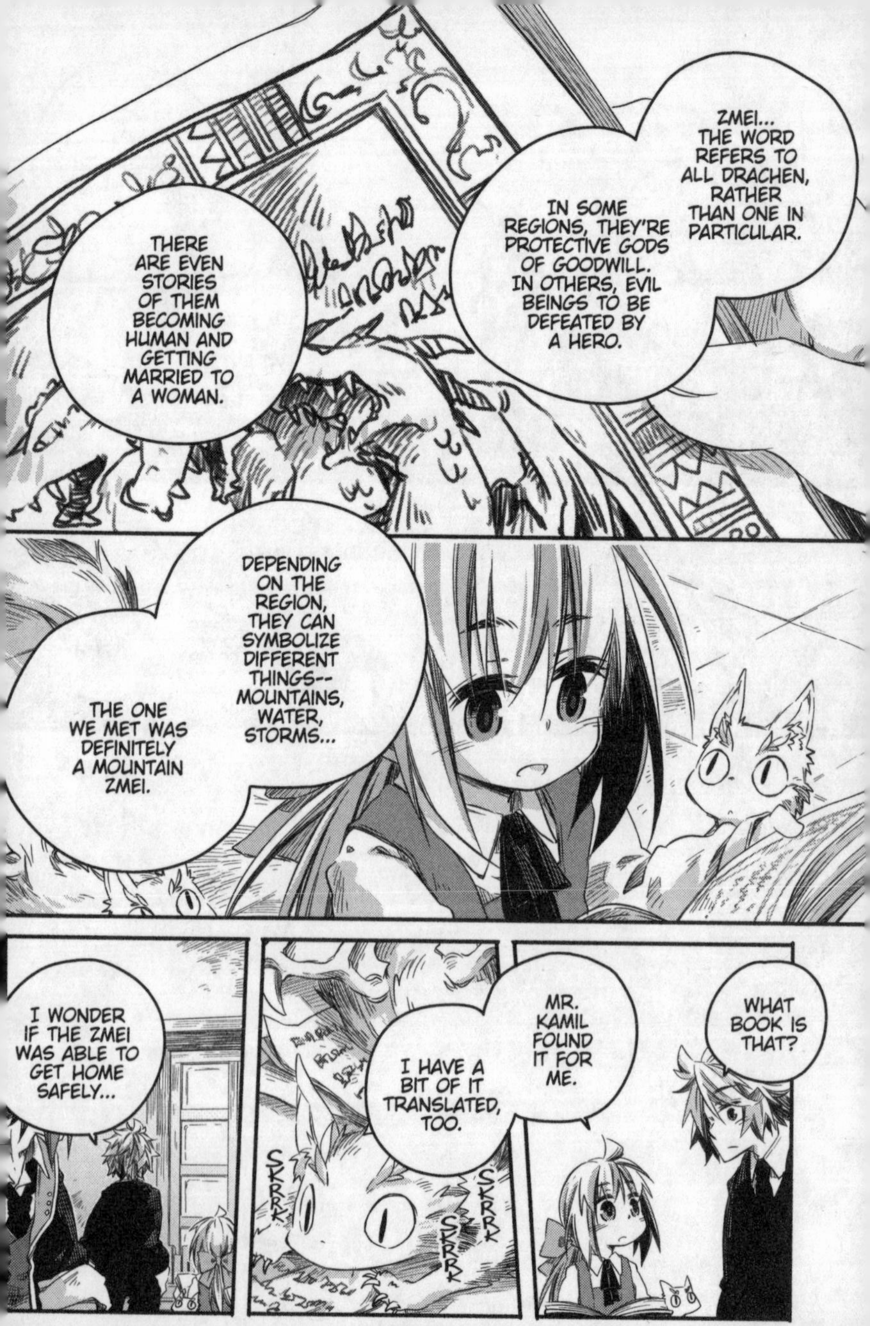
ZMEI... THE WORD REFERS TO ALL DRACHEN, RATHER THAN ONE IN PARTICULAR.
IN SOME REGIONS, THEY'RE PROTECTIVE GODS OF GOODWILL. IN OTHERS, EVIL BEINGS TO BE DEFEATED BY A HERO.
THERE ARE EVEN STORIES OF THEM BECOMING HUMAN AND GETTING MARRIED TO A WOMAN.
DEPENDING ON THE REGION, THEY CAN SYMBOLIZE DIFFERENT THINGS--MOUNTAINS, WATER, STORMS...
THE ONE WE MET WAS DEFINITELY A MOUNTAIN ZMEI.
WHAT BOOK IS THAT?
MR. KAMIL FOUND IT FOR ME.
I HAVE A BIT OF IT TRANSLATED, TOO.
SKRRK
SKRRK
SKRRK
I WONDER IF THE ZMEI WAS ABLE TO GET HOME SAFELY...

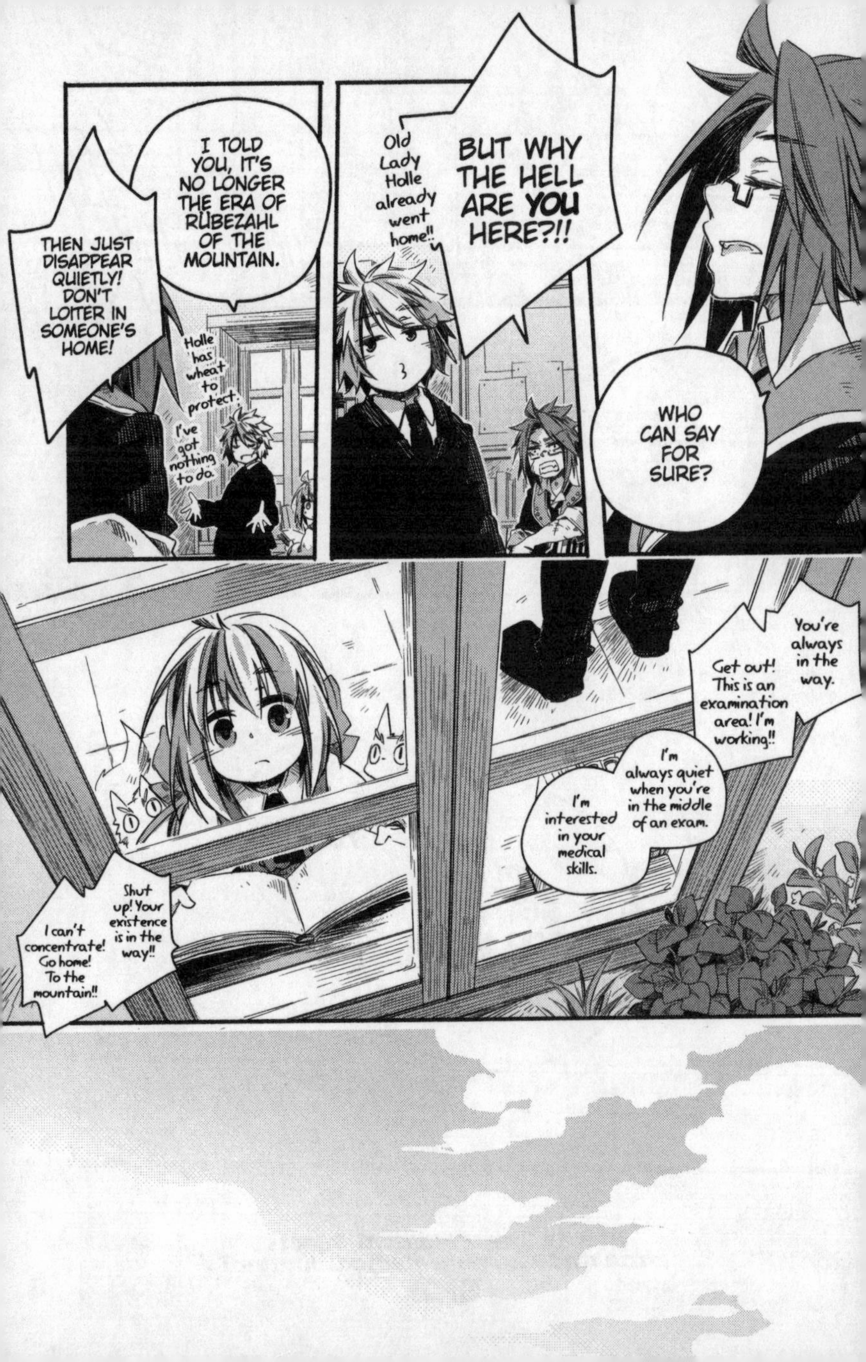
BUT WHY THE HELL ARE YOU HERE?!!
Old Lady Holle already went home!!
WHO CAN SAY FOR SURE?
I TOLD YOU, IT'S NO LONGER THE ERA OF RÜBEZAHL OF THE MOUNTAIN.
THEN JUST DISAPPEAR QUIETLY! DON'T LOITER IN SOMEONE'S HOME!
Holle has wheat to protect.
I've got nothing to do.
You're always in the way.
Get out! This is an examination area! I'm working!!
I'm always quiet when you're in the middle of an exam.
I'm interested in your medical skills.
Shut up! Your existence is in the way!!
I can't concentrate! Go home! To the mountain!!

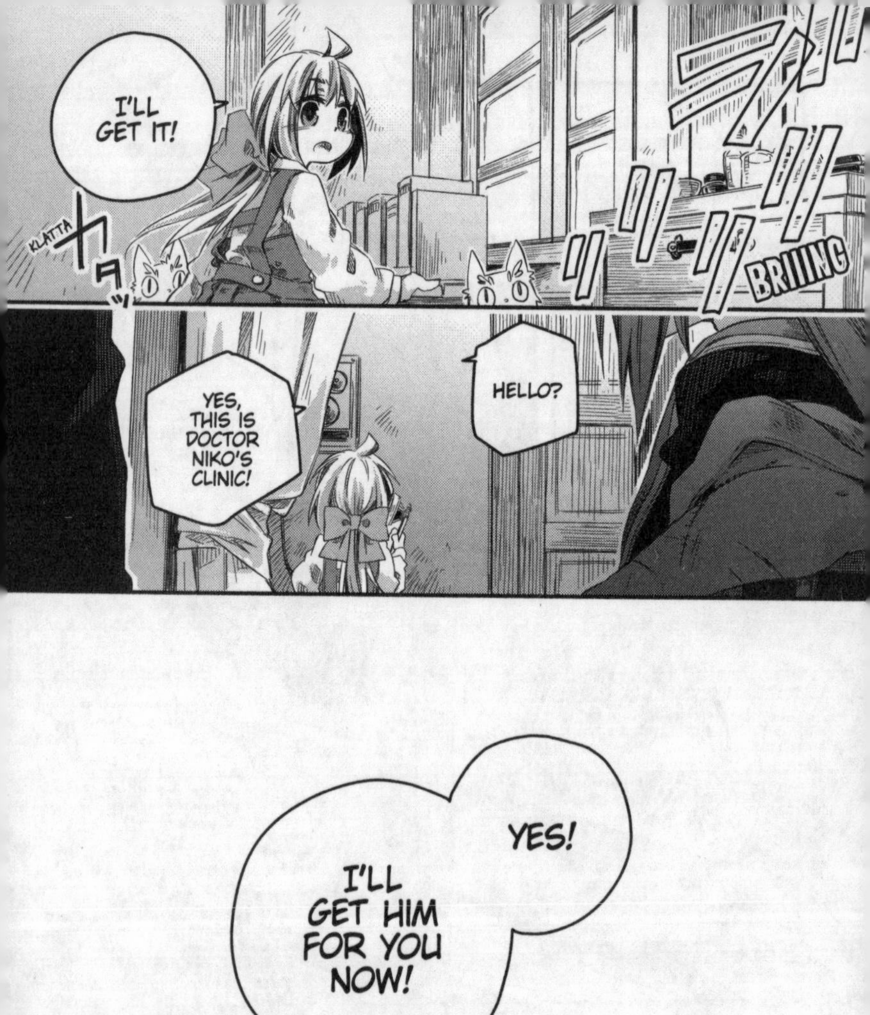
BRIIING
I'LL GET IT!
KLATTA
HELLO?
YES, THIS IS DOCTOR NIKO'S CLINIC!
YES! I'LL GET HIM FOR YOU NOW!

How to Treat Magical Beasts: Mine and Master's Medical Journal

END

Thank you for reading to the very end!!

I had some trouble gathering all the materials I needed to write the story, so things were a little difficult for a while there.

I wanted to get the narrative to a certain place before the series finished, so I'm relieved I was able to reach that point before things wrapped up.

I hope to see you again in a different work!

—Kaziya

There was a puk in every chapter this time, too!! Please find them.

Assistants for Chapters 24 and 25: Asakura Koyuki-san and Satoumi Fumakana-san. Thank you!!

I saw it!!
This was the work of Rübezahl!!
CHATTER
And Rübezahl's the one who turned that monster into flowers?
That's right!!
He's an herbalist, too! No mistake!!
CHATTER
CHATTER
I guess Rübezahl did have a lot of stories involving herbs...
Was he protecting us?
Is he a... good guy?
and he's not always doing bad things.
PWOP
The god of flowers!!
PWOP PWOP...
So this is how legends slowly change.
IRK
This is all your fault!
Maybe I should go cause another ruckus!!

SEVEN SEAS ENTERTAINMENT PRESENTS

How to Treat Magical Beasts

Mine and Master's Medical Journal

story and art by **KAZIYA** **VOLUME 5**

TRANSLATION
Angela Liu

ADAPTATION
Jaymee Goh

LETTERING AND RETOUCH
Annaliese "Ace" Christman

COVER DESIGN
Hanase Qi

PROOFREADER
Kurestin Armada, Dawn Davis

EDITOR
Jenn Grunigen

PREPRESS TECHNICIAN
Rhiannon Rasmussen-Silverstein

PRODUCTION ASSISTANT
Christa Miesner

PRODUCTION MANAGER
Lissa Pattillo

MANAGING EDITOR
Julie Davis

ASSOCIATE PUBLISHER
Adam Arnold

PUBLISHER
Jason DeAngelis

WATASHI TO SENSEI NO GENJUU SHINRYOUROKU VOL. 5

Originally published in Japan in 2020 by MAG Garden Corporation, Tokyo.
English translation rights arranged through TOHAN CORPORATION, Tokyo.

Seven Seas press and purchase enquiries can be sent to Marketing Manager Lianne Sentar at press@gomanga.com. Information regarding the distribution and purchase of digital editions is available from Digital Manager CK Russell at digital@gomanga.com.

ISBN: 978-1-64505-448-1

Printed in Canada

First Printing: March 2021

10 9 8 7 6 5 4 3 2 1

FOLLOW US ONLINE: ***www.sevenseasentertainment.com***

READING DIRECTIONS

This book reads from ***right to left***, Japanese style. If this is your first time reading manga, you start reading from the top right panel on each page and take it from there. If you get lost, just follow the numbered diagram here. It may seem backwards at first, but you'll get the hang of it! Have fun!!

1
2
3
4
5
6
7
8
9

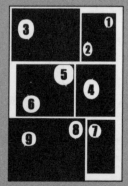